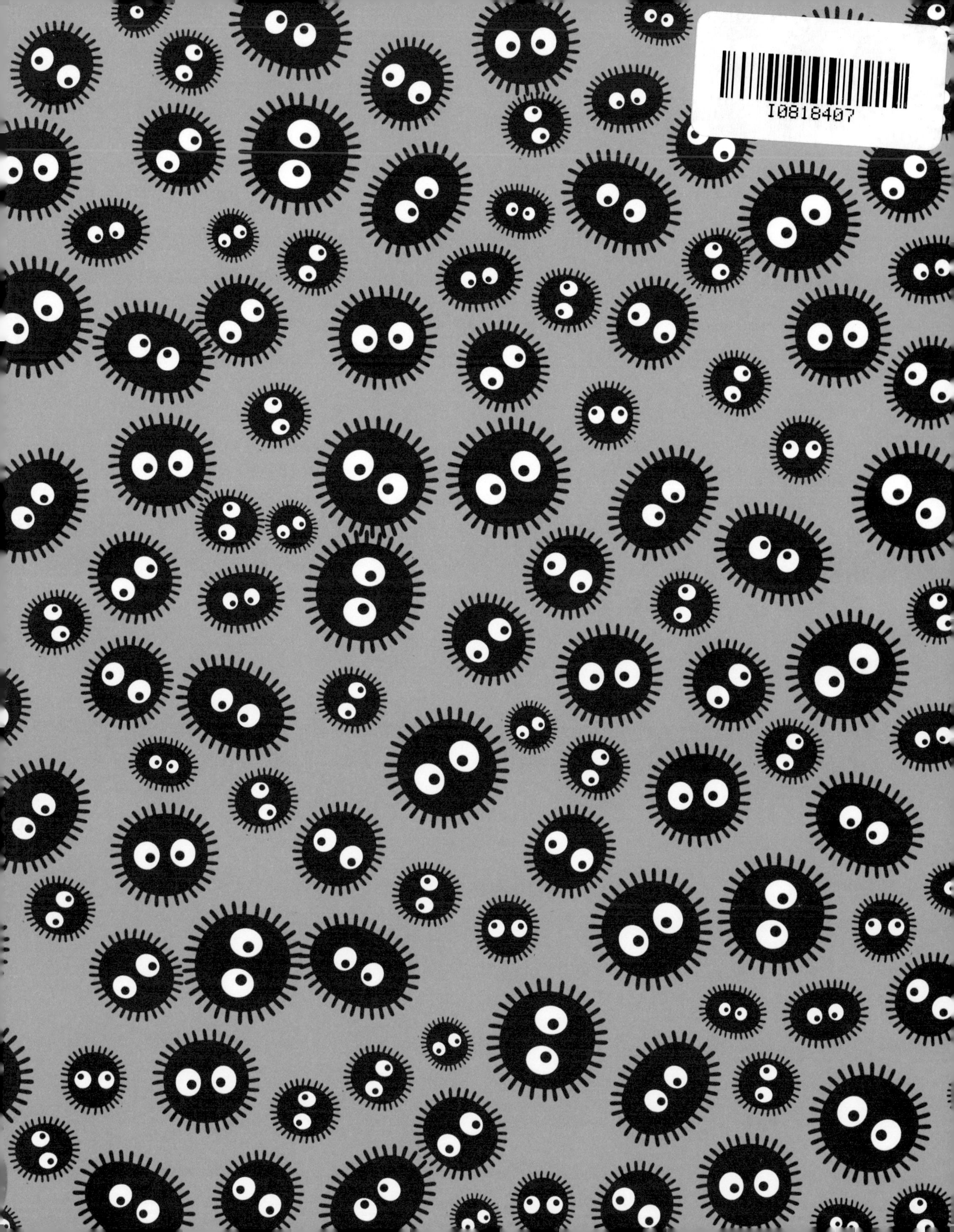

MY NEIGHBOR HAYAO

ART INSPIRED BY THE FILMS OF

MIYAZAKI

ISBN 978-2-37495-1355

Texts: respective authors

Director of publication: Rodolphe Lachat
Cernunnos logo design: Mark Ryden
Book design: Benjamin Brard

Published in 2020 by Cernunnos, an imprint of ABRAMS.

Printed and bound in China
10 9

Abrams books are available at special discounts when purchased in quantity for premiums and promotions as well as fundraising or educational use. Special editions can also be created to specification. For details, contact specialsales@abramsbooks.com or the address below.

Abrams® is a registered trademark of Harry N. Abrams, Inc.

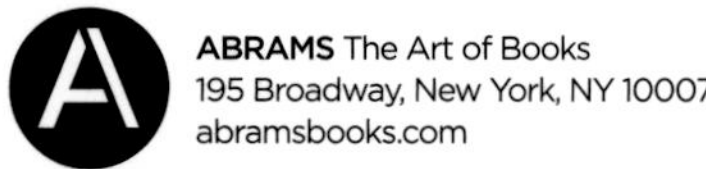

ABRAMS is represented in the UK and Europe by Abrams & Chronicle Books, 22-24 Ely Place, London EC1N 6TE and Média-Participations, 57 rue Gaston Tessier, 75166 Paris, France.
abramsandchronicle.co.uk and media-participations.com
info@abramsandchronicle.co.uk

MY NEIGHBOR HAYAO
ART INSPIRED BY THE FILMS OF MIYAZAKI

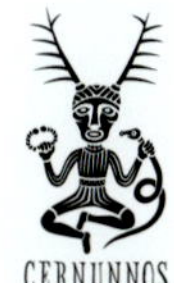

TABLE OF CONTENTS

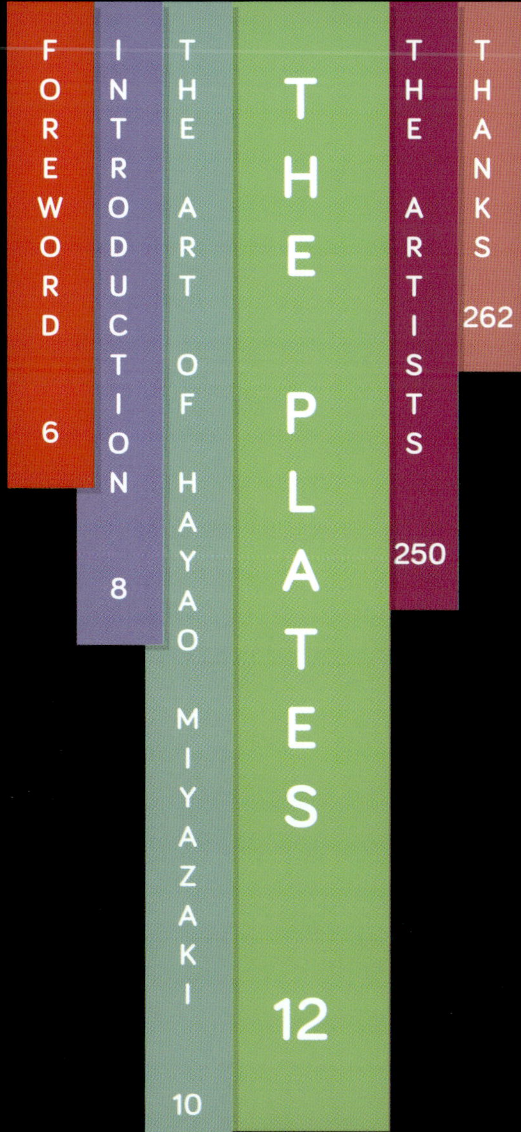

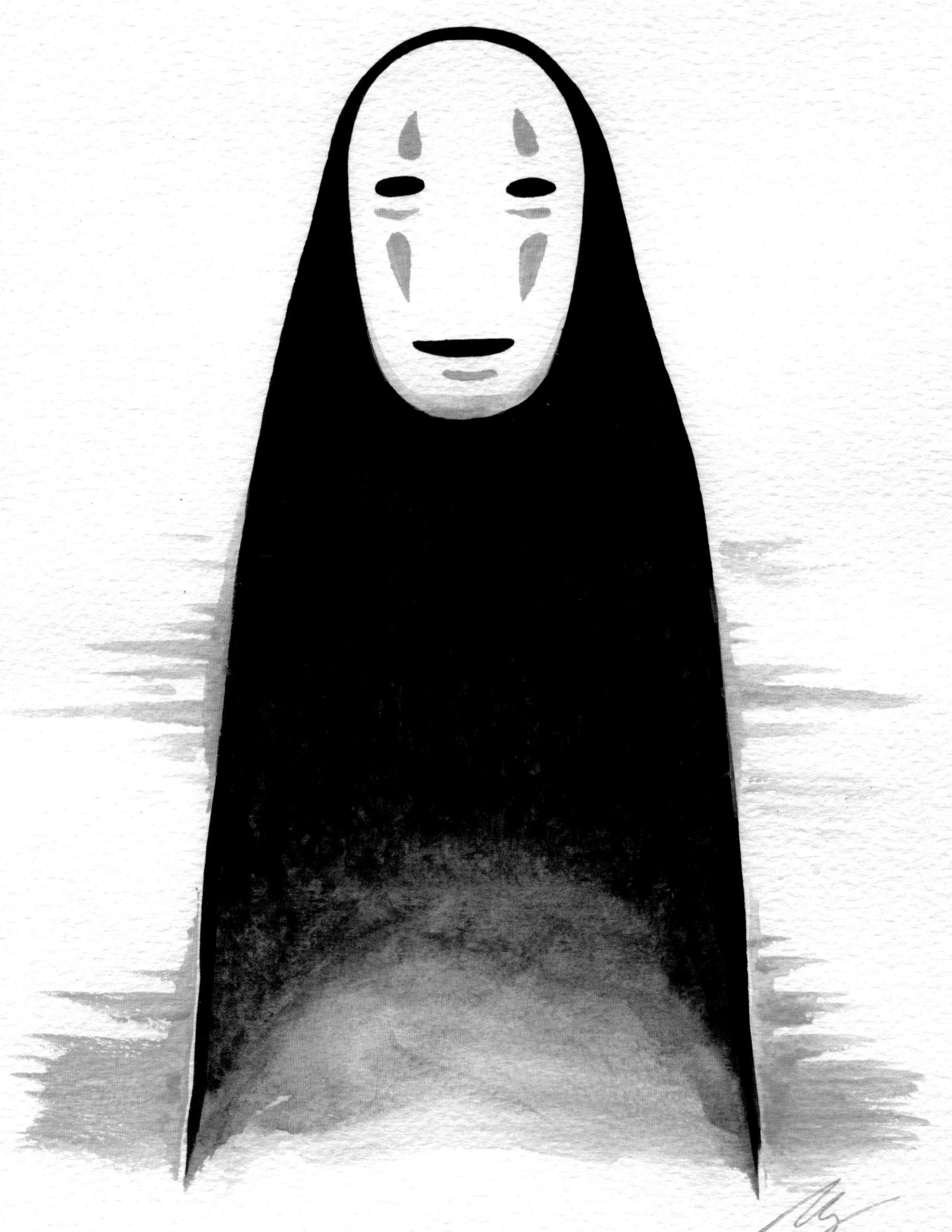

FOREWORD

The heartfelt, magical, hilarious, soulful, astounding and exhilarating work of master Hayao Miyazaki has profoundly touched and influenced thousands of artists and filmmakers from all over the world. I know *Spirited Away* changed me as a filmmaker and is one of the reasons I made *The Book of Life*. Miyazaki's films have allowed us a personal and privileged view into the window of his very soul. And in that reflection we have seen ourselves. His films are a true triumph of the perfect balance of art and craft.

But more importantly, they are triumph of the human spirit. The world is a much better place having had Hayao Miyazaki's work to guide and inspire us all for generations to come.

His legacy is forever and after.

Viva Miyazaki!

Jorge Gutierrez
Filmaker of *El Tigre* and *The Book of Life*

RHYS COOPER
No Face
Watercolor and ink on paper. 8 x 10".

INTRODUCTION

It's a cool and breezy January night in San Francisco. A long queue snakes its way down Leavenworth Street, makes a sharp left onto Sutter and traverses one full city block to an intimate and cozy gallery space at the corner of Jones. The hundreds of film and art lovers who have come out for the evening are both eager and patient, most have been in line for over an hour or two and many are in costume.

A young woman wearing a white fur headpiece with red face paint stands patiently behind a couple in matching grey terry-cloth outfits with beige tummies and long whiskers. A child, no older than twelve years old, clutches a small wooden broom and stuffed black cat as her parents adjust the red bow in her hair. Passersby stop to ogle, both confused and bemused by the length of the line and the colorful inhabitants who comprise it.

The year is 2017 and it's the opening night reception of the first annual Miyazaki-inspired art show. Inside the intimate gallery space on Sutter Street, the walls of the Spoke Art gallery are covered from floor to ceiling with an eclectic mix of paintings, prints and sculptures. The exhibition is hung salon-style, partly because the overwhelming number of artworks demands it and partly because the content of the artworks on view is so diverse that there's no way to present it in anything resembling a linear fashion.

Paintings created in acrylic or oil paints on canvas and wood panel hang beside graphite drawings and watercolor paintings on paper. On various pedestals, sculptures made from metal, felt and mixed media are scattered about. One can even find hand cut paper, collage, needlepoint and assemblage peppered throughout the exhibition.

Along the back wall of the gallery a diverse range of limited edition prints are on view. Many of these were created with analog hand printing methods, such as serigraphy, while other, more complicated designs warranted state-of-the-art archival pigment printing.

Over the course of the evening, we welcomed hundreds of very patient and enthusiastic attendees with thousands more visiting during the exhibition's three-week run. The following year, we traveled the show to Hashimoto Contemporary in New York City's Lower East Side and the following year the exhibition ventured to Honolulu, Hawaii, as part of the POW! WOW! urban arts festival. As the exhibition toured, it grew larger and larger, like a gluttonous No-Face, taking on new works and new artists, and bringing in new fans as the word spread.

The eclectic and varied nature of the artworks found throughout this book should not come as a surprise to anyone who's followed Hayao Miyazaki's storied fifty-plus year career. From his television work with Toei Animation in the early 1960s to his "final film" with Studio Ghibli in 2013, Hayao Miyazaki has created an unparalleled body of work, an ouevre that spans generations, transcends genres and elevated a previously under appreciated medium as true cinema.

Over the course of the next two hundred or so pages, you'll revisit a rustic countryside inhabited by a mysterious, smiling and cuddly creature. You'll travel back hundreds of years to the Muromachi period with a girl raised by wolves. You'll fly over the Mediterranean with a porcine pilot and you'll dine at a bathhouse inhabited by the gods.

Of course, the creatures, gods, children, heroines, forests, flying machines and spirits that you'll encounter here are not identical to the ones you may remember. Some of the works shown are more literal and representational, characters you know and love albe, it depicted through a new medium. Others are more open to individual artistic interpretation, unique spins on our shared cultural memory, the creation of something that is both eerily recognizable and familiar-though unusual and foreign.

This is, of course, the nature of visual art. Much as when stories are passed down from generation to generation, they grow, evolve and adapt, so too does visual art. Young artists cull from those who came before and in turn influence the next generation themselves.

Miyazaki himself is part of this lineage, as are Johanna Spyri (author of *Heidi: Her Years of Wandering and Learning*, published 1880) Eiko Kadono (author of *Kiki's Delivery Service*, published 1985) and Diana Wynne Jones (author of *Howl's Moving Castle*, published 1986). The telling and retelling of stories is instrumental to Miyazaki's own creative process as he propels these new, updated narratives forward to influence those who come after him.

In fact, there's a scene in *Kiki's Delivery Service* that comes to mind, wherein our young witch has lost her powers and must be consoled by her older and wiser friend, the artist Ursula. In discussing her own artistic block and how it's similar to Kiki's recent loss of magic, Ursula describes a time when she was Kiki's age and had lost her drive to create.

"I realized that my art up to then was a copy of someone else, things I had seen somewhere. I decided I had to discover my own style" Urusula sagely advises Kiki, and of course, the advice works.

While many autobiographical references can be found throughout Miyazaki's films, from his mother's fight with tuberculosis when Miyazaki was a child to his father's family business making airplane parts for the Japanese war effort during WWII, it is, in my opinion, this brief exchange between Ursula and Kiki that resonates for me as being one of the more personal, "albeit" subtile, autobiographical notes.

I wonder if it's Ursula's advice that helped propel Miyazaki upwards from his position as a lowly "in-between artist" at Toei Animation in 1963 to his co-founding of Studio Ghibli more than twenty years later in 1985. In many ways, the duality between Ursula and Kiki implies that they're two sides of the same coin, a point driven home in the original Japanese language version of the film as both characters are played by the same voice actor, Minami Takayama.

While I can't speak for Miyazaki myself, after three years of curating and touring this exhibition I can confidently say that the hundreds of artists who have contributed to our show (and subsequently to this book) have all, like both Ursula and Kiki, have discovered their own styles as well, while still paying homage to the brilliant work that inspires us.

Ken Harman Hashimoto
Curator

THE ART OF HAYAO MIYAZAKI

Was it because he witnessed the ugliness of war as a child that Miyazaki has brought so much beauty to Japanese animation? Tokyo-born filmmaker Hayao Miyazaki originally dreamed of becoming a *mangaka*, or Japanese comic book artist, and being the next Osamu Tezuka. Considered the father of modern manga, Tezuka was the author of more than seven hundred series–including *Astro Boy, Buddha, Kimba the White Lion* and *Phoenix*–and roughly seventy films and animated series. He was young Hayao's earliest source of inspiration. "My head still spins today at the thought of comparing myself to such a giant, next to whom I was nothing," Miyazaki told an interviewer from the French newspaper *Libération* in 2014. But the little boy who dreamed of rivalling Tezuka ended up becoming a master in his own right: the first (and to this day only) Japanese to win an Academy Award for best animated feature, for *Spirited Away*. Miyazaki and Tezuka share a love of nature and a visceral hatred of war, along with a deep interest in Western culture. Both also amassed large fanbases among youth audiences before gradually moving toward more adult narratives. "Cinema was a strange and distant medium to me," Miyazaki has said. "What's more, I took part in hardly any of the major movements of the time. I was so much in my cartoonist's bubble that I missed out on it all. [...] Being free, living a free life, that was my obsession when I was young. But working as a *mangaka* is like slavery. Only once I discovered animation did I break free of that nightmare. Basically, I didn't need to be a *mangaka* anymore." Who would have thought that the future creator of *Princess Mononoke* would be so disgusted by the study of art that he refused to attend art school? Instead, he chose to study economics, even if it meant being a mediocre student (which he was), so that he could concentrate on personal projects. He was eventually hired by Toei Animation at age twenty-two in the 1960s and went on to found Studio Ghibli in 1985.

Like his longtime creative partner Isao Takahata, he has favored hand-drawn animation throughout his career. He mastered watercolor, pencil drawing, painting and colorizing, having held practically every job in the industry: storyboard artist, animator, screenwriter and director. After fifty years of work and dedication, Miyazaki has become a god of Japanese animation.

In perfecting his own art and visual world, Miyazaki was influenced by Asian and Western animated classics such as *Panda and the Magic Serpent*, Lev Atamanov's 1957 *The Snow Queen*, and *The King and the Mockingbird* (originally released as *La Bergère et le Ramoneur* in 1952). An admirer of Antoine de Saint-Exupéry, Miyazaki has often cited *The Little Prince, Night Flight* and *Wind, Sand and Stars* as sources of inspiration. Indeed, he returns to the figure of the aviator in

Castle in the Sky and *Porco Rosso*, and calls it into question in *The Wind Rises*. An avid reader of fantasy, science fiction and mystery novels, Miyazaki incorporates elements of "lowbrow" literature into many of his films. In addition to Maurice Leblanc, to whom he pays homage in *Lupin the Third: The Castle of Cagliostro*, his imagination was also fed by Anglophone writers such as Lewis Carroll, Ursula K. Le Guin and Diana Wynne Jones (author of *Howl's Moving Castle*). Celebrated Franco-Belgian comic book artist Jean Giraud AKA Moebius was another major influence, and we see traces of his flying hero Arzak in the manga *Nausicaä of the Valley of the Wind*. The links between Miyazaki and Giraud's work were the focus of a joint exhibition at Monnaie de Paris in 2004. In Miyazaki's films, literary retellings and references are blended with elements from Japanese narrative culture and the filmmaker's personal memories and themes. Environmental concerns and a critique of consumerism interweave in such complex tales as *Nausicaä*, *Princess Mononoke* and *Spirited Away*. A passion for aviation ended up blossoming into a vast poetic universe, one elevated by superb drawings, an innovative aesthetic and musical scores by Joe Hisaishi. As anime scholar Marie Pruvost-Delaspre once explained in an interview on France Inter: "Miyazaki's work contains some quite astonishing camera movement that we rarely see in animation. Miyazaki and Takahata really were the first to pursue that kind of depth of field."

Another of Miyazaki's strengths lies in his highly distinctive, instantly recognizable visual style. His narratives often incorporate endearing creatures–such as Totoro–that occasionally transform into ferocious beasts. "Adults think of a child's imagination as being all cute, fluffy teddy bears, the kind of things they like," Miyazaki explained in *Positif* magazine. "But children are drawn to the monstrous. [...] For them to grow, they have to be confronted with a darkness, which, to adults, can appear inherently bad." Totoro, Porco Rosso, No-Face and Haku the dragon have since entered the global pop culture canon. The power of Miyazaki's art has allowed it to be embraced on every continent thanks to its universal values and strong female characters. Though the representation of women in film is just now starting to evolve, Miyazaki was ahead of his time in creating iconic heroines like Chihiro, Kiki, Mononoke, Sheeta and Sophie. Far from waiting for a Prince Charming to come to their rescue, Miyazaki's female characters are beloved for their maturity and selflessness in the face of danger. In this regard, Nausicaä is one of the greatest heroines of Japanese cinema. *Nausicaä of the Valley of the Wind* is an epic odyssey, brilliantly drawn and written, that blends science fiction and fantasy and continues to be one of the best ecological fables ever to take comic book form. Miyazaki is among the rare artists to have found success not just in film but also in publishing and television. He has become as much a giant of animation as Tezuka was of manga, and he remains a master of the twentieth- and twenty-first-century imagination. His influence on today's creators, no matter the genre, is becoming more evident with each passing year and is already beginning to bear fruit.

Lloyd Chery
Journalist

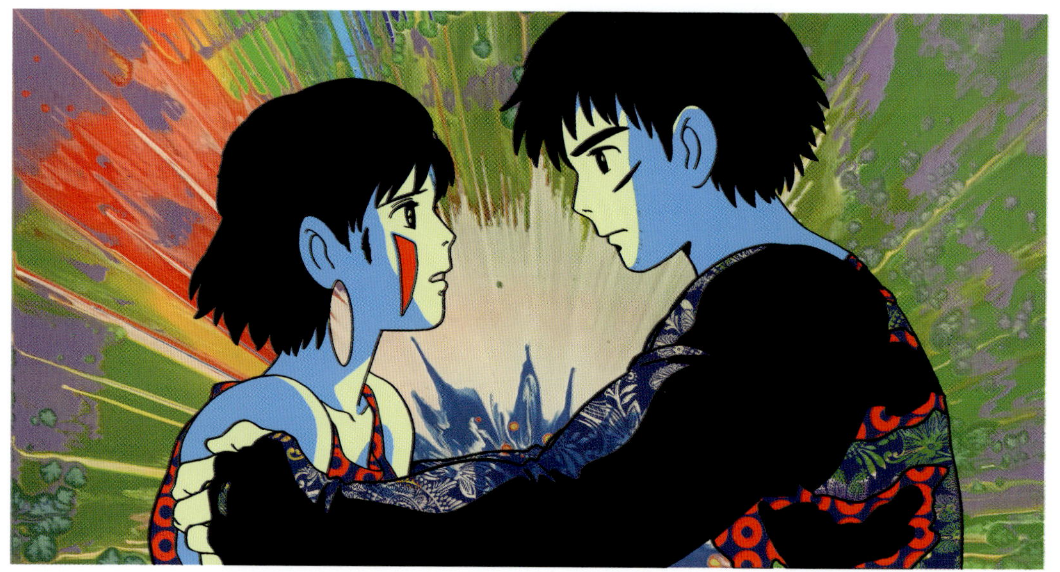

MATT DYE / BLUNT GRAFFIX

Princess Mononoke

Spin art over holographic foil with 5 color screen print. 23.75 x 11.5".

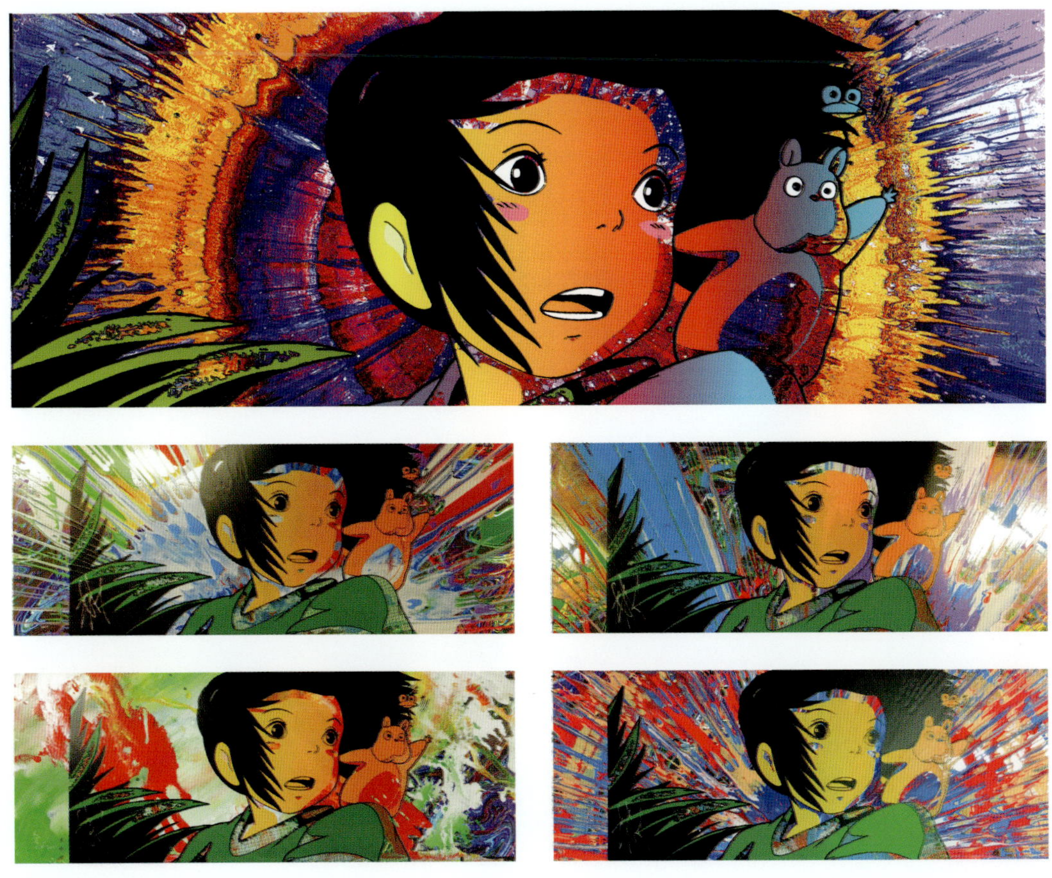

Chihiro

Centrifuge on foil - hand pulled screen prints. 26 x 10".

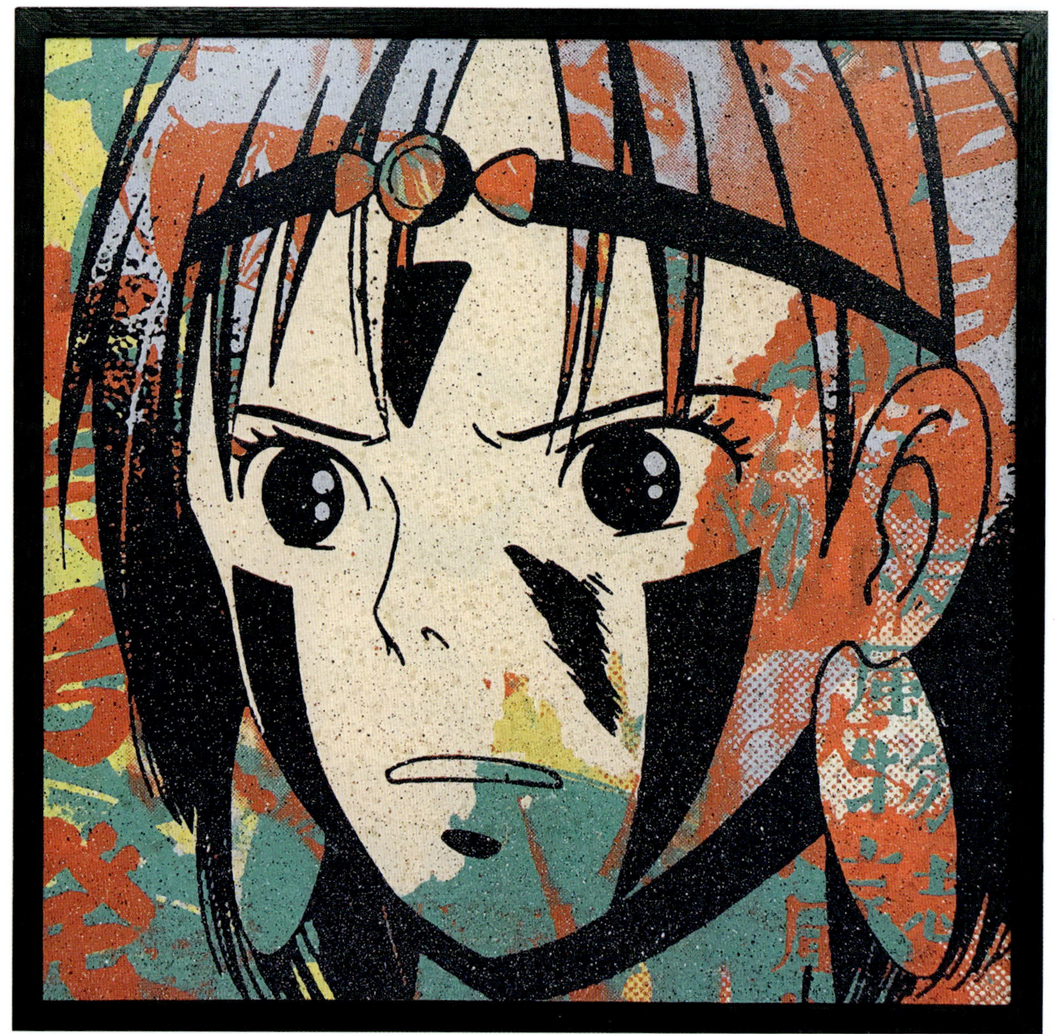

GREG GOSSEL

San

Screen print, collage, acrylic, and enamel on wood panel. 10 x 10".

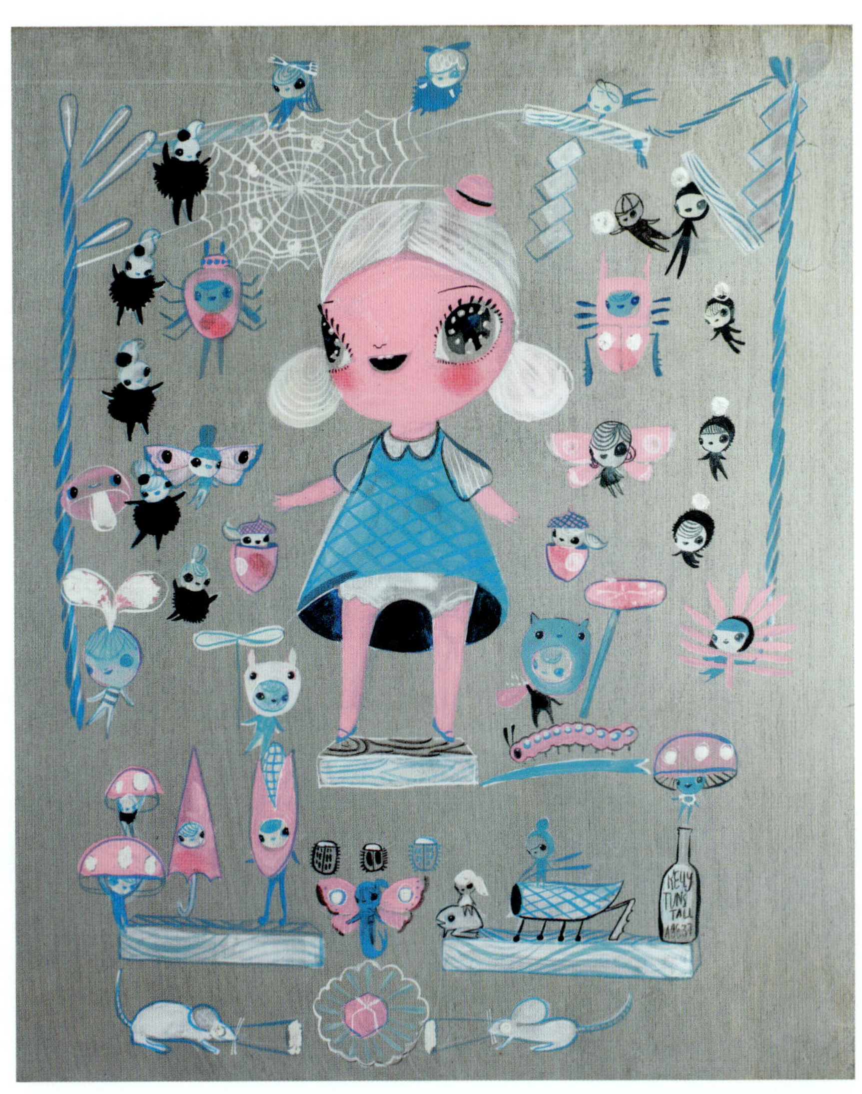

KELLY TUNSTALL

Totoro the Musical

Acrylic and white gold leaf on panel. 16 x 20".

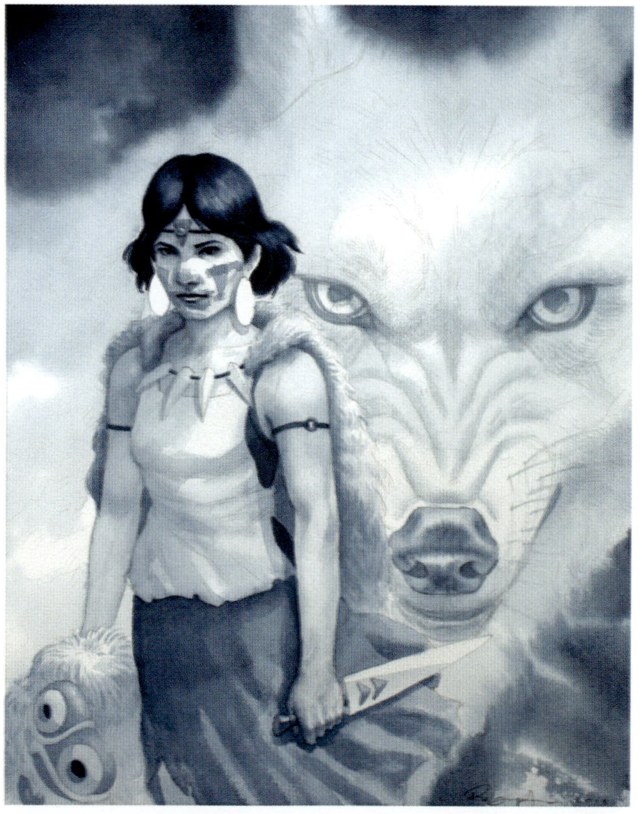

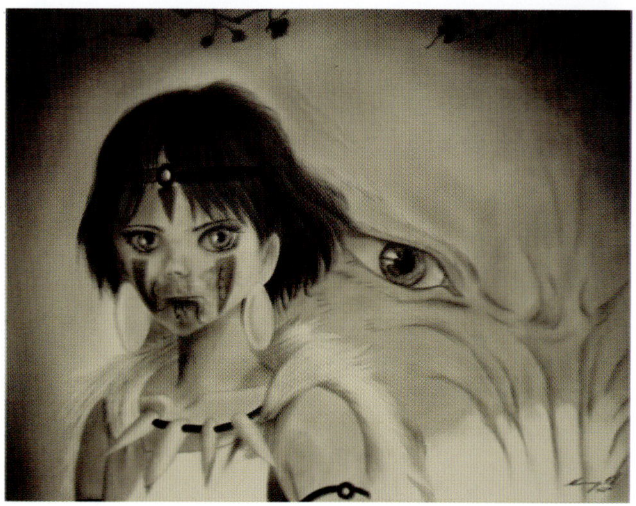

REUBEN NEGRON

TOP LEFT

The Wolf Girl

Watercolor. 11 x 14".

HARRY MICHALAKEAS

BOTTOM LEFT

The Earth Doesn't Belong to Man, Man Belongs to the Earth

Pastel, carbon, graphite and ink on Bristol. 11 x 14".

RIGHT PAGE

Kiki's Delivery Service

Pastel, carbon and charcoal. 12 x 16".

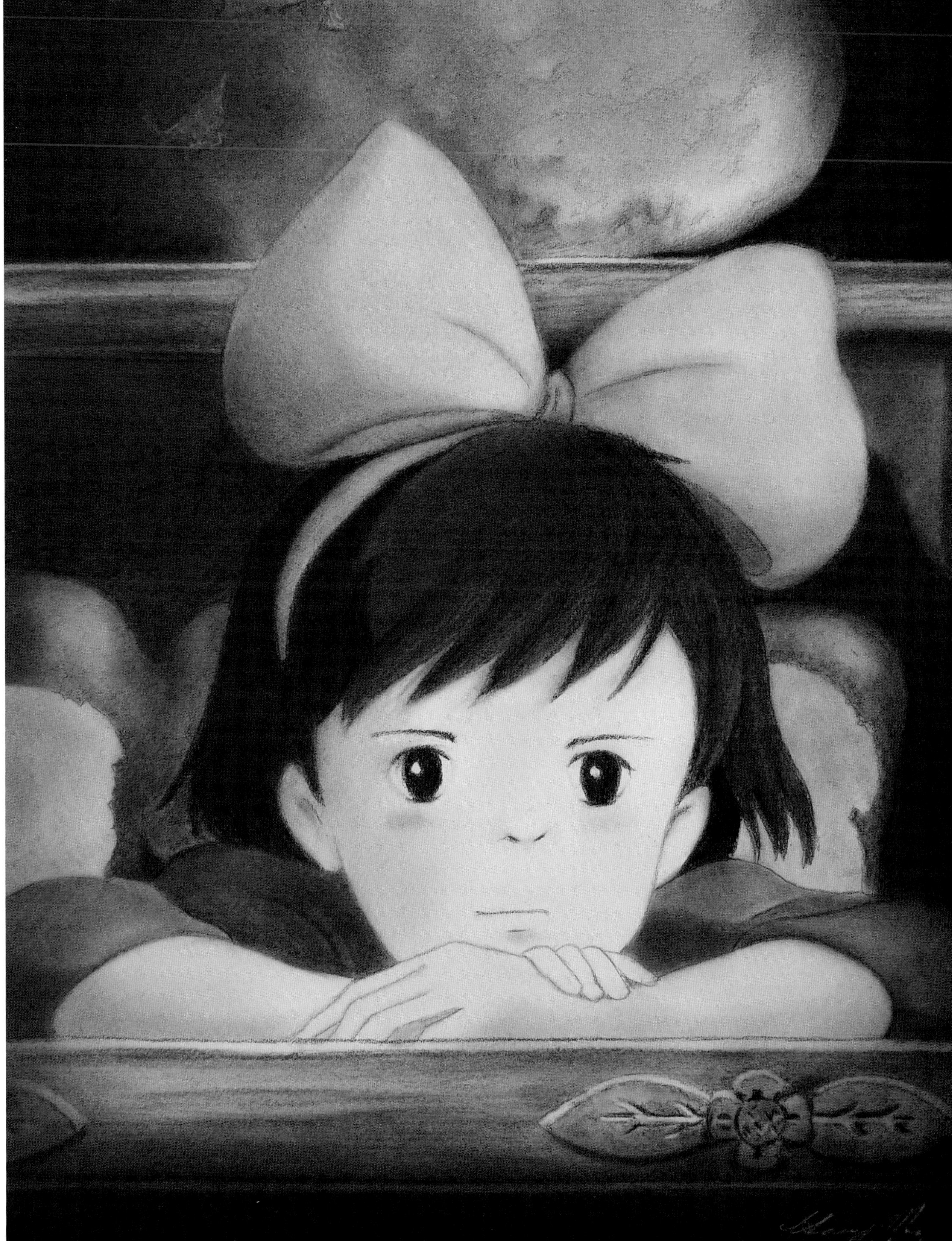

EDWIN USHIRO

RIGHT PAGE

Wrapping Ends Up
Mixed media on acetate. 5 x 7".

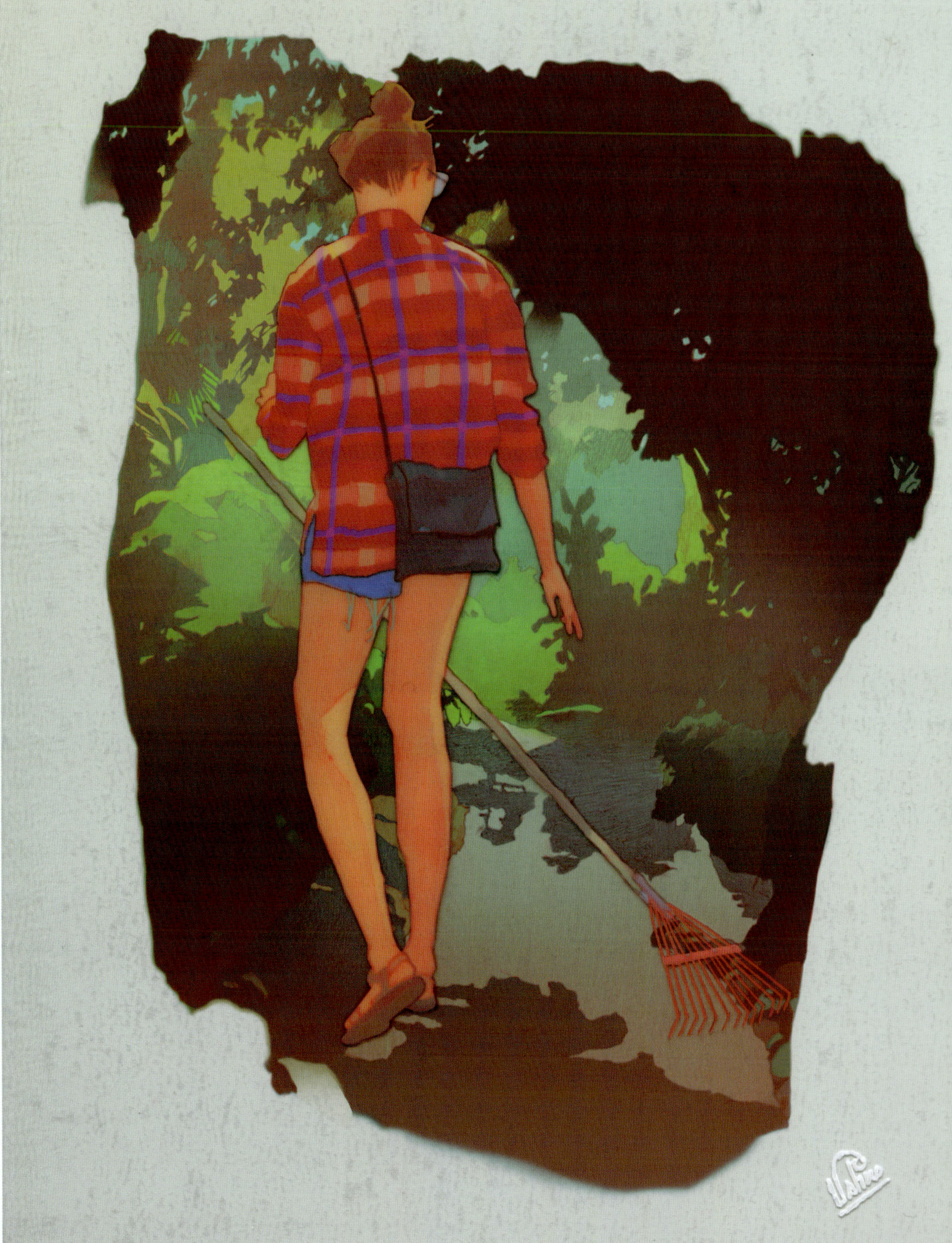

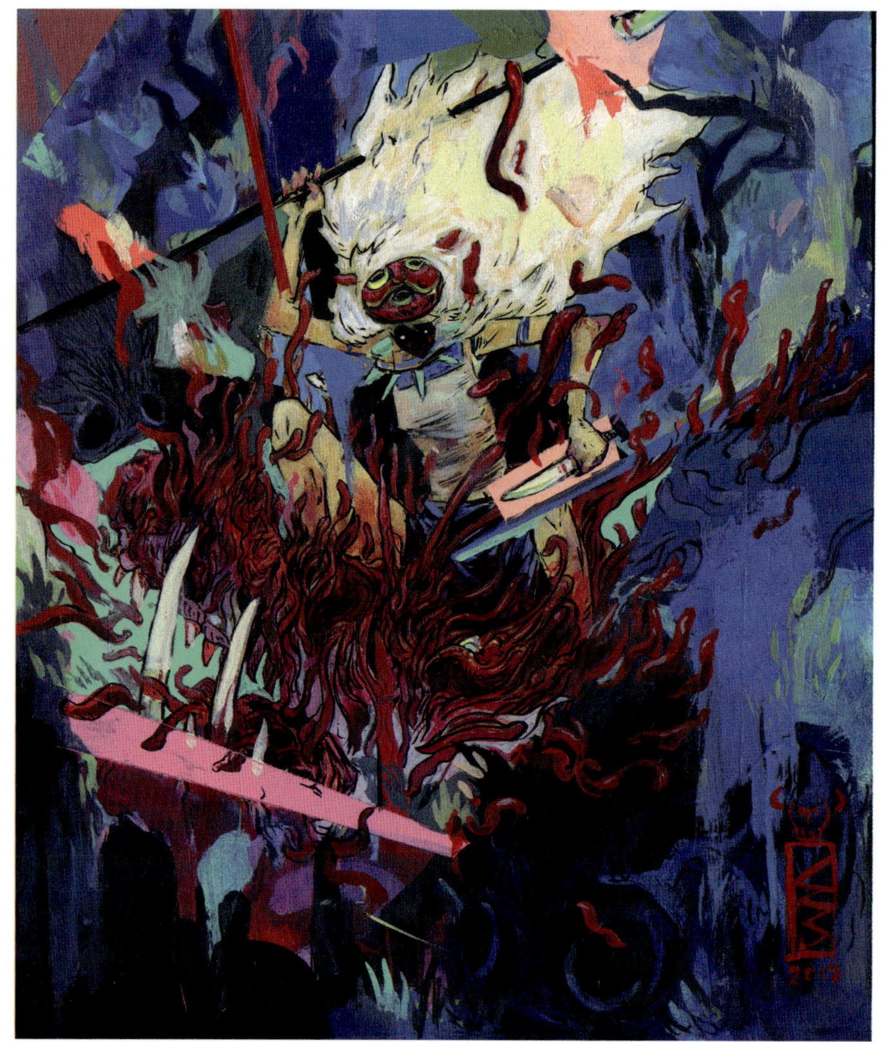

ERIC BONHOMME

ABOVE

Consumed

Acrylic on wood. 11 x 14".

RIGHT PAGE

Out of my Way!

Acrylic on board. 16 x 20".

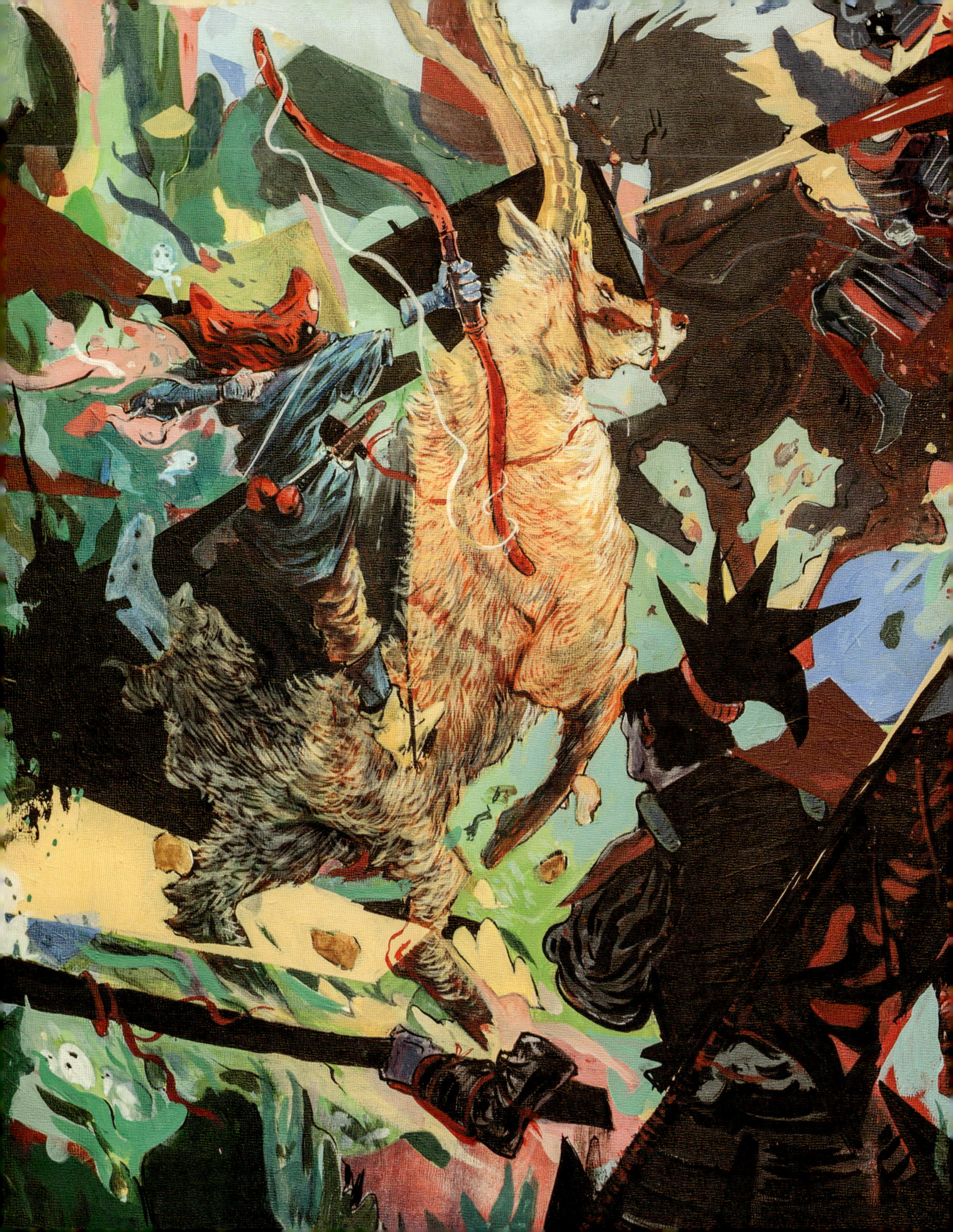

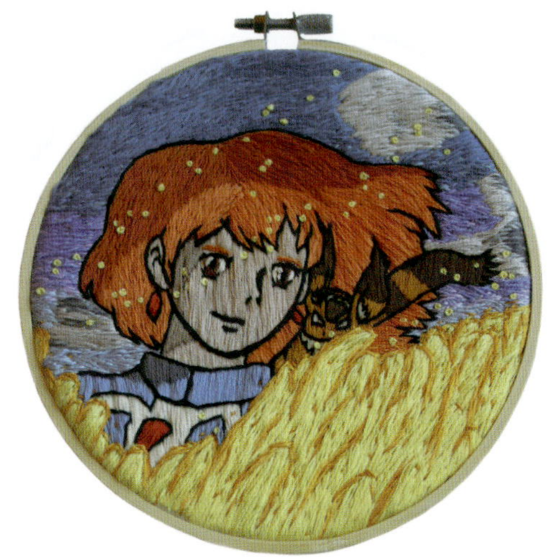

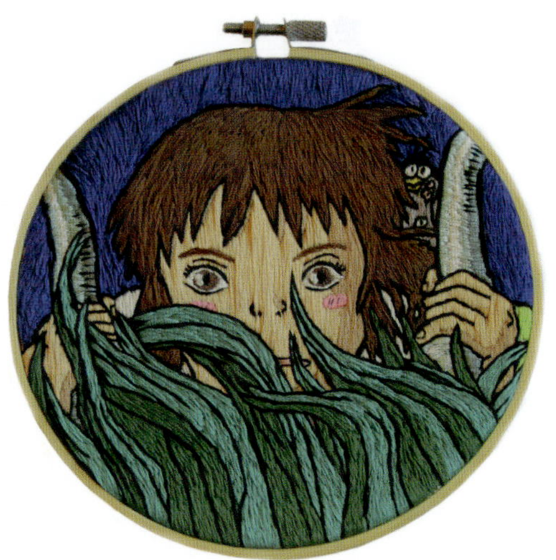

LIZ VOWLES

TOP LEFT

Ohmu Embrace

Embroidery floss on cotton fabric.
6" diameter.

TOP RIGHT

Kohaku River

Embroidery floss on cotton fabric.
6" diameter.

BRANDAN STYLES

RIGHT PAGE

Howls Moving Castle

Acrylic on hand cut wood.
12 x 8.5 x 3.5".

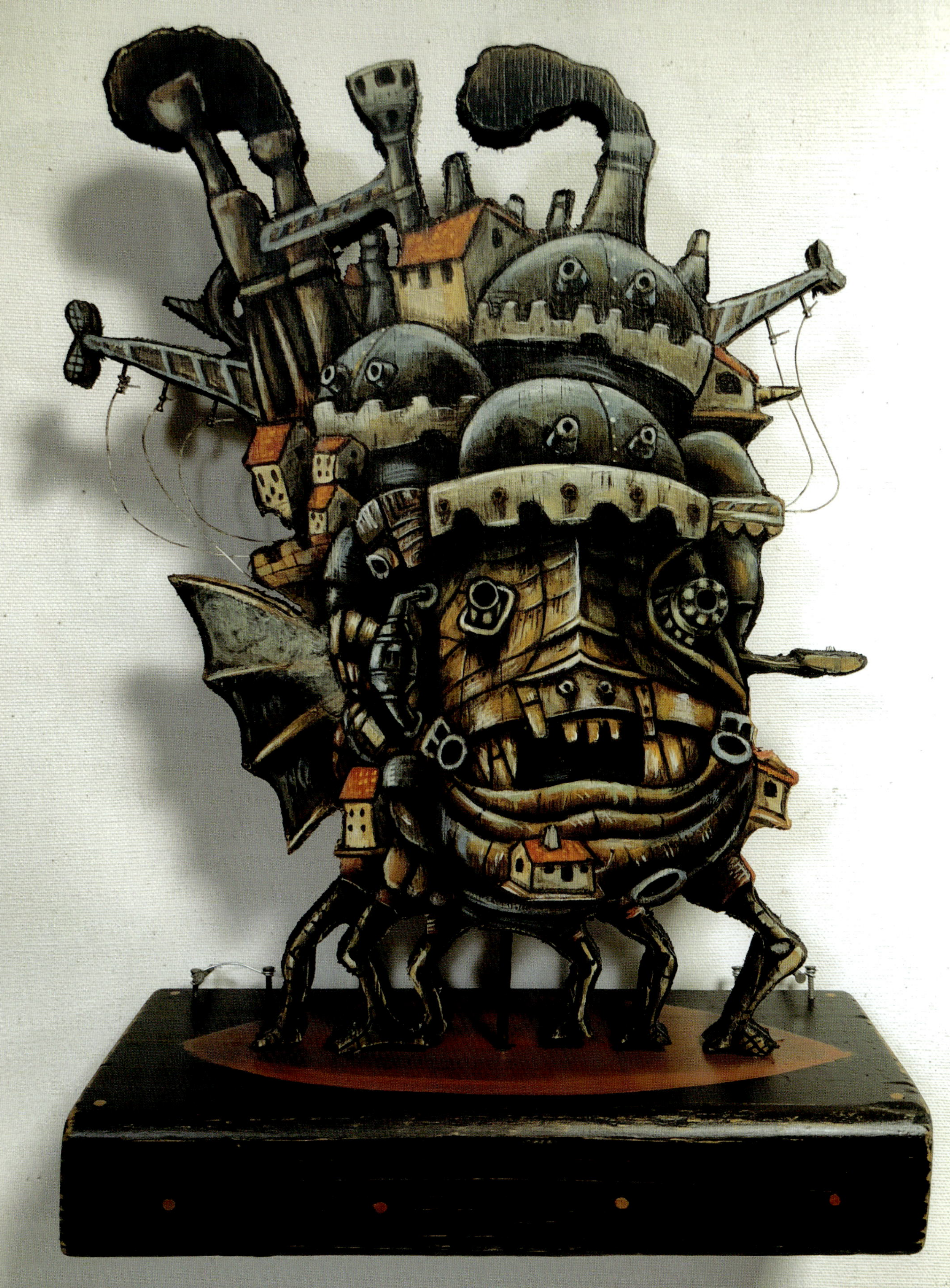

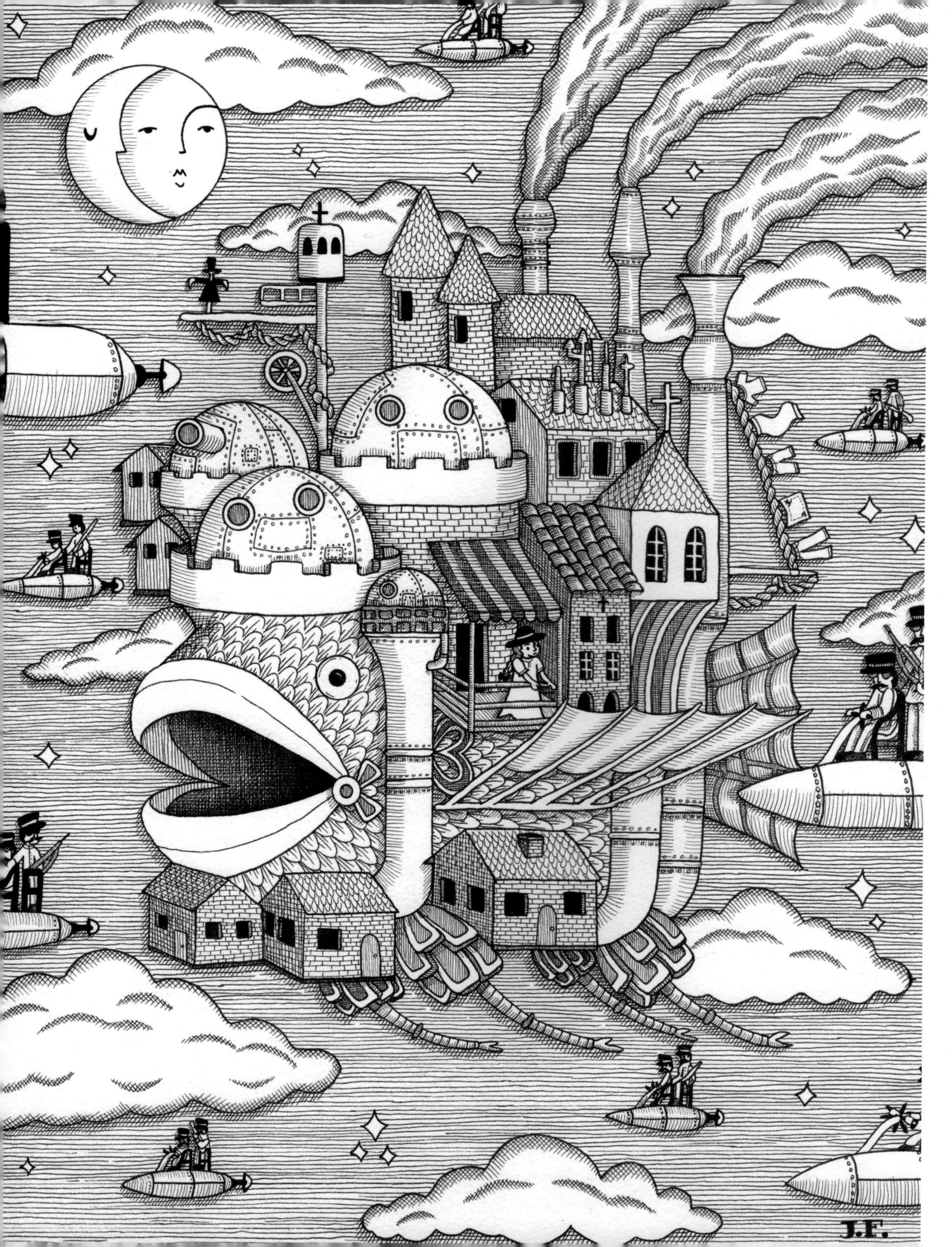
J.F.

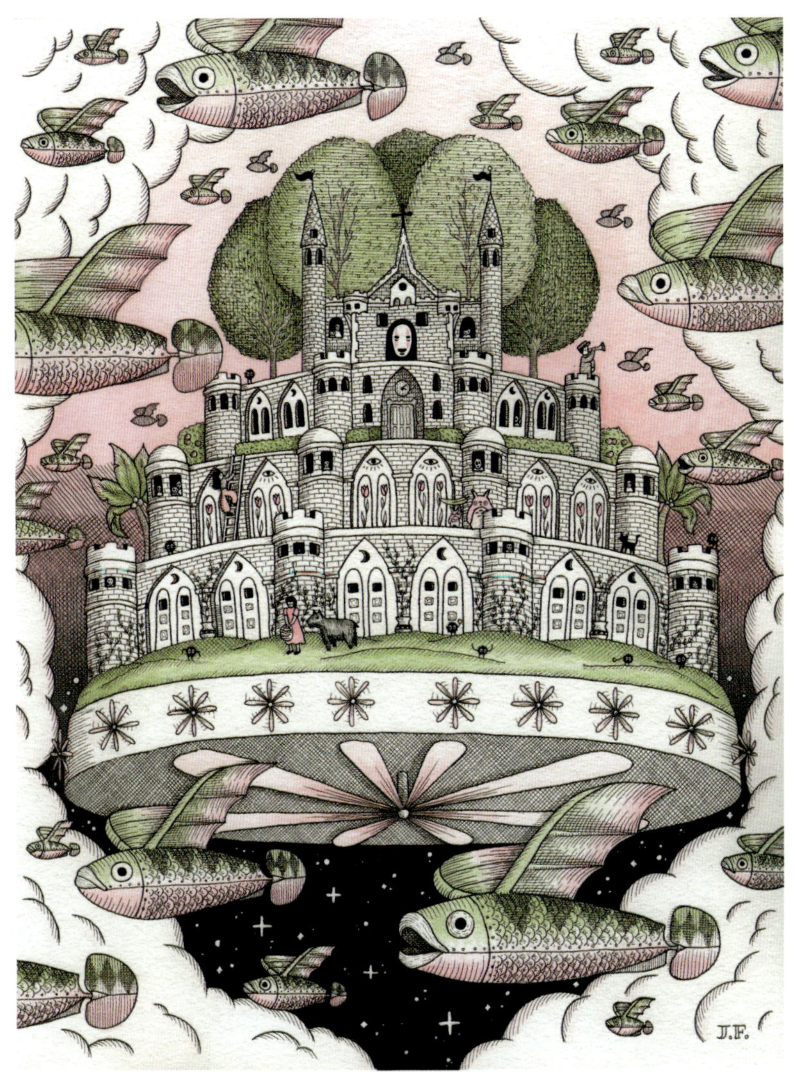

JAYDE CARDINALLI

ABOVE

Fish's Moving Castle

Ink on paper. 12 x 16".

LEFT PAGE

Fish's Flying Castle

Ink on paper. 12 x 16".

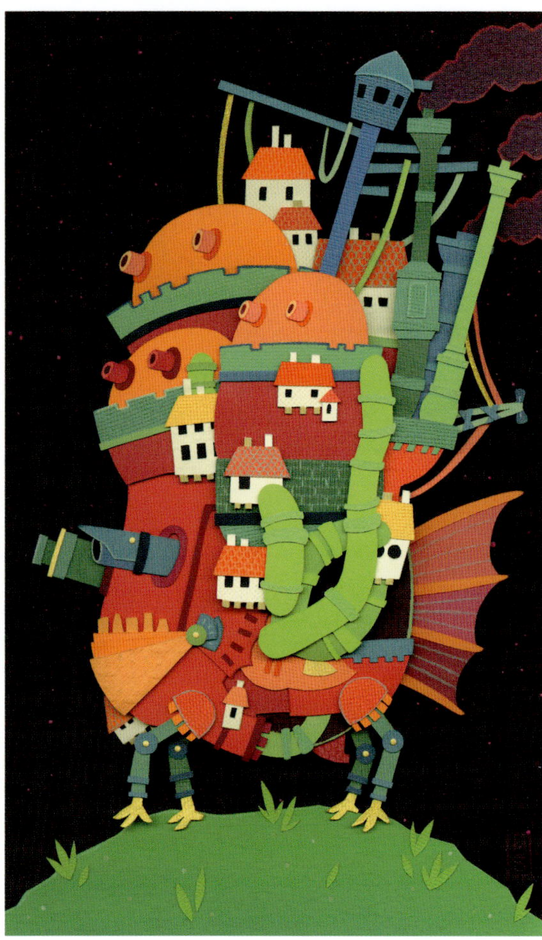

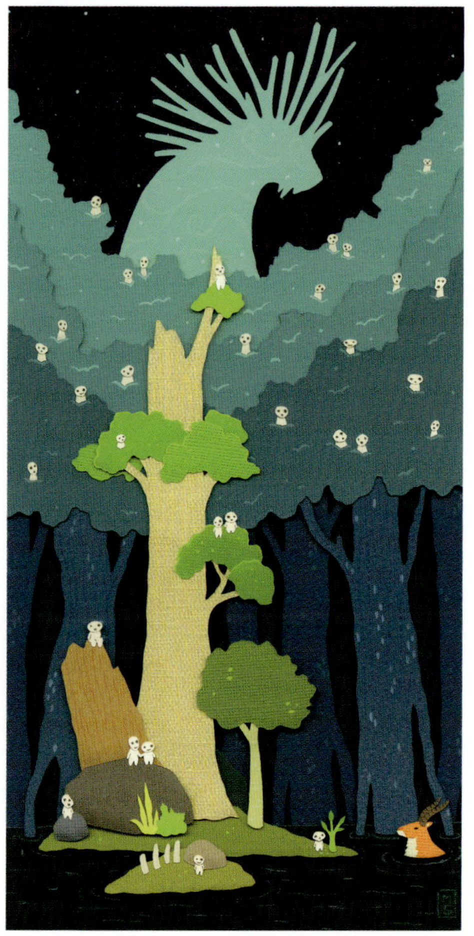

MEGHAN STRATMAN

LEFT

Howl's Castle

Paper collage. 6 x 10".

RIGHT

The Forest Spirit

3D paper collage. 6 x 12".

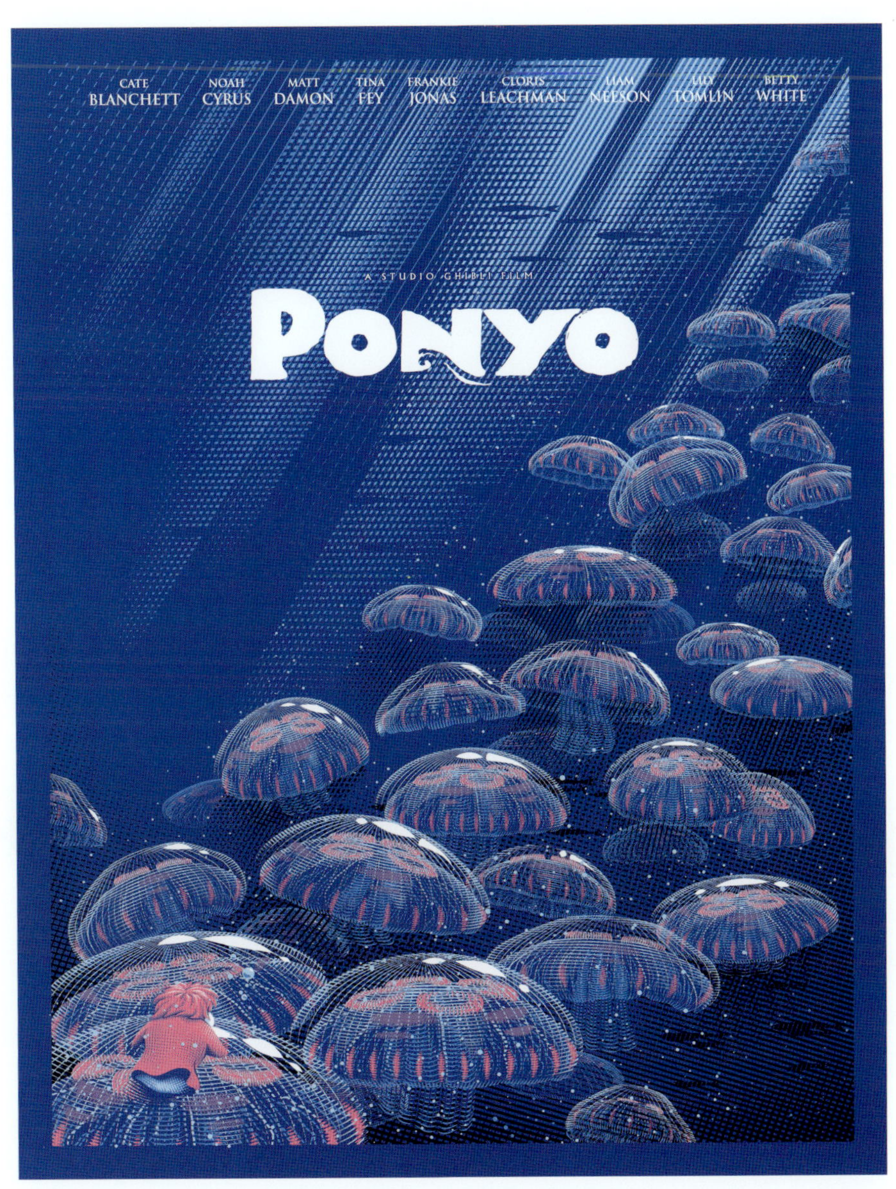

TRACIE CHING

Ponyo

Silkscreen print. 18 x 24".

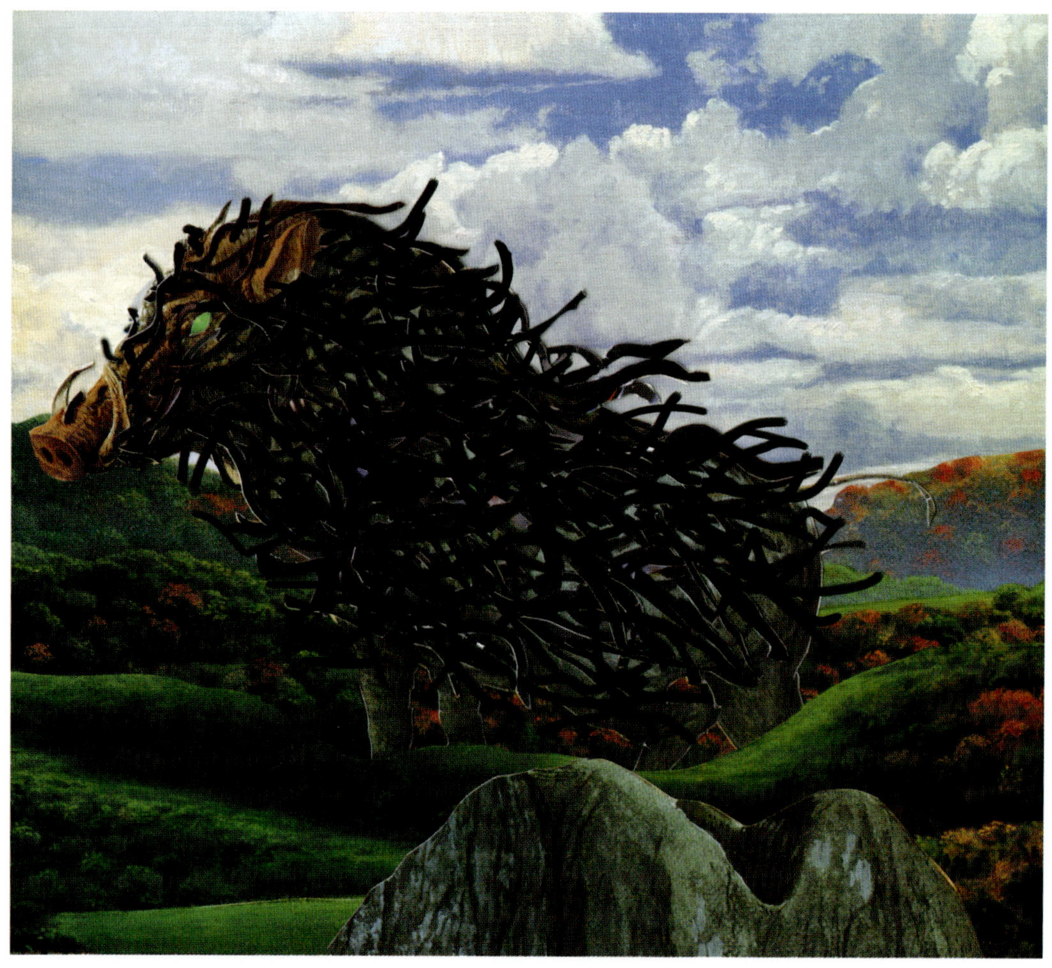

MICHAEL TUNK

ABOVE

Nago the Boar Demon
Collage. 16 x 12".

RIGHT PAGE

Shishi Gami the Forest Spirit
Collage. 17 x 21".

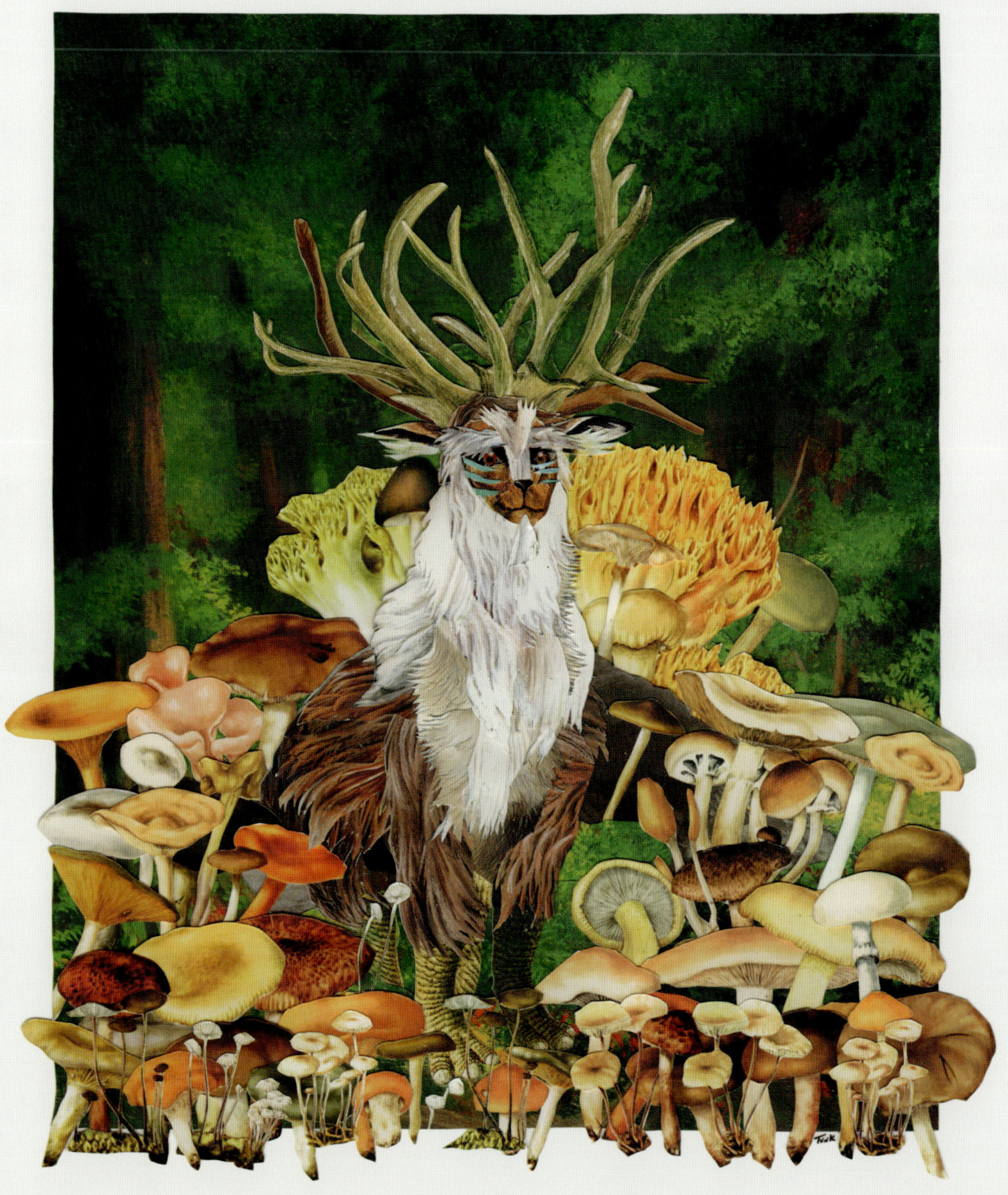

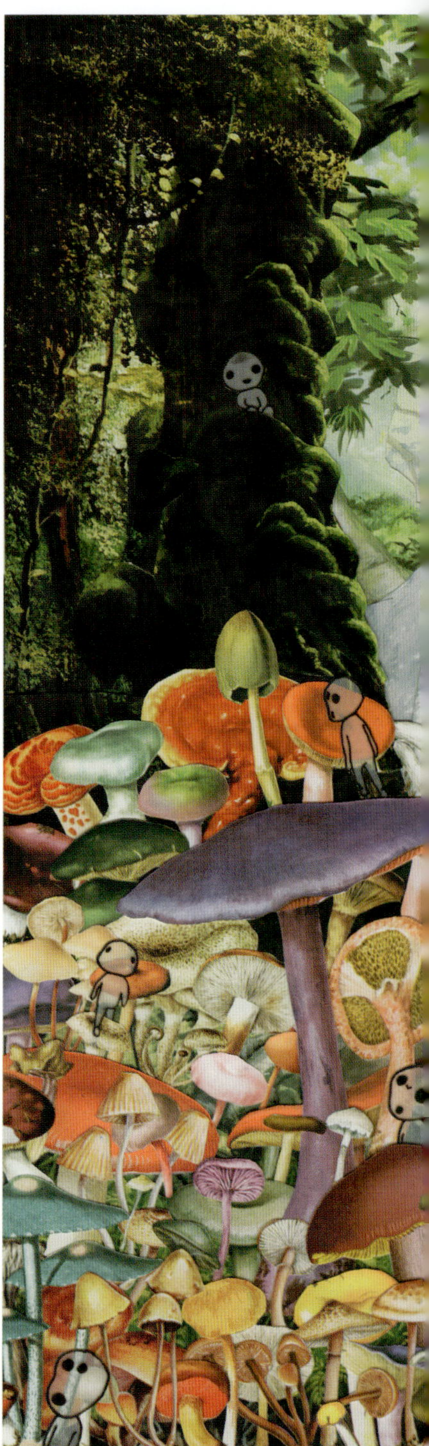

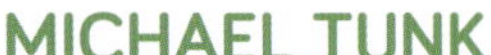

Mononoke Hime

Analog collage with Micron pen and vellum paper. 19 x 16".

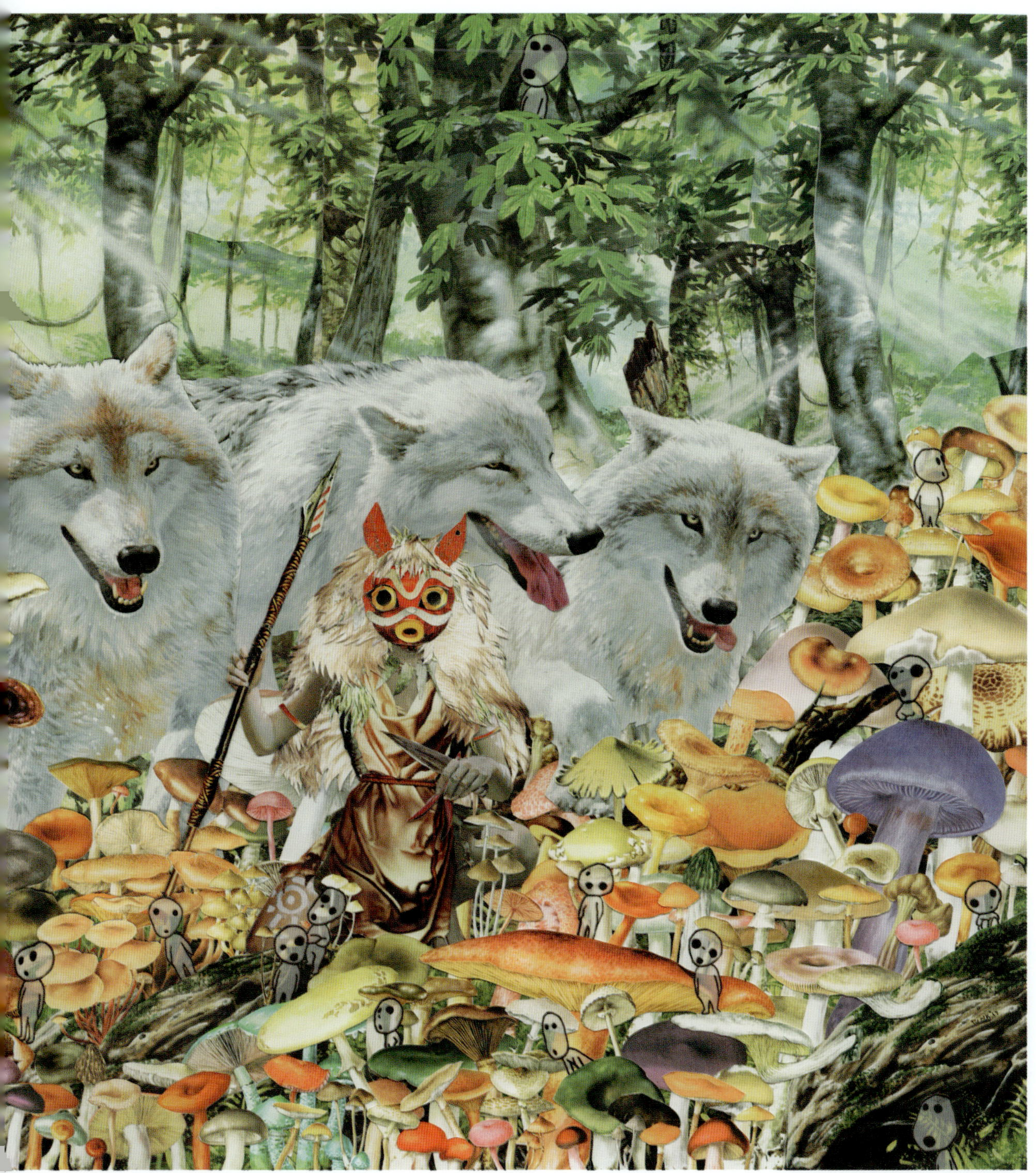

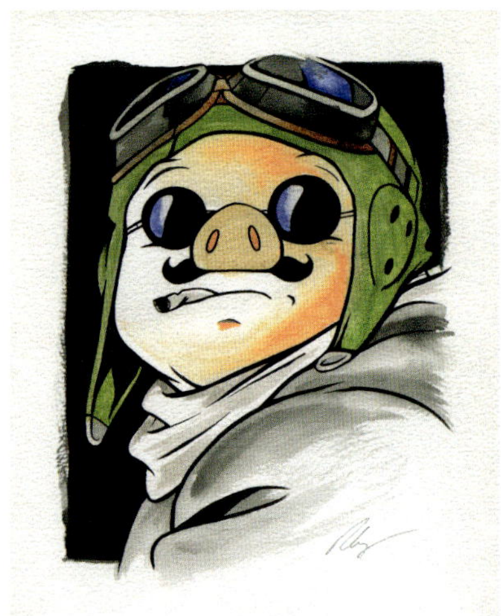

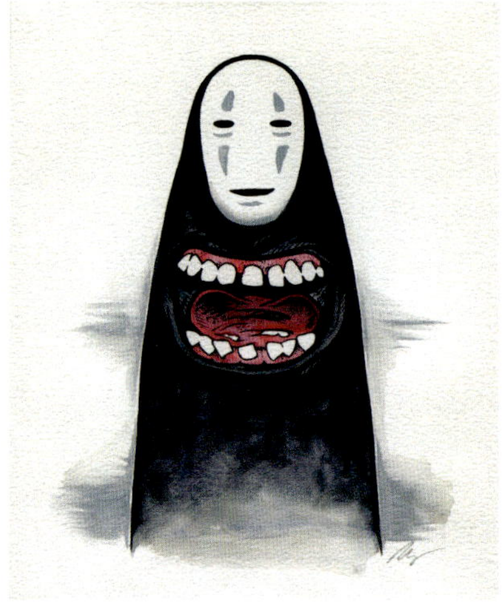

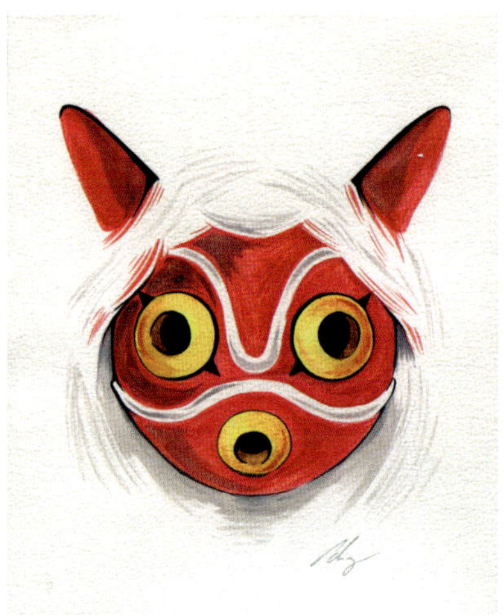

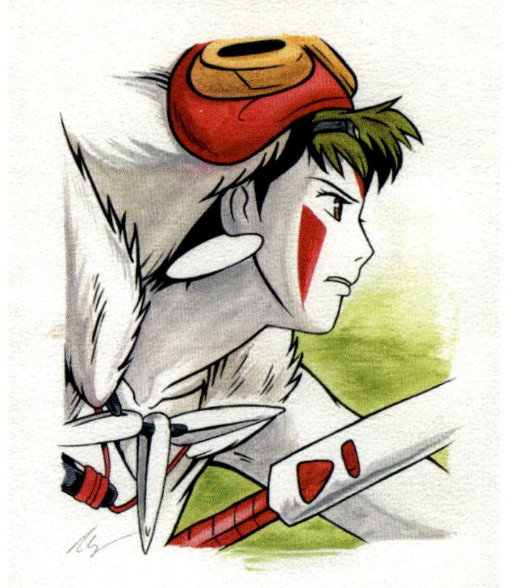

RHYS COOPER

TOP LEFT

Porco Rosso

Watercolor and ink on paper.
8 x 10".

TOP RIGHT

No Face is Hungry

Watercolor and ink on paper.
8 x 10".

RIGHT PAGE

Soot Sprites

Watercolor and ink on paper.
8 x 10".

BOTTOM LEFT

Masked Princess

Watercolor and ink on paper.
8 x 10".

BOTTOM RIGHT

Mononoke

Watercolor and ink on paper.
8 x 10".

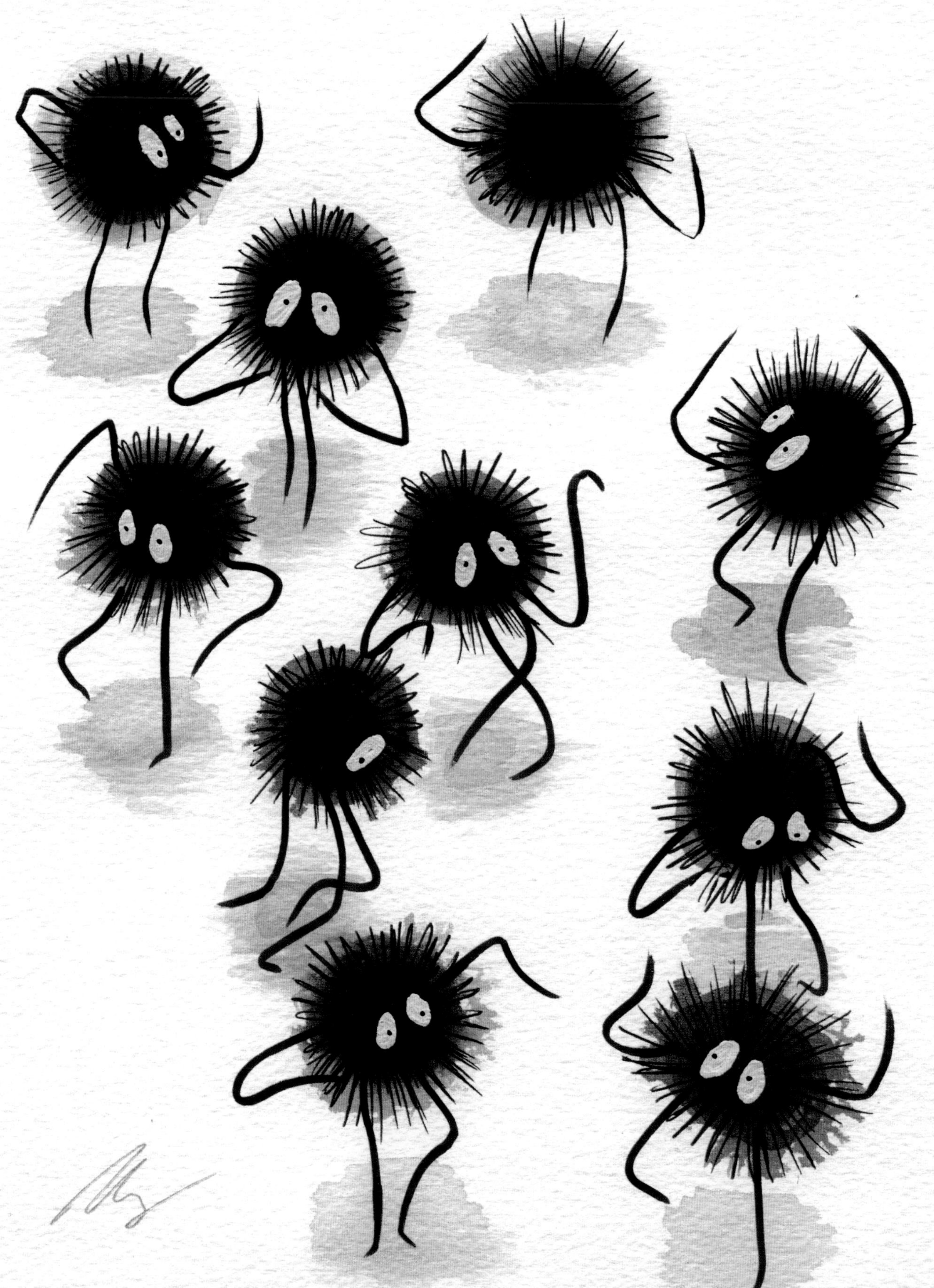

RIGHT PAGE

ALLISON REIMOLD

Kiki

Gouache, acrylic and graphite on vellum. 8 x 10".

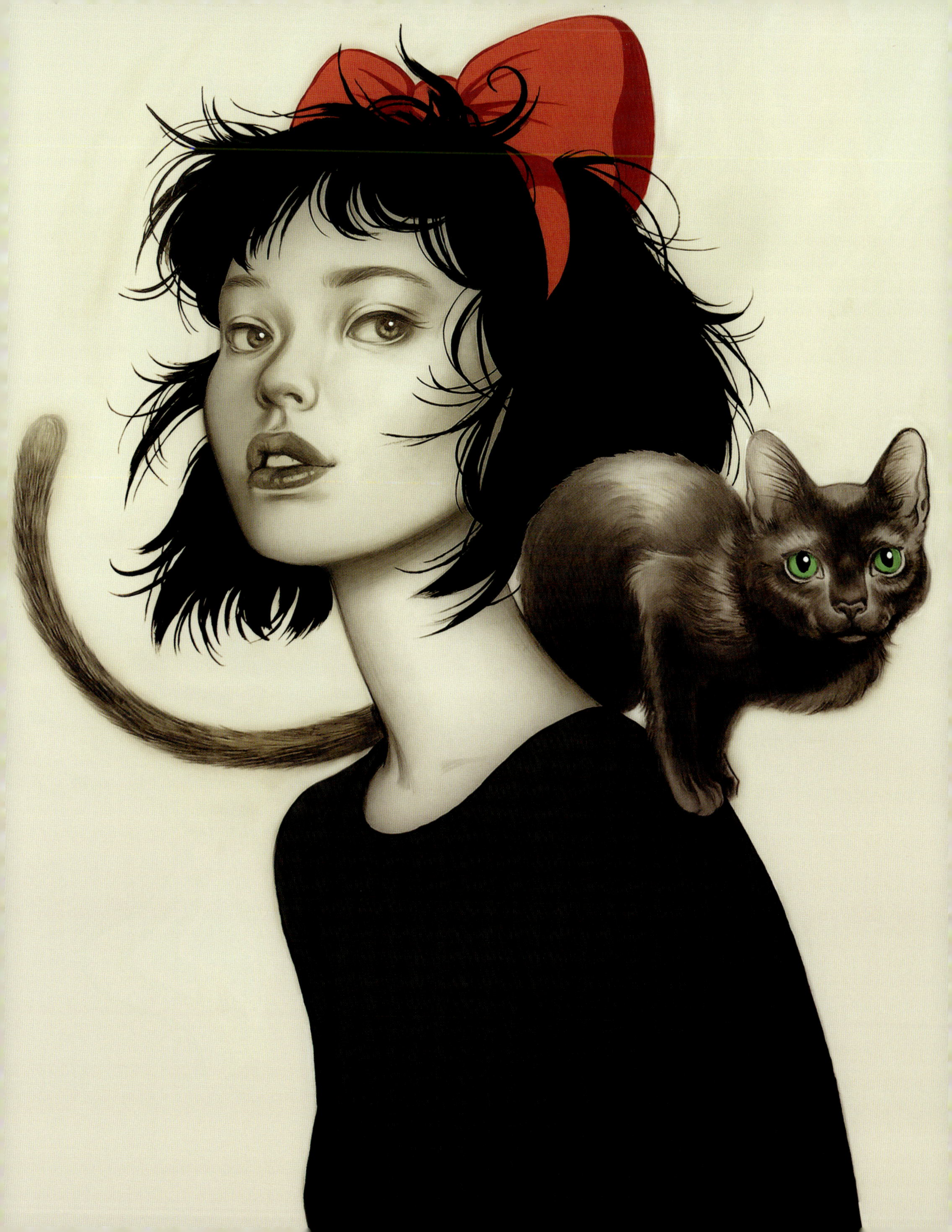

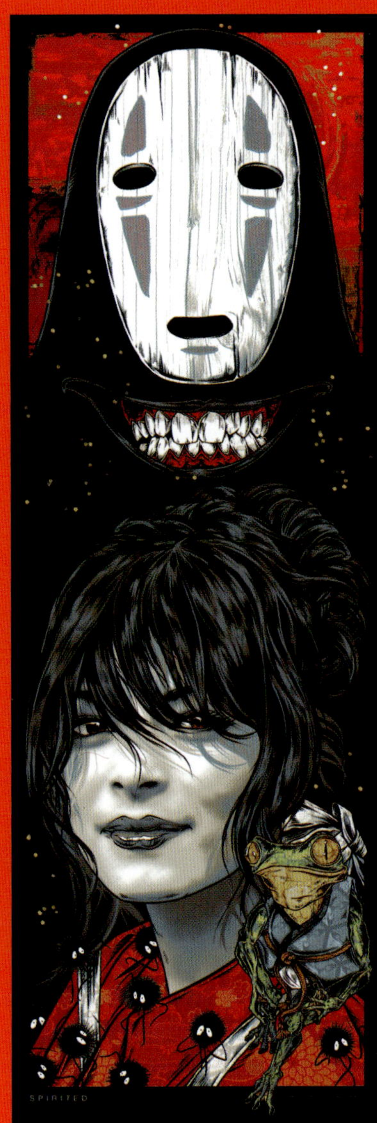

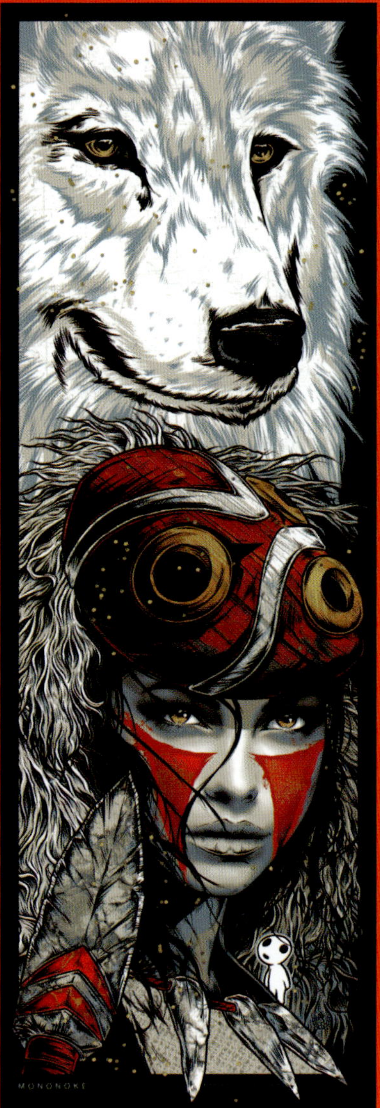

RHYS COOPER

MAX DALTON

LEFT
Spirited
Seven-color screen print. 12 x 36".

RIGHT
Mononoke
Seven-color screen print. 12 x 36".

RIGHT PAGE
Kamikakushi
Archival pigment print. 18 x 24".

千と千尋の神隠し

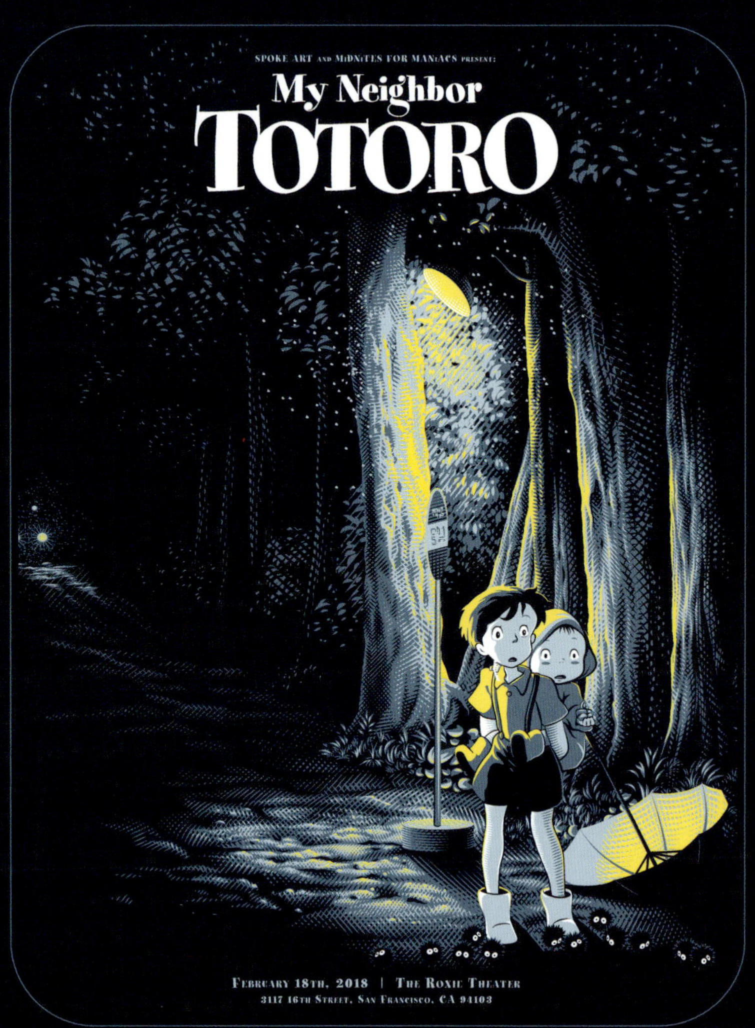

TRACIE CHING

ABOVE

My Neighbor Totoro
Five-color screen print. 18 x 24".

RIGHT PAGE

Princess Mononoke
Five-color screen print. 18 x 24".

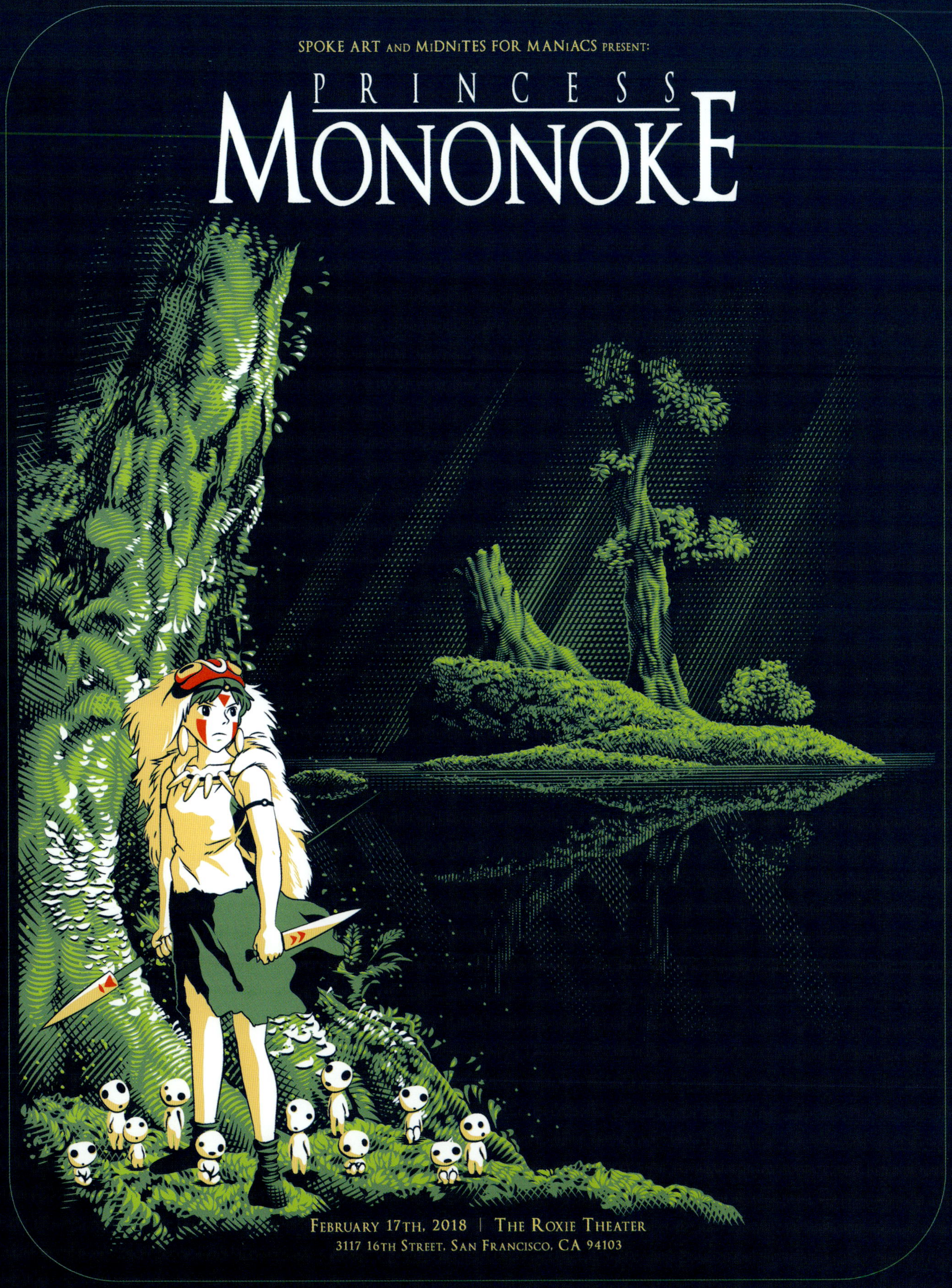

SPOKE ART AND MIDNITES FOR MANIACS PRESENT:

PRINCESS MONONOKE

FEBRUARY 17TH, 2018 | THE ROXIE THEATER

3117 16TH STREET, SAN FRANCISCO, CA 94103

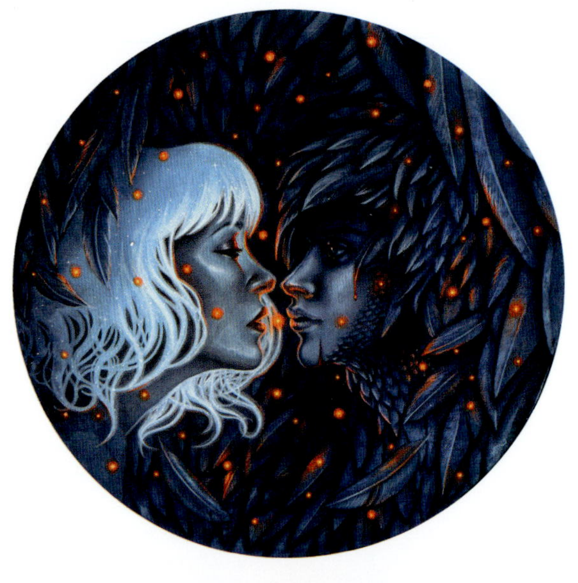

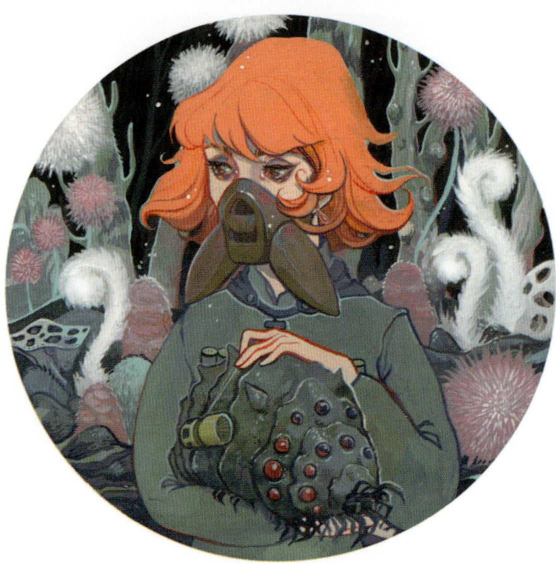

KELLY MCKERNAN

TOP

Starlight

Watercolor and acryla gouache on panel. 12" diameter.

AUDRA AUCLAIR

BOTTOM

Spore

Gouache on paper. 10" diameter.

STACEY AOYAMA

RIGHT PAGE

Ponyo's Run

Archival pigment print. 18 x 24".

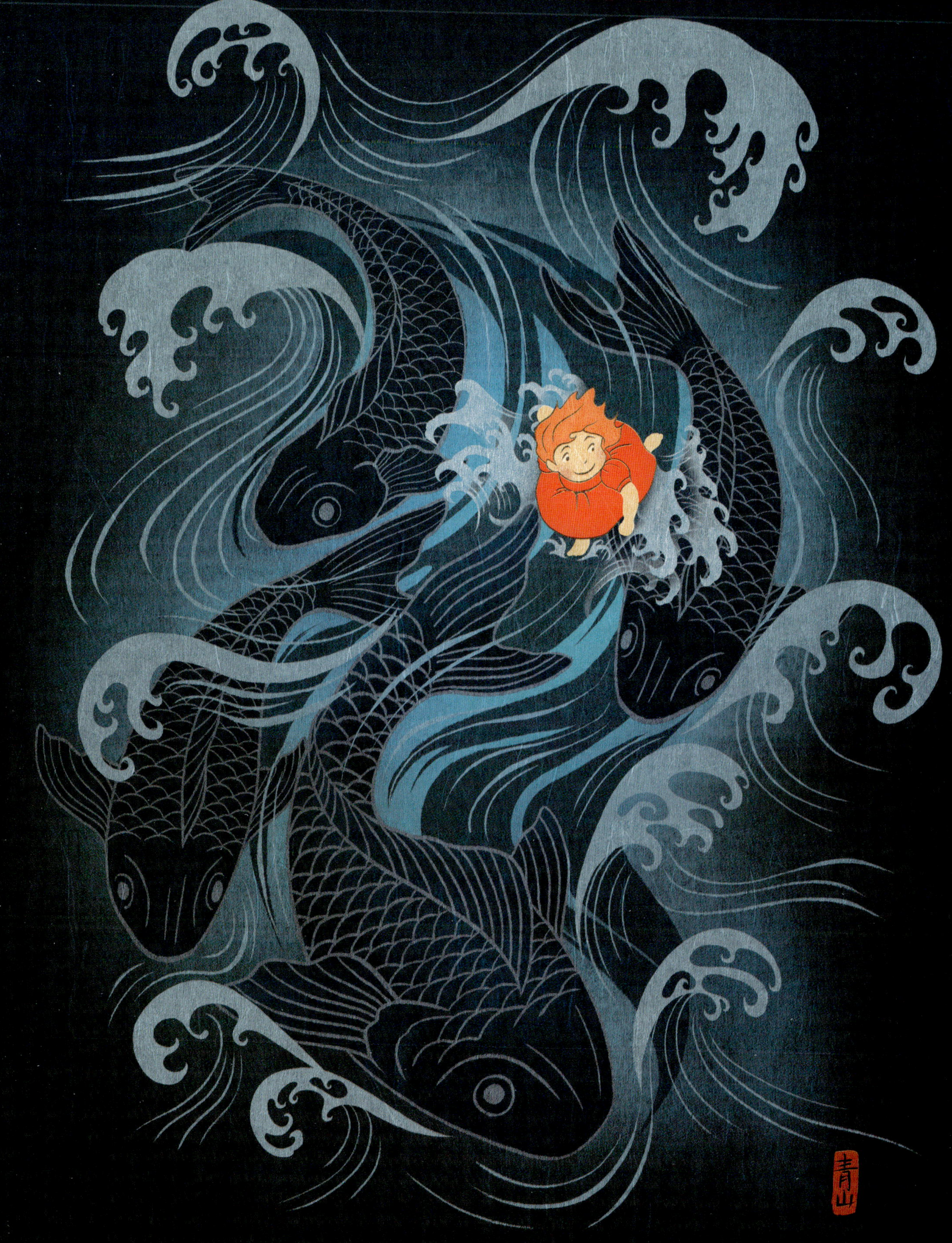
青山

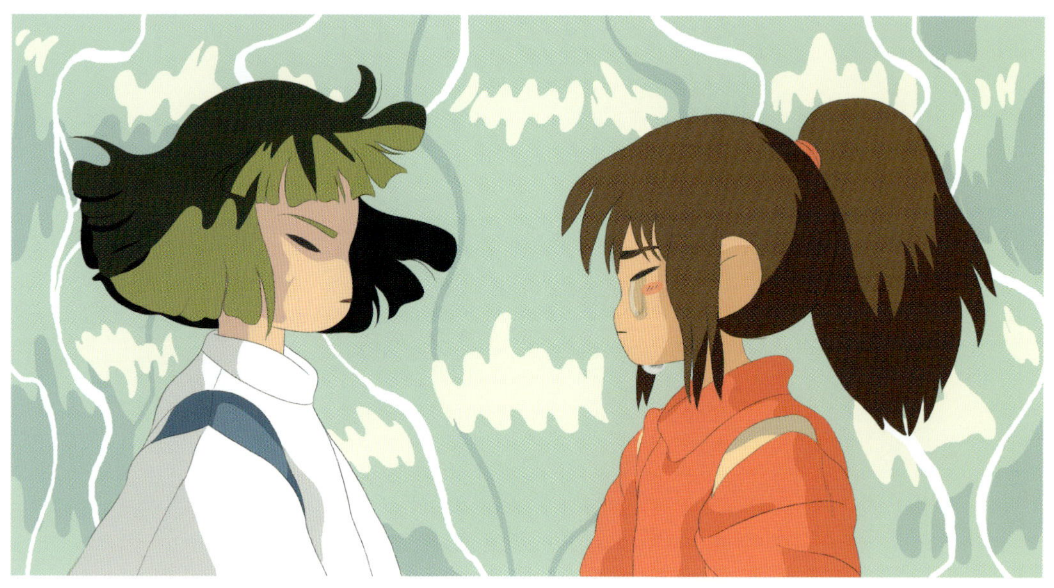

IVONNA BUENROSTRO

ABOVE
Sen
Archival pigment print. 24 x 18".

RIGHT PAGE
The Wind Rises
Archival pigment print. 24 x 18".

LE VENT SE LÈVE, IL FAUT TENTER DE VIVRE

風立ちぬ

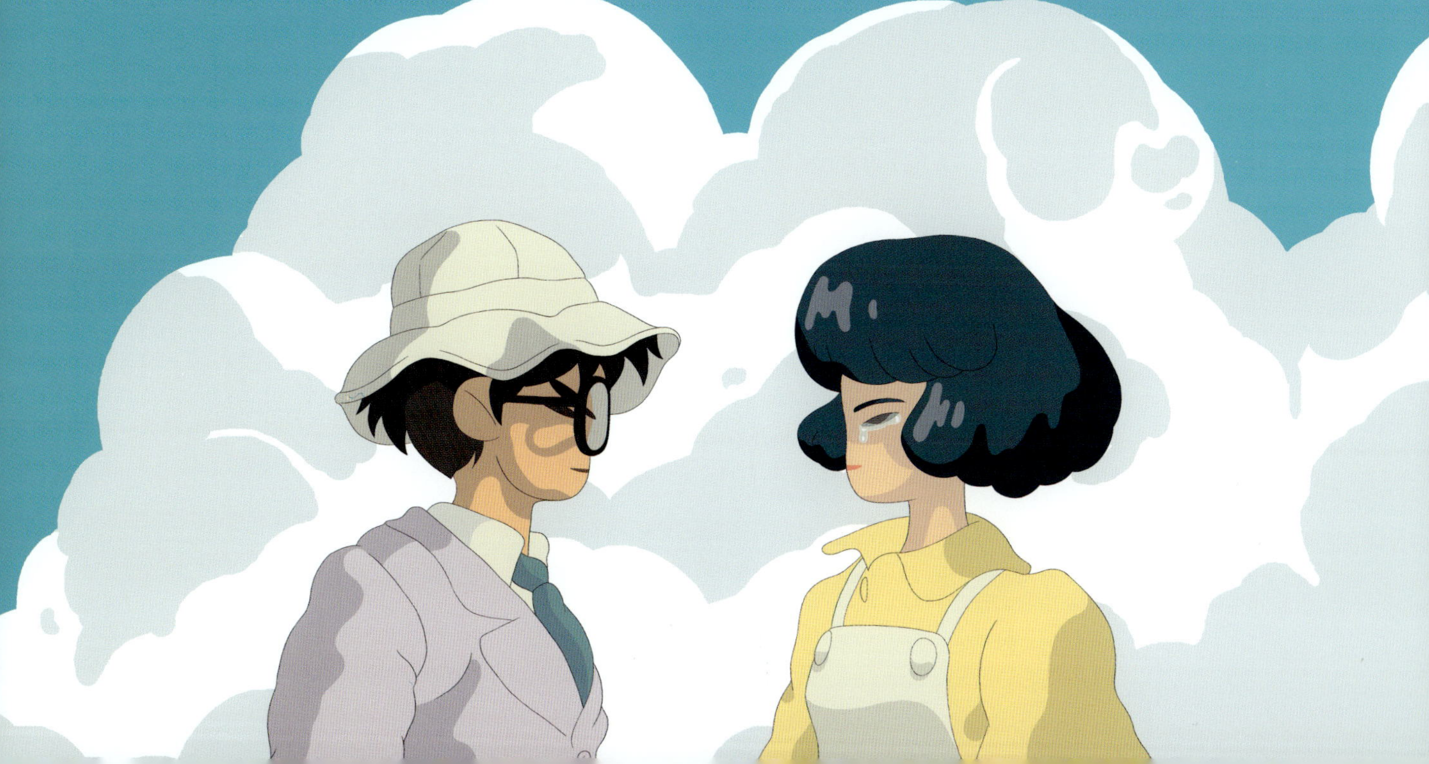

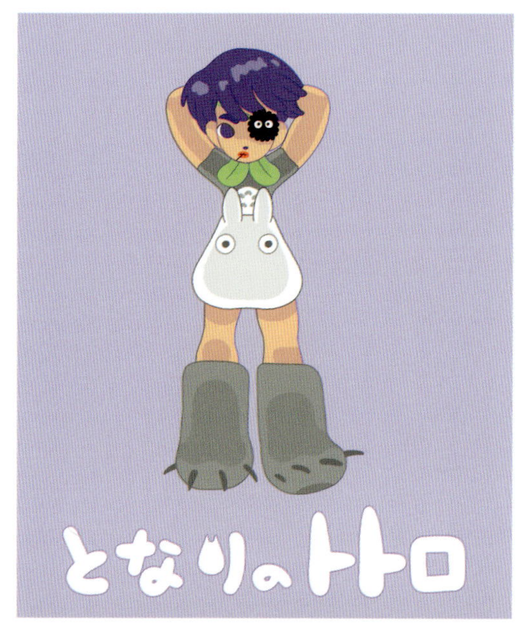

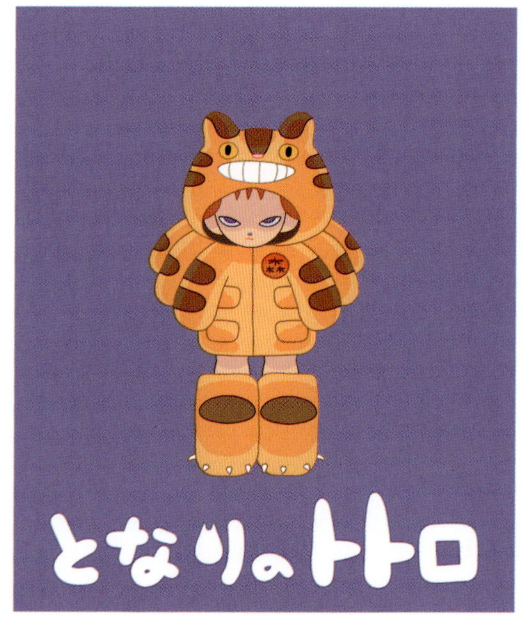

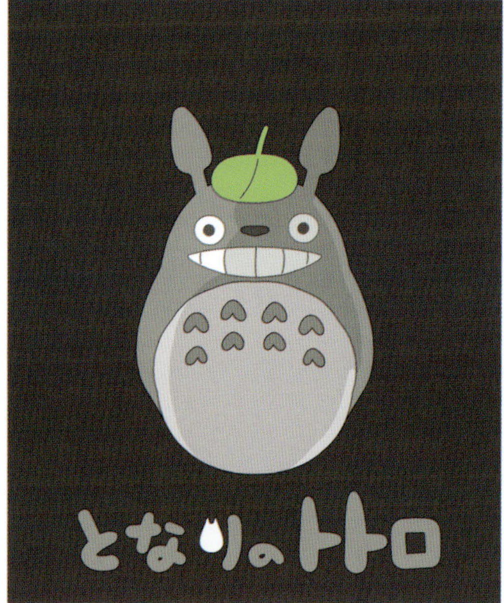

IVONNA BUENROSTRO

TOP LEFT

Satsuki

Archival pigment print. 8 x 10''.

TOP RIGHT

Mei in Catbus Coat

Archival pigment print. 8 x 10''.

LEFT

Totoro

Archival pigment print. 8 x 10''.

RIGHT PAGE

Ponyo Ramen Noodles

Archival pigment print. 16 x 20''.

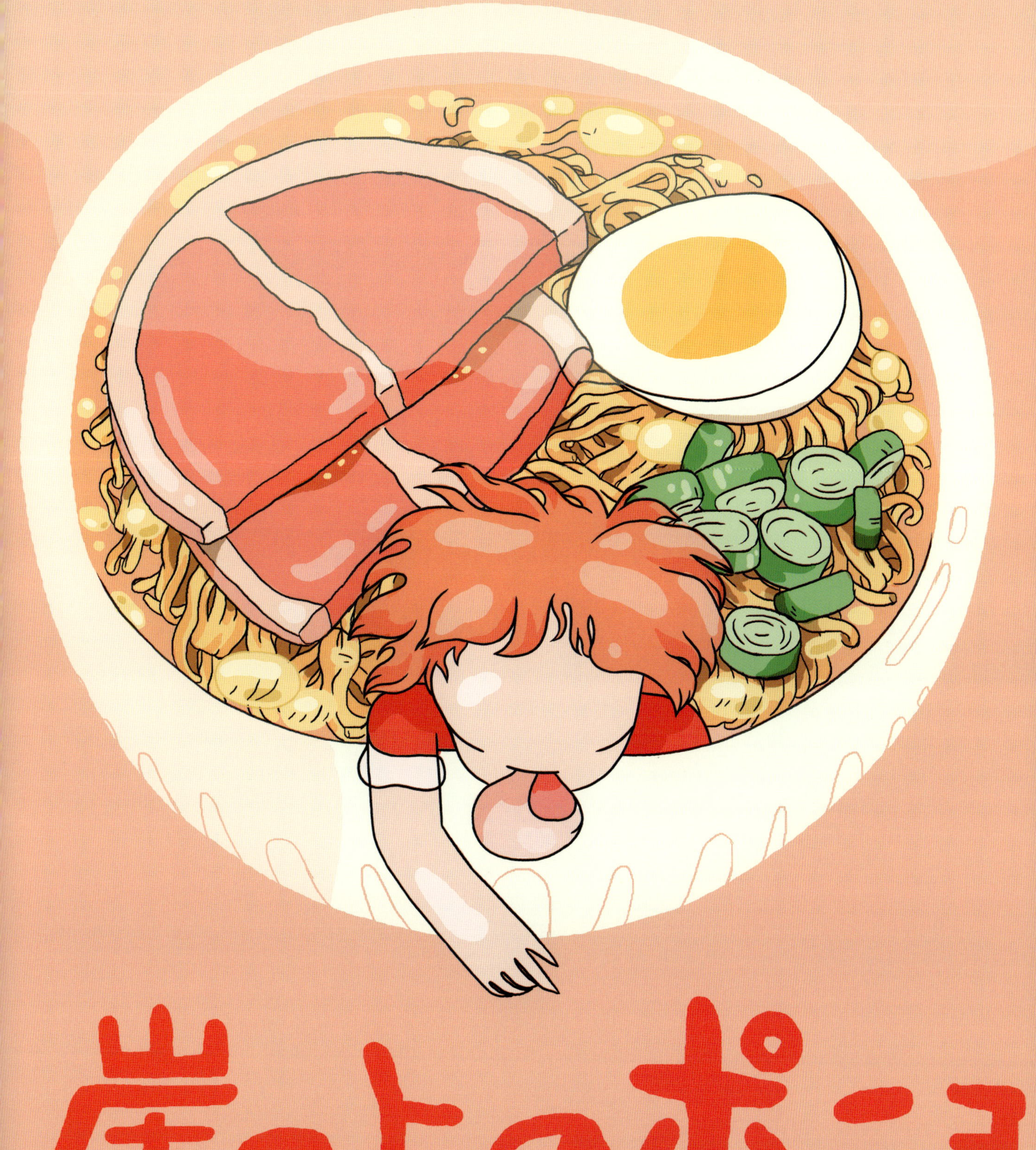
崖の上のポニョ

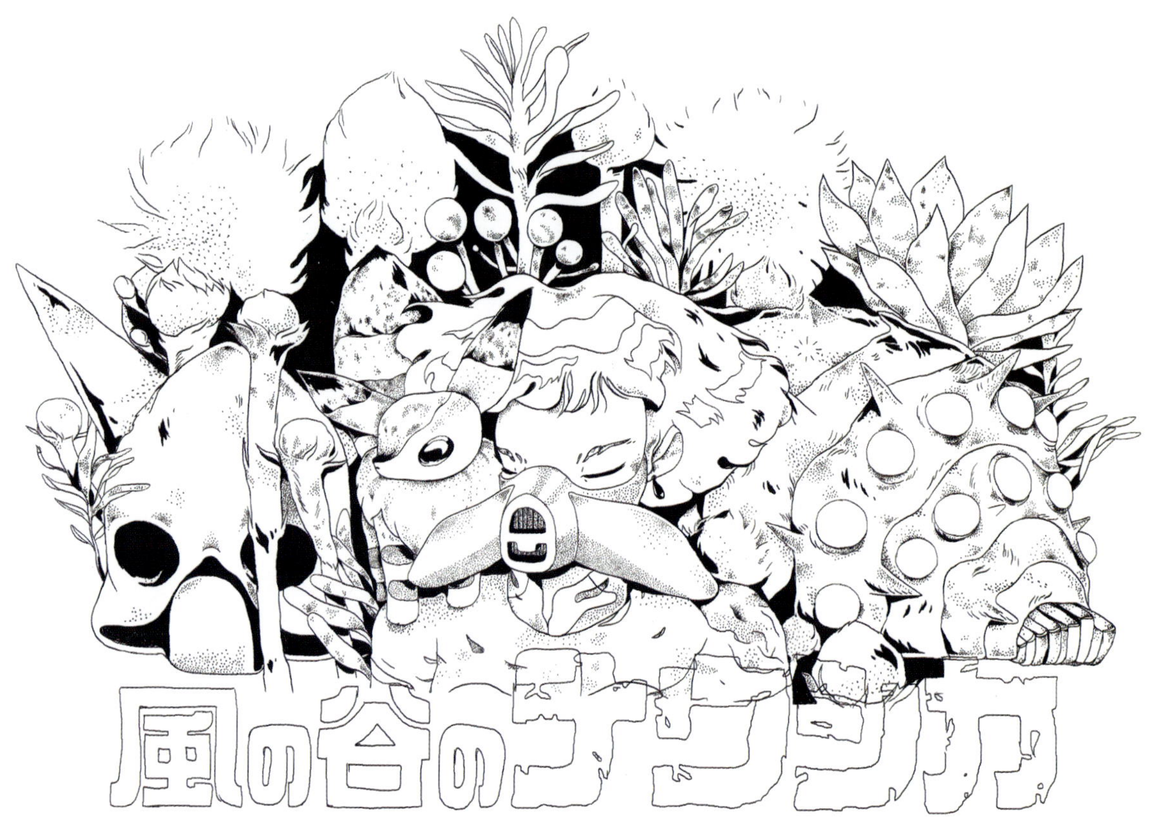

ABOVE

IVONNA BUENROSTRO

Nausicaa

Archival pigment print. 19 x 13".

RIGHT PAGE

IVONNA BUENROSTRO

San

Archival pigment print. 20 x 16".

もののけ姫

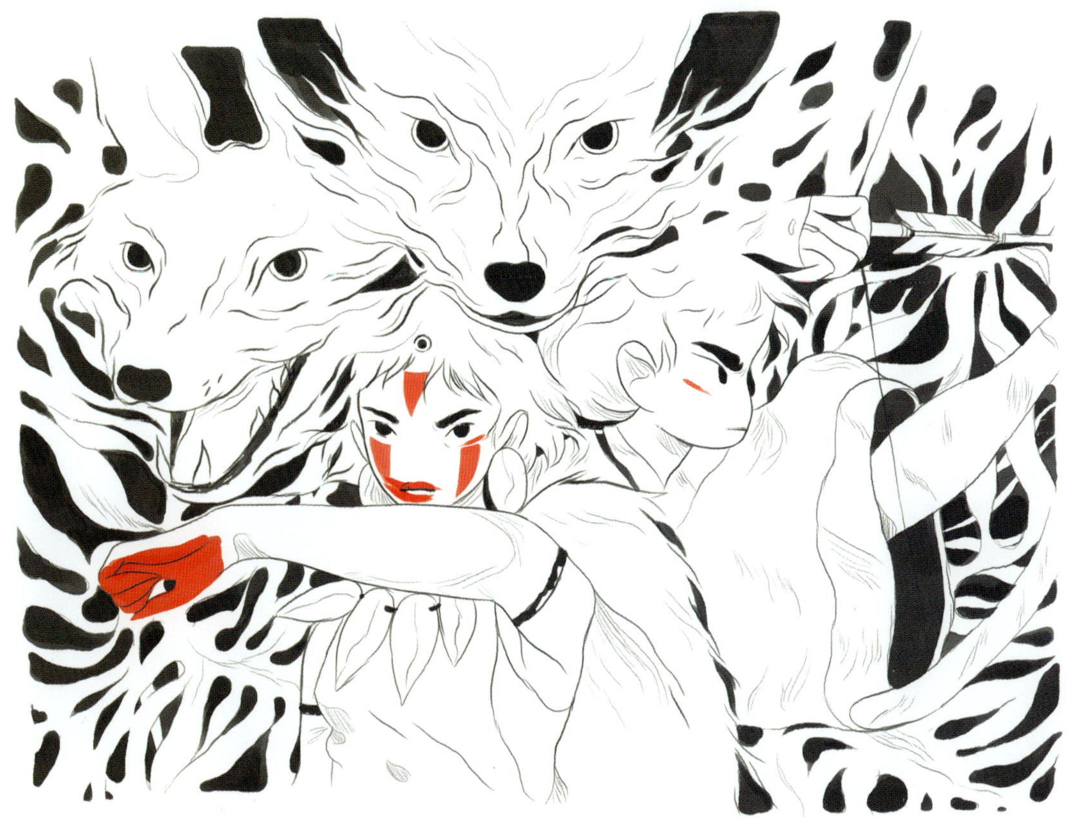

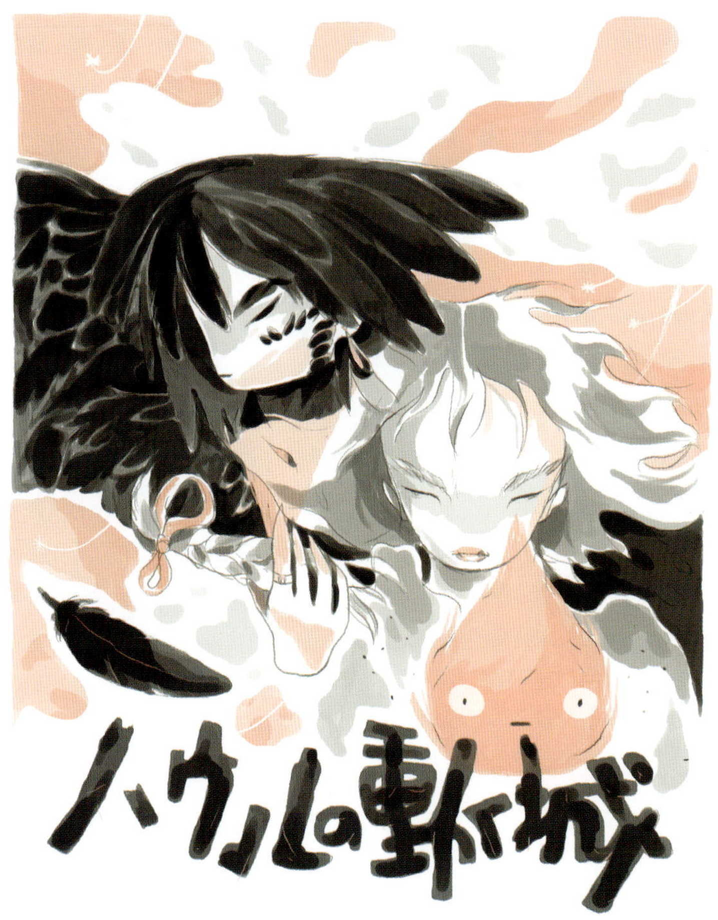

IVONNA BUENROSTRO

ABOVE

Sophie, Your Hair Looks Just Like Starlight

Archival pigment print. 16 x 20".

RIGHT PAGE

Miss Witch

Archival pigment print. 11 x 14".

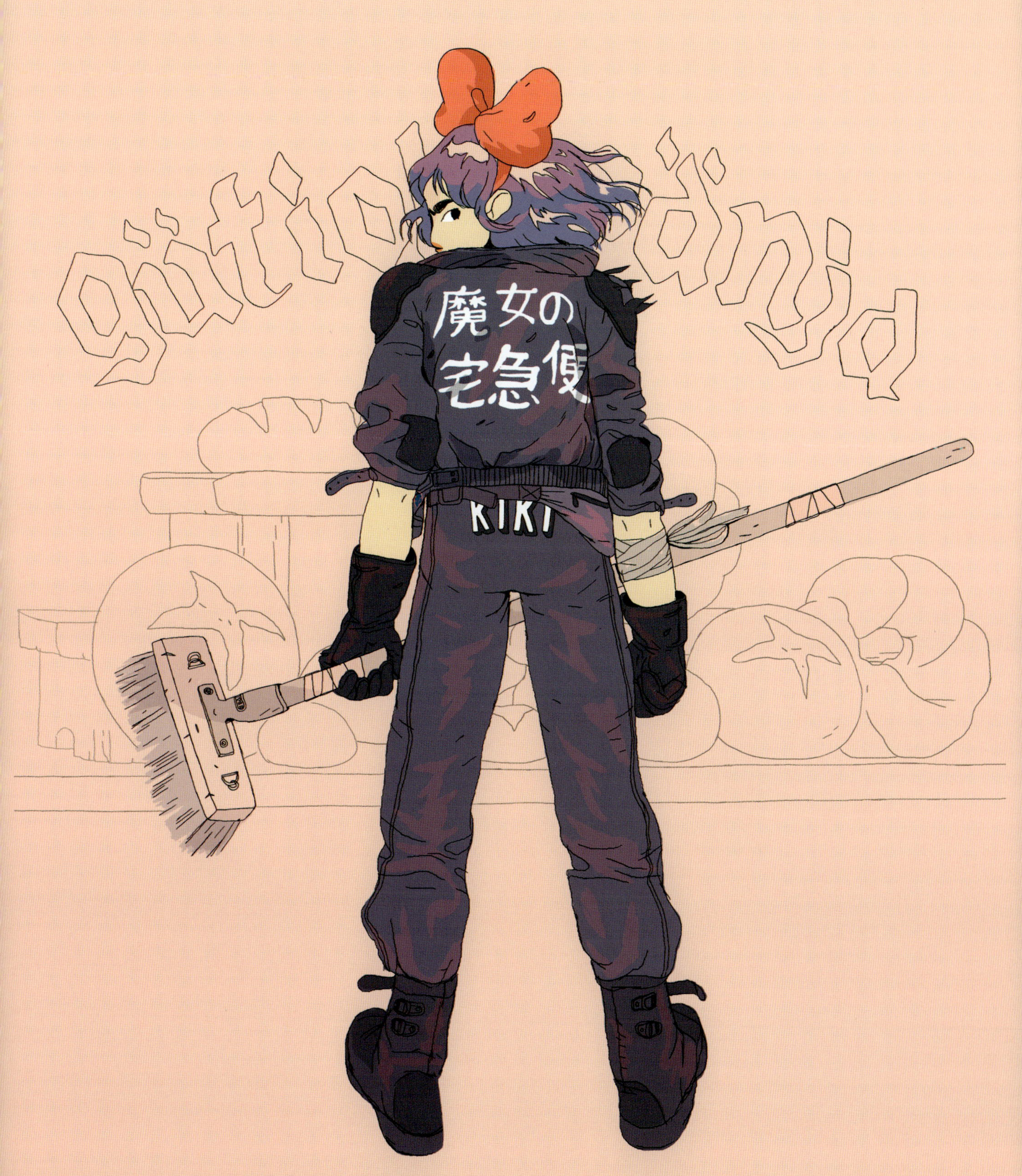
魔女の
宅急便
KIKI

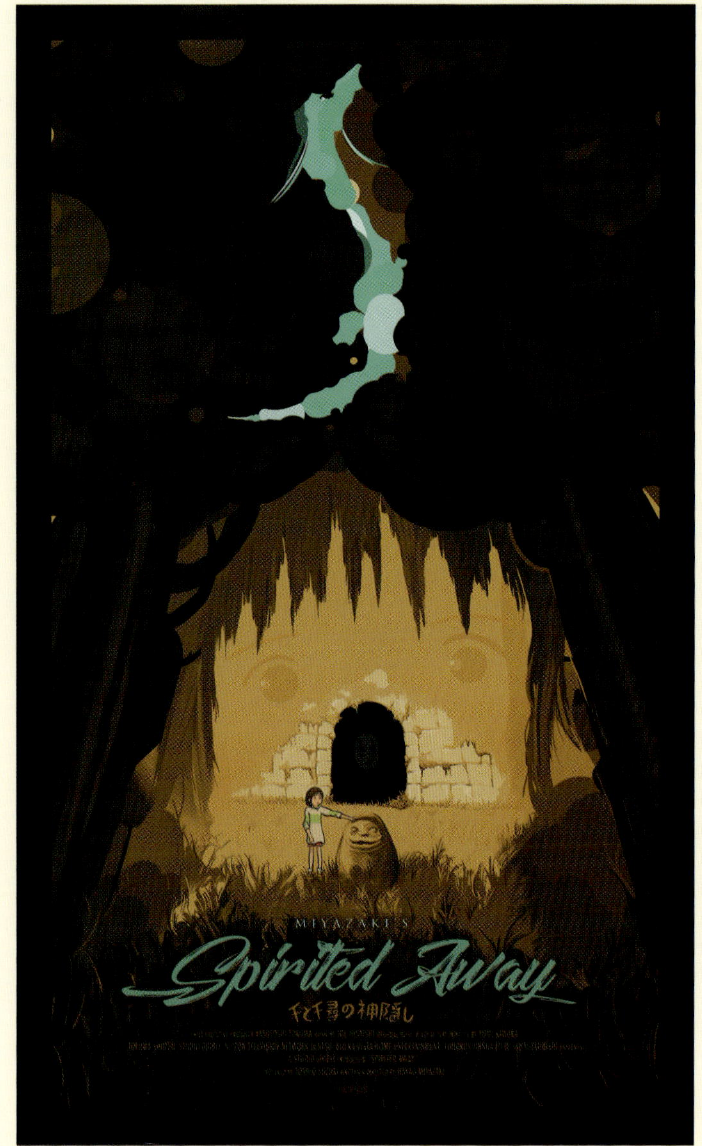

SCOTT HOPKO

ABOVE

**Spirited Away -
A Journey's End (Variant)**
Archival pigment print. 14 x 24".

DAN GRISSOM

RIGHT PAGE

Secret Place
Screen print. 16 x 20".

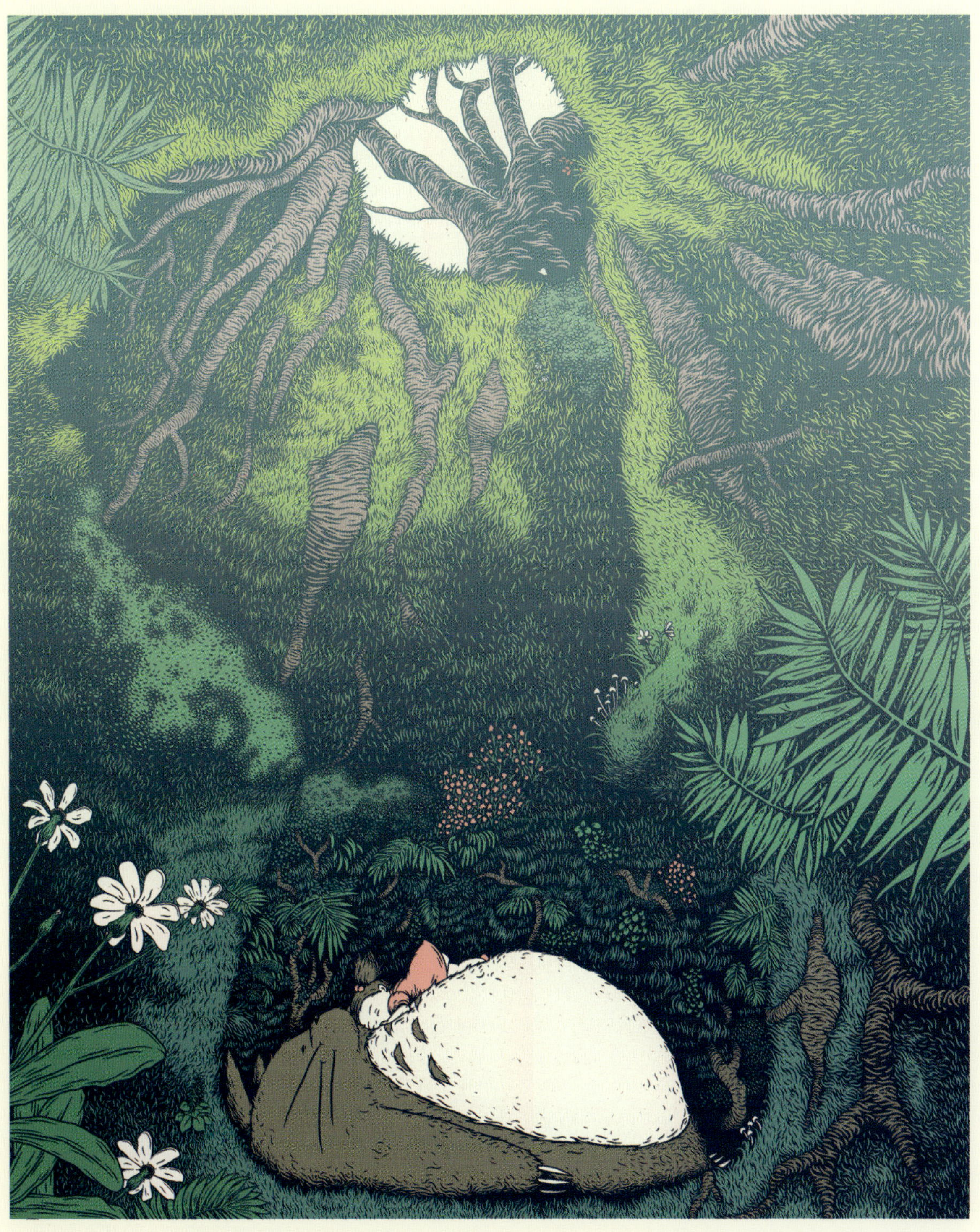

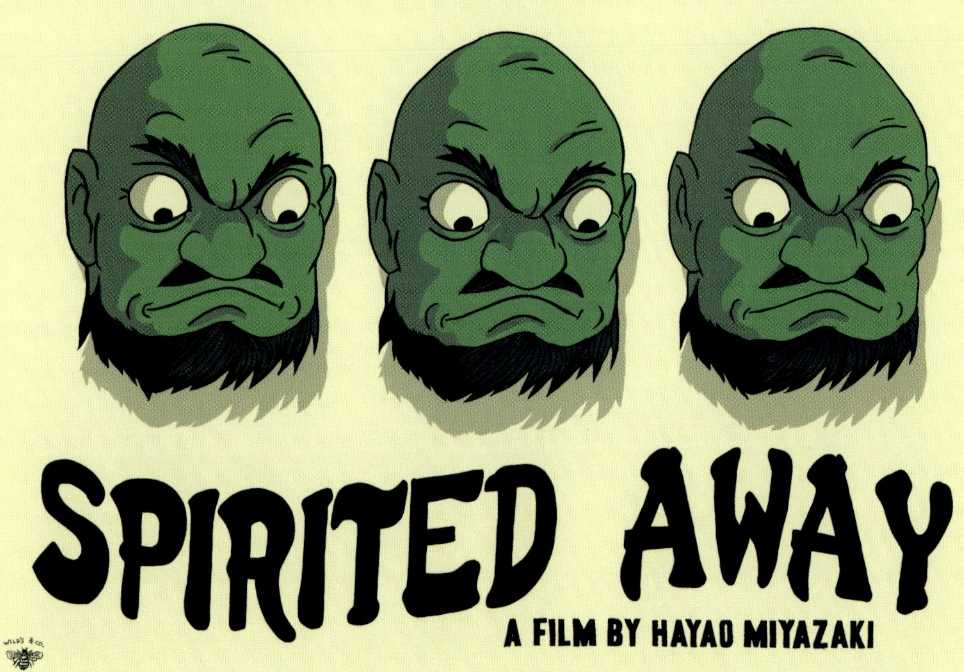

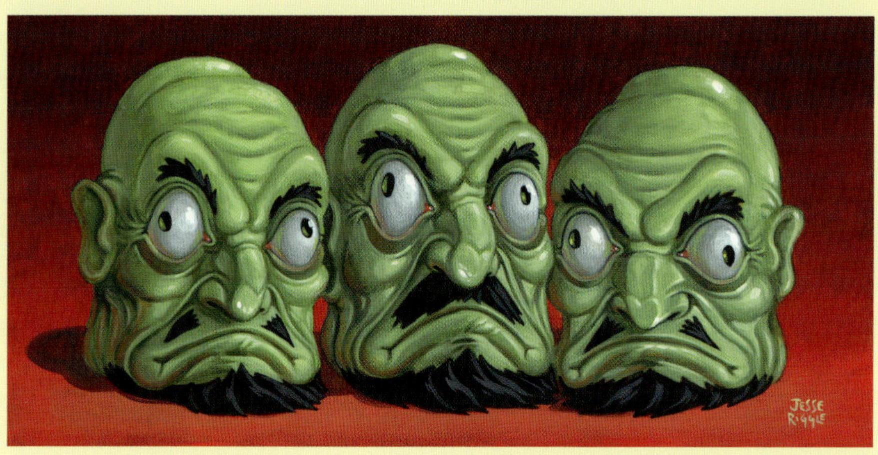

CHRIS WALKER

TOP

Spirited Away
Gouache on board. 28 x 20".

JESSE RIGGLE

BOTTOM

Kashira
Acrylic on panel. 12 x 6".

BEAU BERKLEY

RIGHT PAGE

Procession of the Spirits
Marker and colored pencil on Bristol paper. 16 x 20".

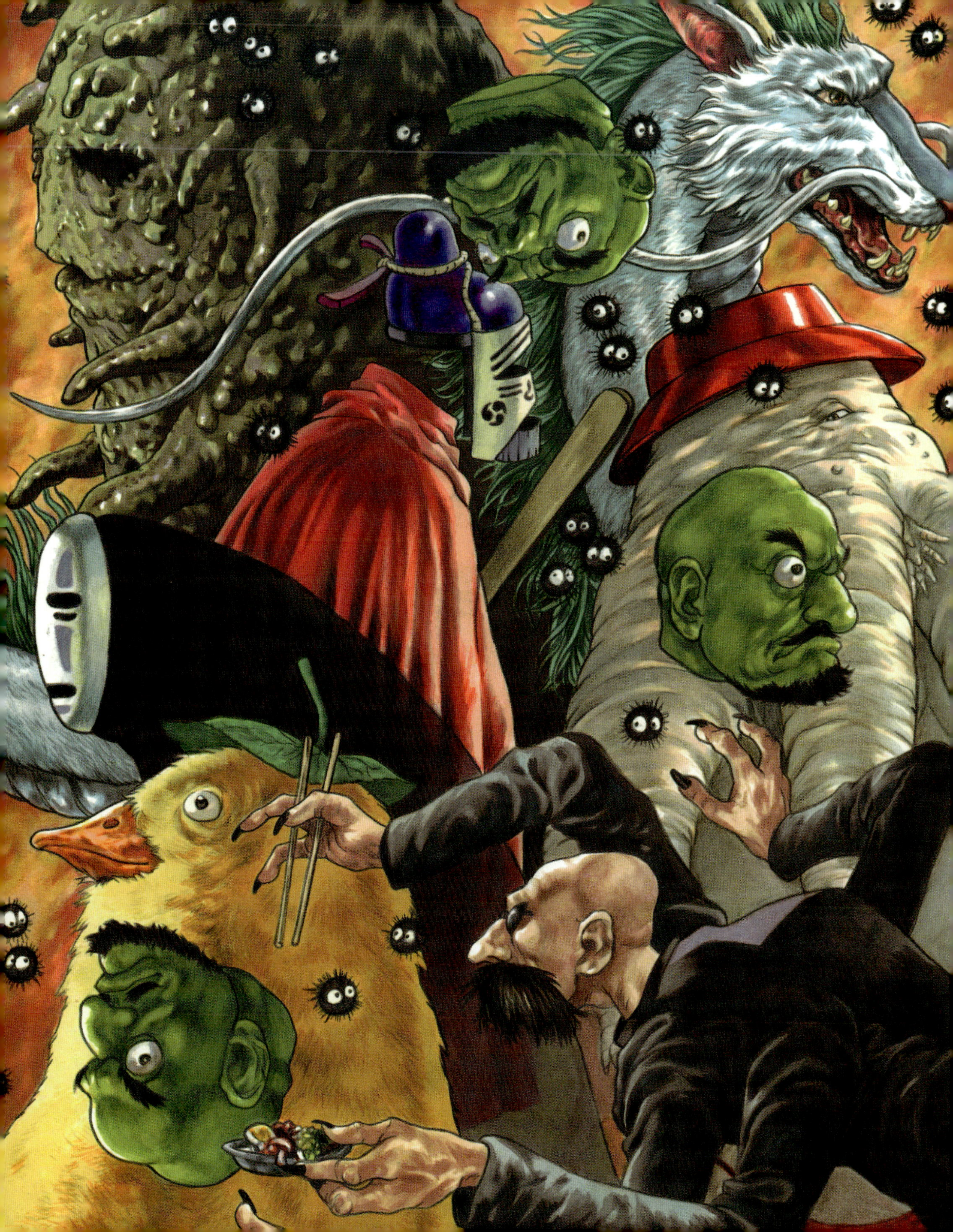

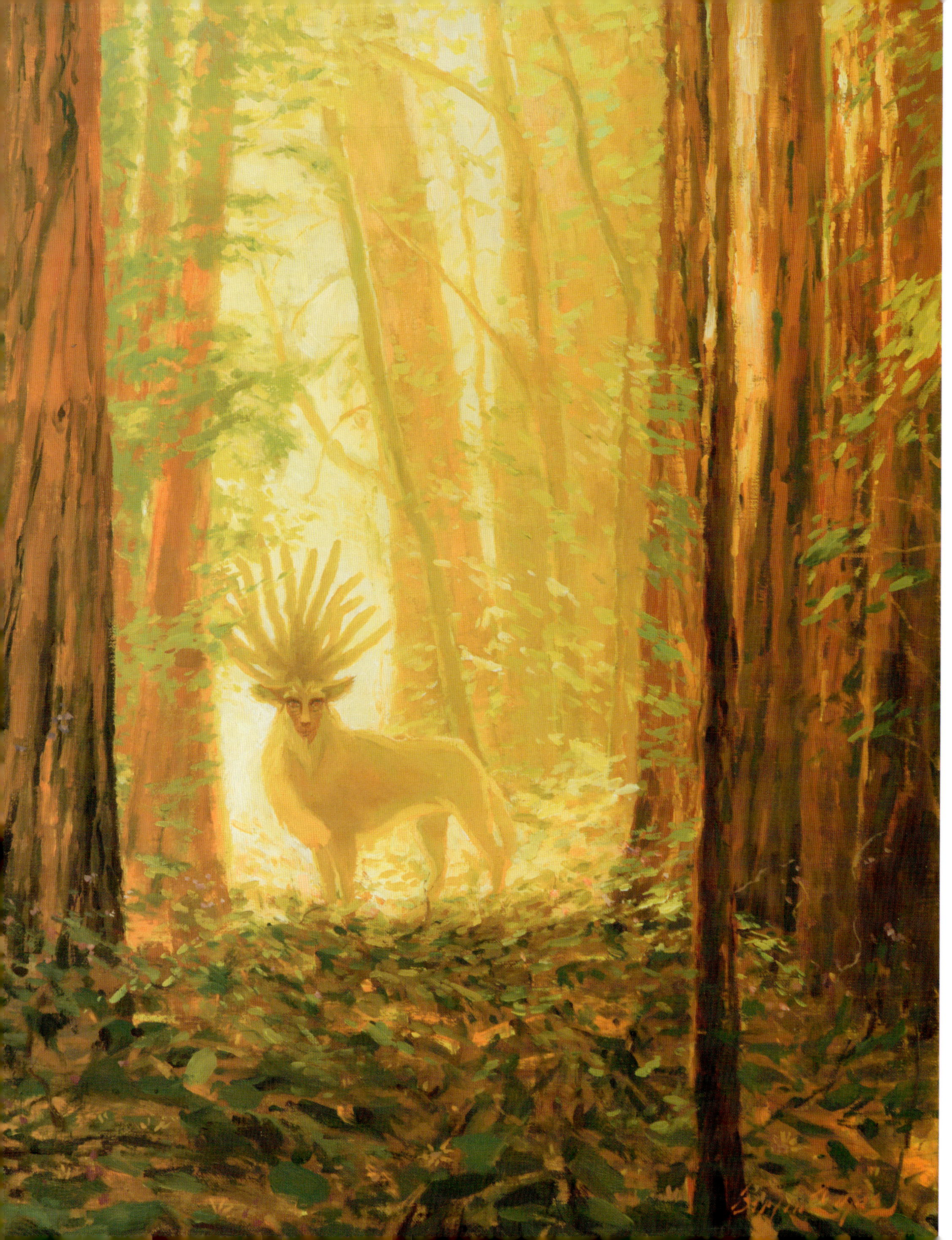

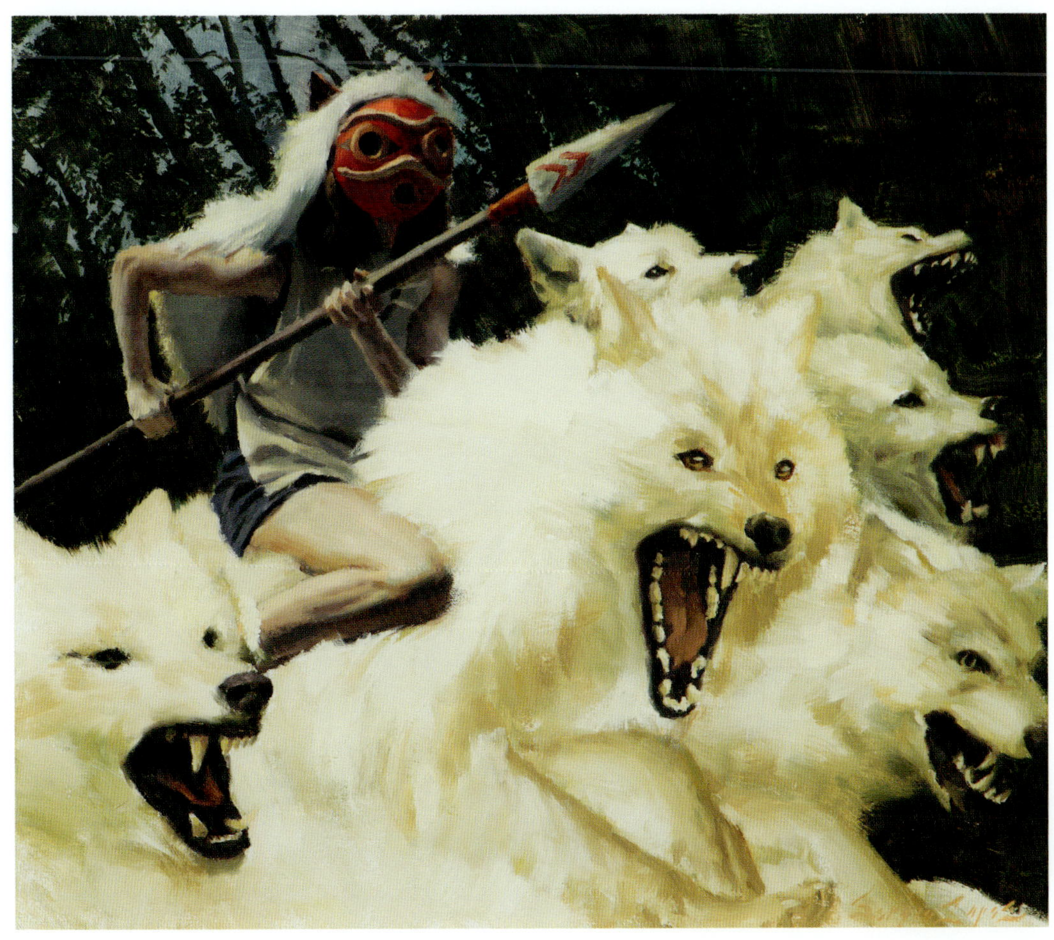

SERGIO LOPEZ

LEFT PAGE

Shishigami

Oil on canvas board.
18 x 24".

TOP

Spirit of The Guardian

Oil and canvas mounted on board.
18 x 16".

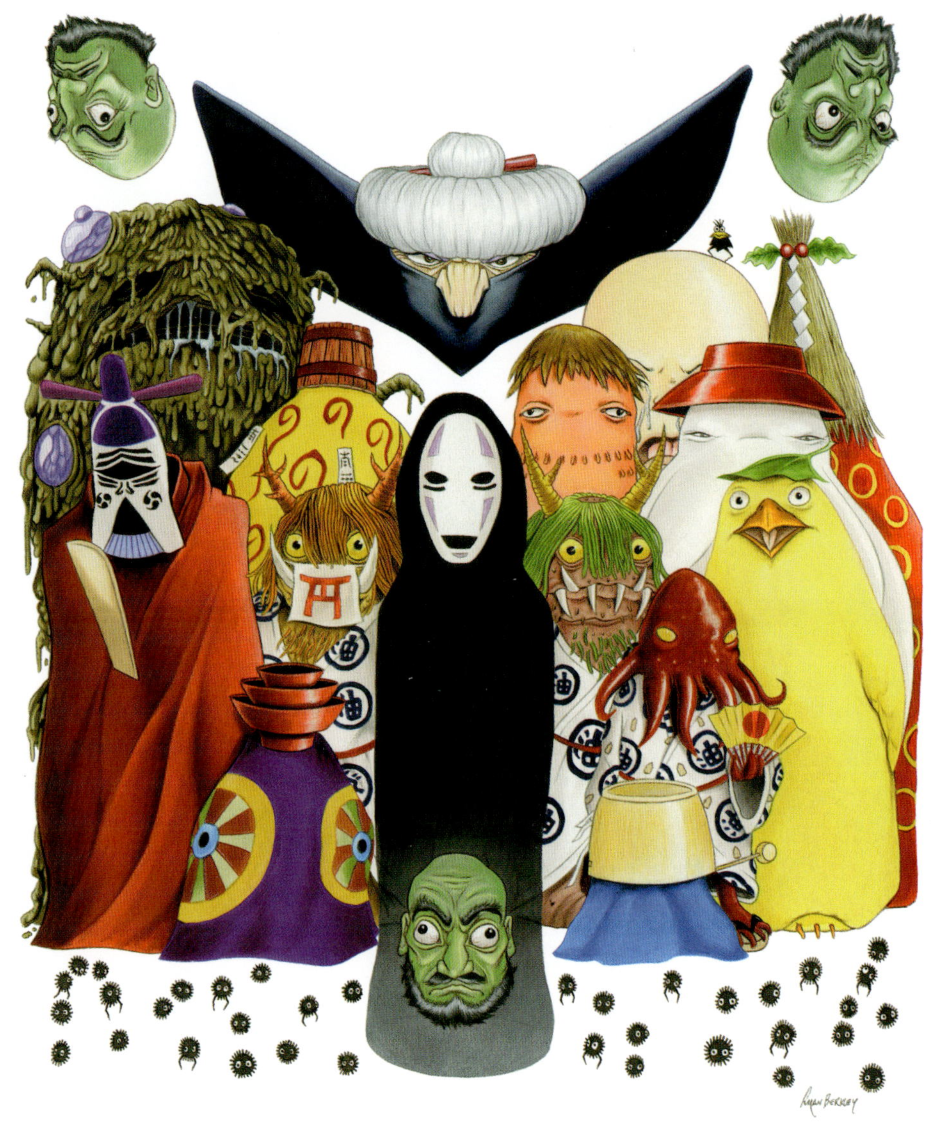

RYAN BERKLEY

ABOVE

Bath Spirits

Marker and colored pencil on paper. 11 x 14".

RIGHT PAGE

Neighbors

Marker and colored pencil. 11 x 14".

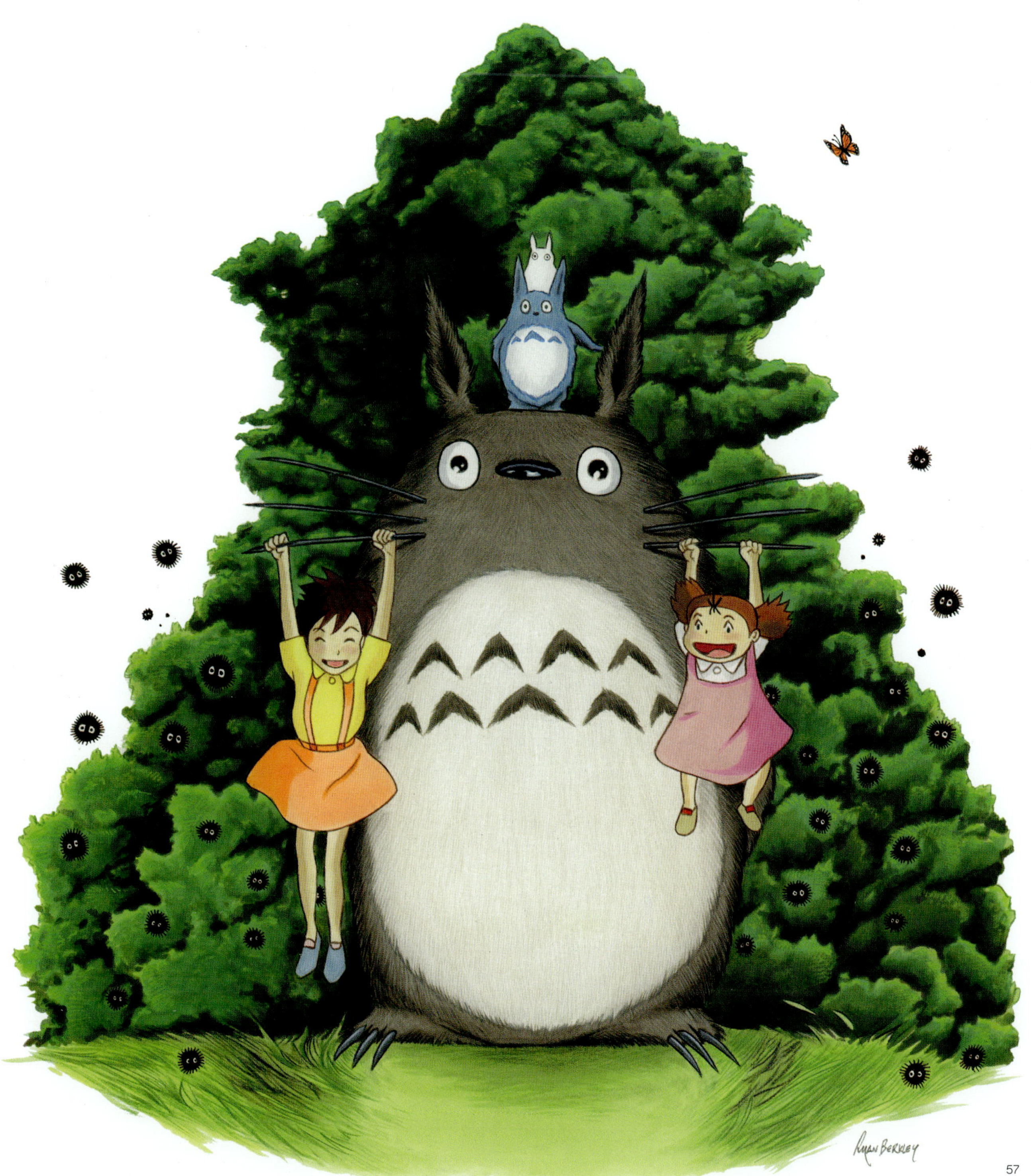

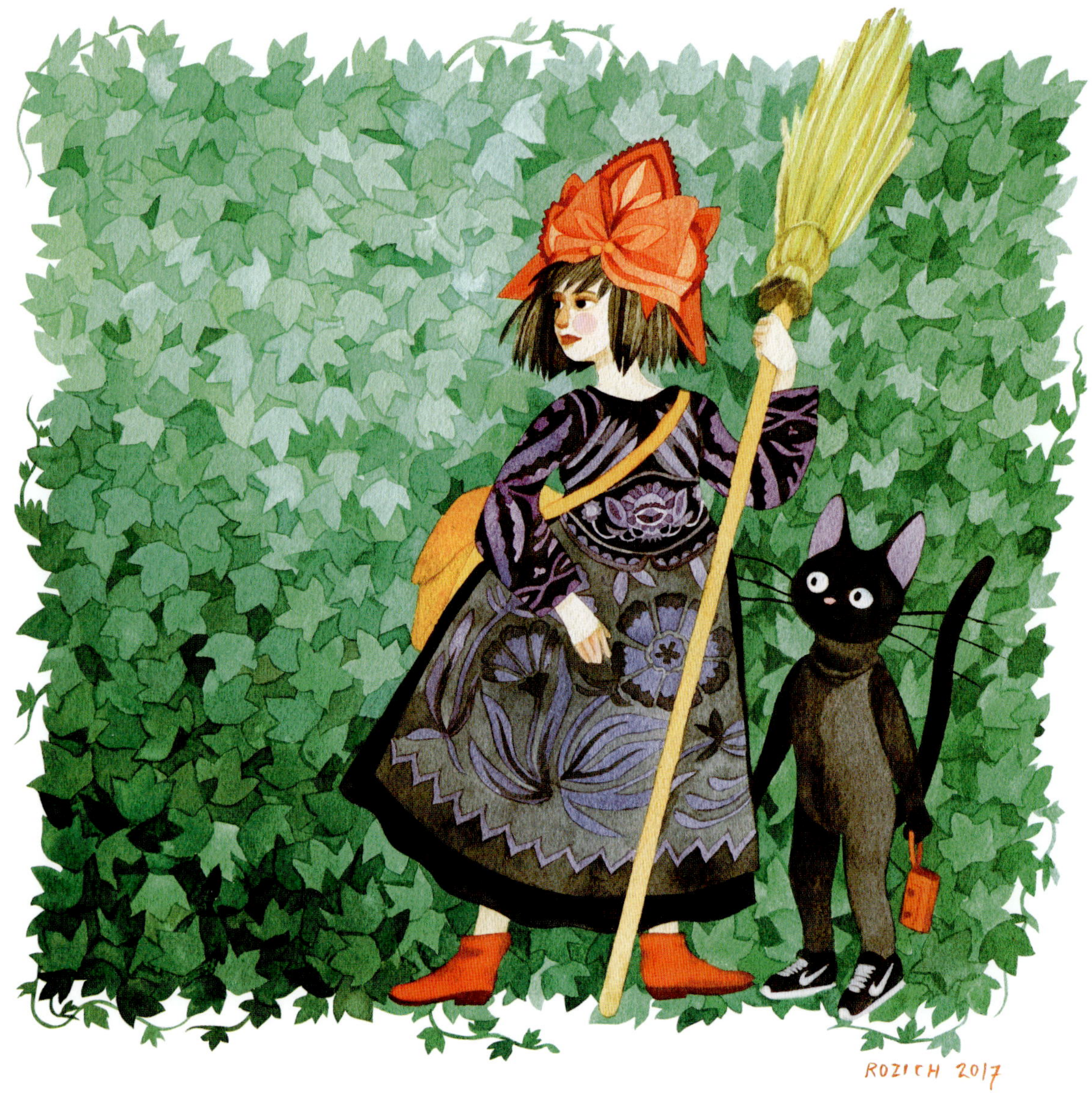

STACEY ROZICH

Kiki's Yardwork Service

Watercolor on paper. 12 x 12".

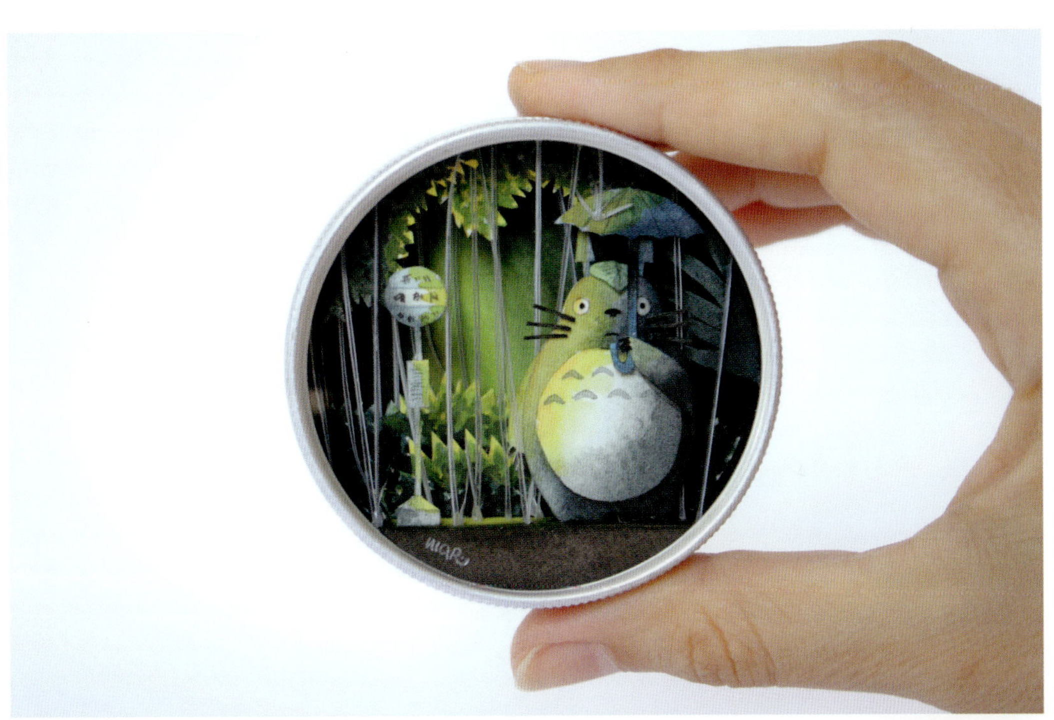

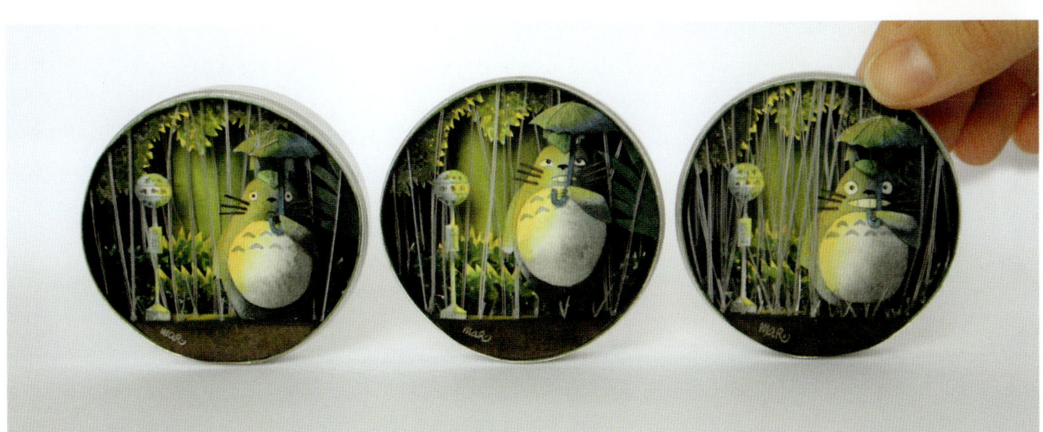

MAR CERDÀ

You Put The Umbrella Over Your Head, Like That I, II & III

Cut paper and watercolor inside metal box. 2.75" in diameter.

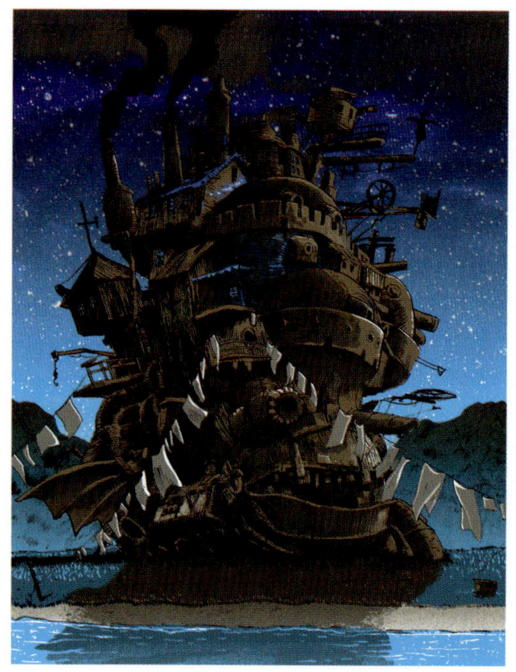

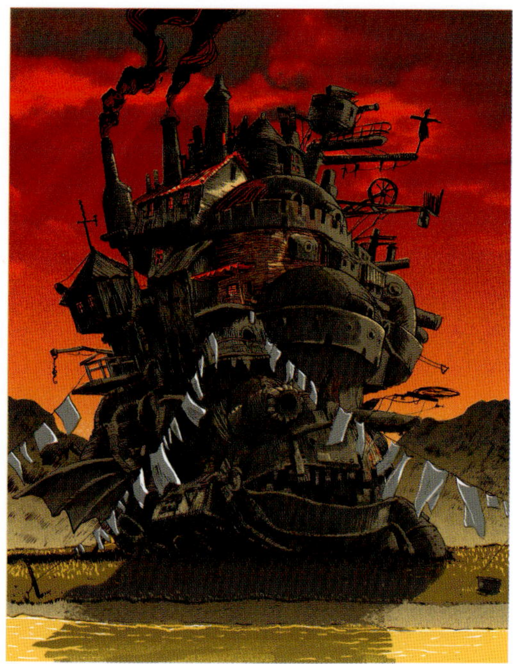

TIMOTHY DOYLE

LEFT

May All Your Bacon Burn (Night Variant)

Screen print. 18 x 24".

RIGHT

May All Your Bacon Burn (Red Variant)

Screen print. 18 x 24".

RIGHT PAGE

May All Your Bacon Burn

Screen print. 18 x 24".

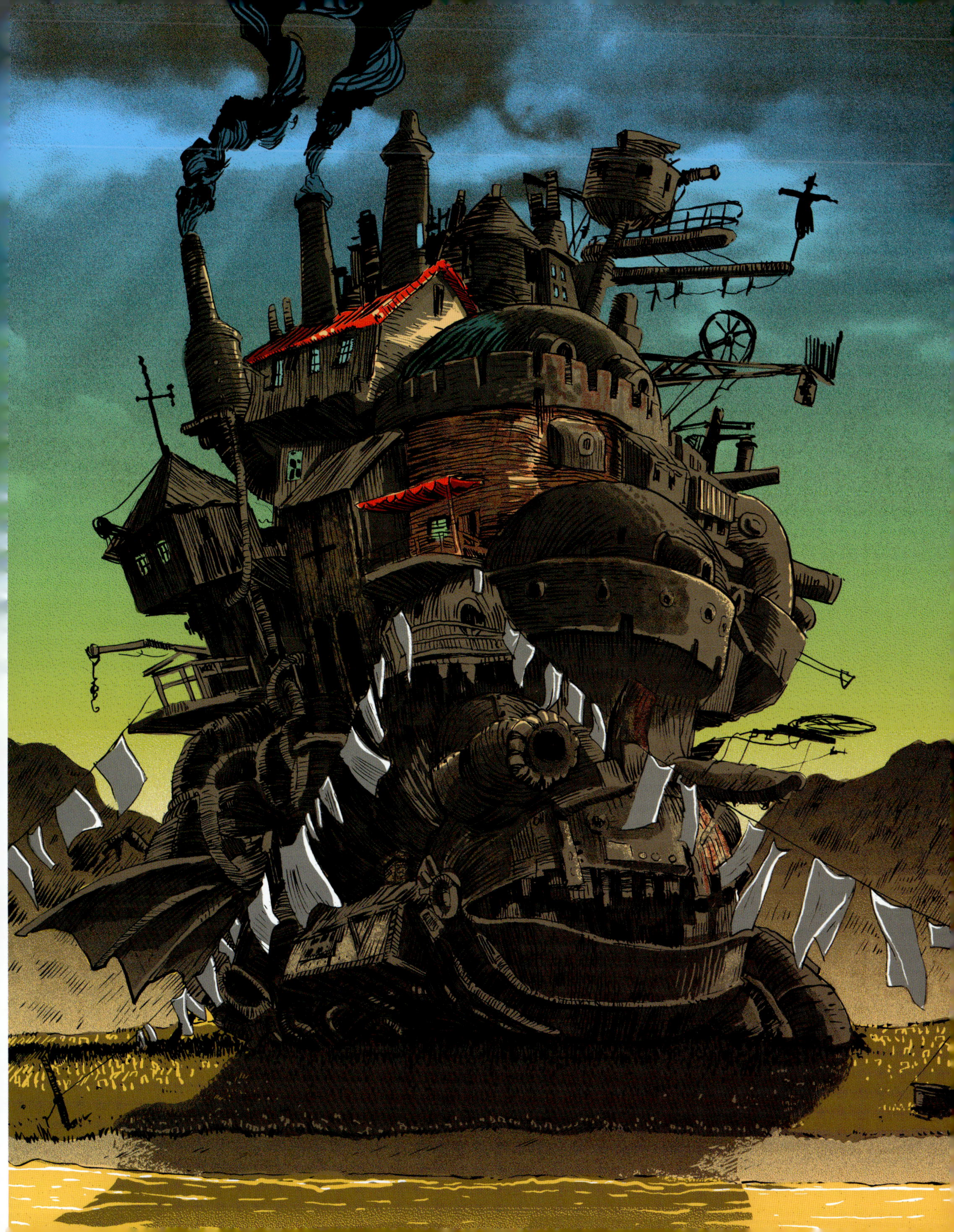

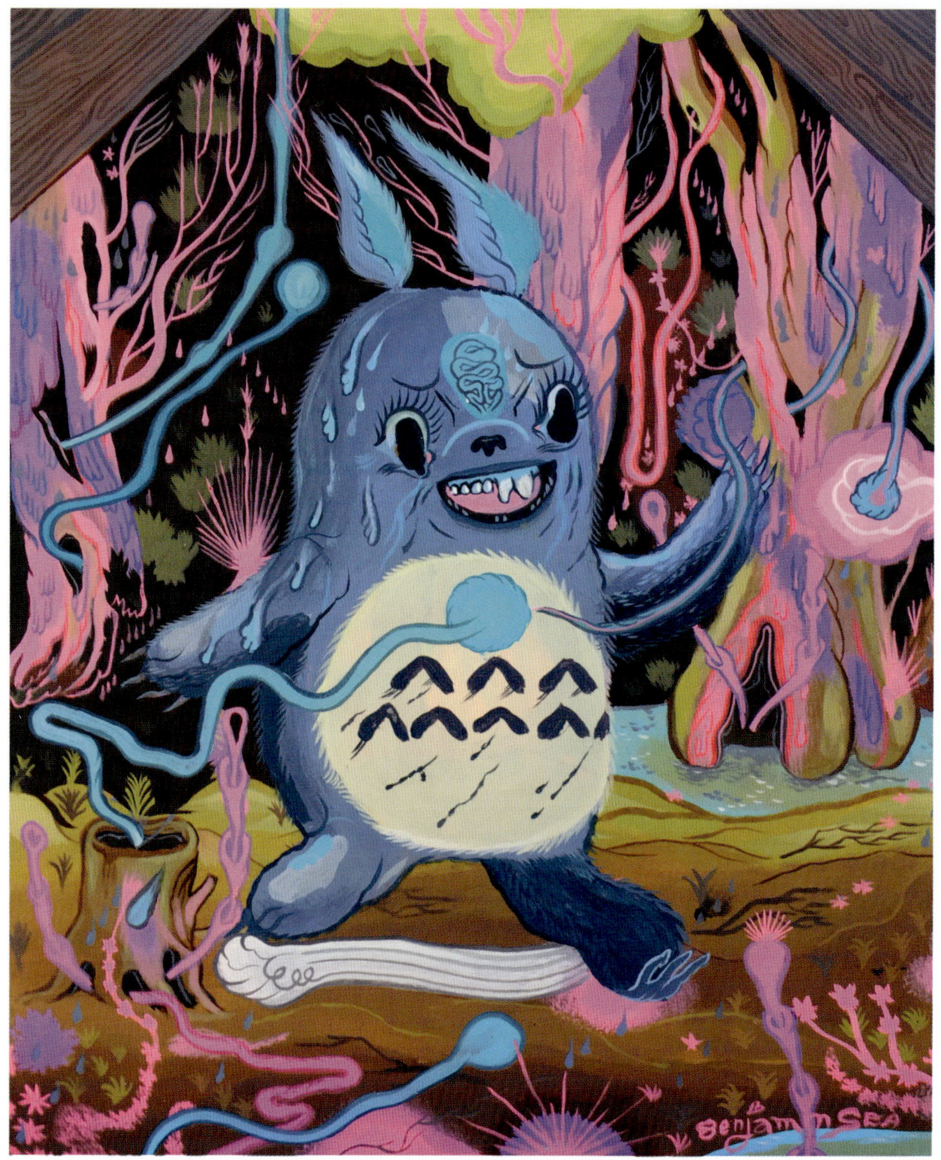

ABOVE

BENJAMIN CONSTANTINE

Spirited Woods

Acrylic and gouache on wood panel.
7.8 x 9.8".

RIGHT PAGE

MAX KAUFFMAN

Village View

Gouache and water based spray paint on panel. 12 x 16".

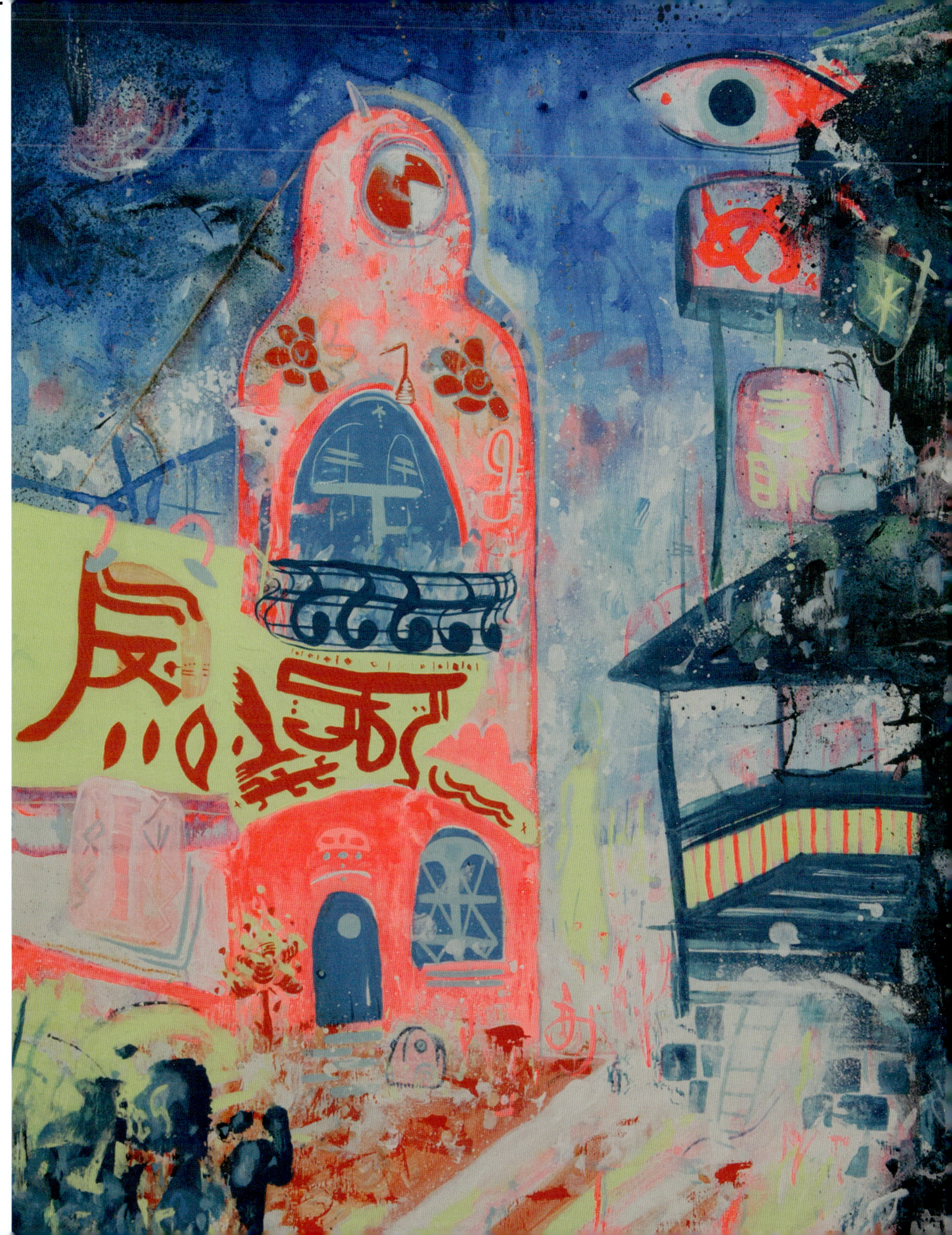

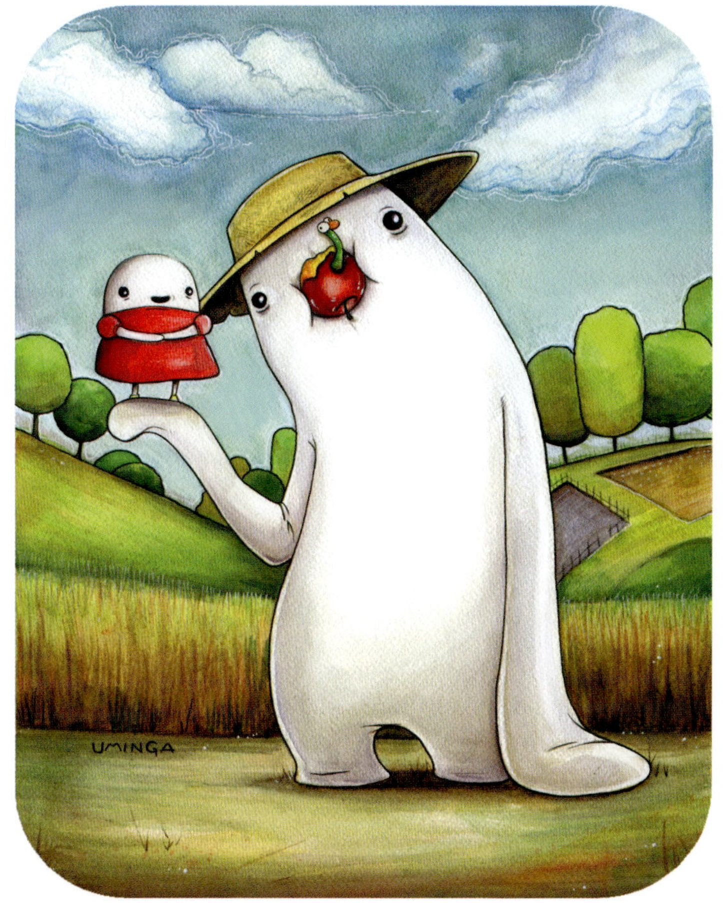

christopher uminga

ABOVE

CHRISTOPHER UMINGA

Mr. Dough & the Egg Princess

Watercolor on paper. 11 x 14".

RIGHT PAGE

CHRIS SKINNER

Laputa's Hidden Corner

Archival pigment print. 14 x 18".

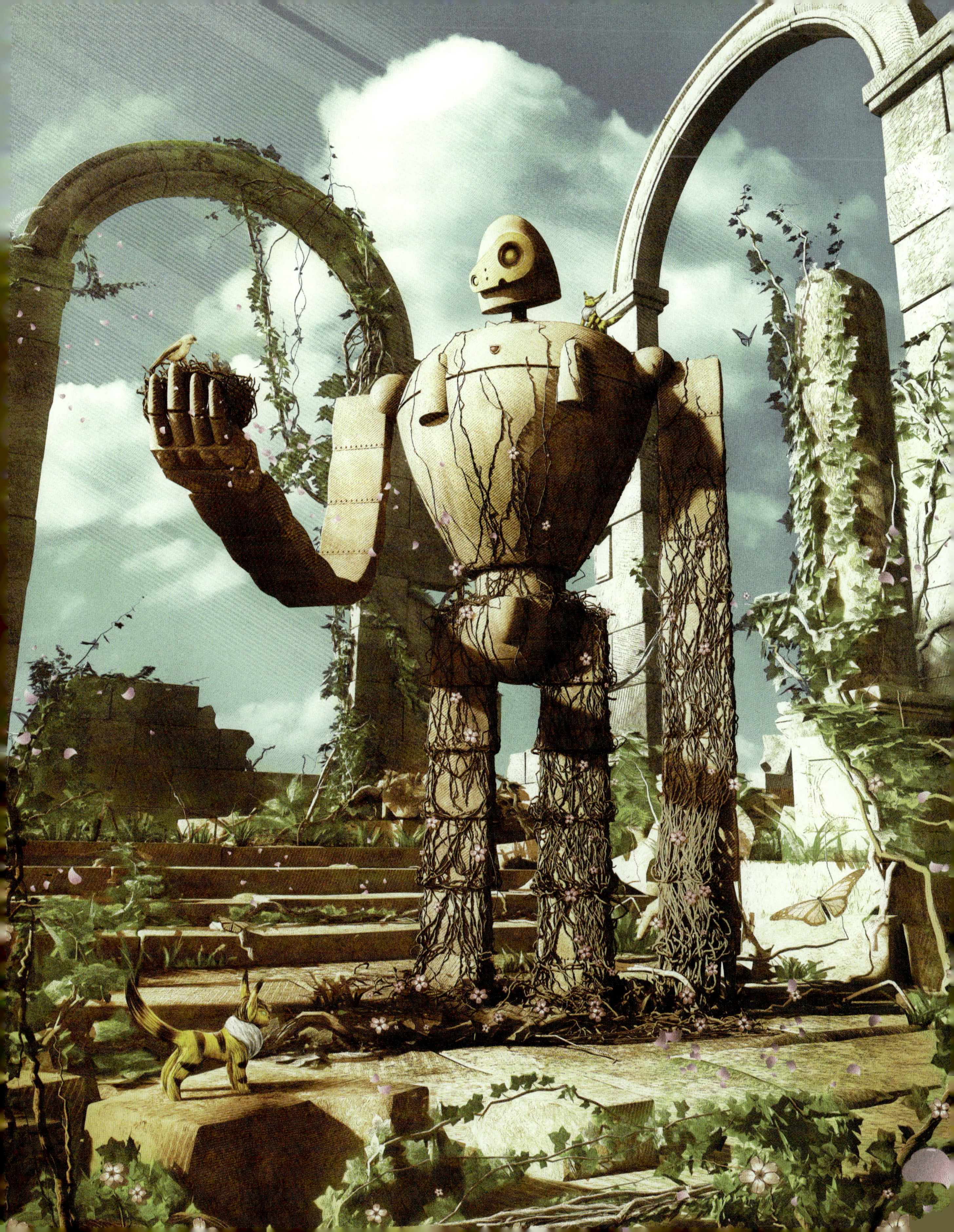

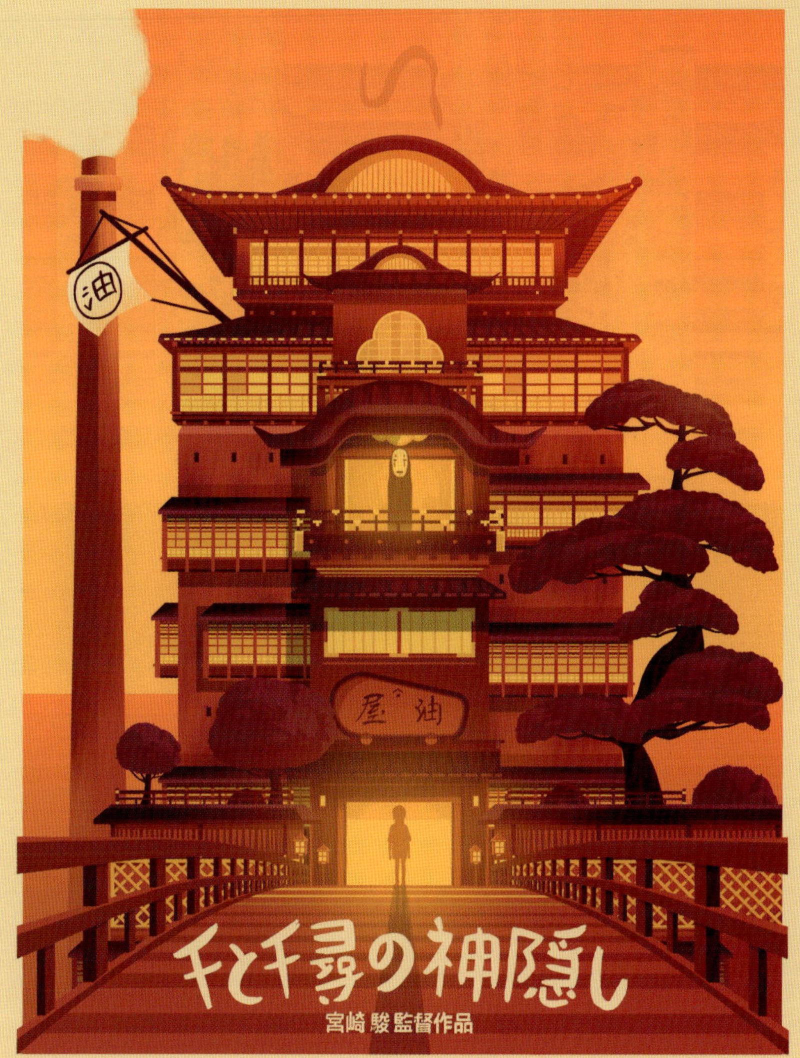

GEORGE TOWNLEY

ABOVE

Spirited Away

Archival pigment print. 18 x 24".

RIGHT PAGE

My Neighbor Totoro

Archival pigment print. 16 x 24".

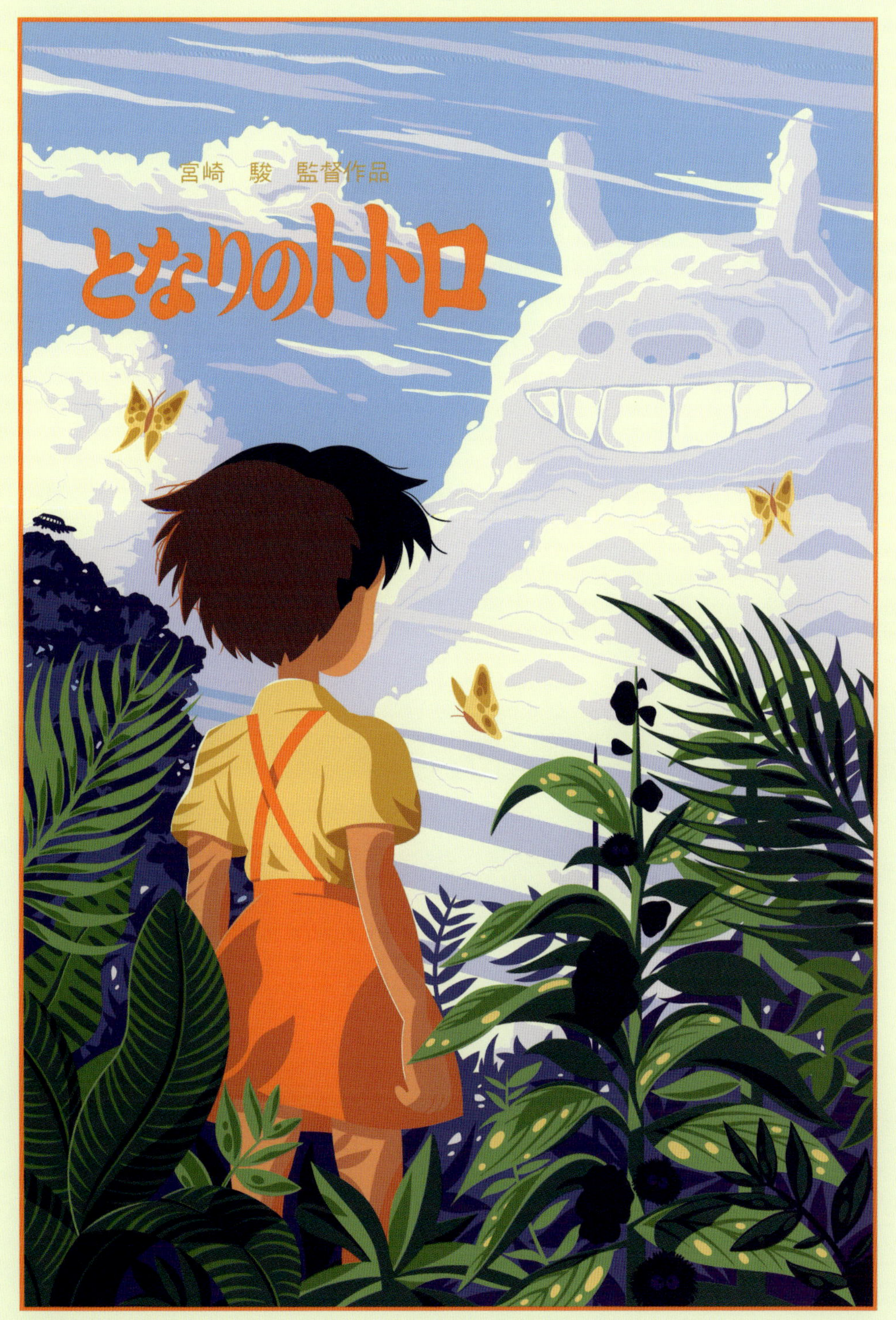
宮崎 駿 監督作品
となりのトトロ

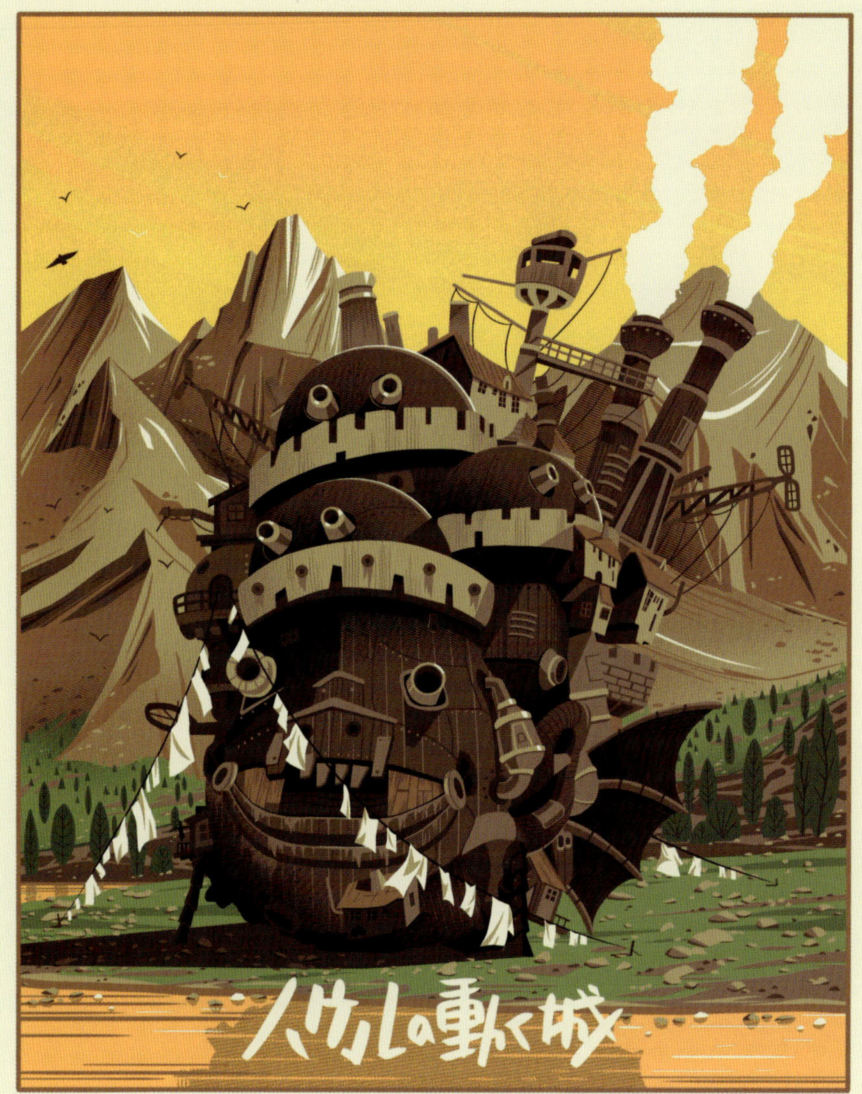

GEORGE TOWNLEY

Howl's Moving Castle
Archival pigment print. 18 x 24".

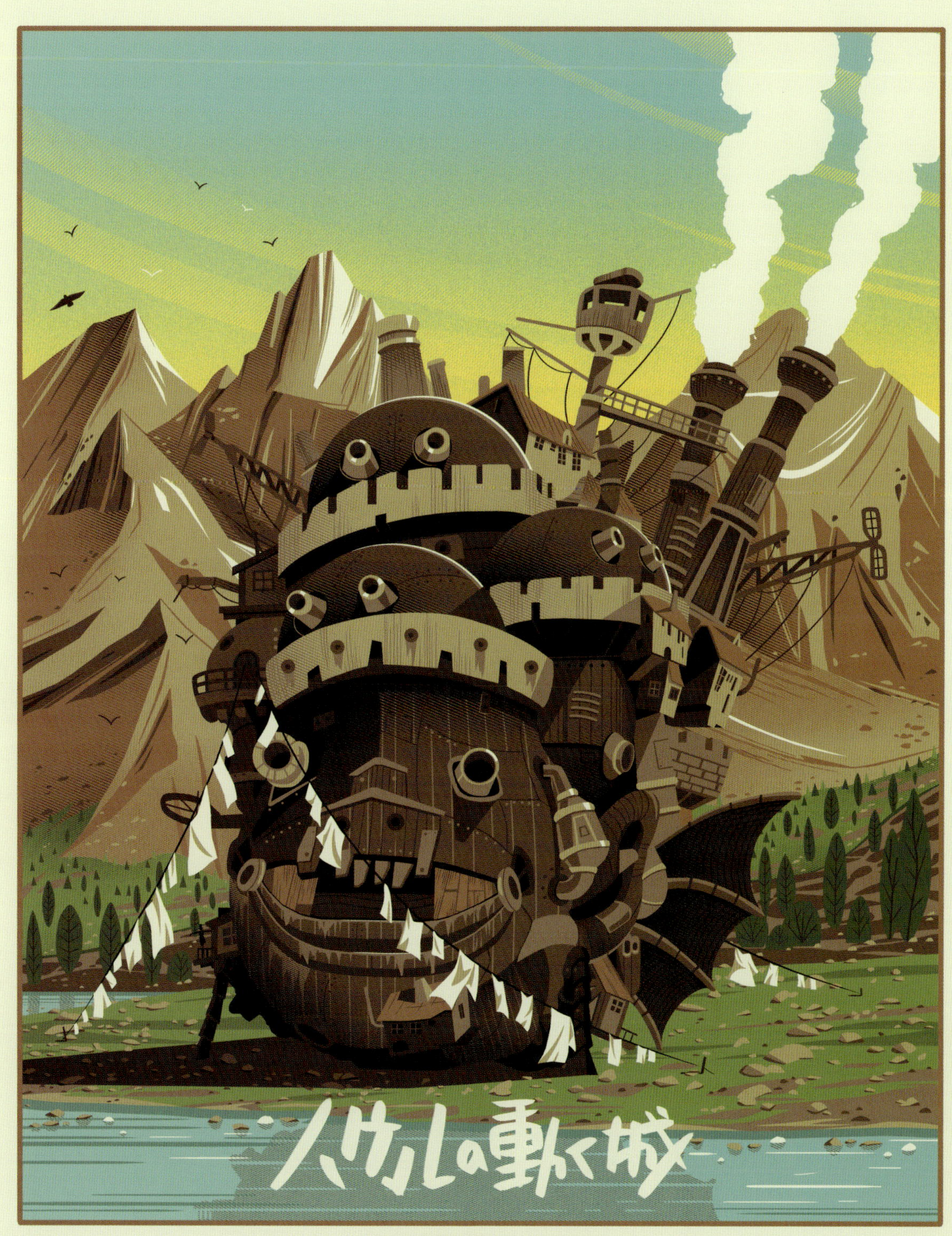

宮崎駿監督作品

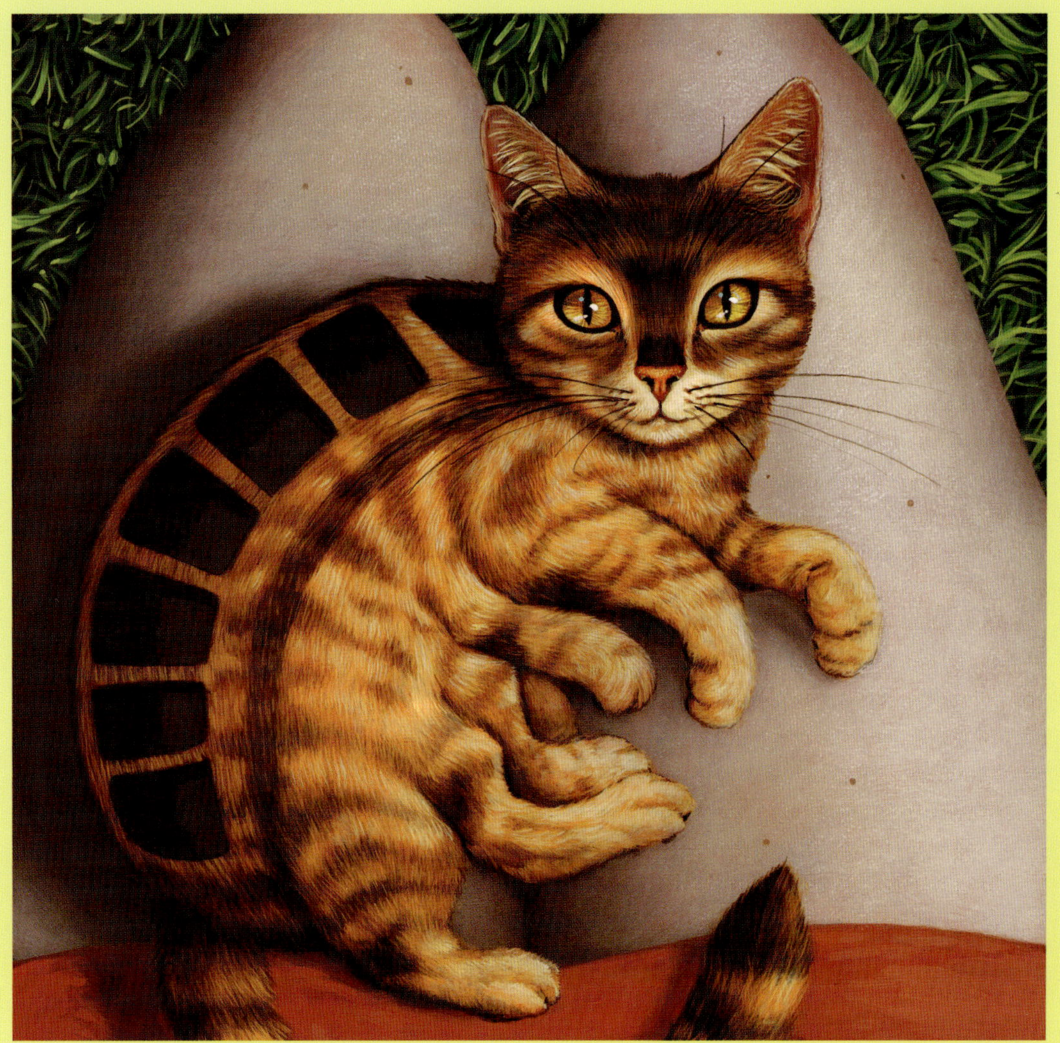

ABOVE

CASEY WELDON

Lil Nekobasu

Acrylic on wood. 14 x 14".

RIGHT PAGE

FERNANDO REZA

The Trees Cry out as they Die

Archival pigment print. 18 x 24".

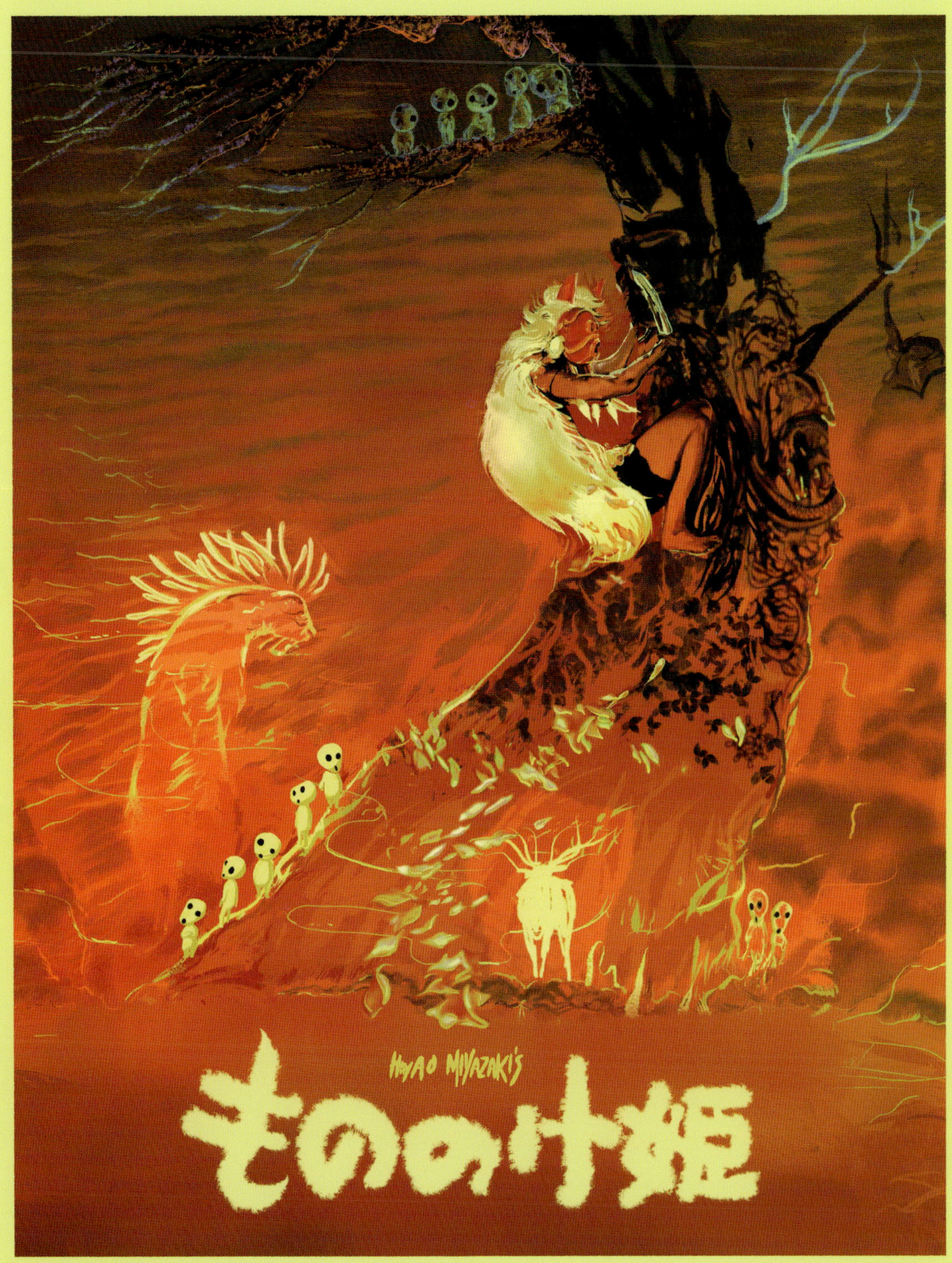
HAYAO MIYAZAKI'S
もののけ姫

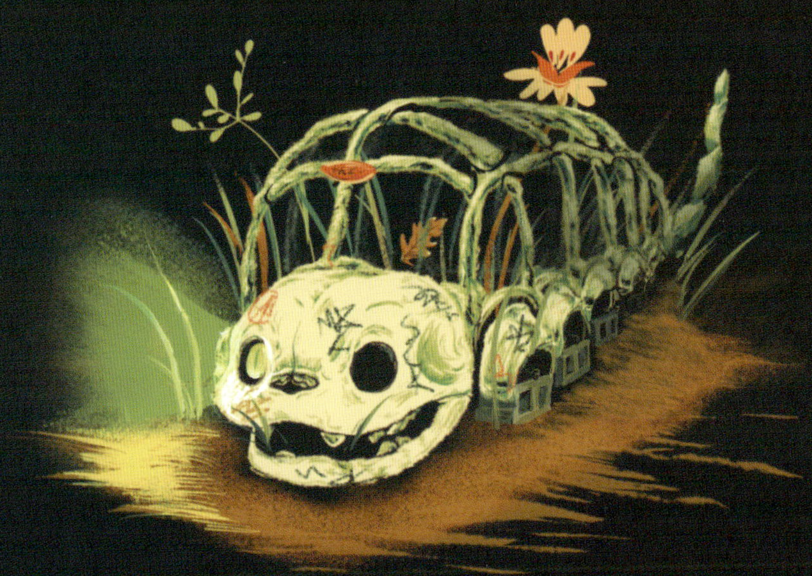

FERNANDO REZA

ABOVE

Out of Service

Archival pigment print. 8 x 8".

RIGHT PAGE

The Cat Bus That Couldn't Slow Down

Archival pigment print. 18 x 24".

KEAUNU REEVES
SANDRA BULLOCK
DENNIS HOPPER
JEFF DANIELS
HIYAO MIYAZAKI'S
SPEED
EXECUTIVE PRODUCER YASUYOSHI TOKUMA SCREENPLAY BY HAYAO MIYZAZAKI & GRAHAM YOST MUSIC BY JOE HISAISHI
TOKUMA SHOTEN PRESENTS A STUDIO GHIBLI PRODUCTION "SPEED"
BASED ON THE SHORT STORY "THE BUS THAT COULDN'T SLOW DOWN" DIRECTED BY HIYAO MIYAZAKI
スタジオジブリ
STUDIO GHIBLI

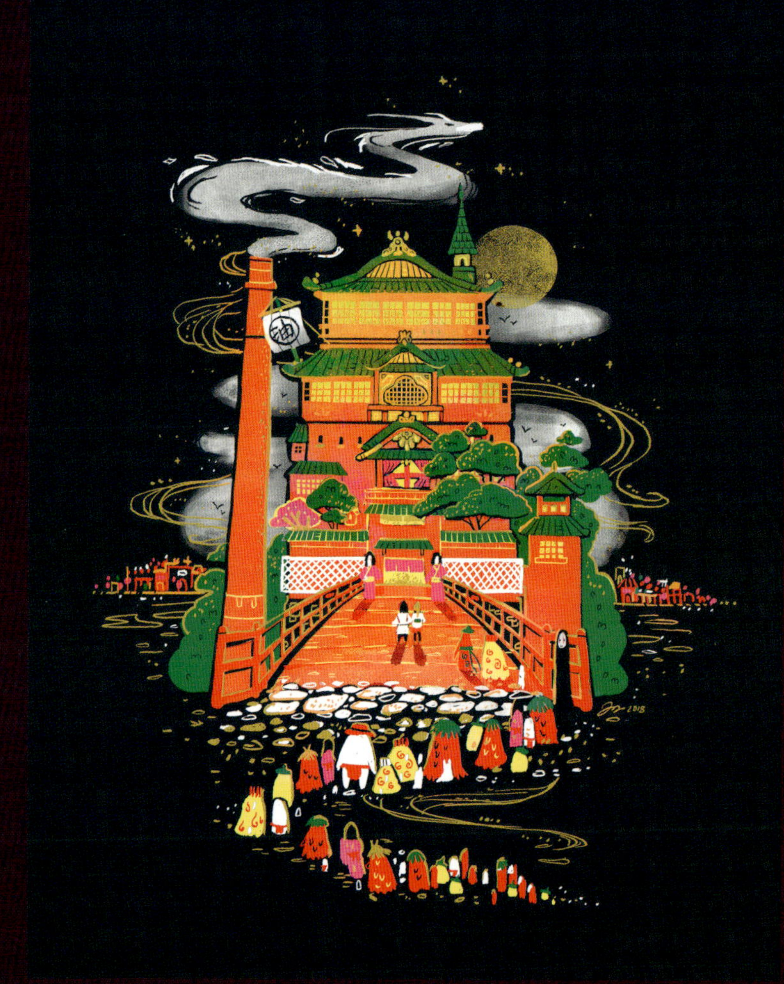

JOSEY TSAO

ABOVE

Spirit's Crossing

Hand-embellished screen print. 18 x 24".

TRACIE CHING

RIGHT PAGE

Spirited Away

Five-color screen print. 18 x 24".

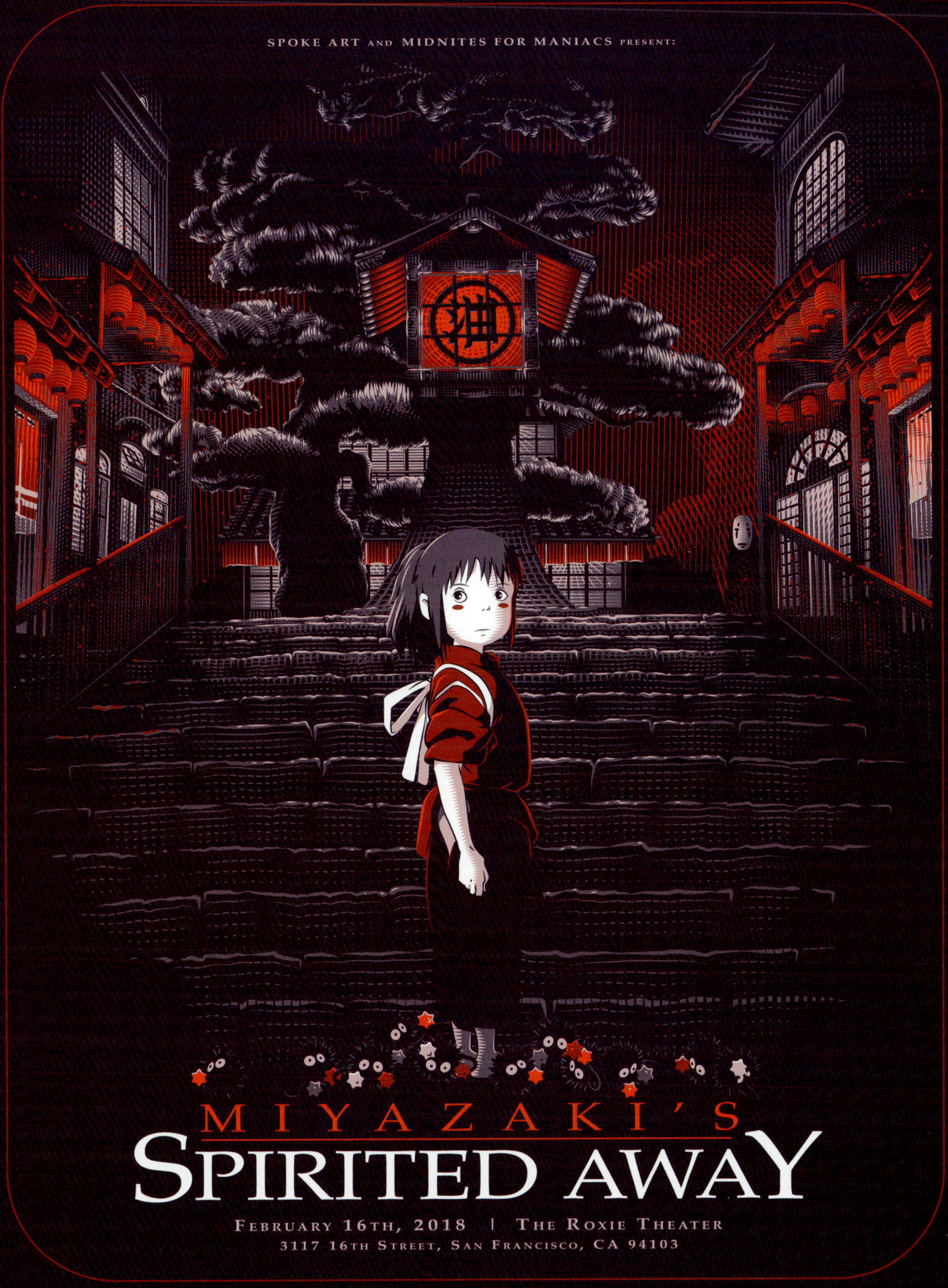

Spoke Art and Midnites for Maniacs present:

Miyazaki's
Spirited Away

February 16th, 2018 | The Roxie Theater
3117 16th Street, San Francisco, CA 94103

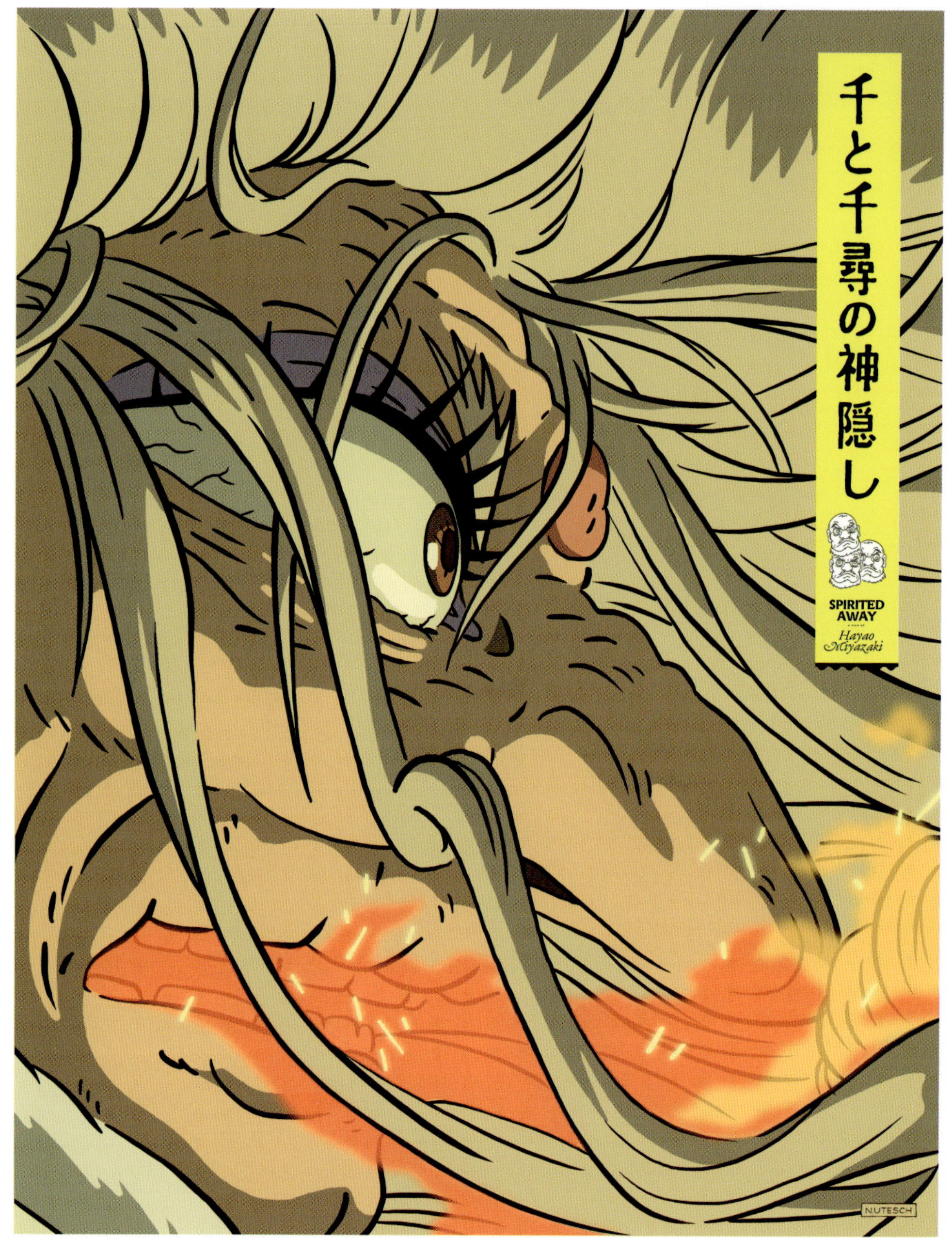

NATE UTESCH

Yubaba

Archival pigment print. 18 x 24".

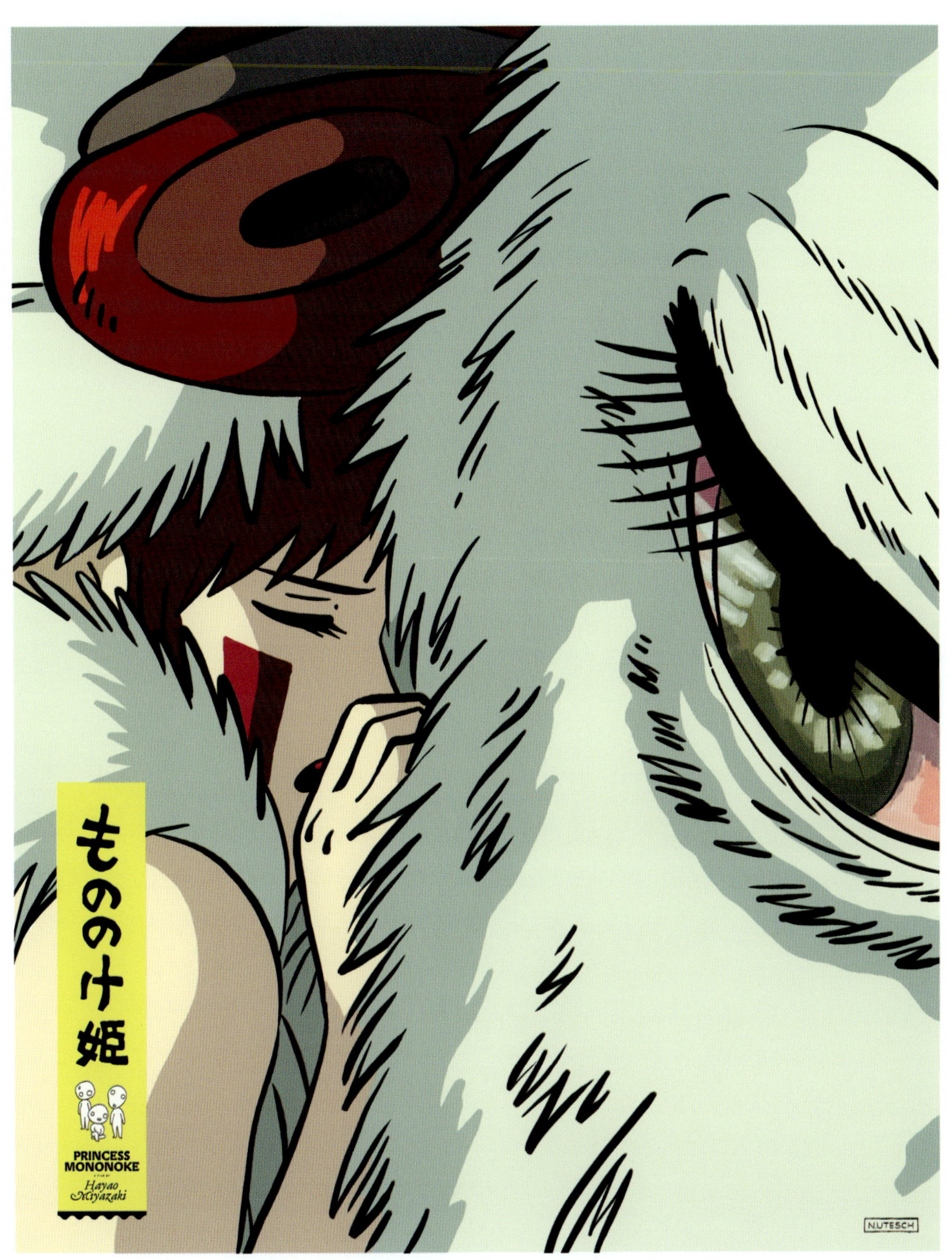

San and Moro
Archival pigment print. 18 x 24".

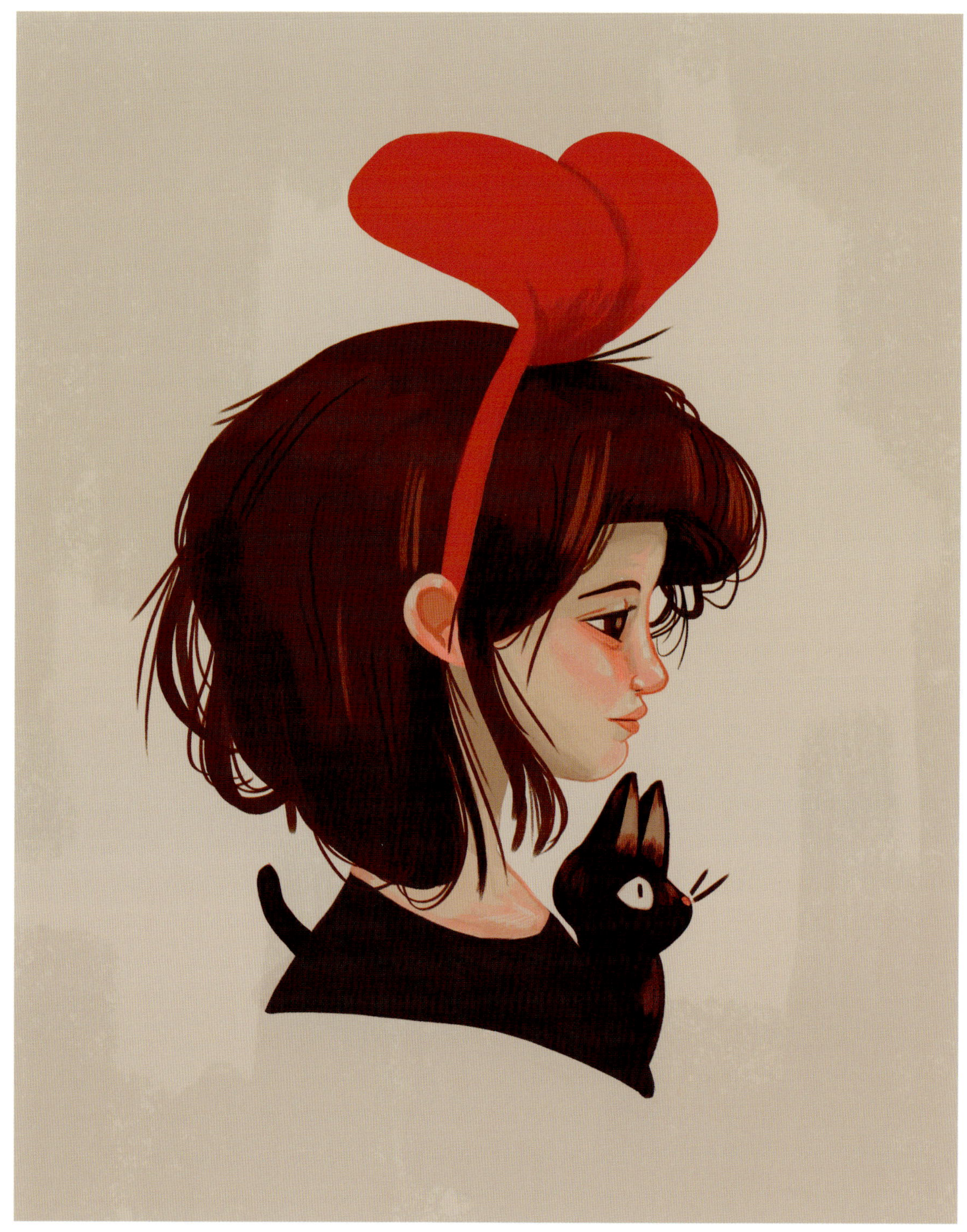

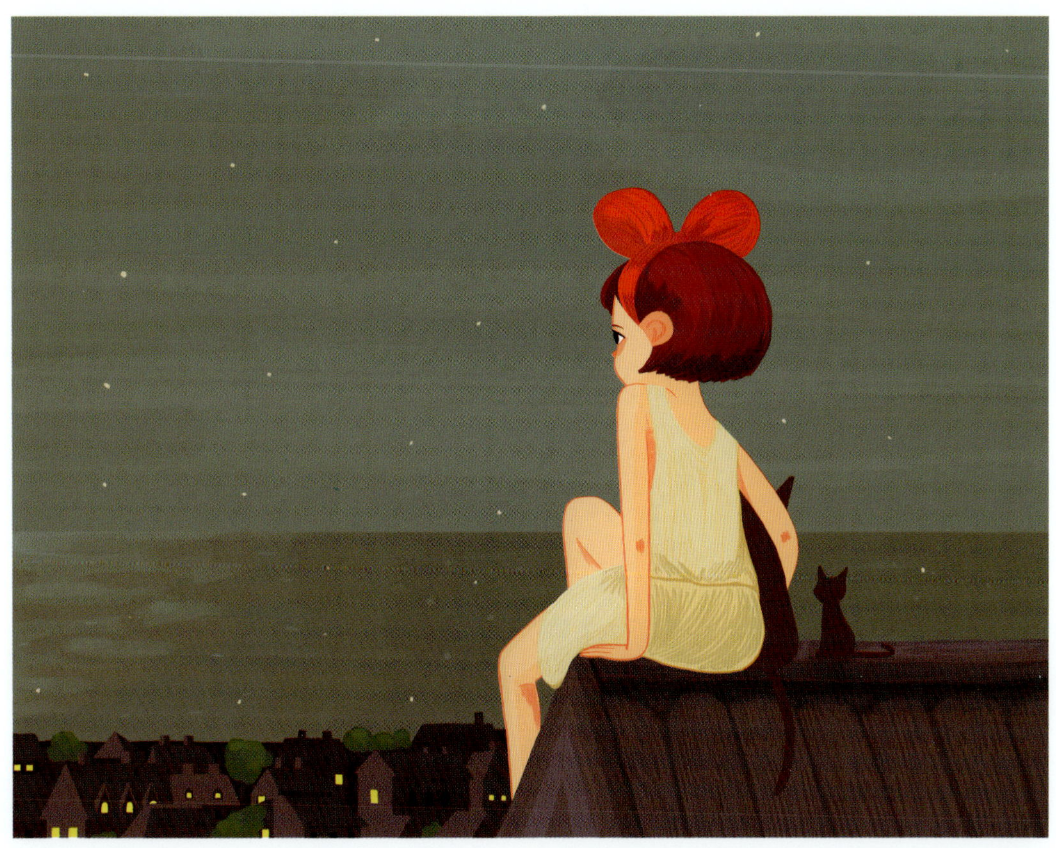

NAN LAWSON

LEFT PAGE

Kiki

Archival pigment print. 8 x 10".

ABOVE

An Evening in Koriko

Archival pigment print. 10 x 8".

RIGHT PAGE

NAN LAWSON

Wolf

Archival pigment print. 8 x 10".

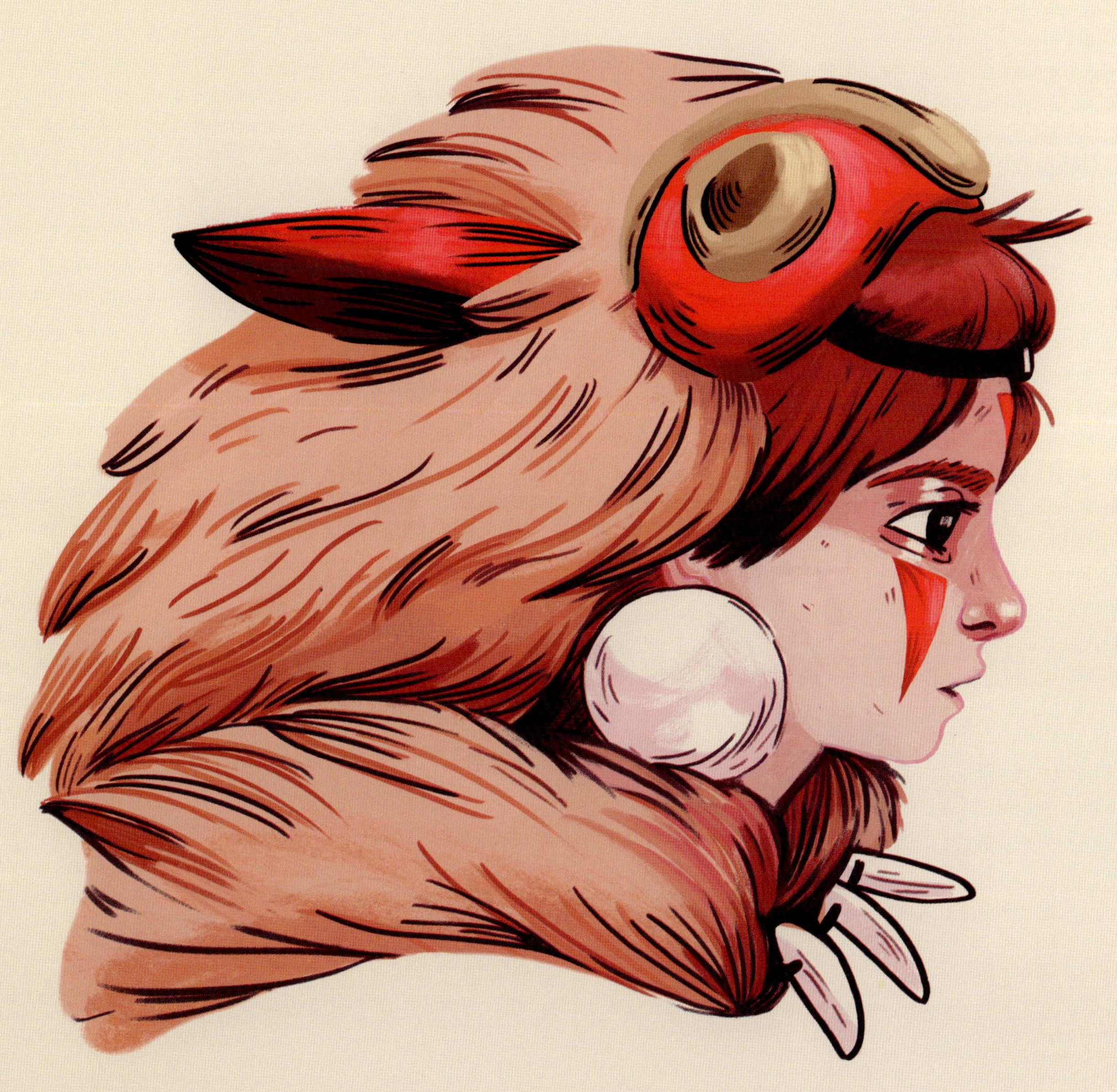

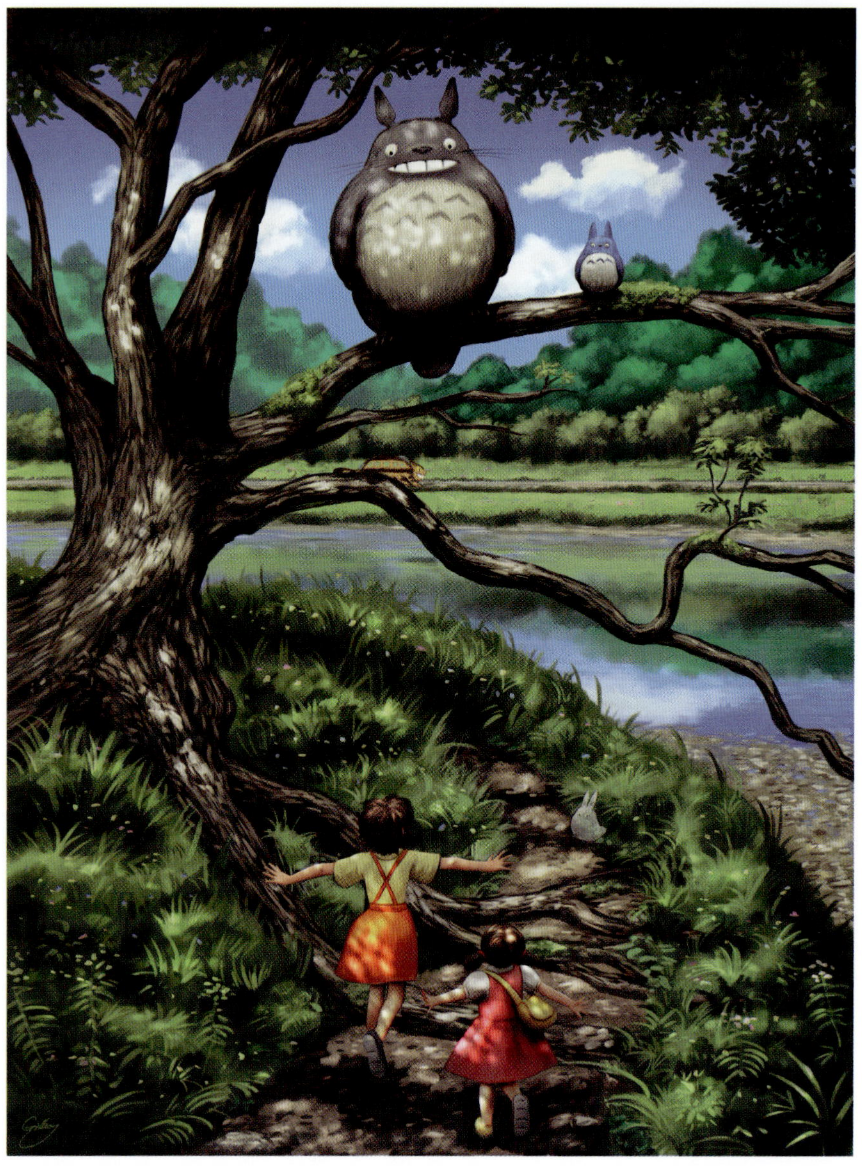

SAM GILBEY

ABOVE

Everybody, Try Laughing. Then Whatever Scares You Will Go Away! (Day Variant)

Archival pigment print. 18 x 24".

RIGHT PAGE

To See With Eyes Unclouded By Hate

Archival pigment print. 18 x 24".

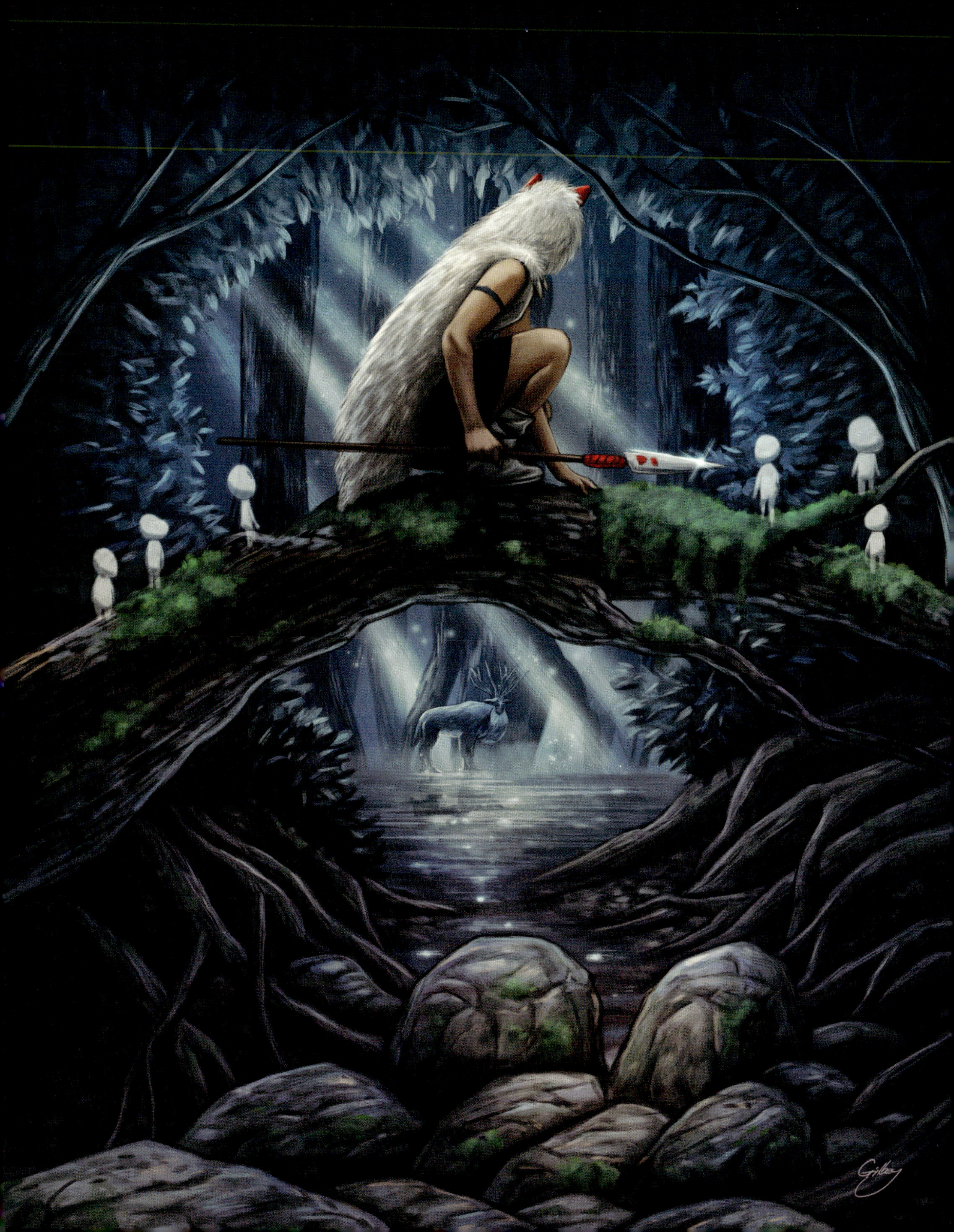

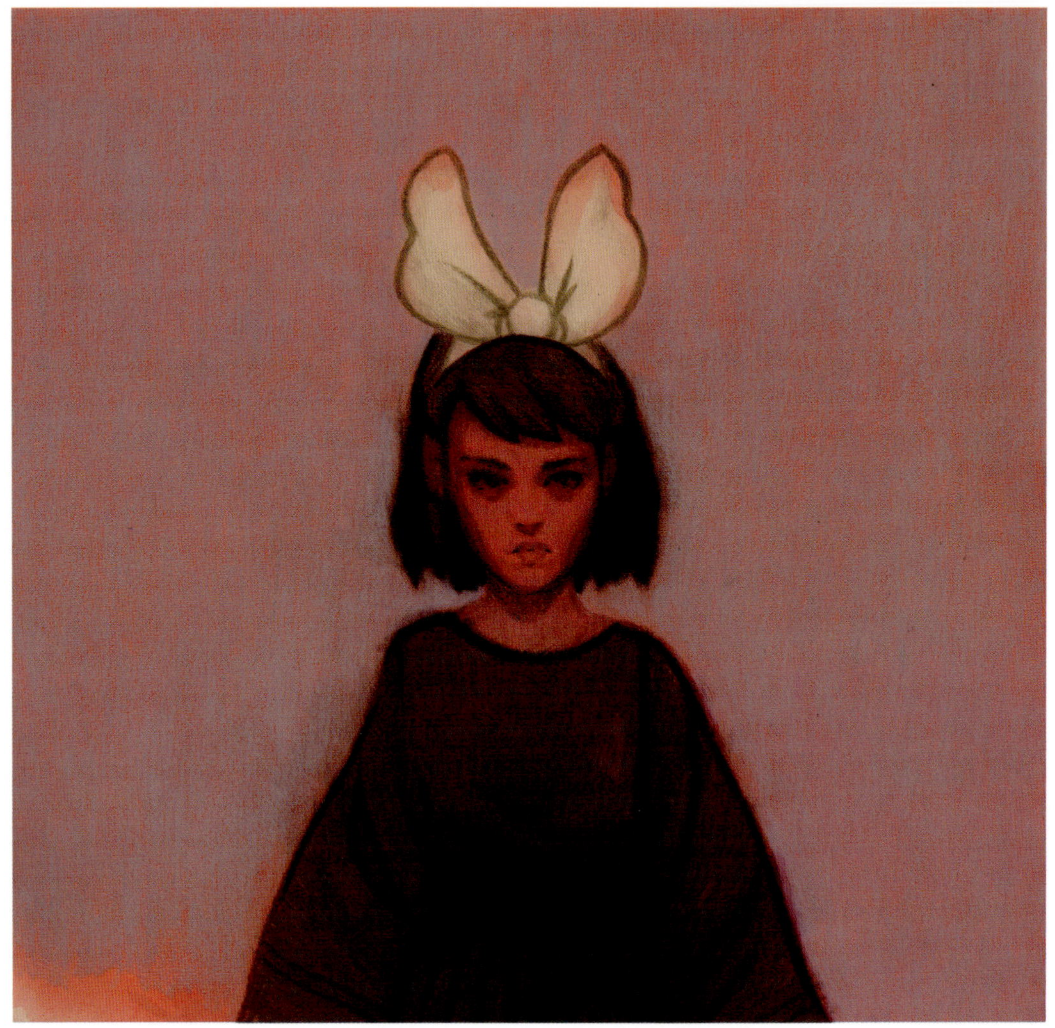

LEONARDO SANTAMARIA

ABOVE

Kiki

Acrylic and colored pencil on paper. 14 x 14".

RIGHT PAGE

Stealing Your Name

Graphite, acrylic, colored pencil, and acrylic gouache on paper. 24 x 30".

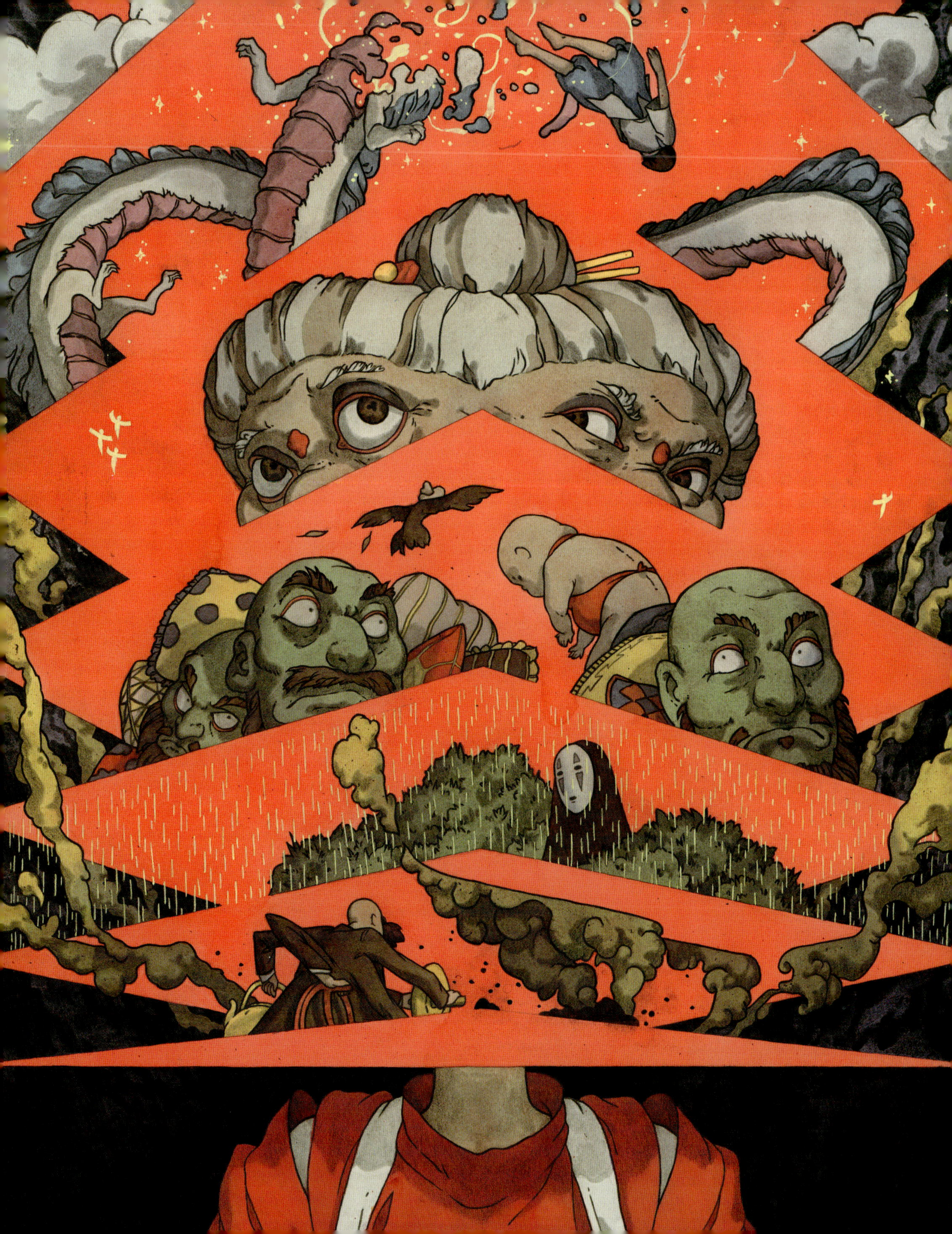

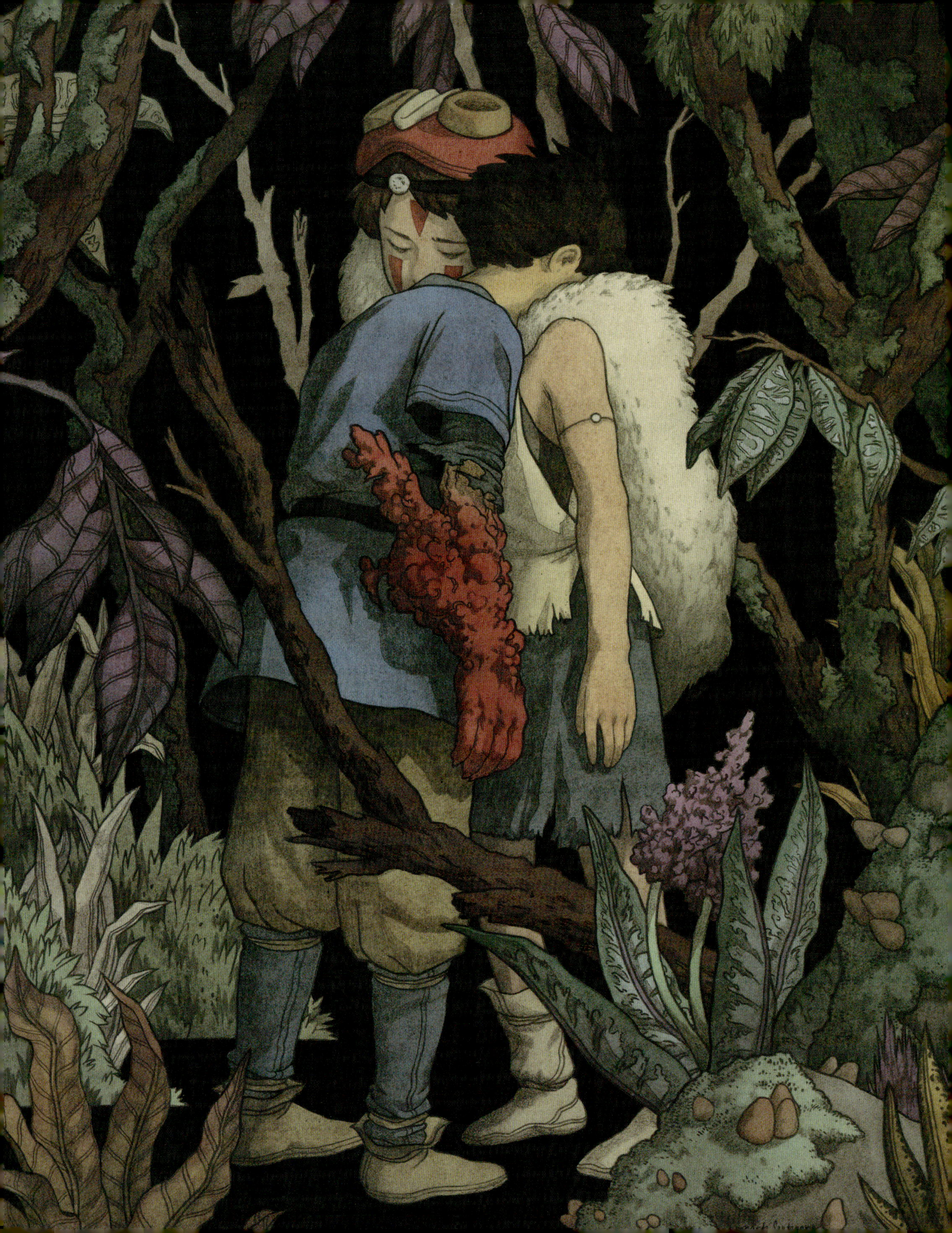

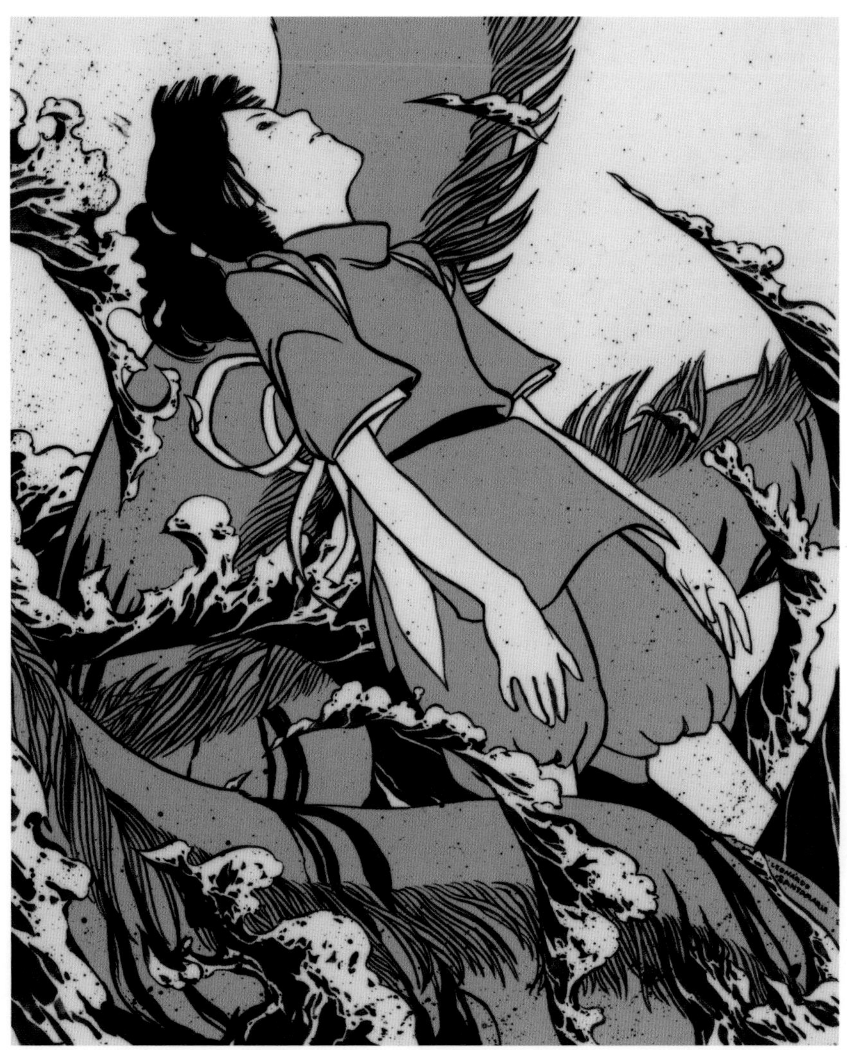

LEONARDO SANTAMARIA

LEFT PAGE

Life is suffering. It is hard. The world is cursed. But still, you find reasons to keep living.

Acrylic, graphite, colored pencil, and ink on paper. 16 x 20".

ABOVE

You Don't Remember Your Name?

Pearlescent ink on polypropylene. 8 x 10".

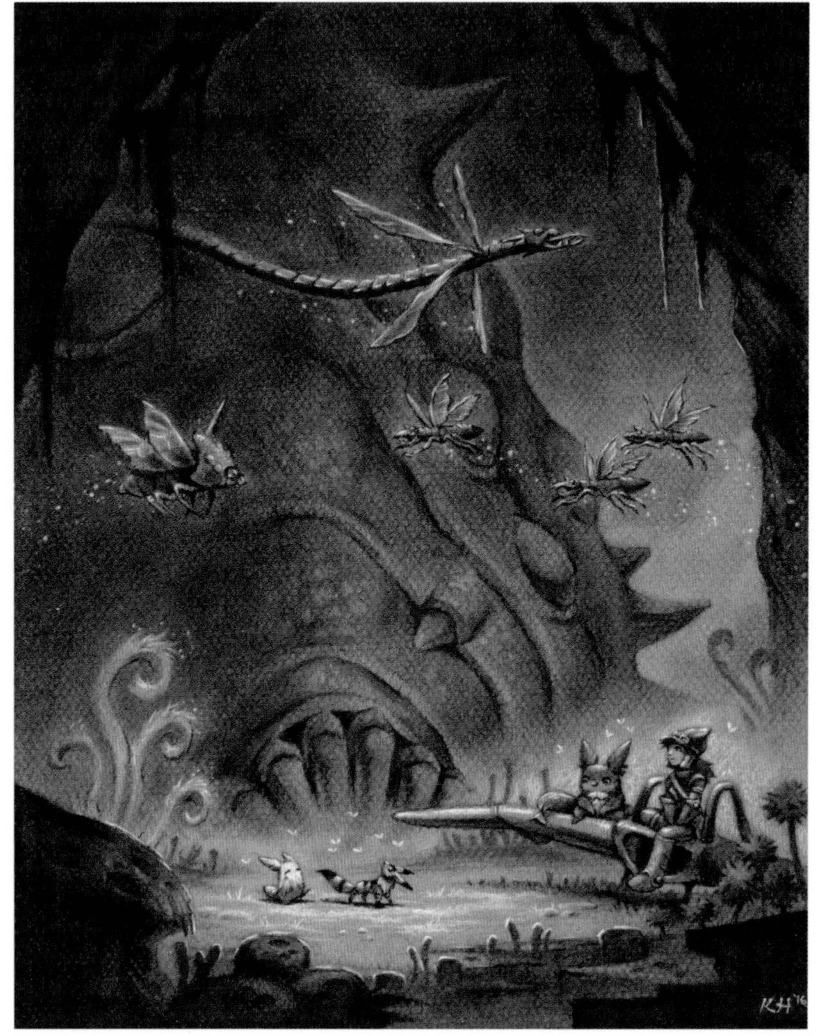

KEVAN HOM

ABOVE

Peace in the Toxic Jungle
Charcoal and white pastel. 8.5 x 11".

RIGHT PAGE

Floating Travelers
Pigment print on canvas. 12 x 16".

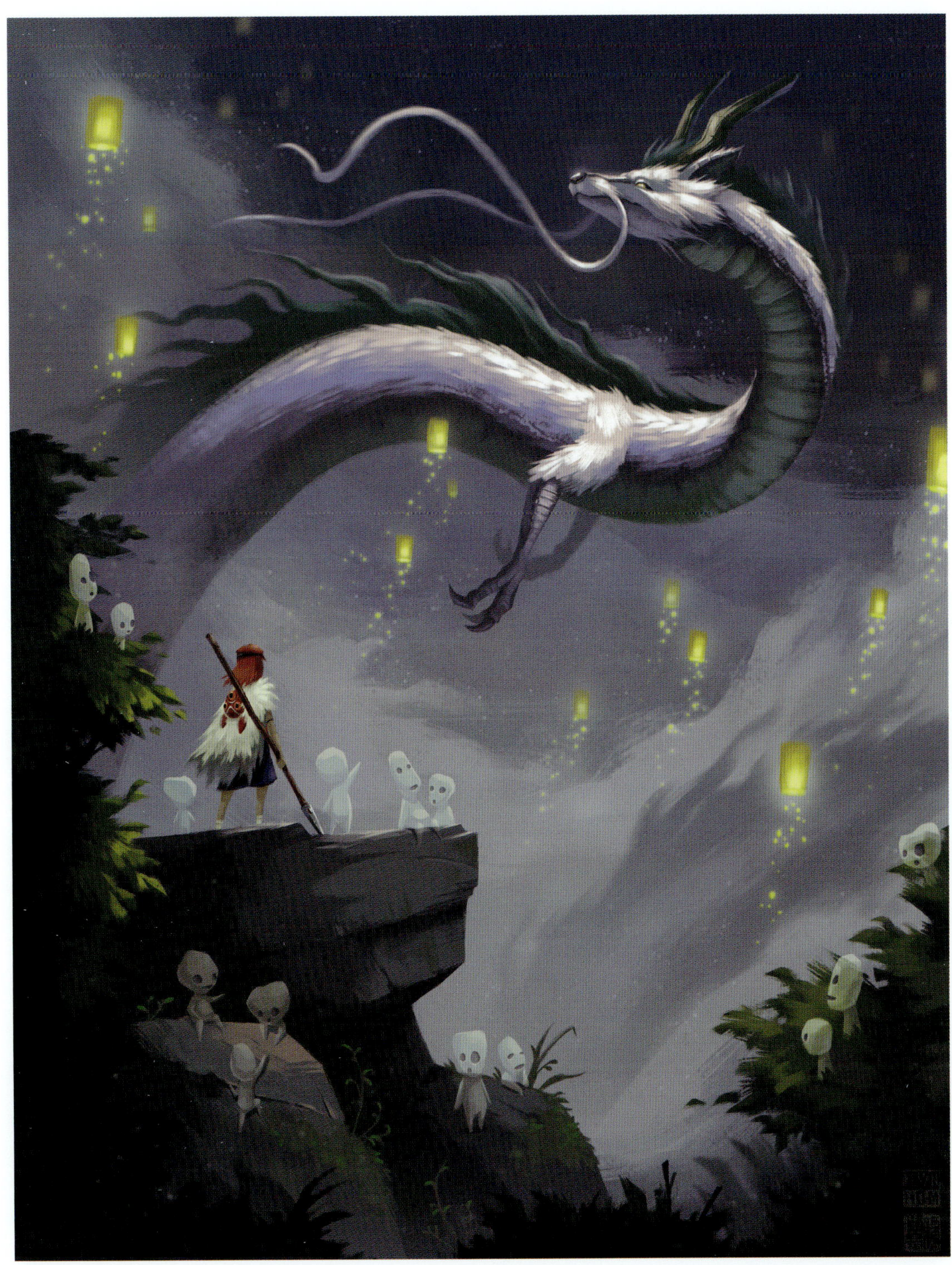

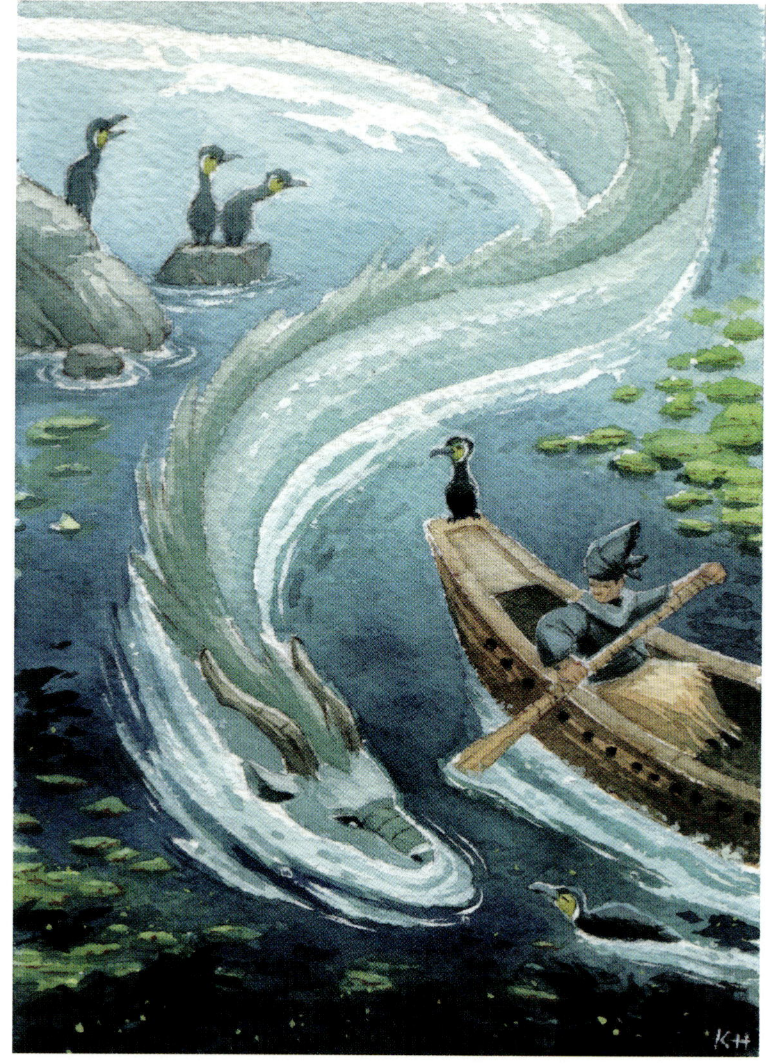

KEVAN HOM

ABOVE

Fishing on the Kohaku River

Watercolor. 5 x 7".

RIGHT PAGE

Radish Spirit's Produce Stall

Watercolor. 5 x 7".

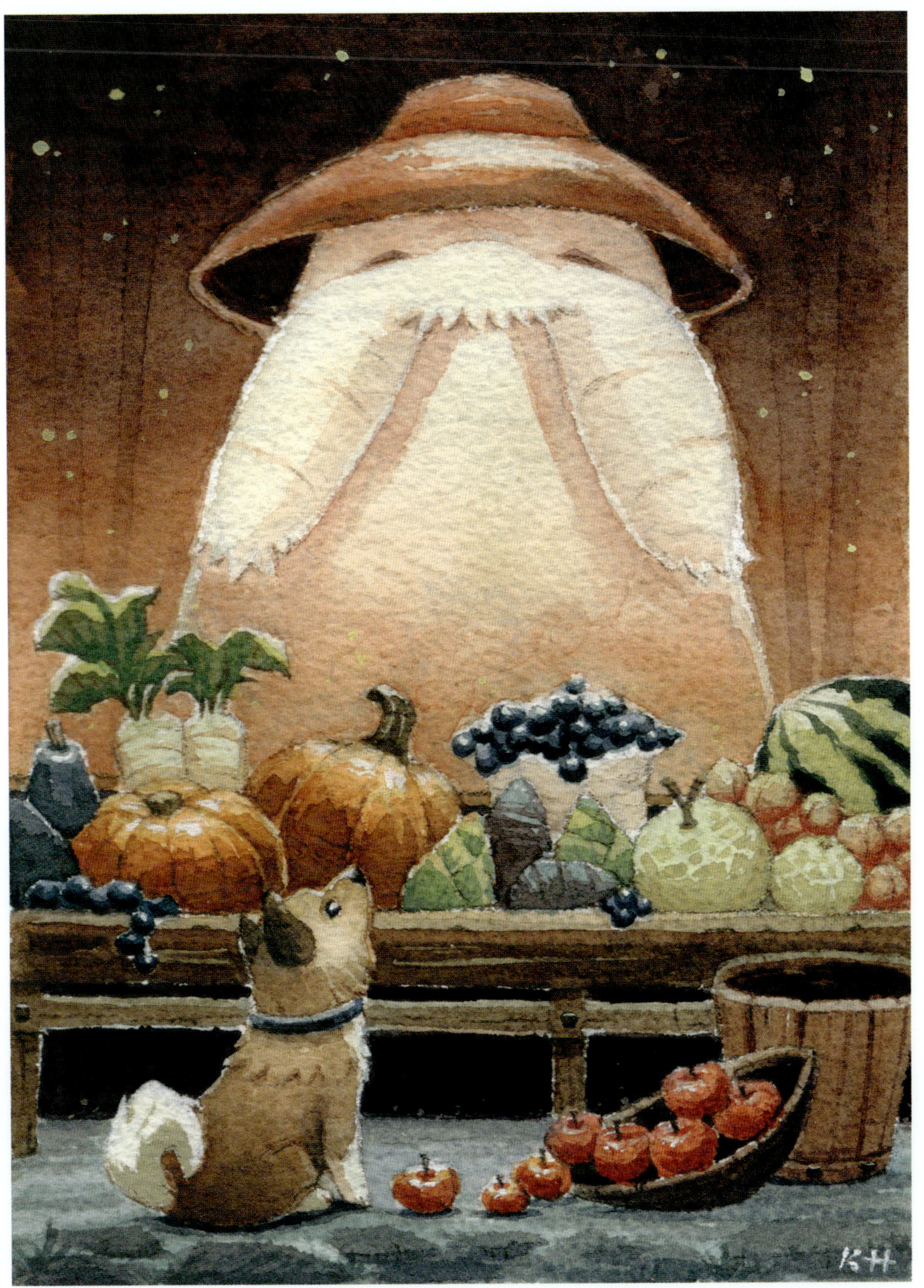
KH

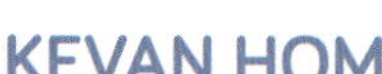

Kittenbus and the Cat Liner

Acrylic on board. 11 x 8.5".

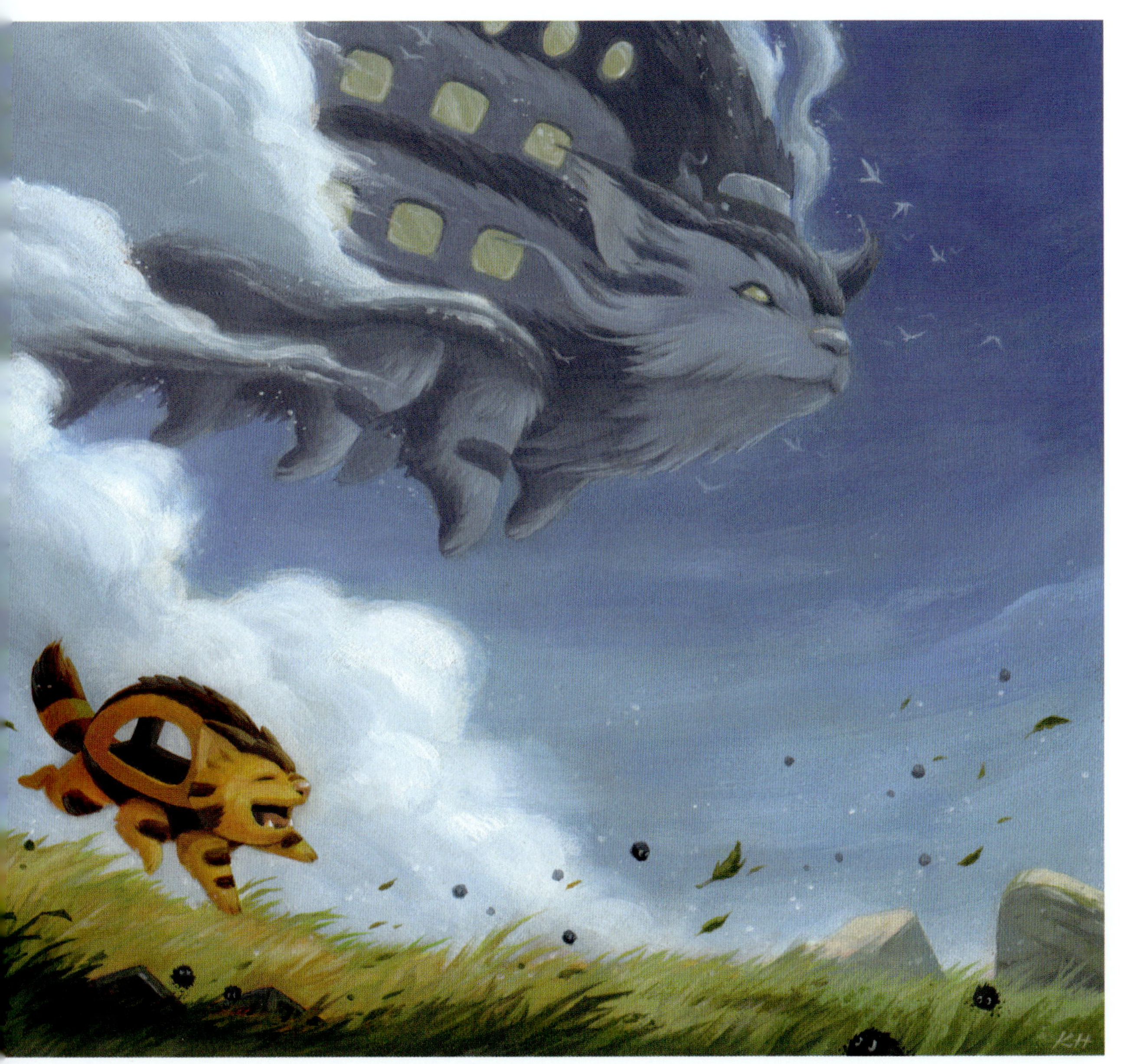

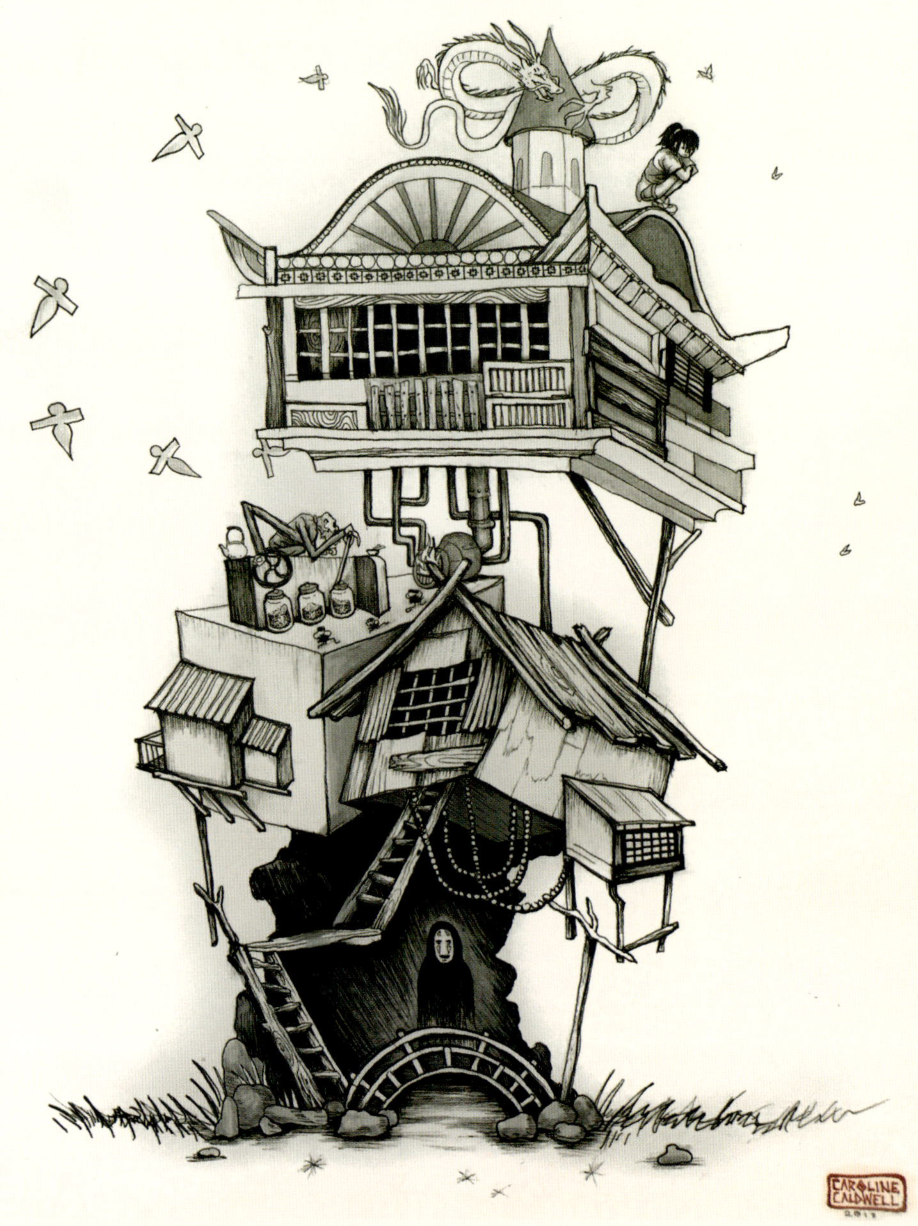

CAROLINE CALDWELL

ABOVE

Spirited Away

Pen, marker and pencil on paper.
13 x 16".

ALLISON REIMOLD

RIGHT PAGE

Chihiro

Graphite and gouache on Mylar.
8 x 10".

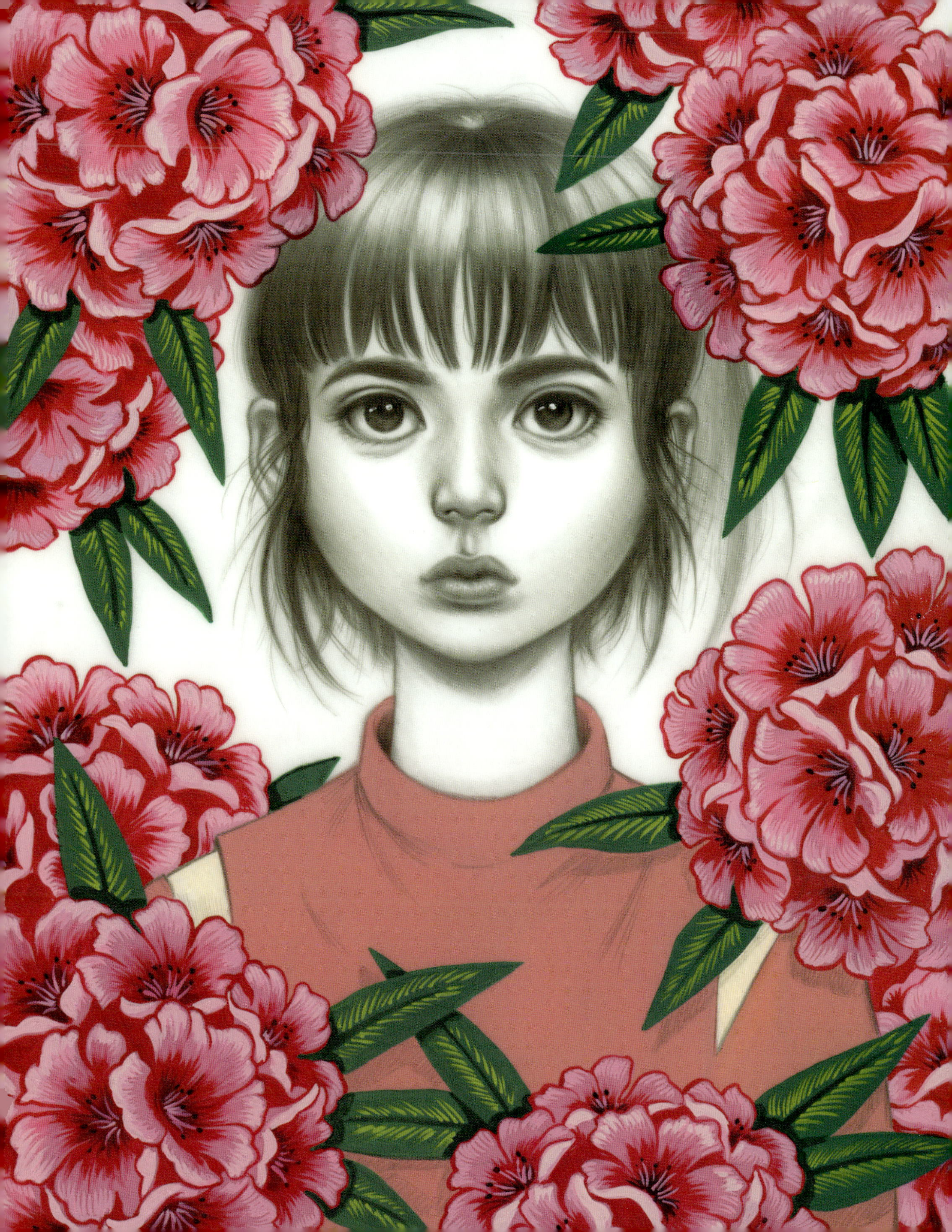

LEILANI BUSTAMANTE

RIGHT PAGE

Haku and Chihiro
Acrylic on board. 11 x 14".

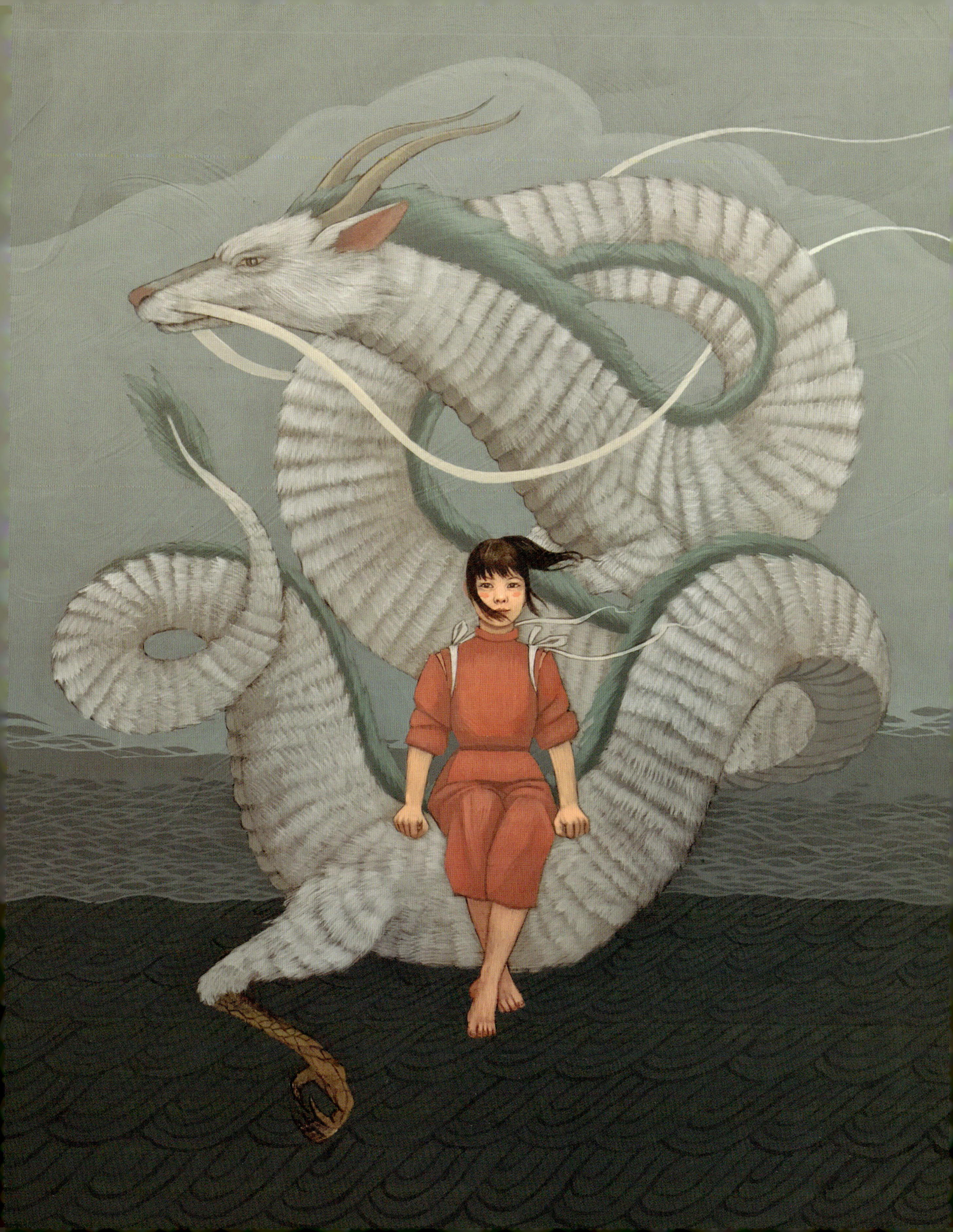

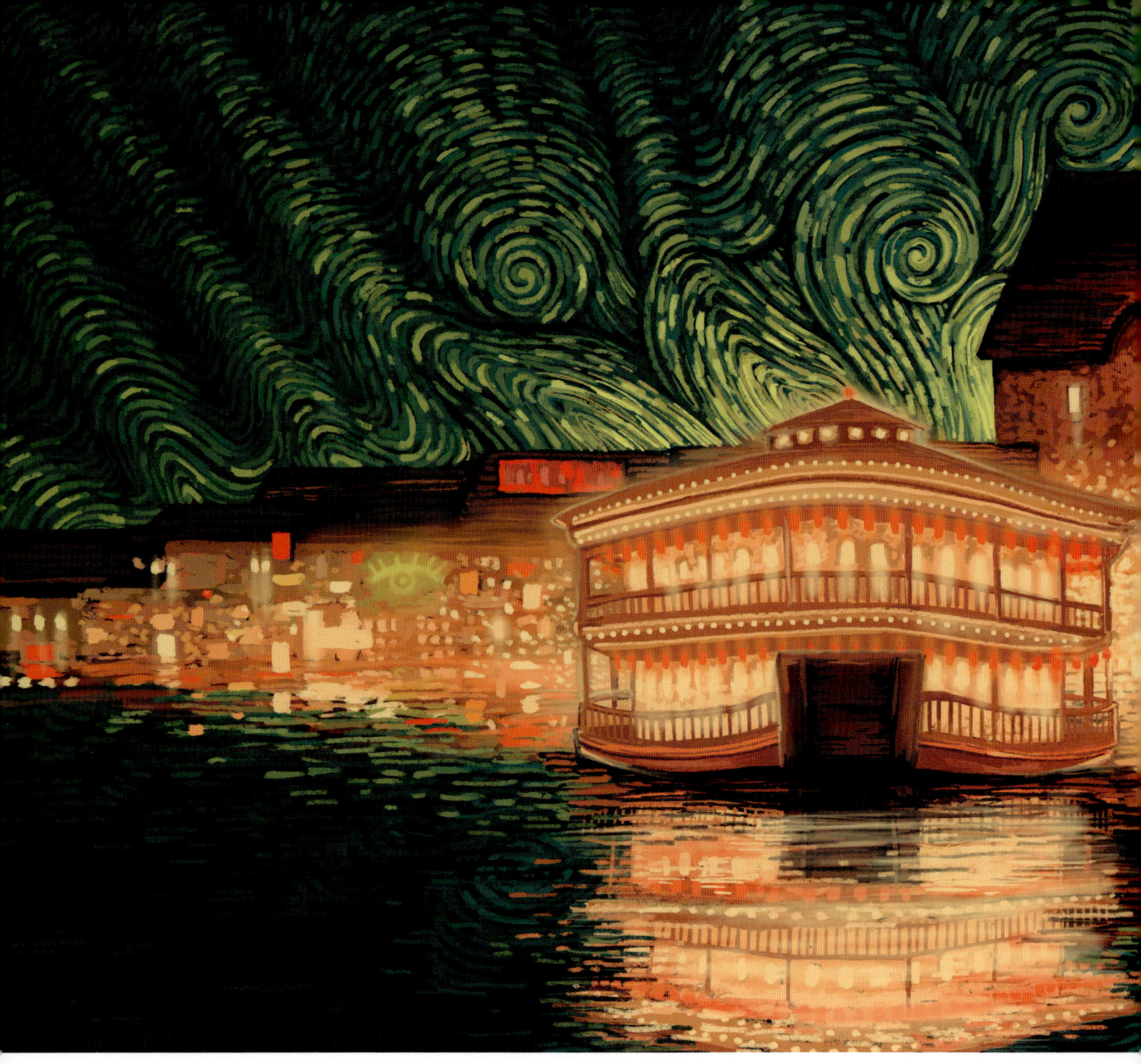

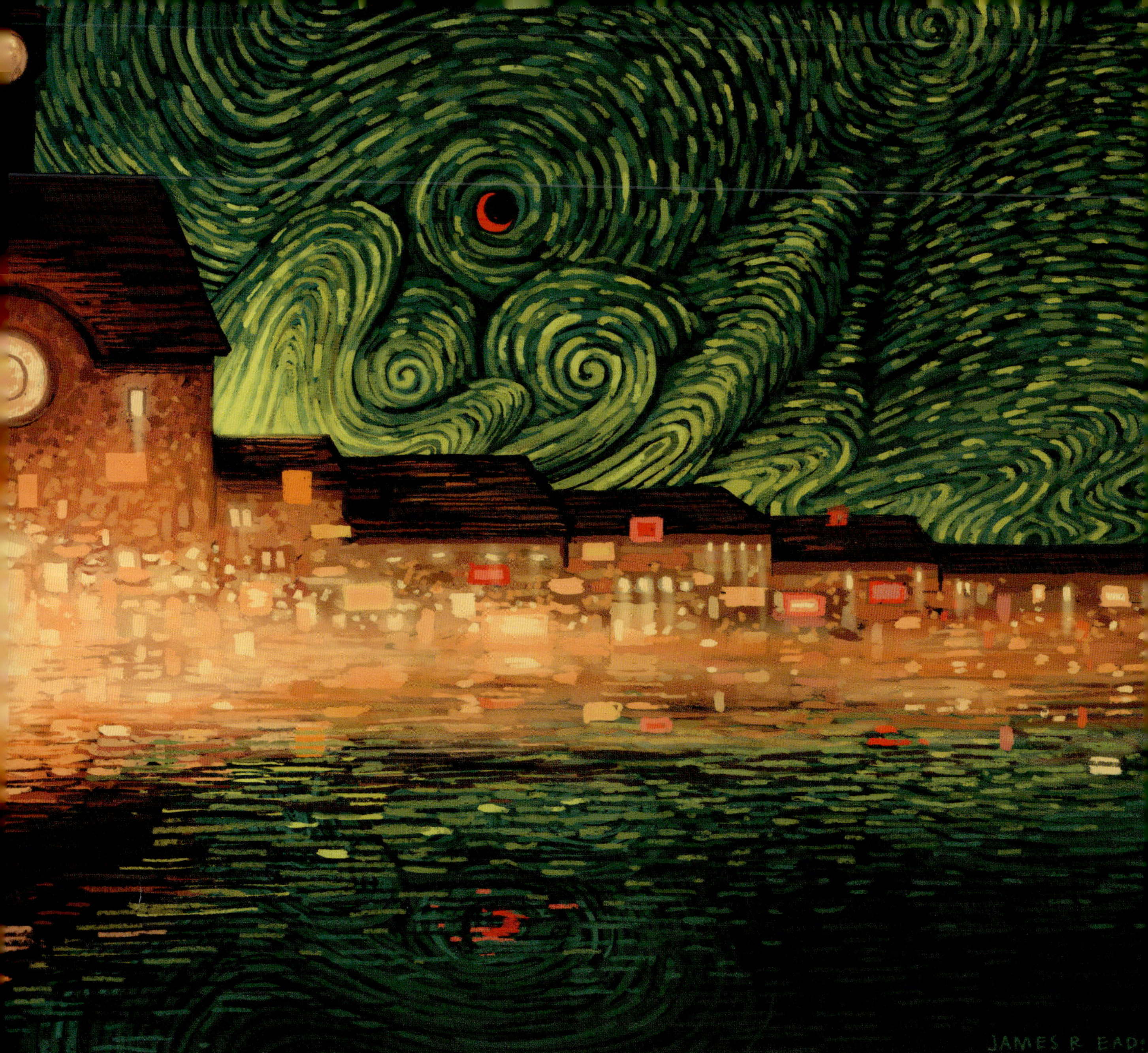

JAMES R. EADS

The Riverboat Spirits

Archival pigment print. 24 x 12''.

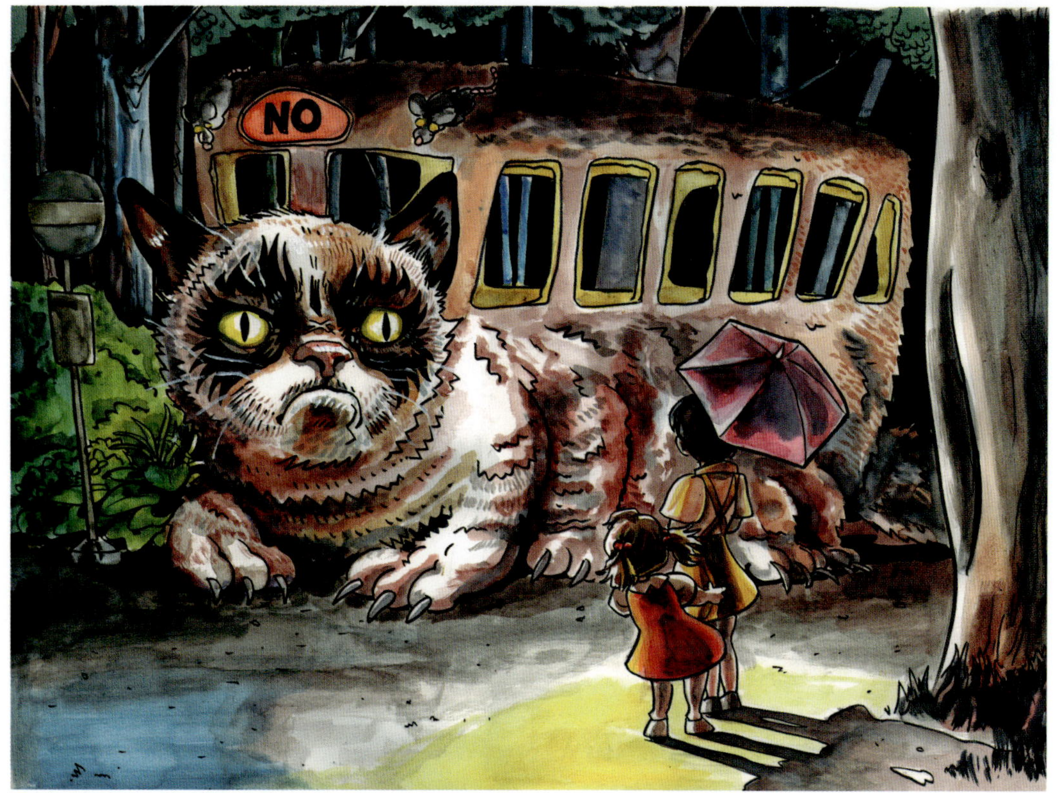

TIMOTHY DOYLE

ABOVE

Out of Service

Watercolor on bristol board. 20 x 16".

GUILLAUME MORELLEC

RIGHT PAGE

Princess Mononoke

Screen print. 18 x 24".

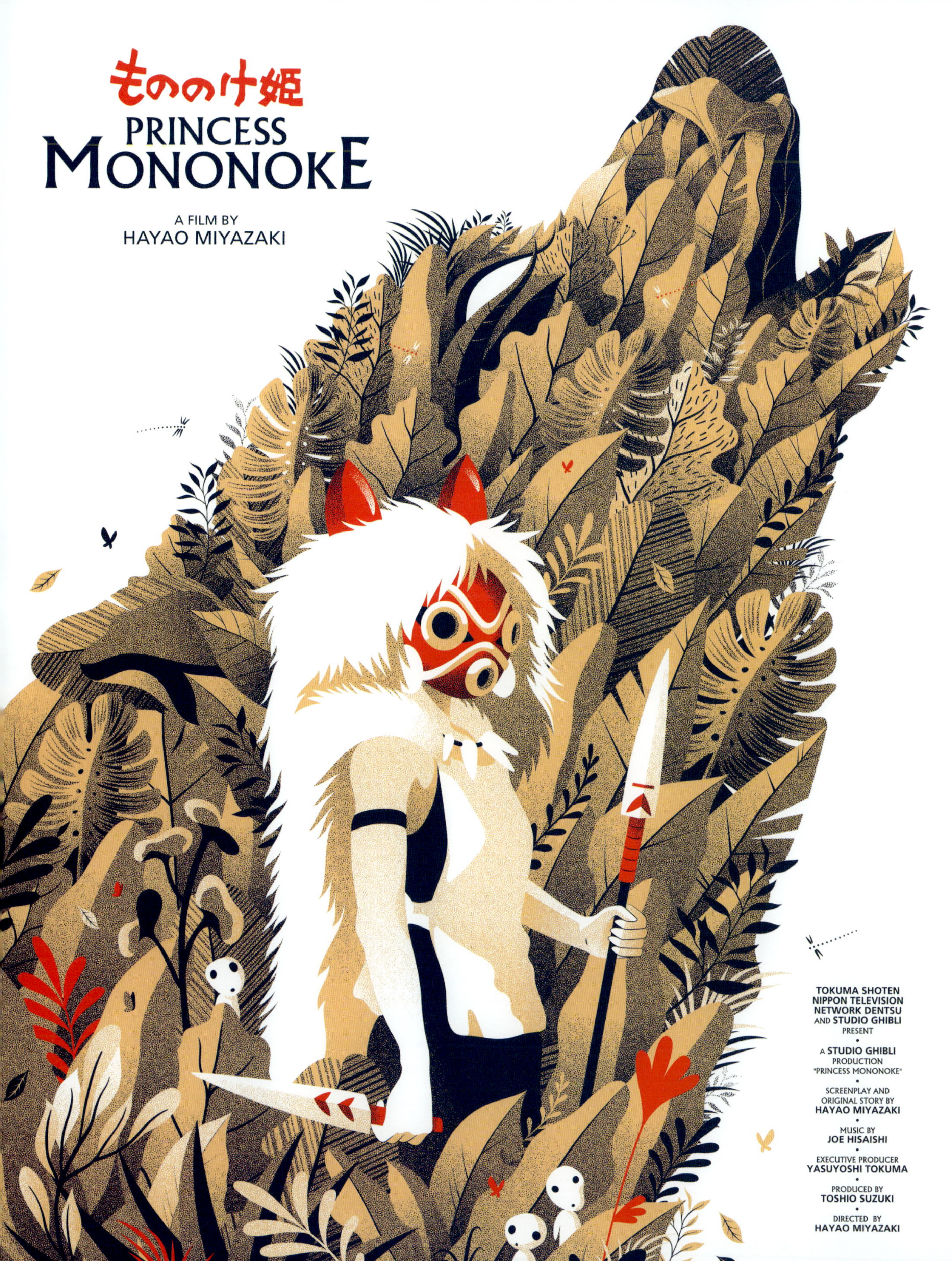
もののけ姫
PRINCESS
MONONOKE
A FILM BY
HAYAO MIYAZAKI
TOKUMA SHOTEN
NIPPON TELEVISION
NETWORK DENTSU
AND STUDIO GHIBLI
PRESENT
A STUDIO GHIBLI
PRODUCTION
"PRINCESS MONONOKE"
SCREENPLAY AND
ORIGINAL STORY BY
HAYAO MIYAZAKI
MUSIC BY
JOE HISAISHI
EXECUTIVE PRODUCER
YASUYOSHI TOKUMA
PRODUCED BY
TOSHIO SUZUKI
DIRECTED BY
HAYAO MIYAZAKI

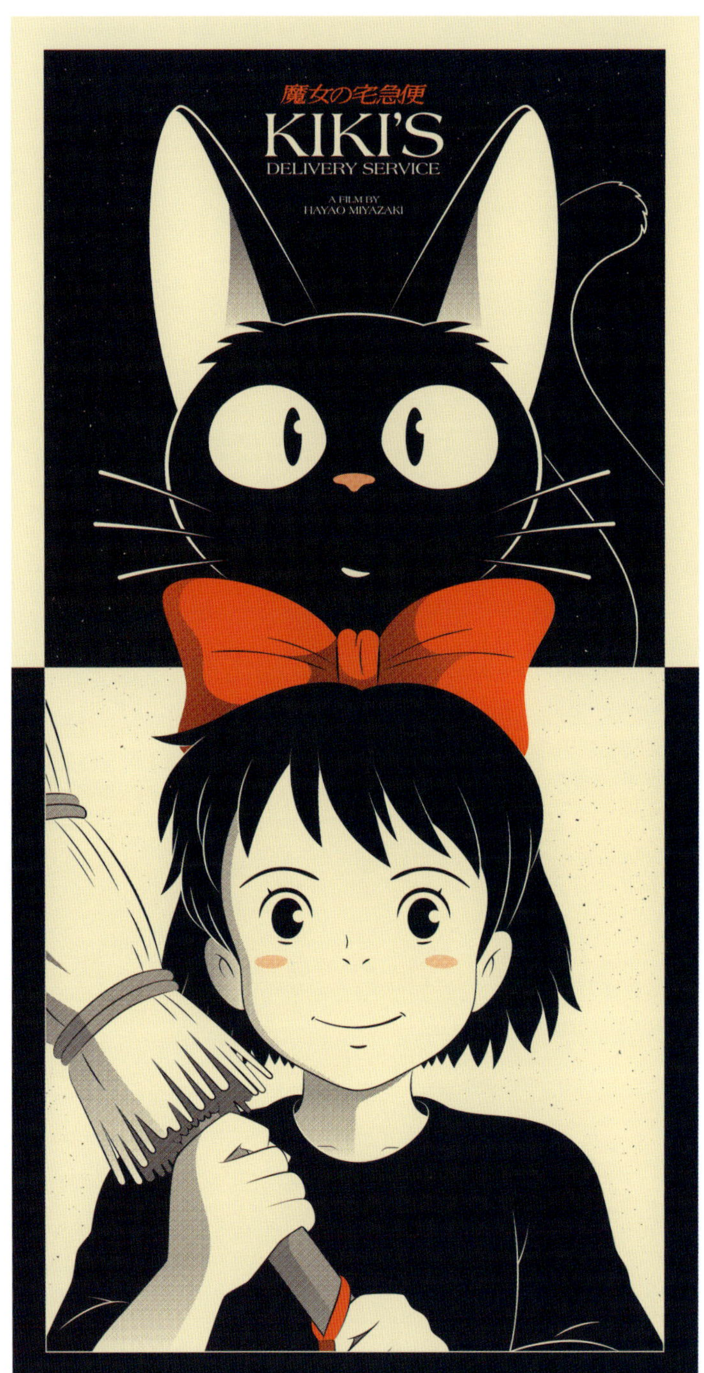

GUILLAUME MORELLEC

LEFT

Kiki's Delivery Service
Two-color screen print. 12 x 24".

RIGHT PAGE

My Neighbor Totoro
Screen print. 18 x 24".

Written & Directed by
HAYAO MIYAZAKI

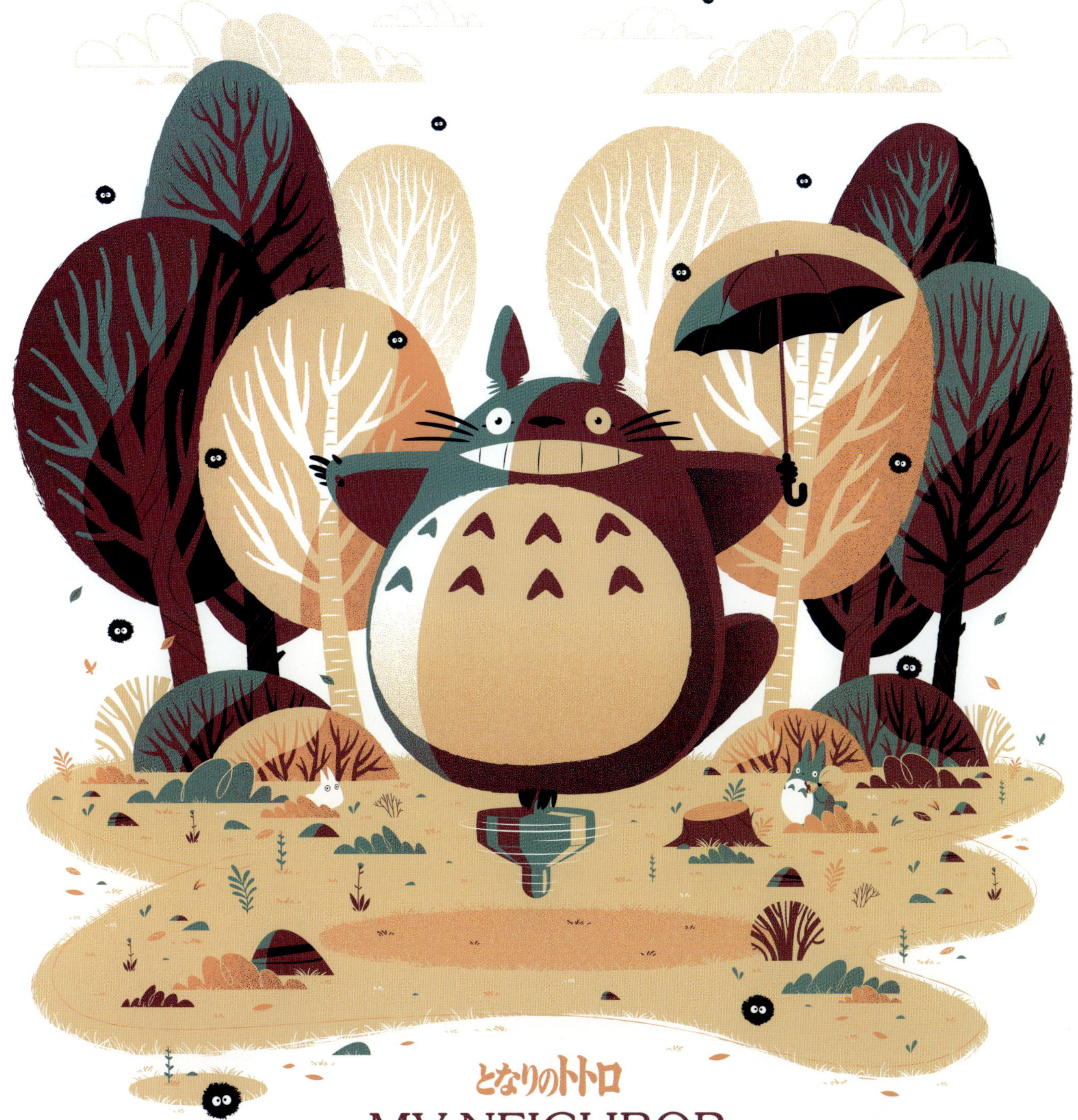

MY NEIGHBOR TOTORO

TOKUMA SHOTEN *presents a* STUDIO GHIBLI *production*
a HAYAO MIYAZAKI *film* "MY NEIGHBOR TOTORO"
Executive Producer YASUYOSHI TOKUMA *Music by* JOE HISAISHI
Original Story & Screenplay by HAYAO MIYAZAKI
Directed by HAYAO MIYAZAKI

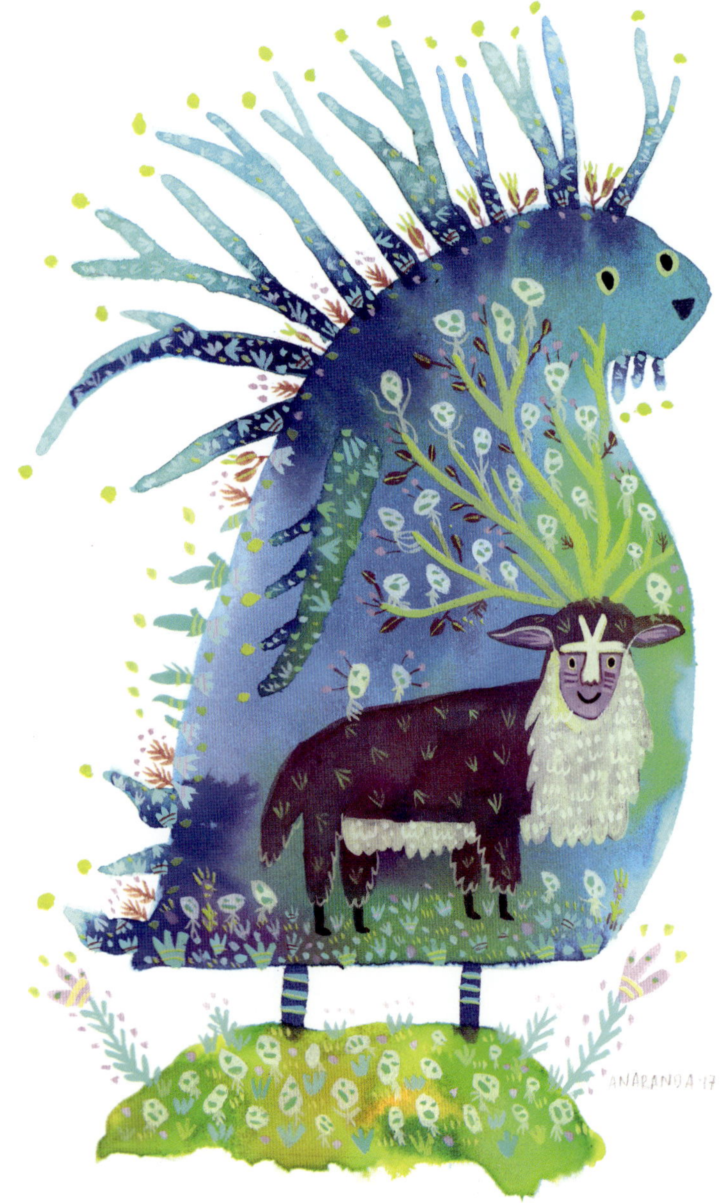

ANA ARANDA

ABOVE

Forest Spirits

Ink and gouache on watercolor paper. 8 x 10".

RIGHT PAGE

Chihiro's Adventure

Watercolor, gouache and gel pen on watercolor paper. 11 x 14".

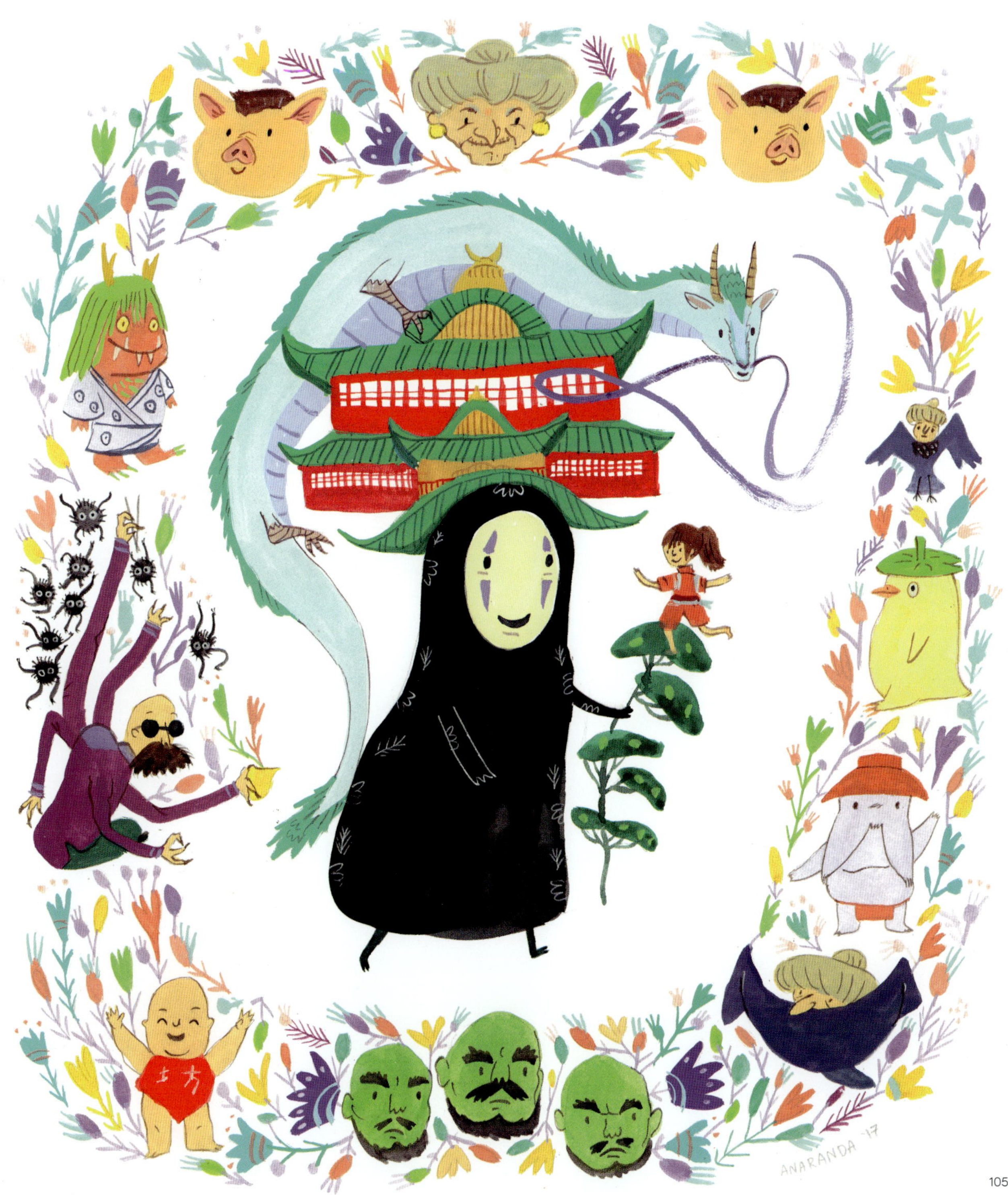
ANARANDA '17

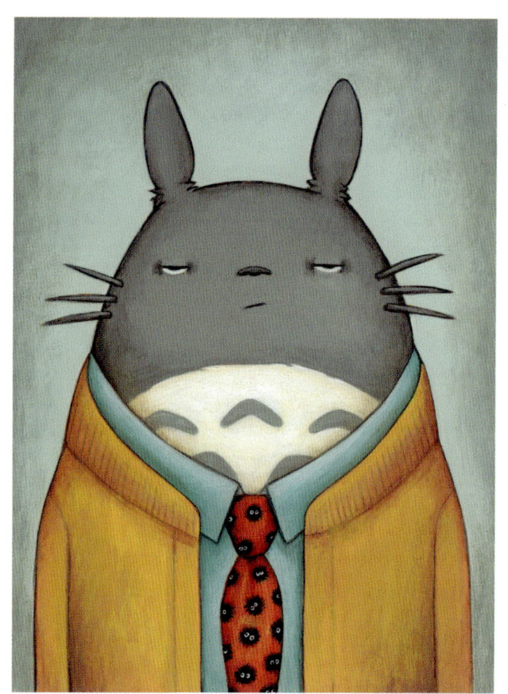

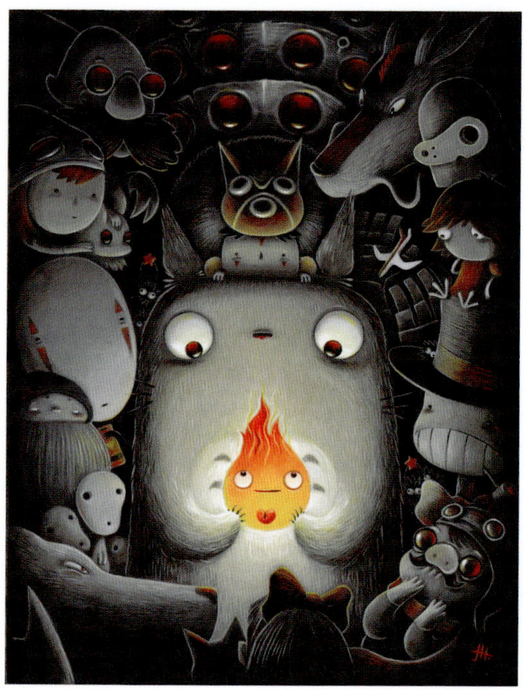

ANNA TILLETT

LEFT

It's a Beautiful Day in the Neighborhood

Acrylic on maple. 5 x 7".

JUSTIN HILLGROVE

RIGHT

I Like Your Spark

Acrylic paint on canvas. 18 x 24".

CROWDED TEETH

RIGHT PAGE

Susuwatari Party

Layered paper. 6 x 14".

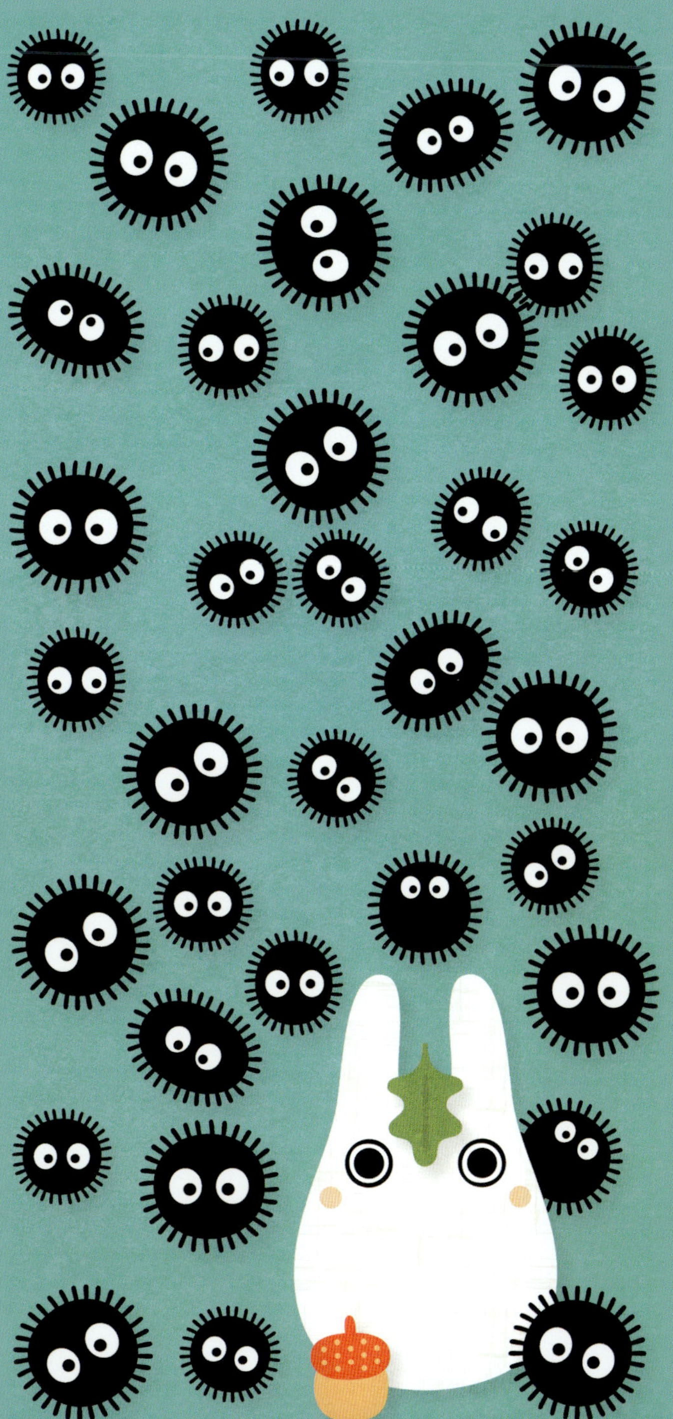

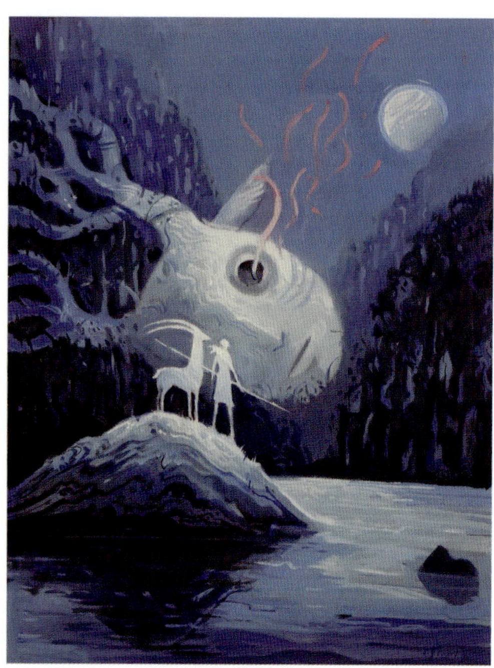

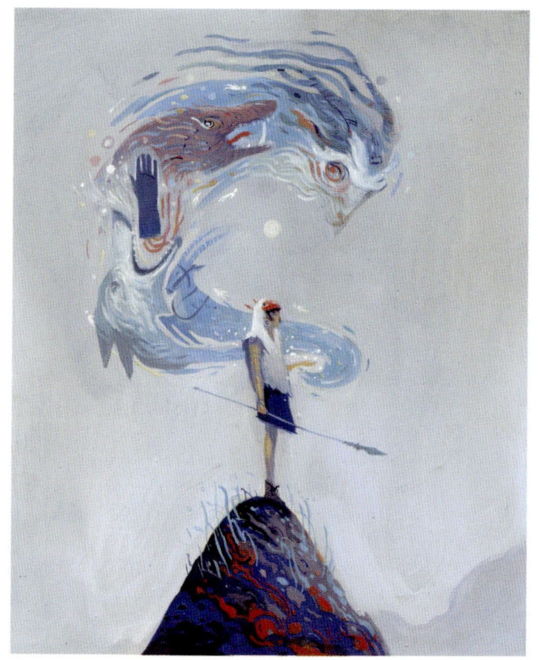

DEAN STUART

LEFT

The Spirit Never Dies
Acrylic on paper. 12 x 16".

RIGHT

Keeping the Spirit
Acrylic on paper. 16 x 20".

RIGHT PAGE

Rise to Meet It, If You Choose
Acrylic on wood panel. 18 x 24".

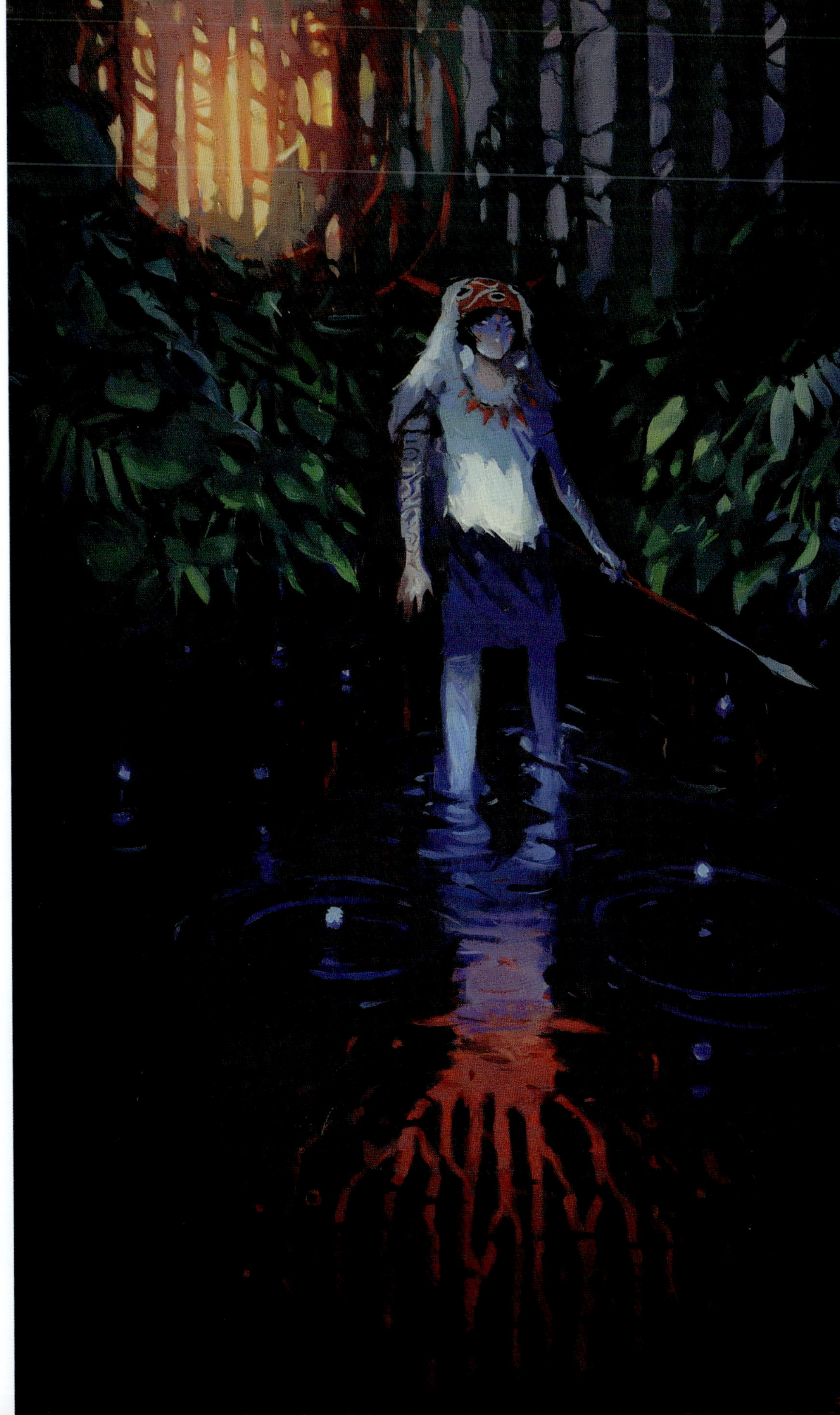

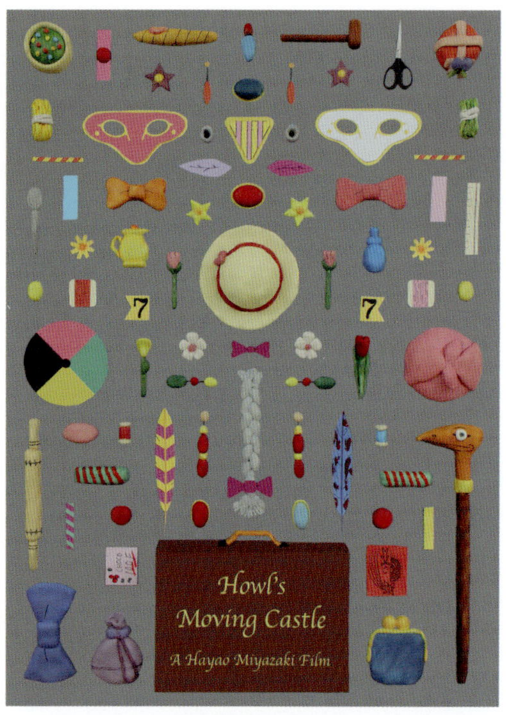

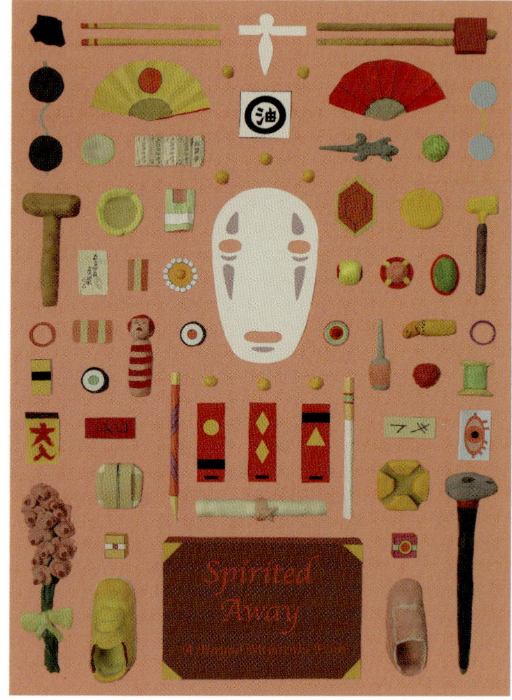

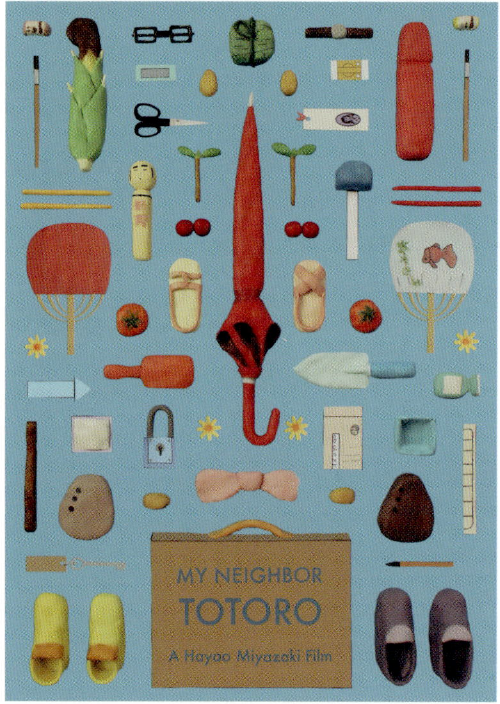

JORDAN BOLTON

TOP LEFT

Howl's Moving Castle

Archival pigment print. 9 x 12".

TOP RIGHT

Spirited Away

Archival pigment print. 9 x 12".

LEFT

My Neighbor Totoro

Archival pigment print. 9 x 12".

RIGHT PAGE

Princess Mononoke

Archival pigment print. 9 x 12".

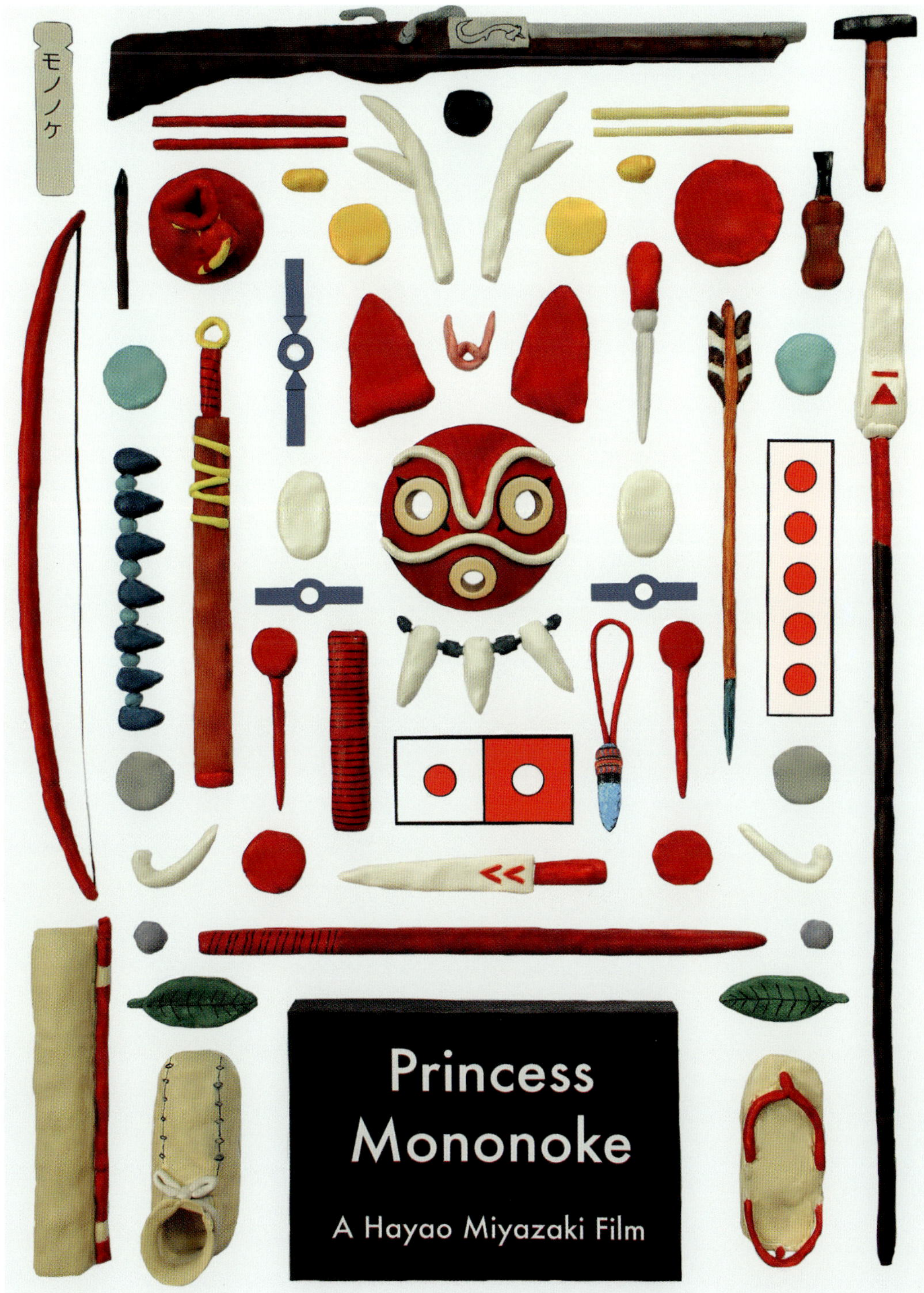
モノノケ
Princess
Mononoke
A Hayao Miyazaki Film

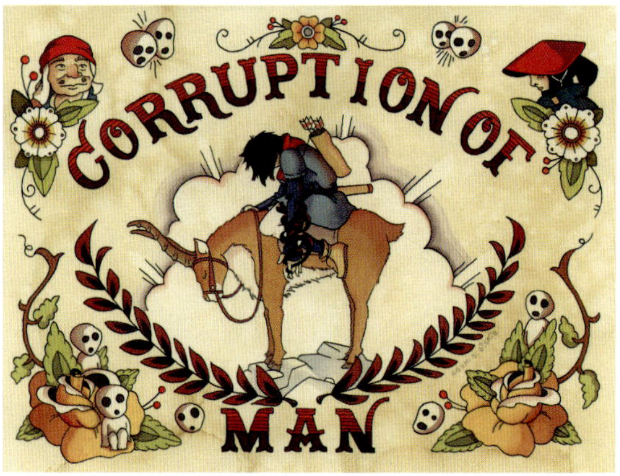

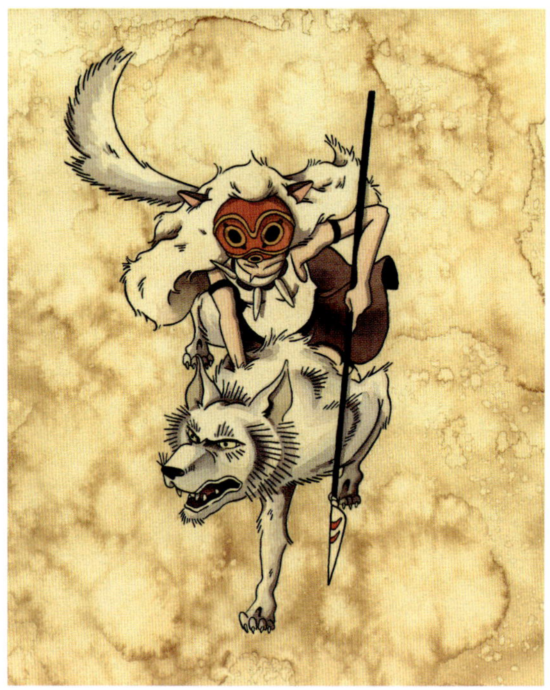

ADAM ZISKIE

TOP

Corruption of Man

Watercolor, ink, coffee on paper. 14 x 11".

BOTTOM

Princess Mononoke

Watercolor and coffee on paper. 8 x 10".

BENNETT SLATER

RIGHT PAGE

The Days of Gods and Demons

Oil on wood. 18 x 24".

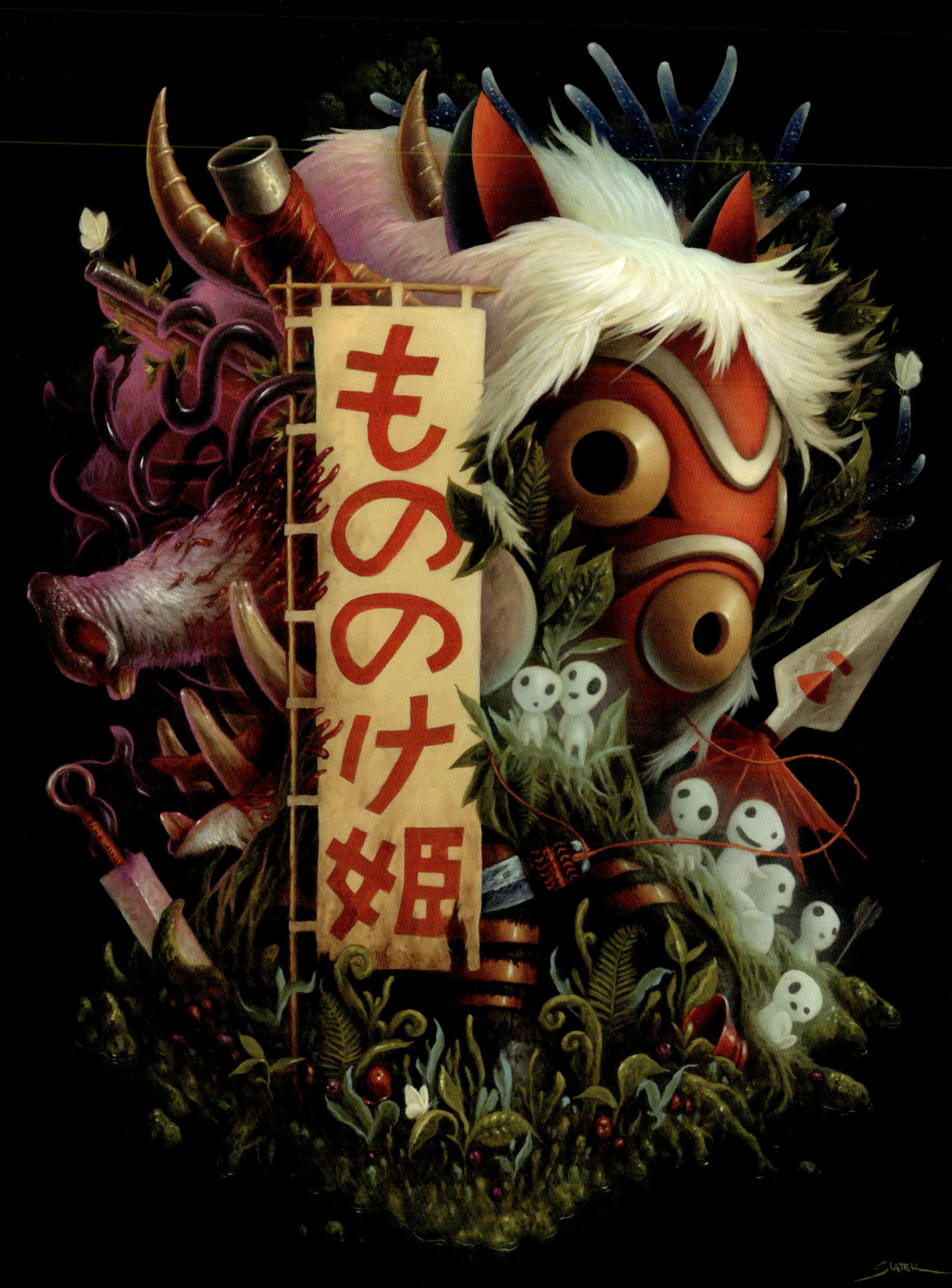
もののけ姫
SLATER

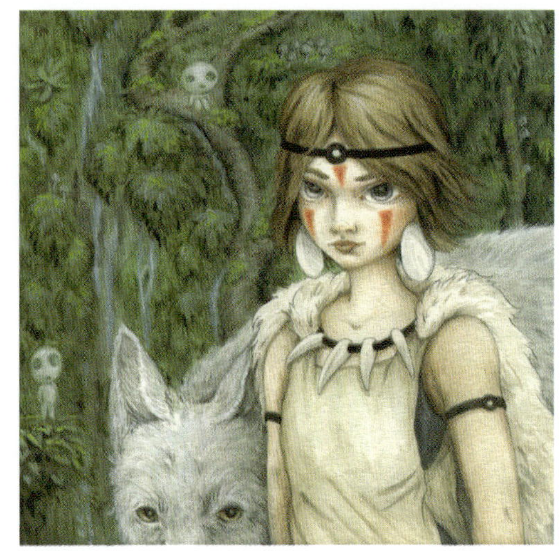

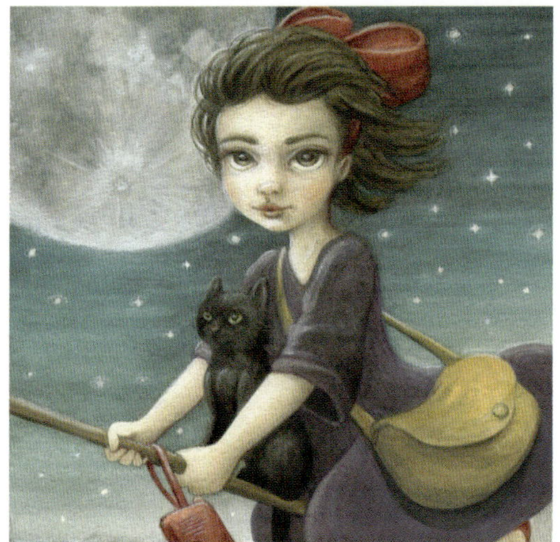

CANDACE JEAN

LEFT

San, The Princess Mononoke

Mixed media. 6 x 6".

RIGHT

Kiki and Jiji

Mixed media. 6 x 6".

BETSY BAUER

RIGHT PAGE

Flight

Digital on canvas print. 16 x 20".

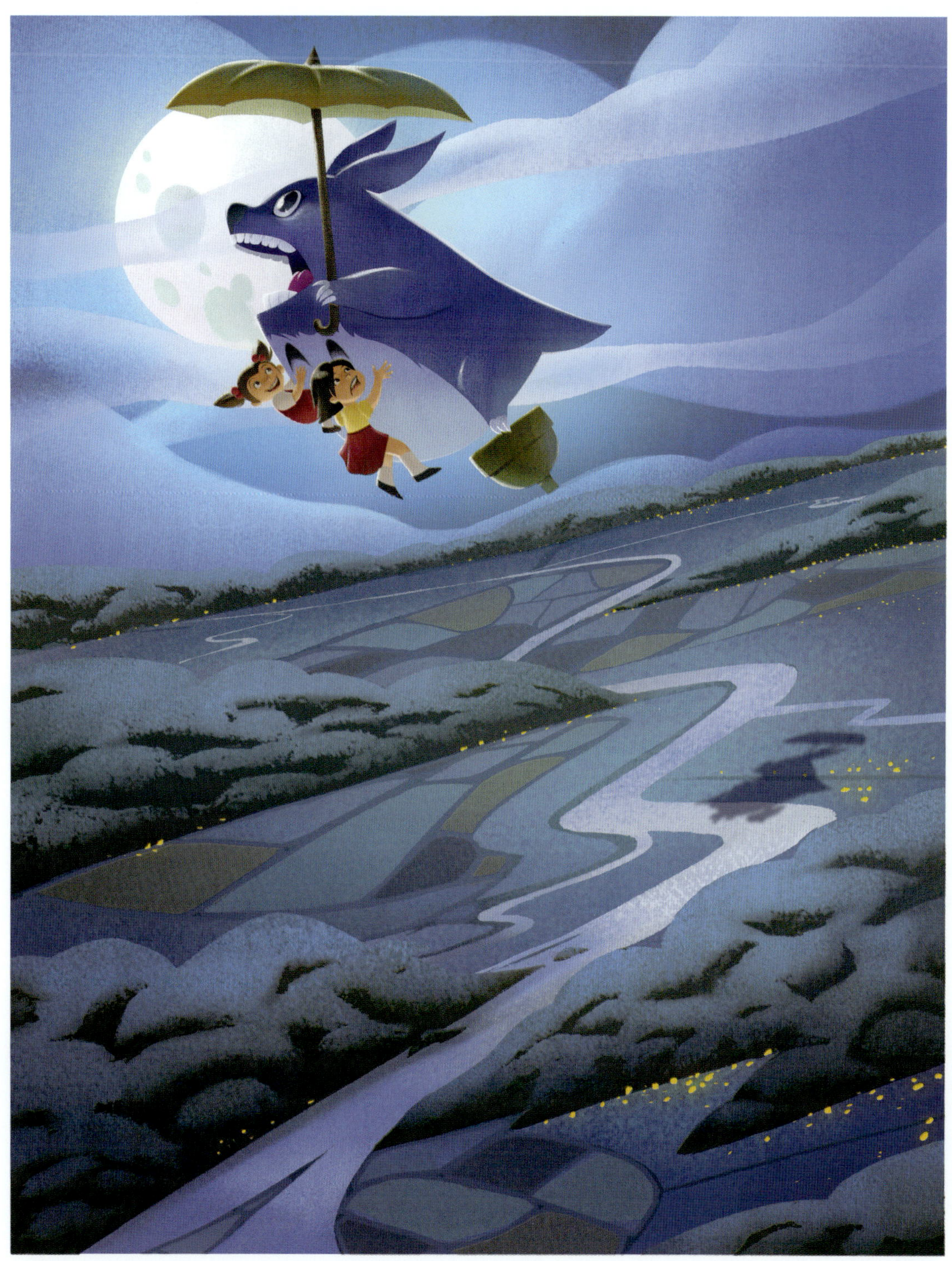

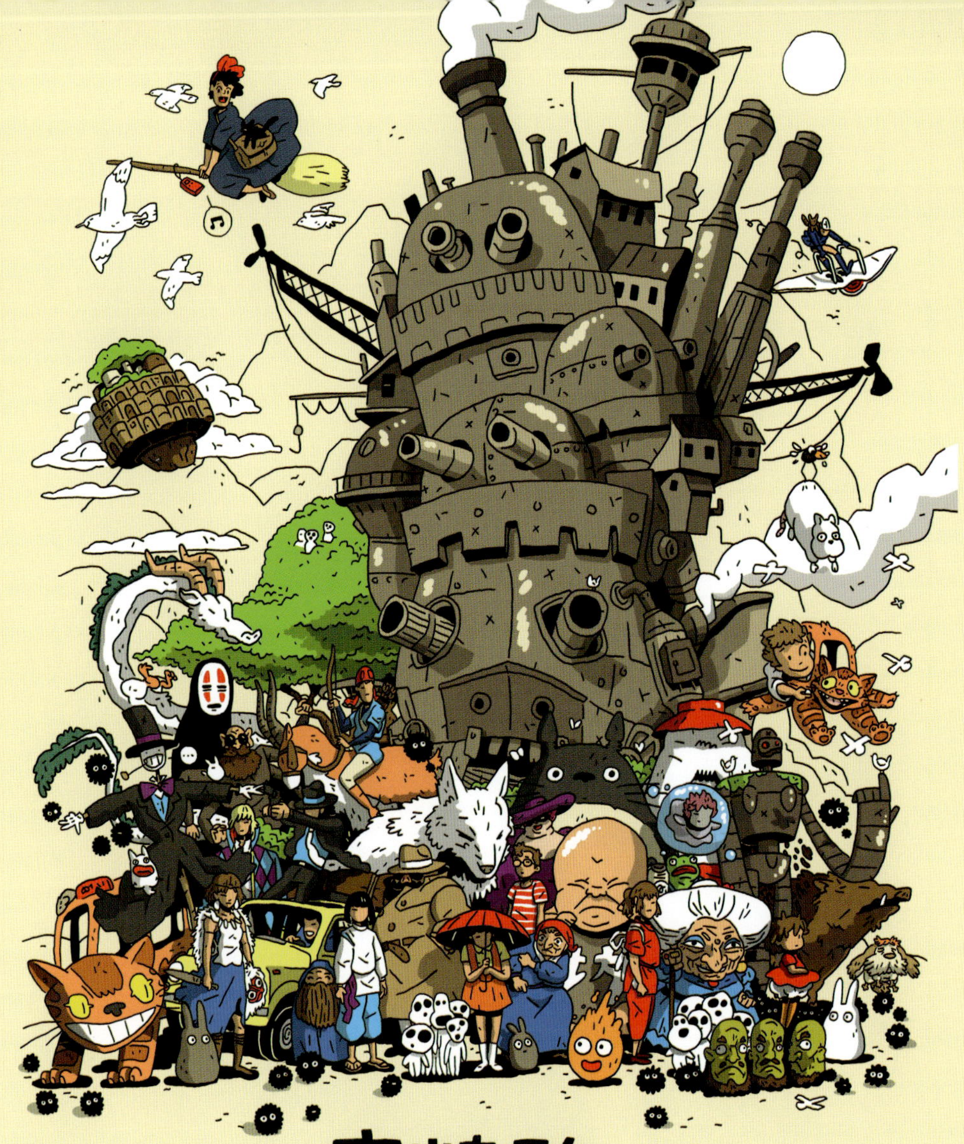

宮崎駿

NICK STOKES

ABOVE

宮崎 駿

Archival pigment print. 18 x 24".

RIGHT PAGE

Do you love me?

Archival pigment print. 11 x 14".

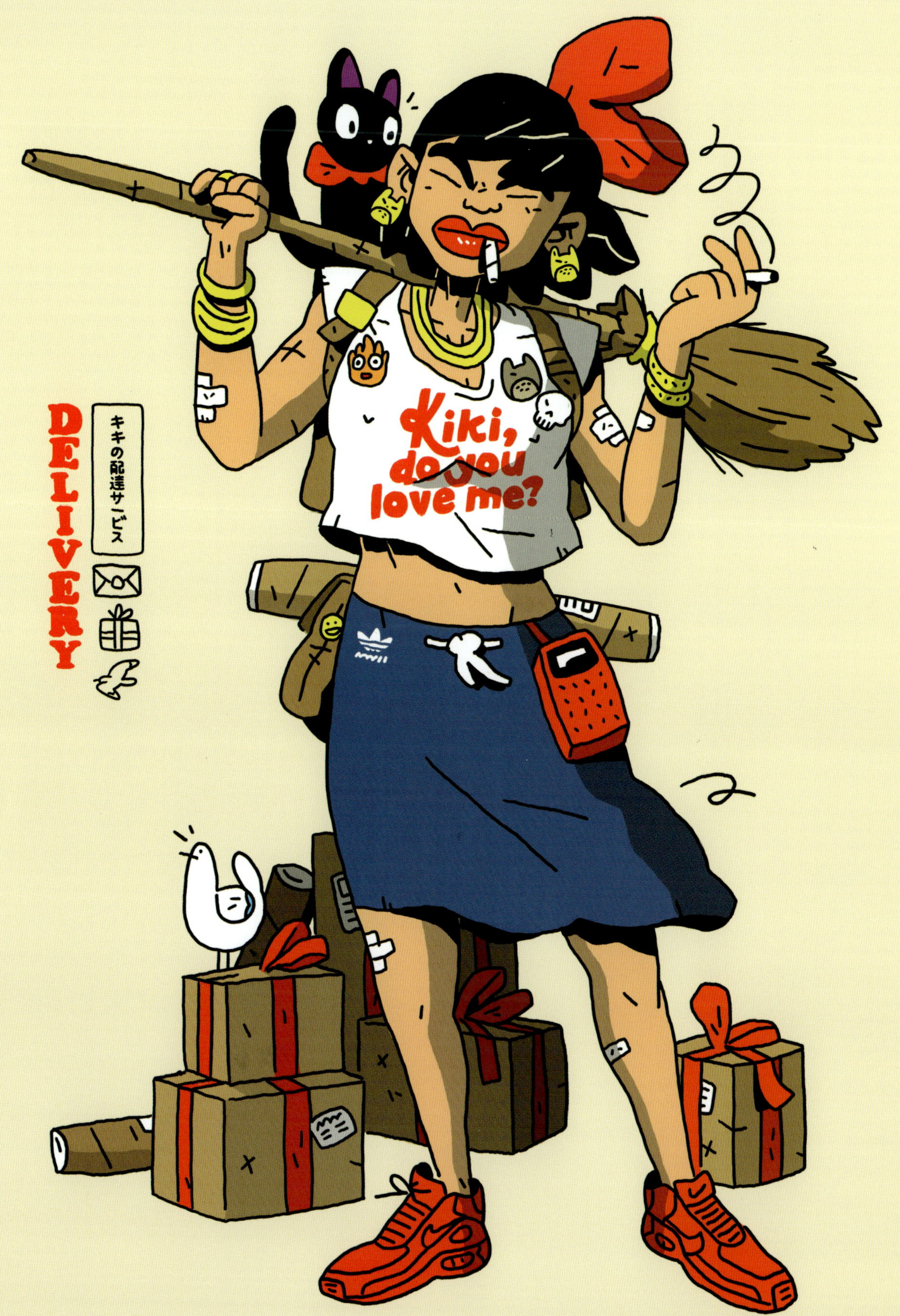
DELIVERY
キキの配達サービス
Kiki, do you love me?

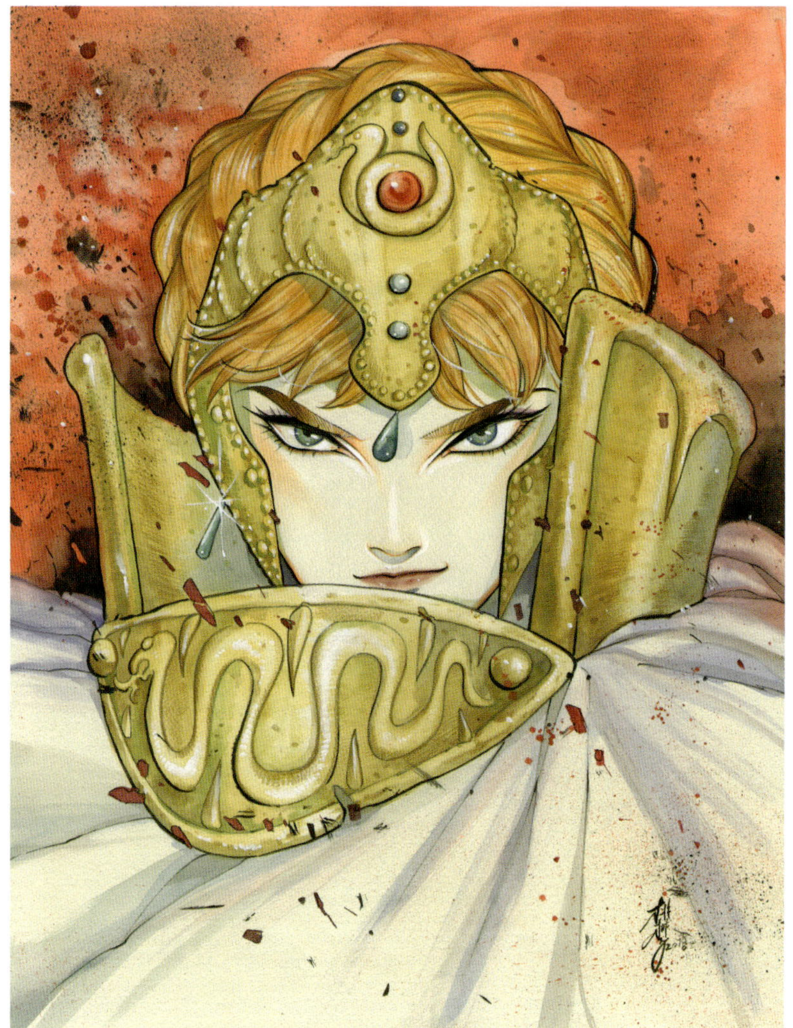

PEACH MOMOKO

ABOVE

Her Highness Kushana

Watercolor, ink and colored pencil. 18 x 24".

RIGHT PAGE

Nausicaa

Watercolor, ink and colored pencil. 18 x 24".

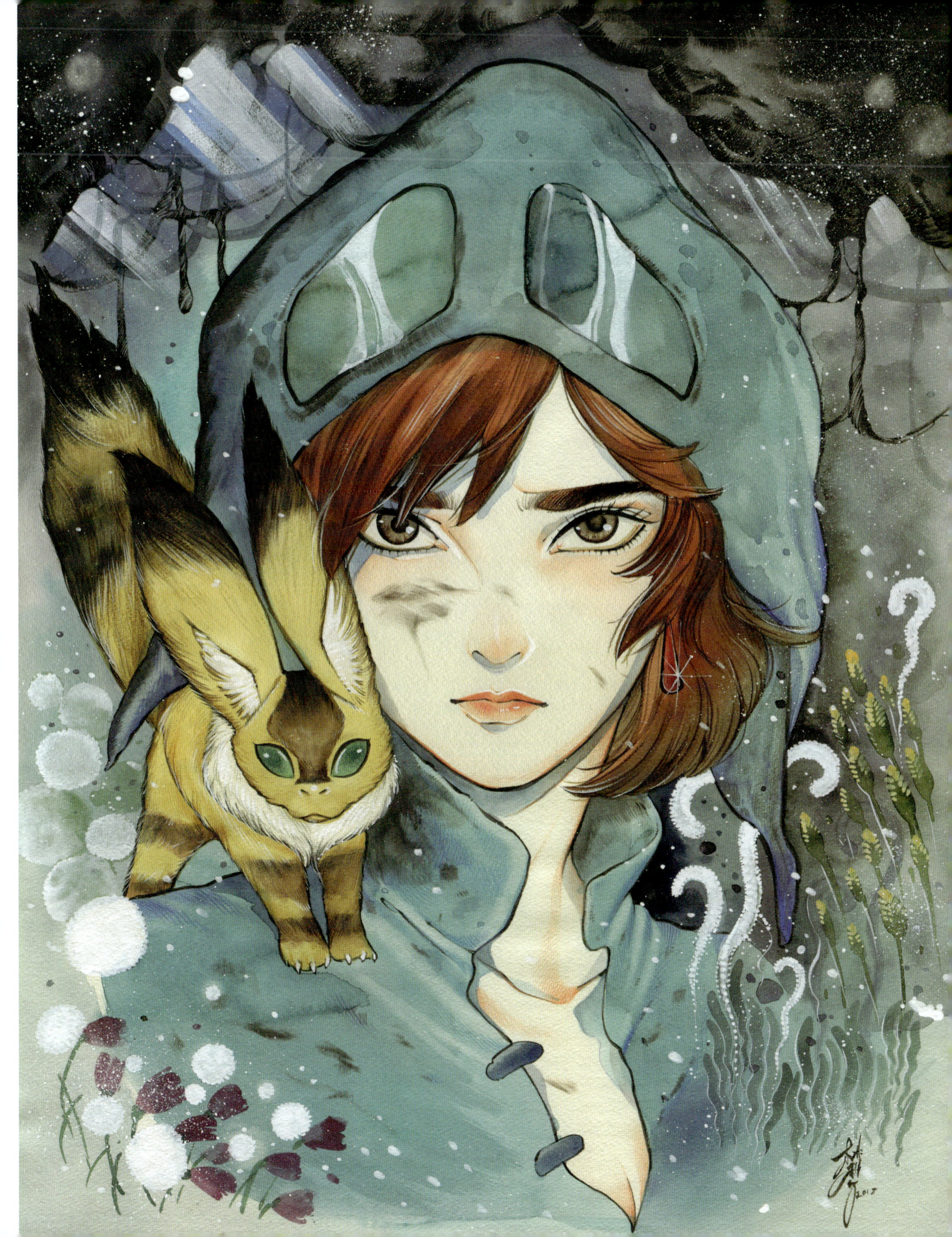

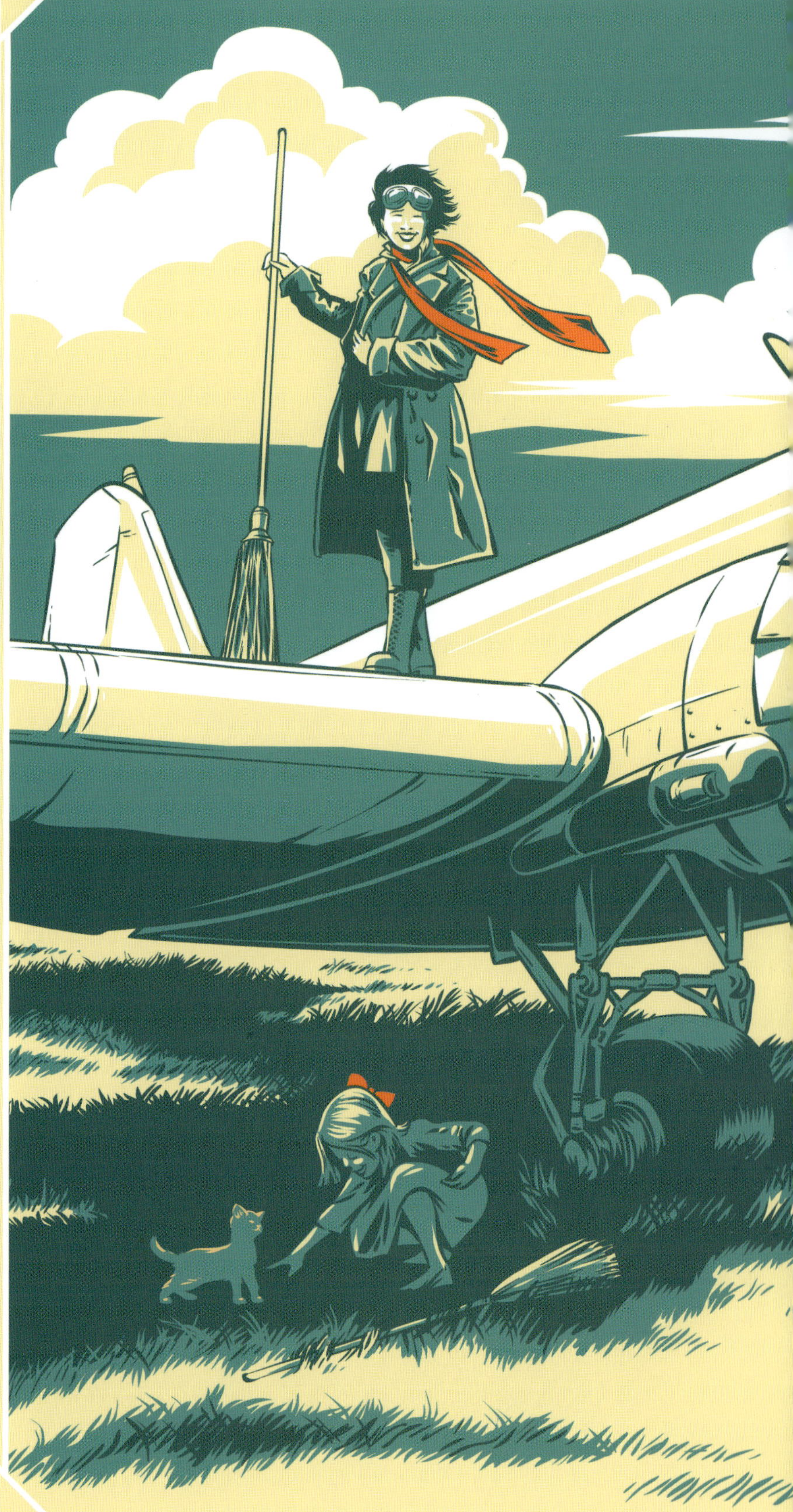

JASON STOUT

Witches in Training

Screen print. 24 x 18".

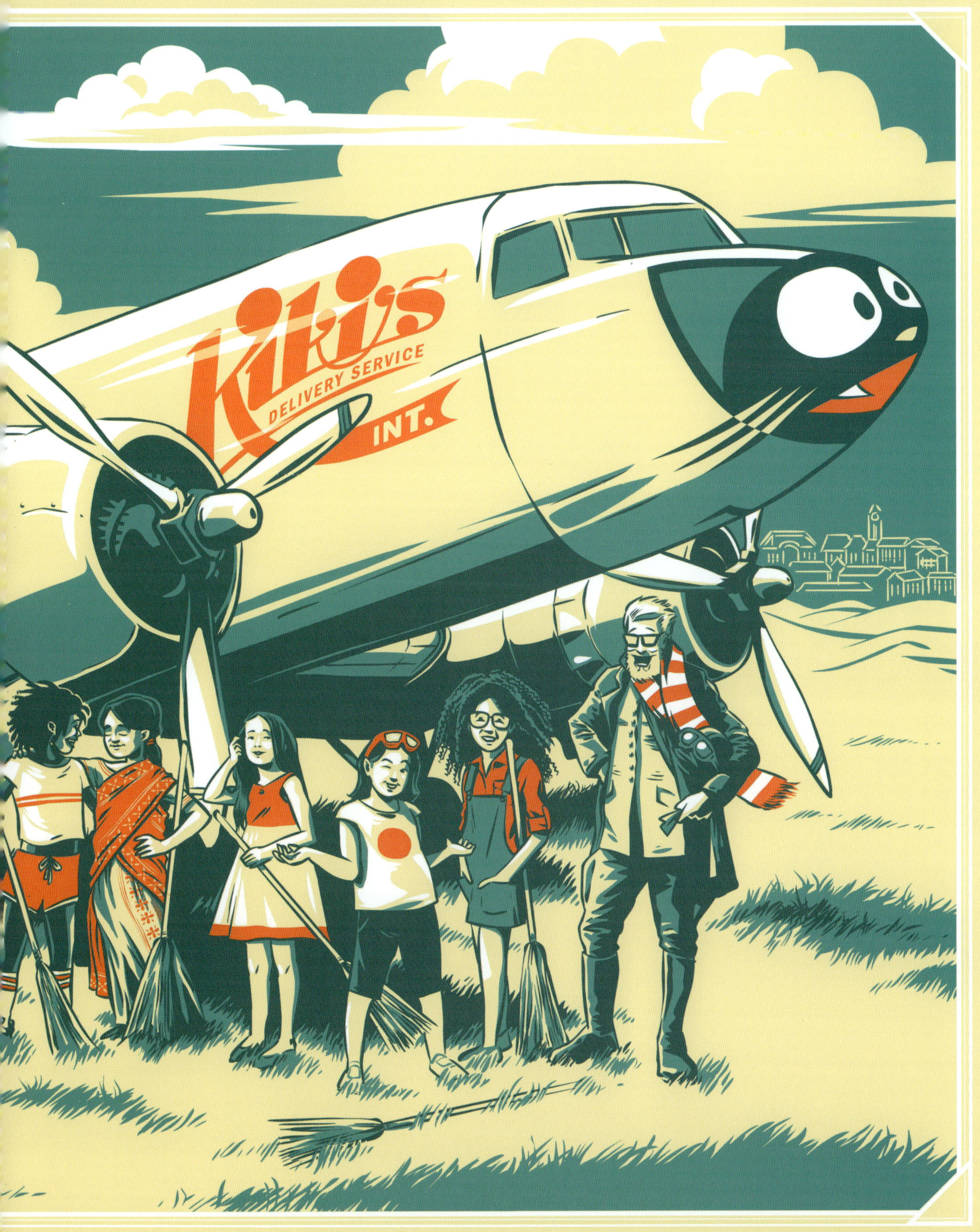
Kiki's
DELIVERY SERVICE
INT.

JUSTIN VAN GENDEREN

RIGHT PAGE

Valley of the Wind

Archival pigment print. 13 x 19".

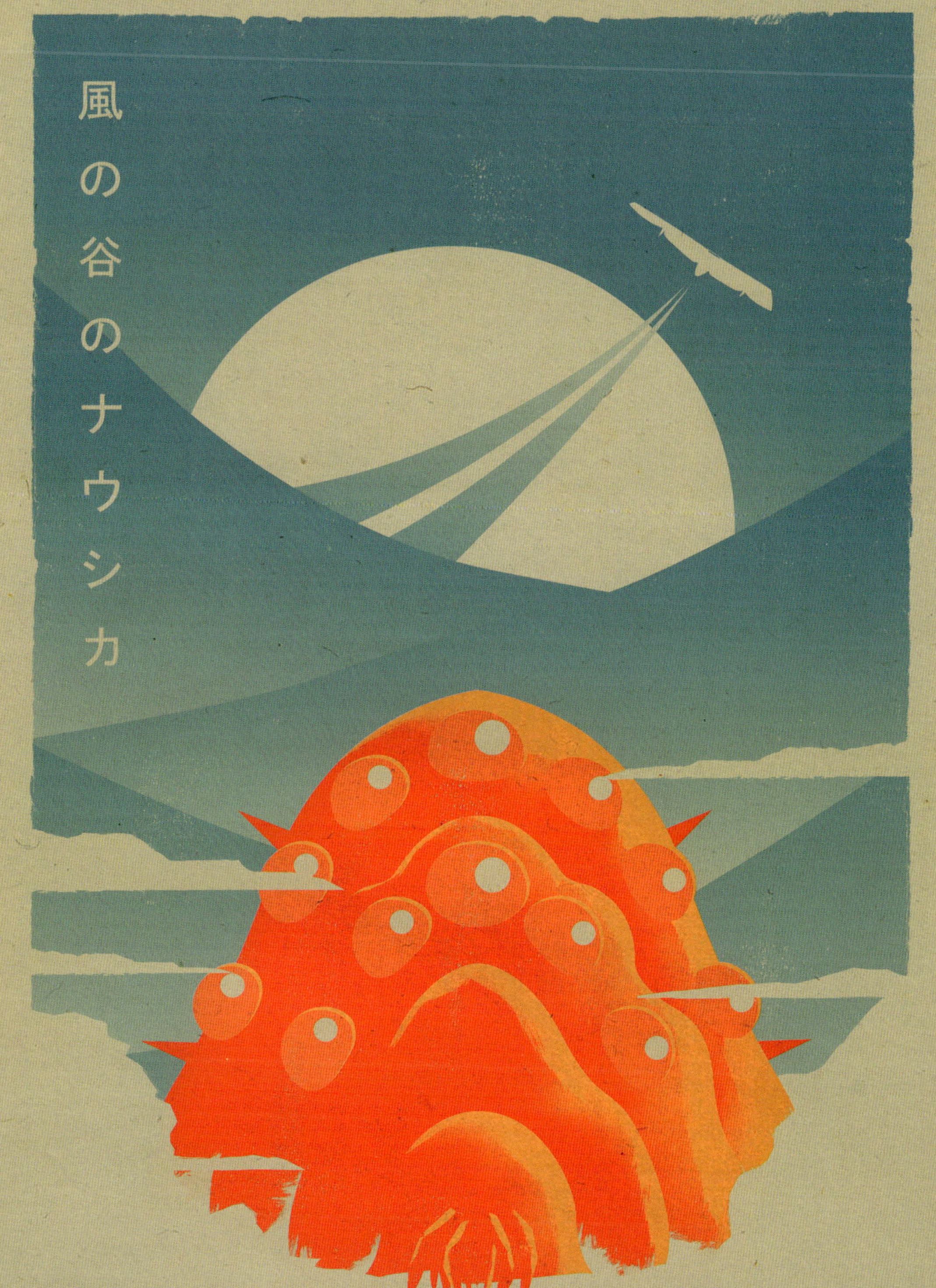
風の谷のナウシカ

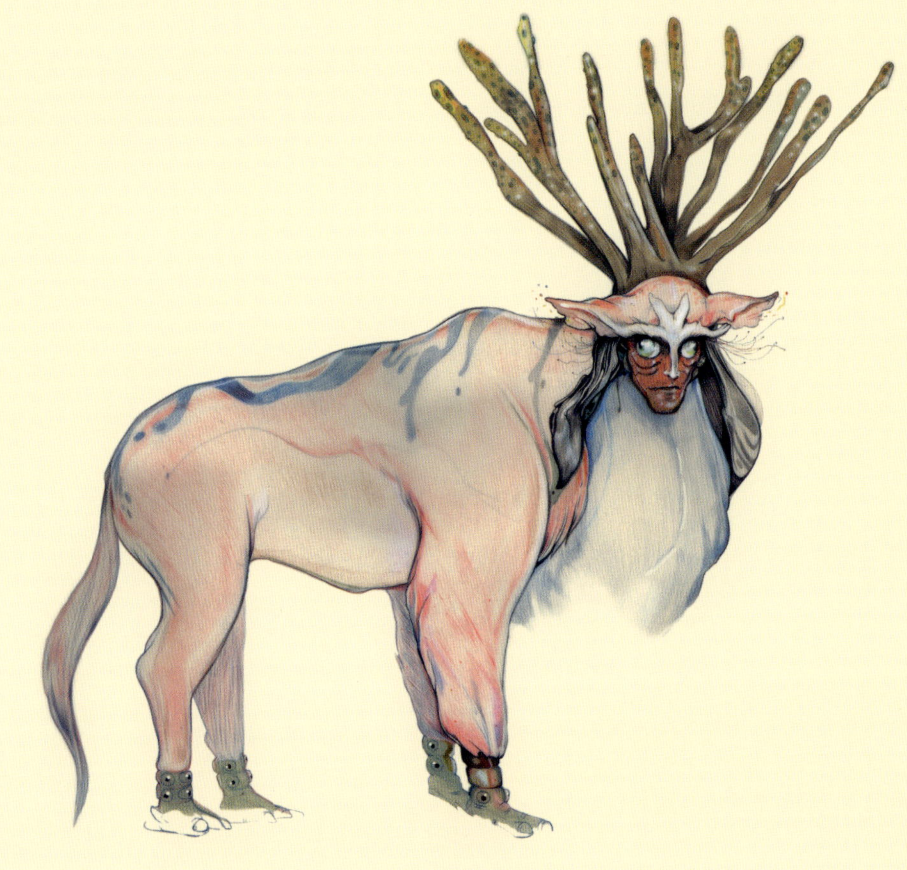

ABOVE

JOSE MERTZ

Return of the Forest Spirit

Watercolor and colored pencil on paper. 18 x 20".

RIGHT PAGE

BRUCE YAN

The Forest Spirit Gives Life and Takes Life Away

Screen print. 18 x 24".

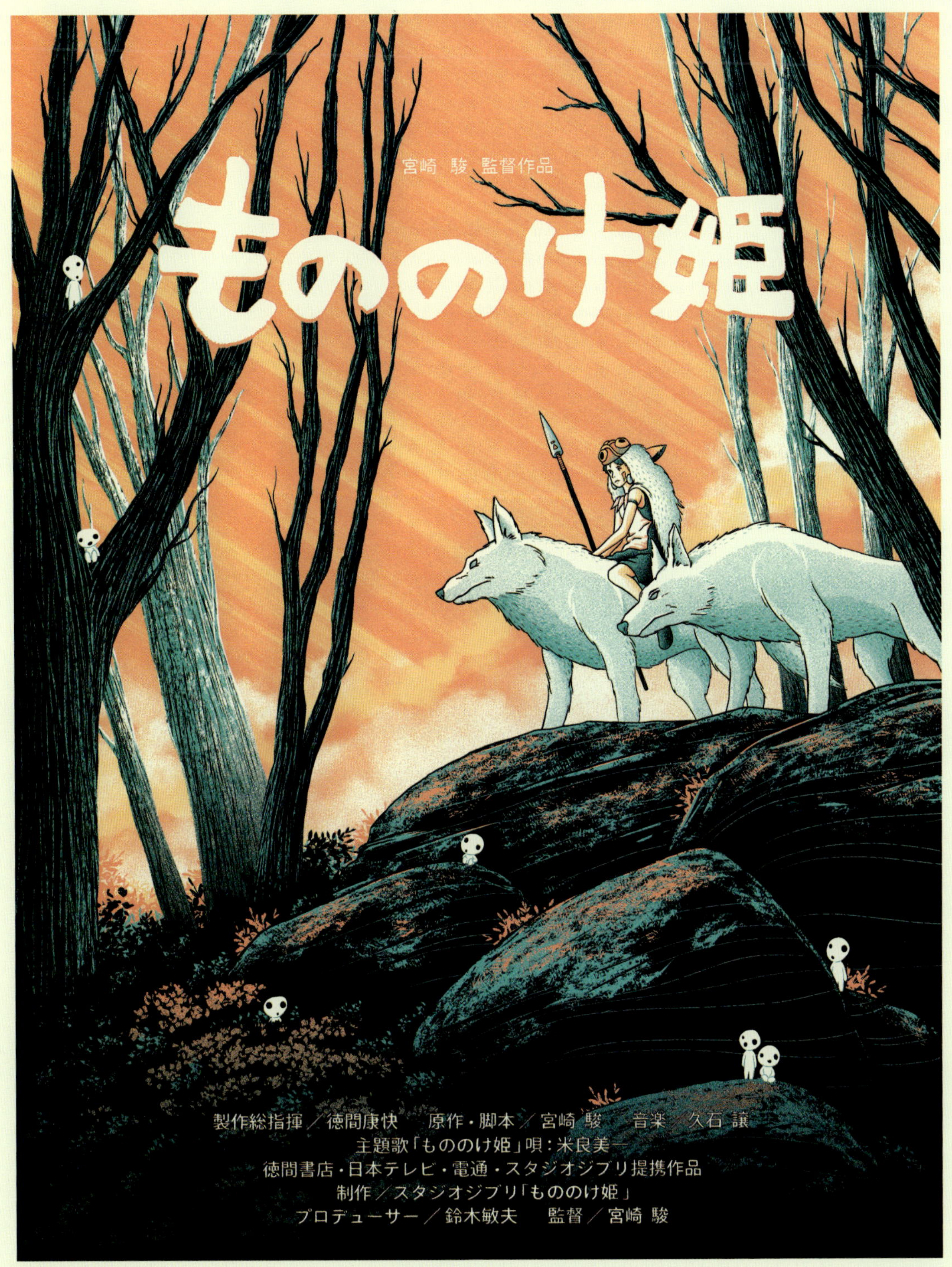
宮崎 駿 監督作品
もののけ姫
製作総指揮／徳間康快　原作・脚本／宮崎 駿　音楽／久石 譲
主題歌「もののけ姫」唄：米良美一
徳間書店・日本テレビ・電通・スタジオジブリ提携作品
制作／スタジオジブリ「もののけ姫」
プロデューサー／鈴木敏夫　監督／宮崎 駿

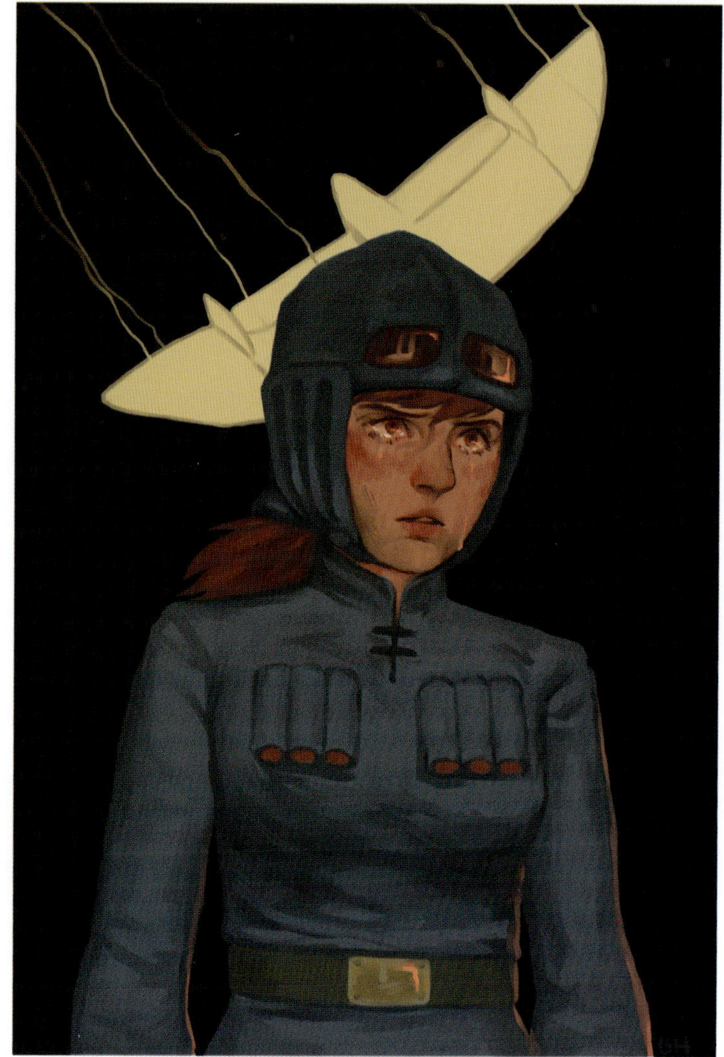

GINA HENDRY

ABOVE

Nausicaä

Archival digital print. 12 x 18".

RIGHT PAGE

The Path of the Wind

Archival digital print. 16 x 20".

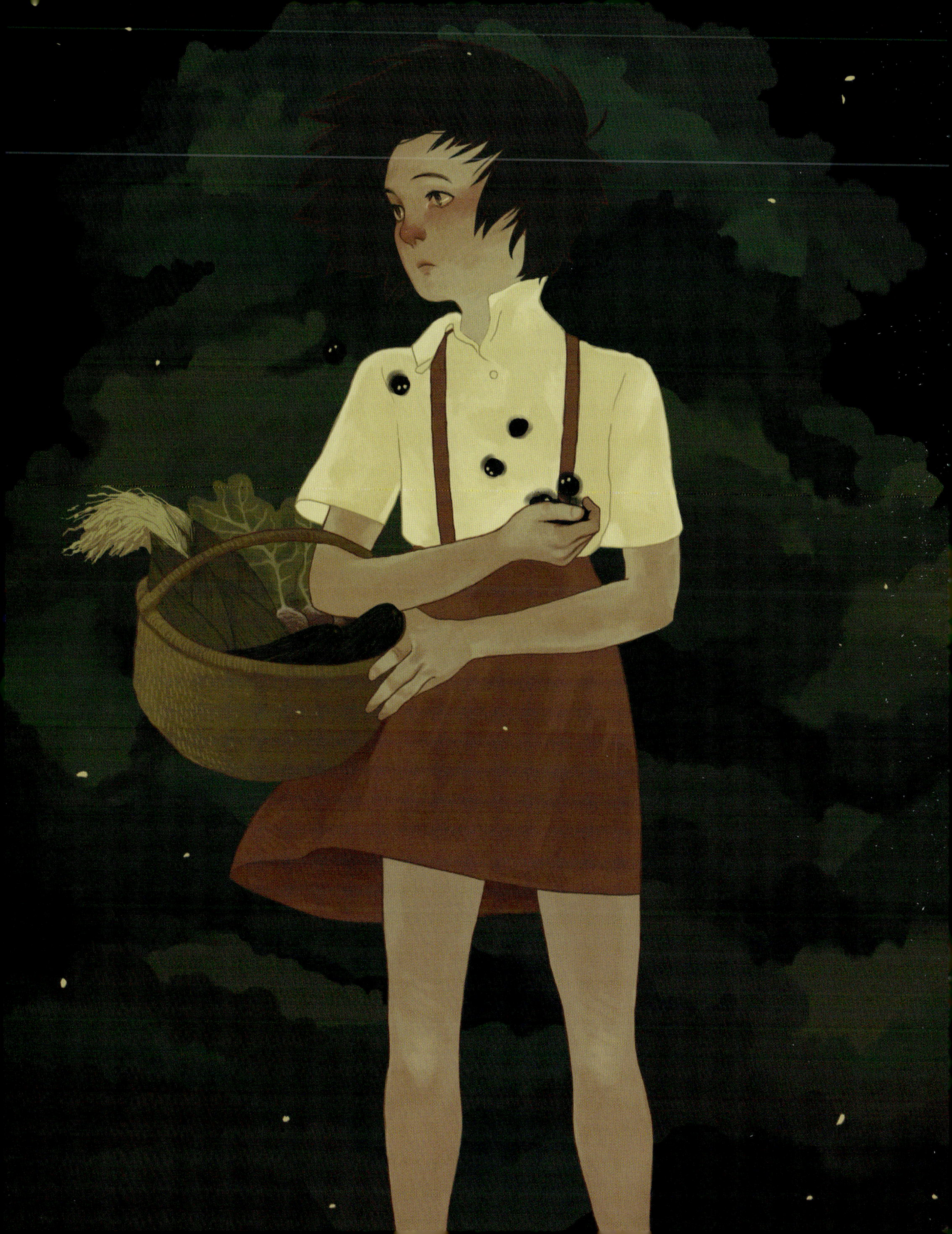

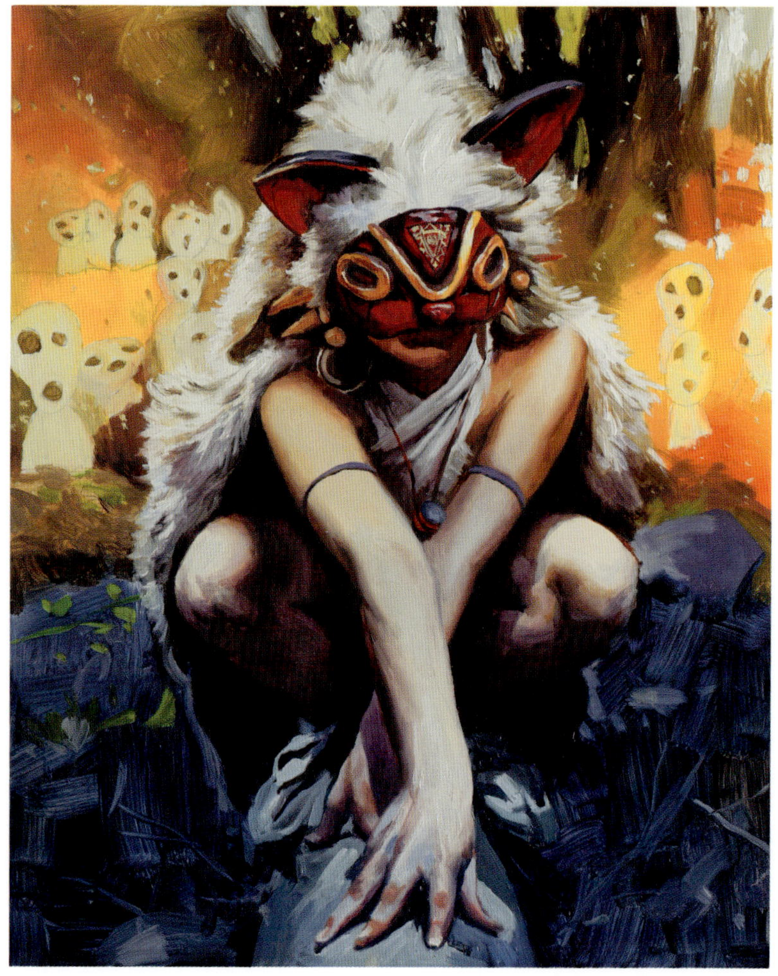

ADAM CALDWELL

ABOVE

San and Kodamas
Meisha Mock designer and model
Oil on panel. 11 x 14".

RIGHT PAGE

San
Meisha Mock designer and model
Oil on canvas. 11 x 14".

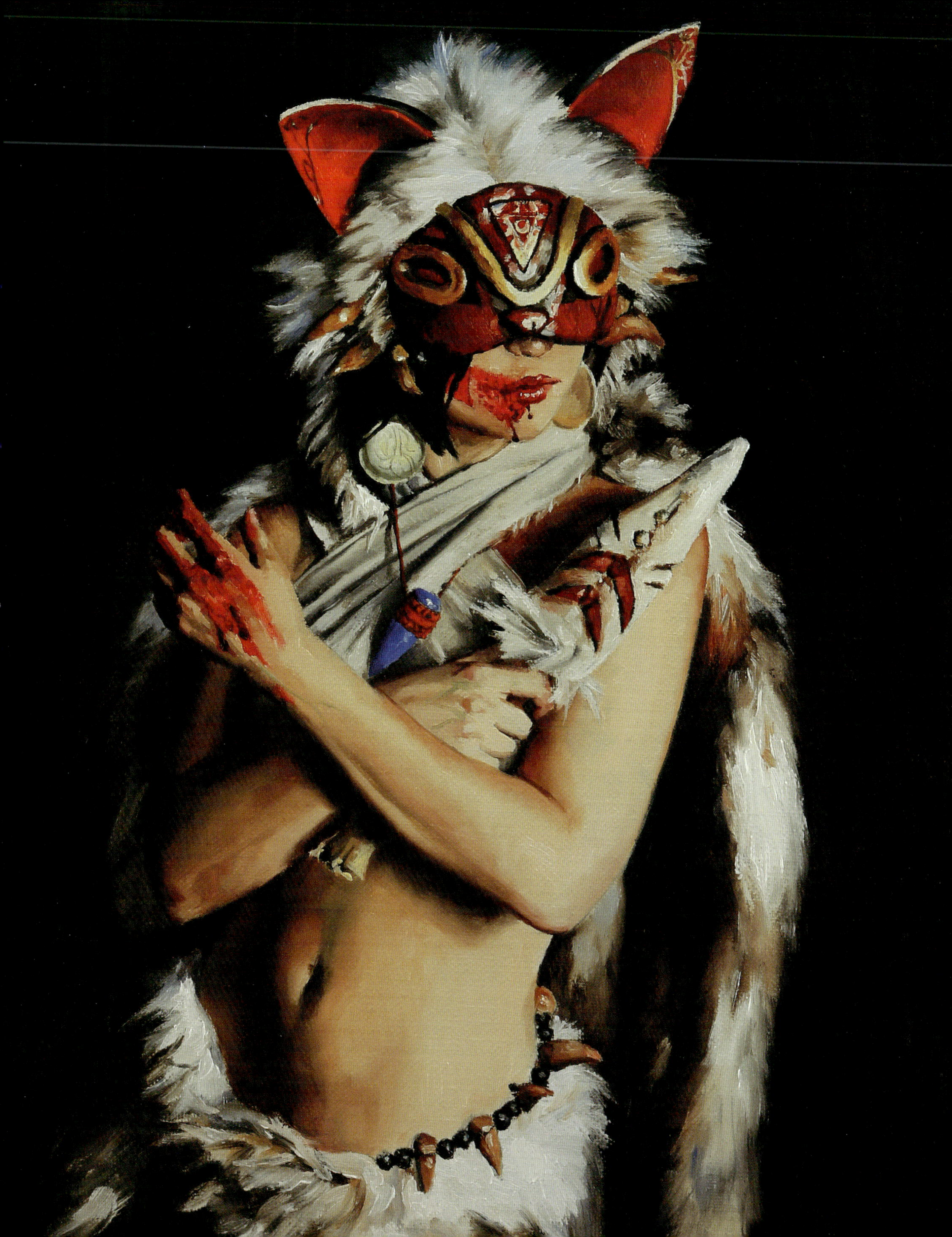

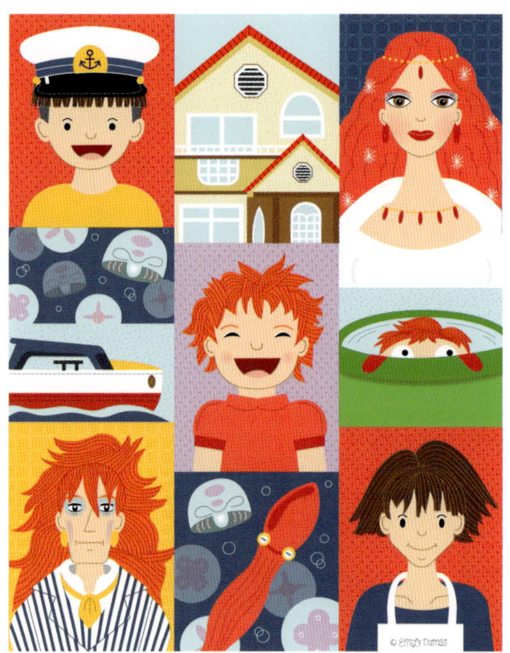

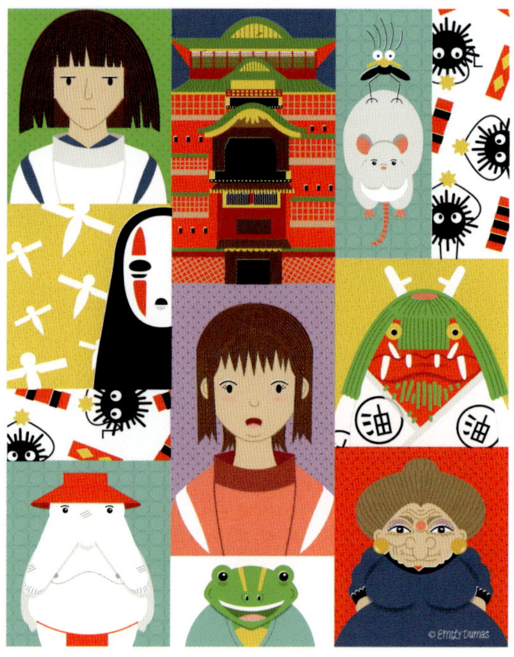

EMILY DUMAS

LEFT

Ponyo's World

Archival digital print. 11 x 14".

RIGHT

Chihiro and Friends

Archival digital print. 11 x 14".

RIGHT PAGE

Friends & Neighbors

Archival digital print. 11 x 14".

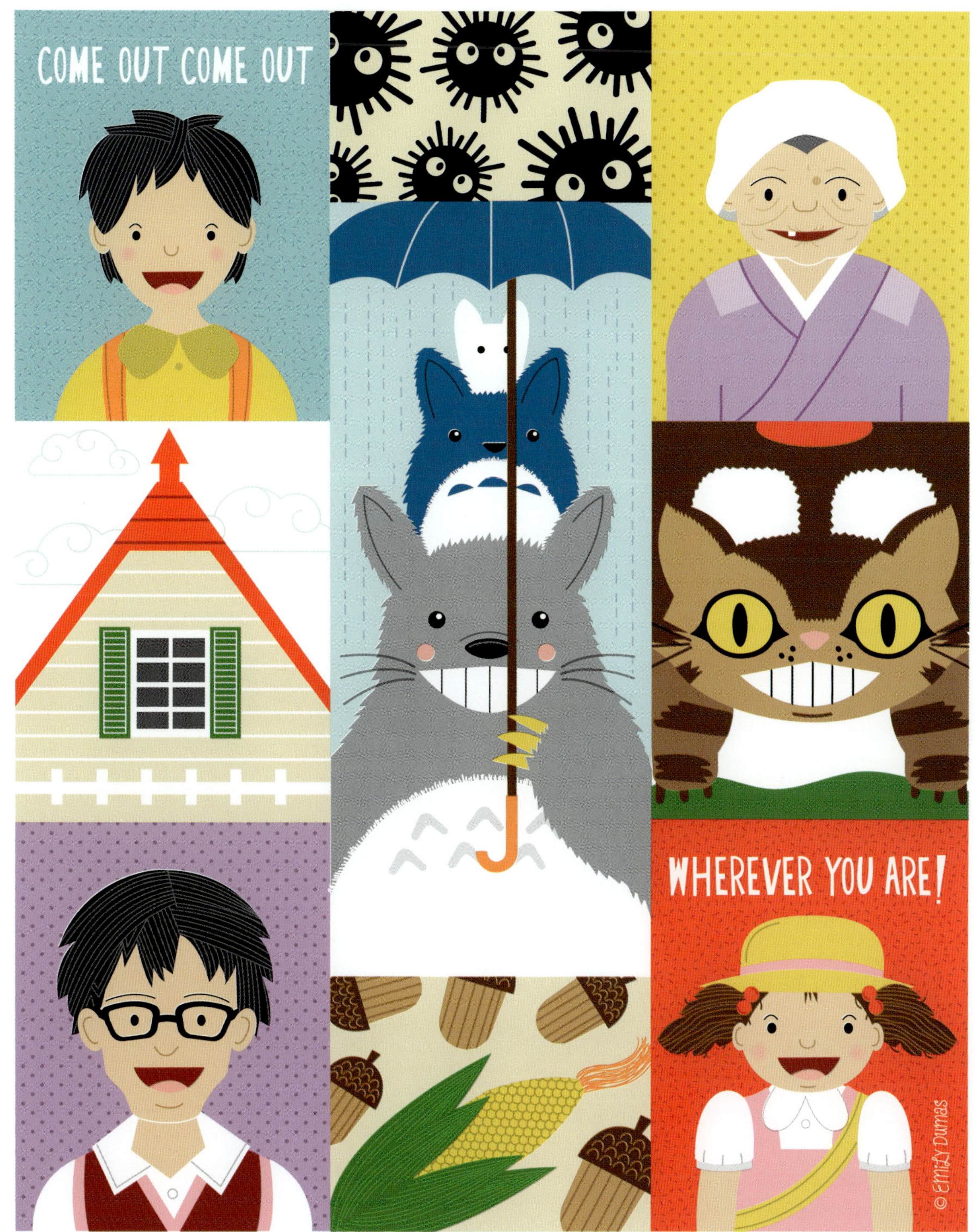
COME OUT COME OUT
WHEREVER YOU ARE!
© Emily Dumas

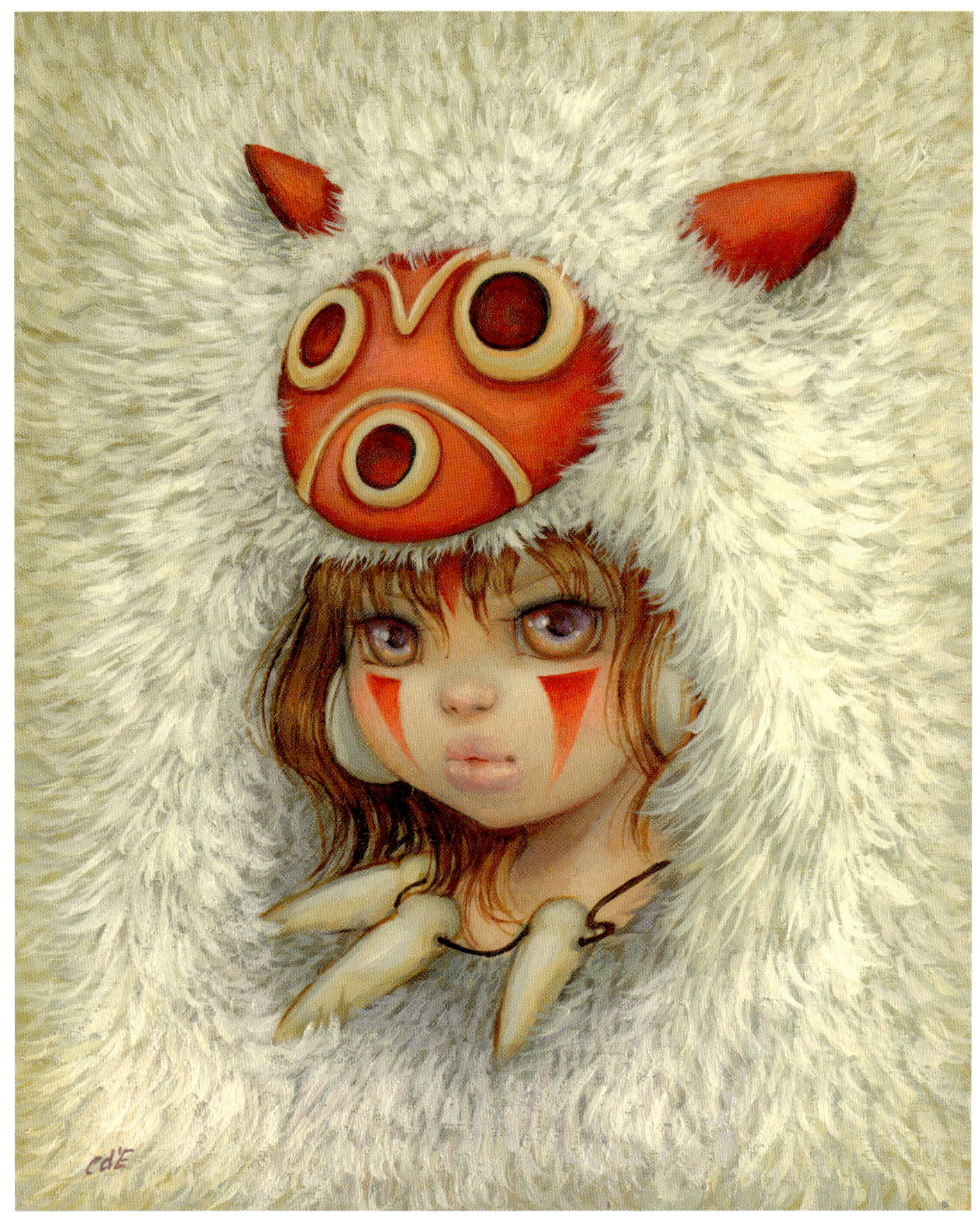

CAMILLA D'ERRICO

Like Mother, Like Daughter

Oil on wood panel. 8 x 10".

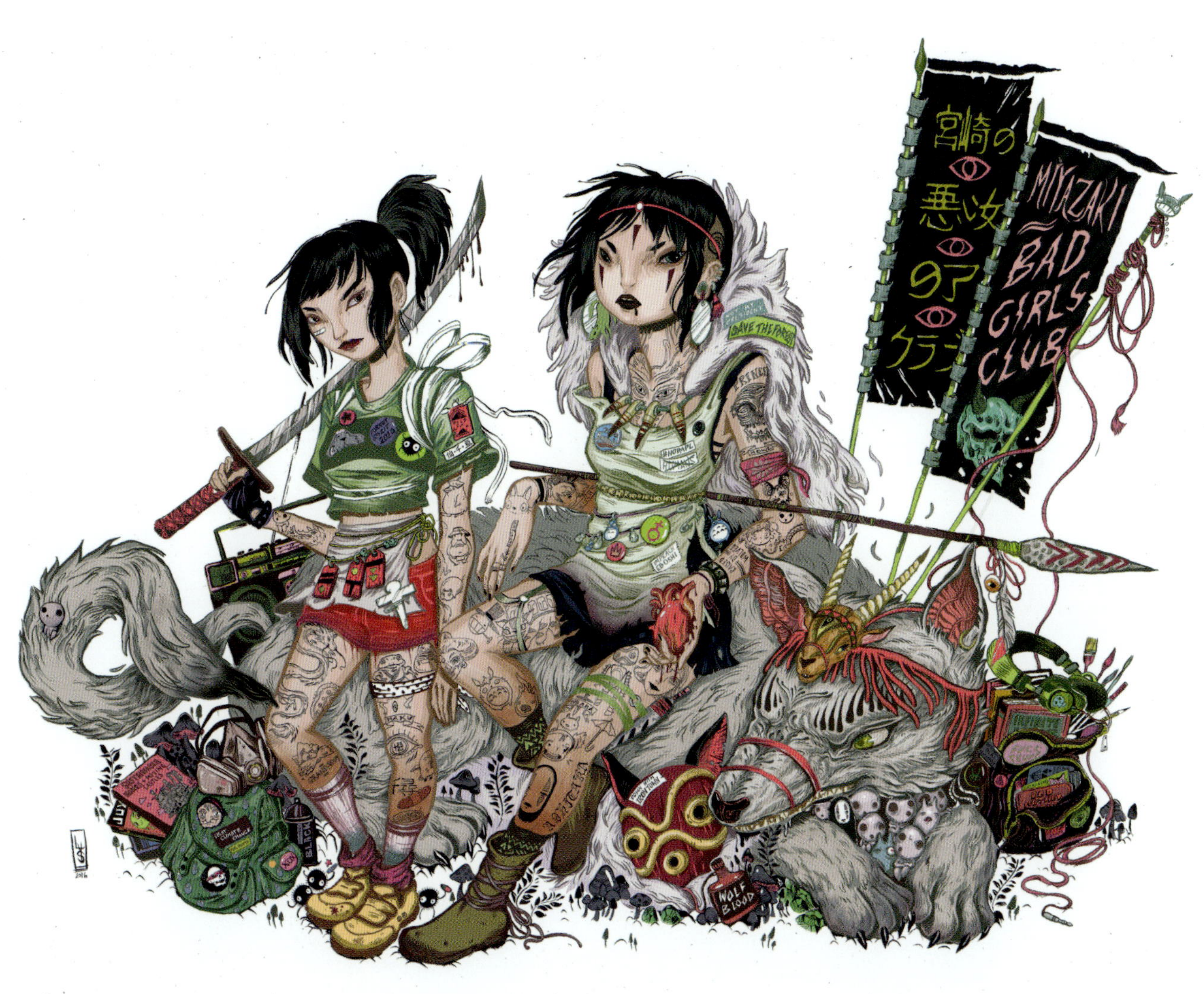

LAUREN YS

Miyazaki Bad Girls Club

Archival pigment print. 24 x 18''.

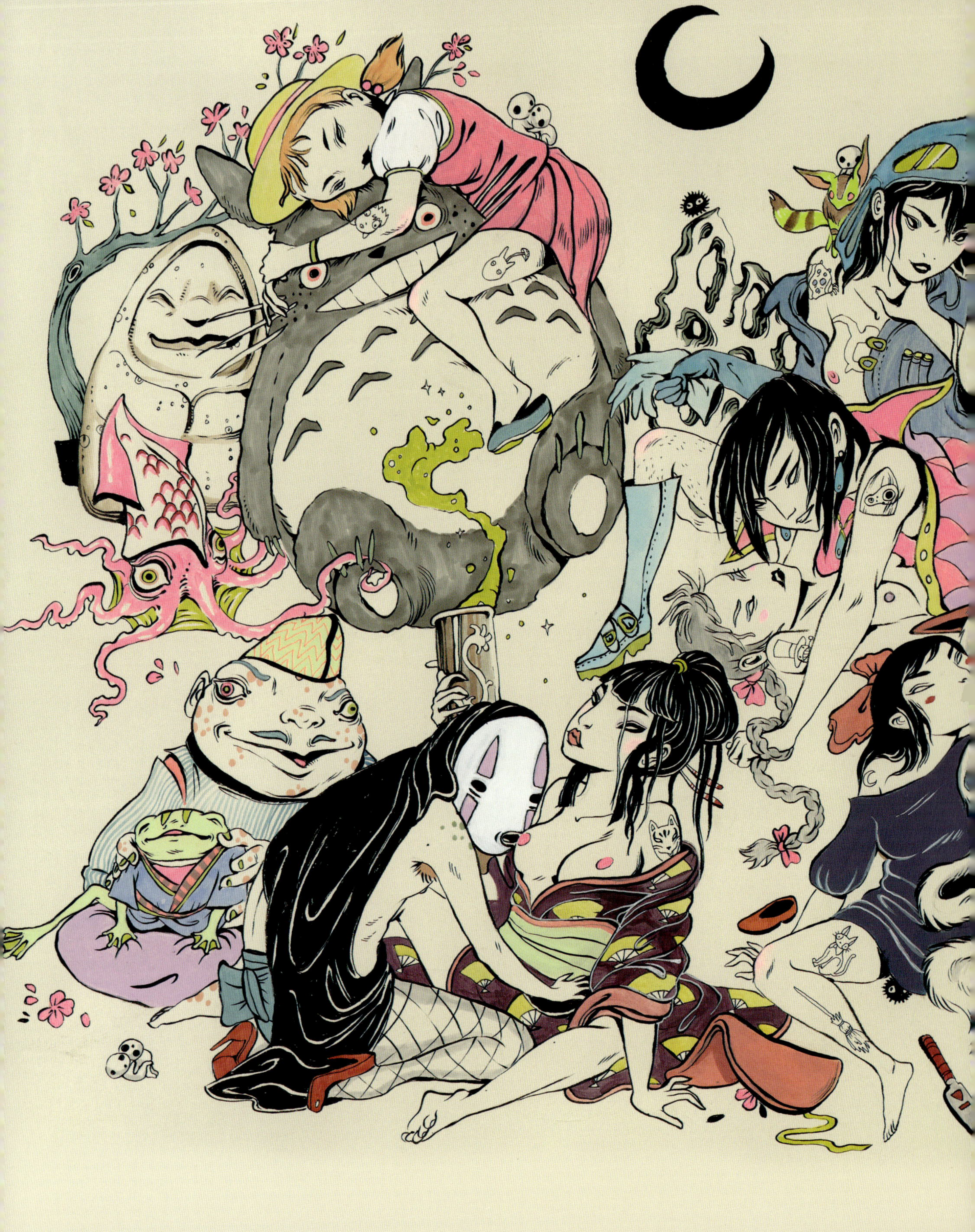

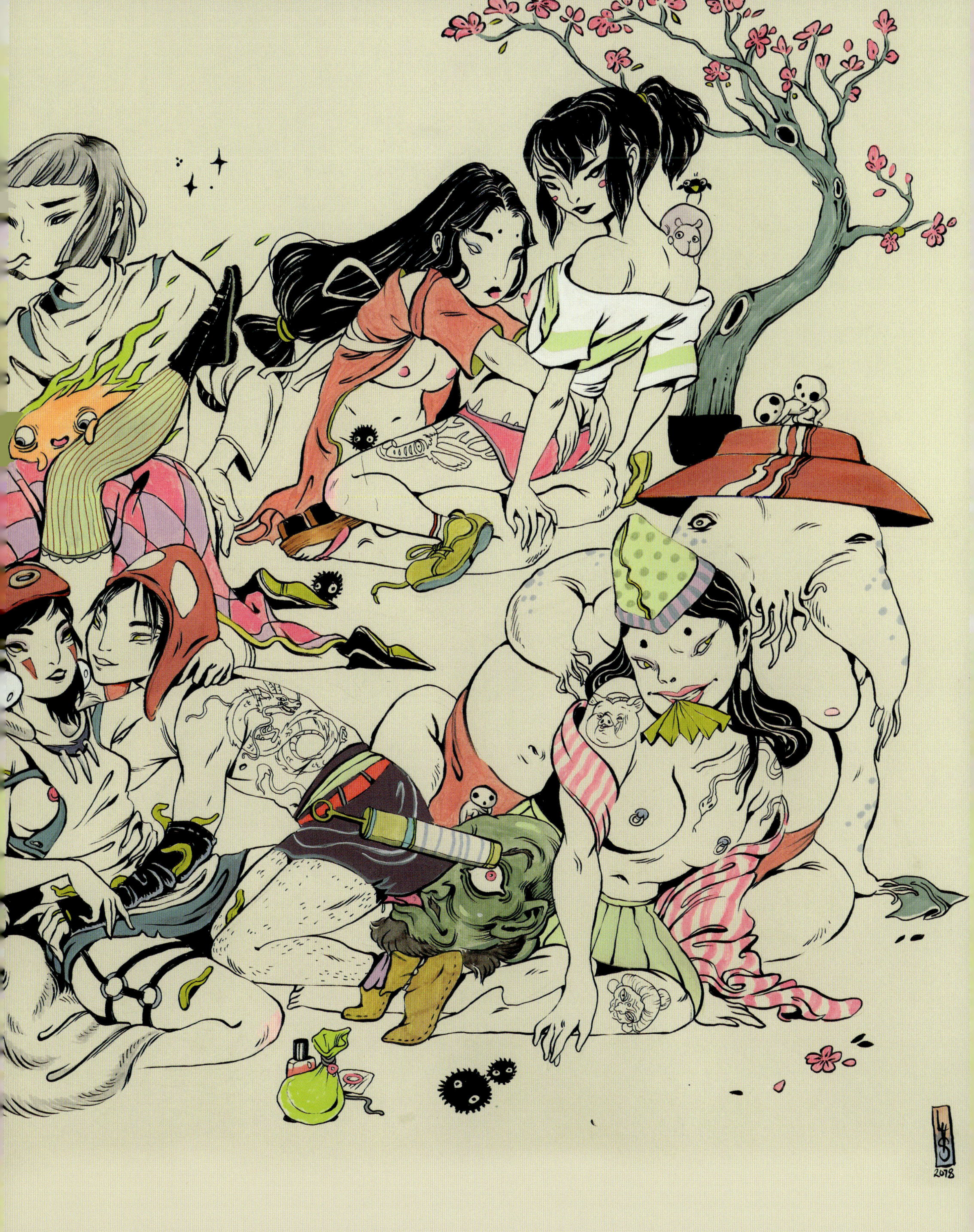

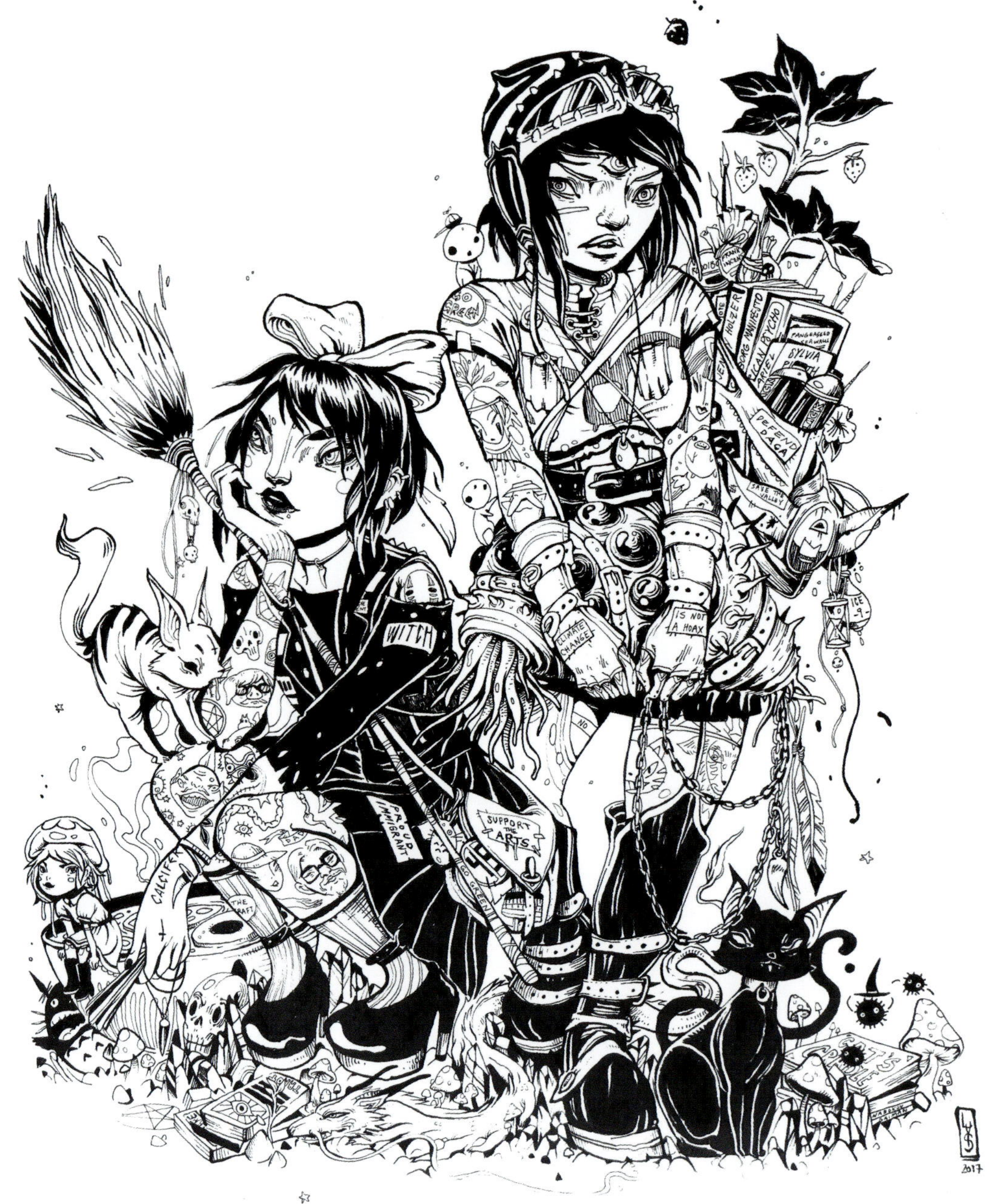

LAUREN YS

J.M. DRAGUNAS

PREVIOUS SPREAD

Miyazaki Shunga

Ink, watercolor and gouache on paper. 36 x 24".

ABOVE

Miyazaki Bad Girl's Club Part II

Ink on paper. 16 x 24".

RIGHT PAGE

Miyazaki Mash

Ink and screentone on Dura-Lar. 11 x 14".

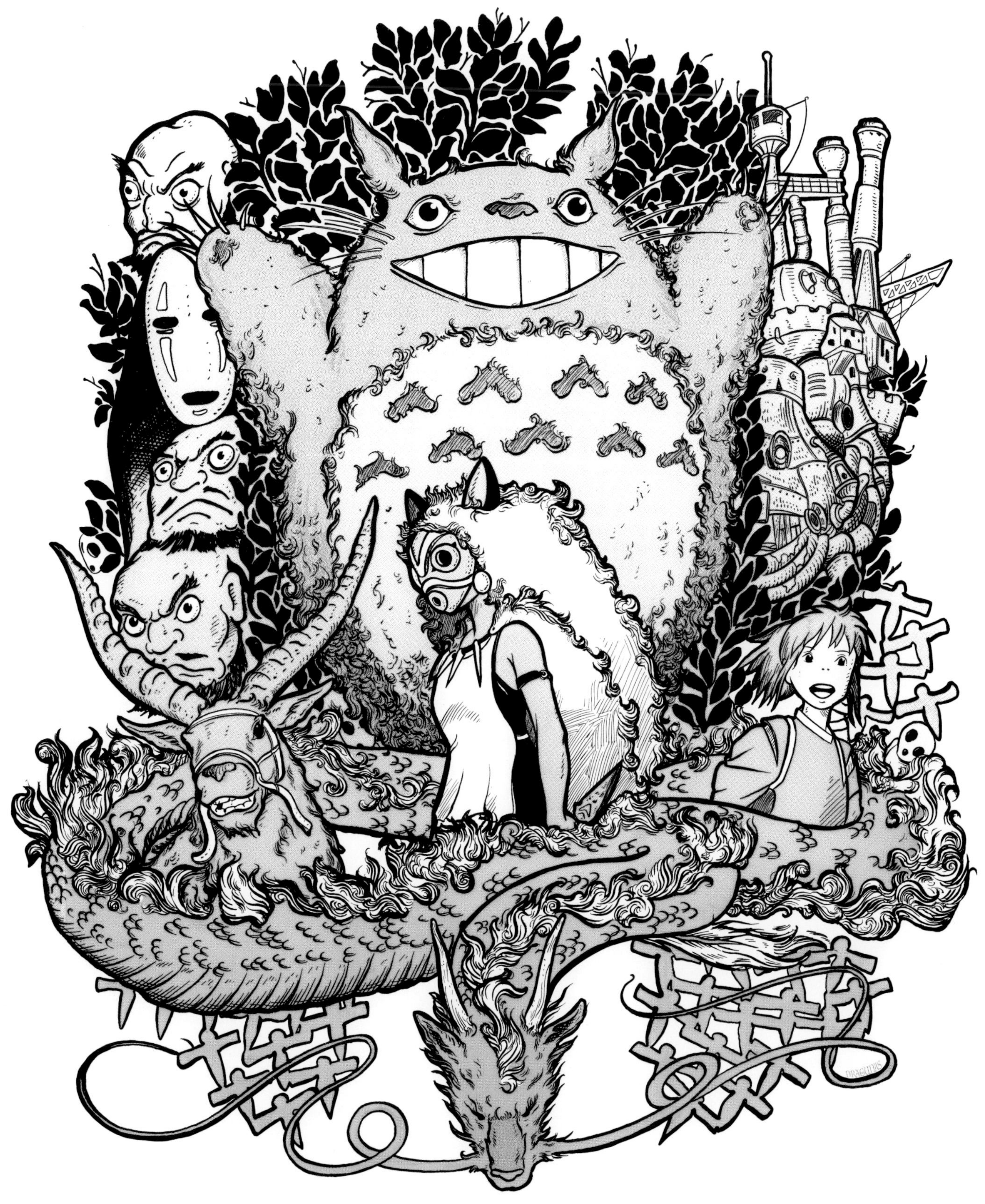

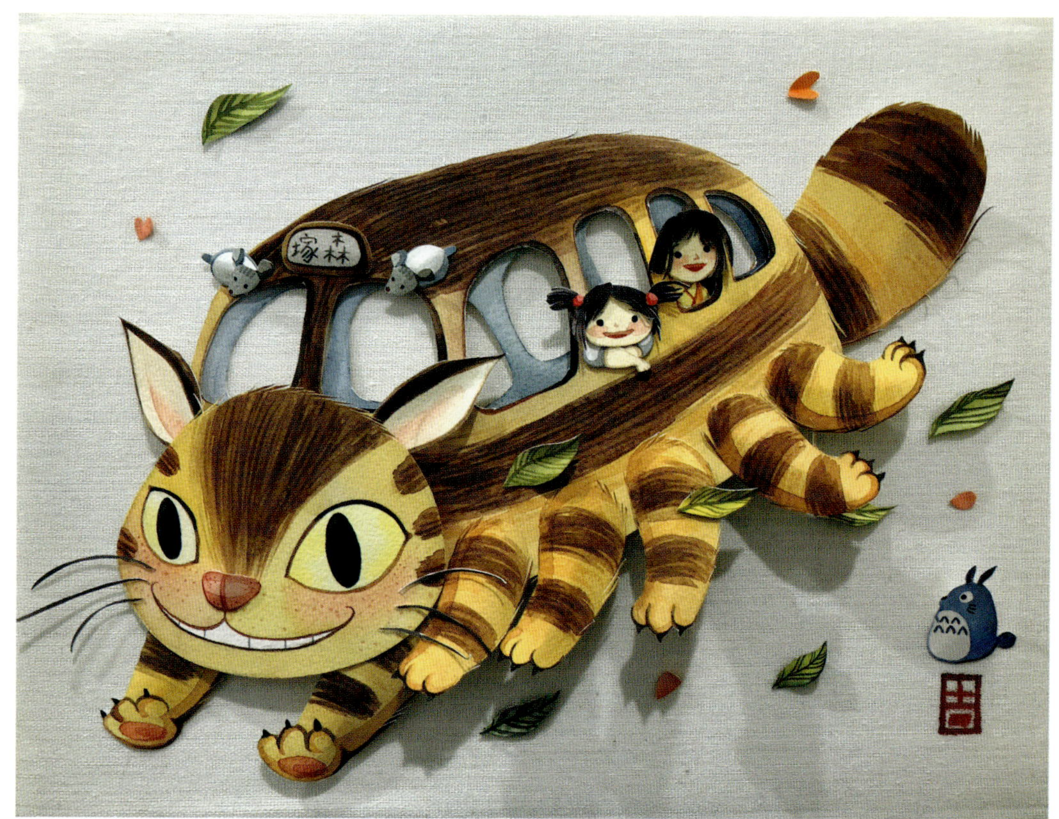

ALINA CHAU

ABOVE

Cat Bus

Watercolor. 14 x 11".

RIGHT PAGE

Totoro

Watercolor. 8 x 11".

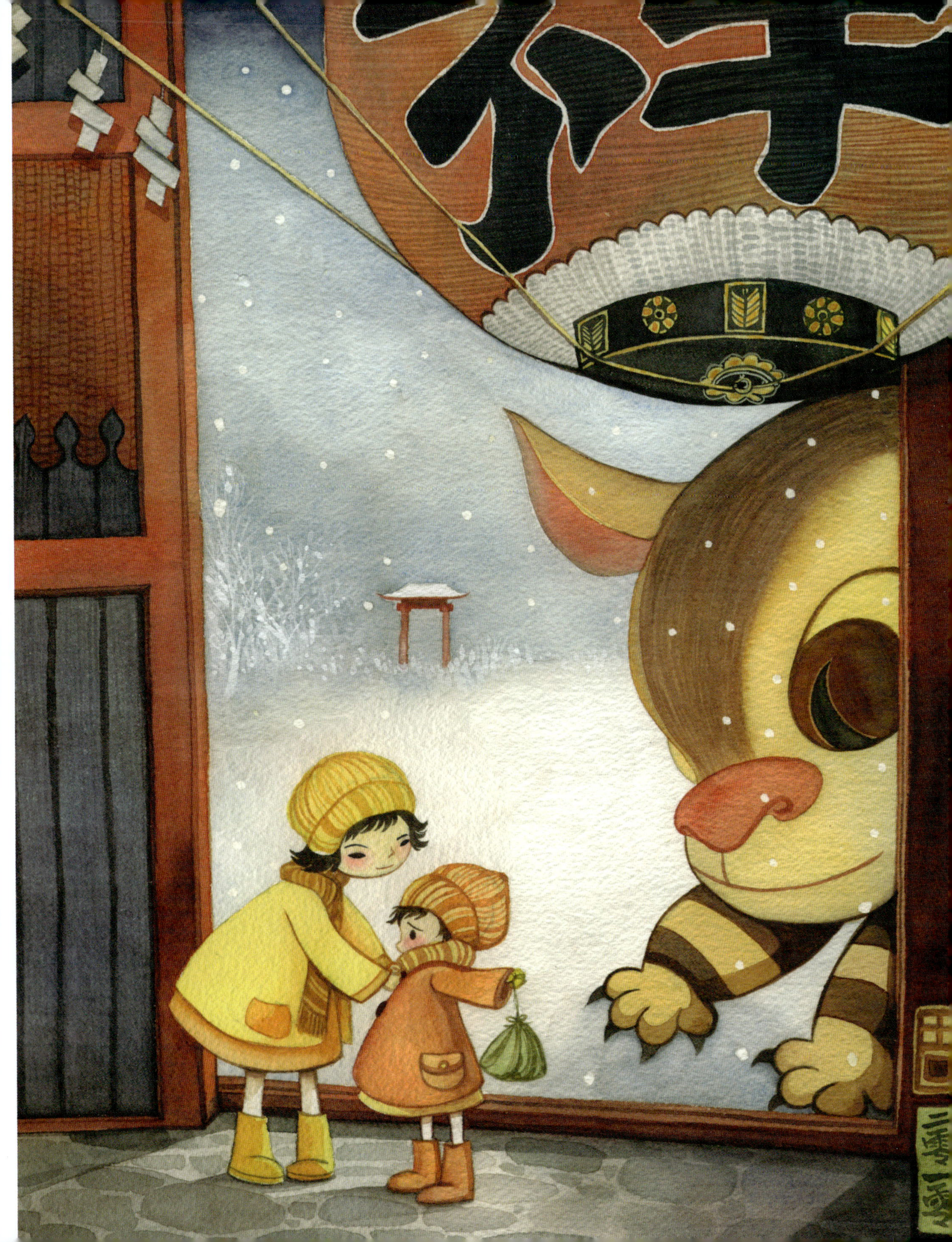

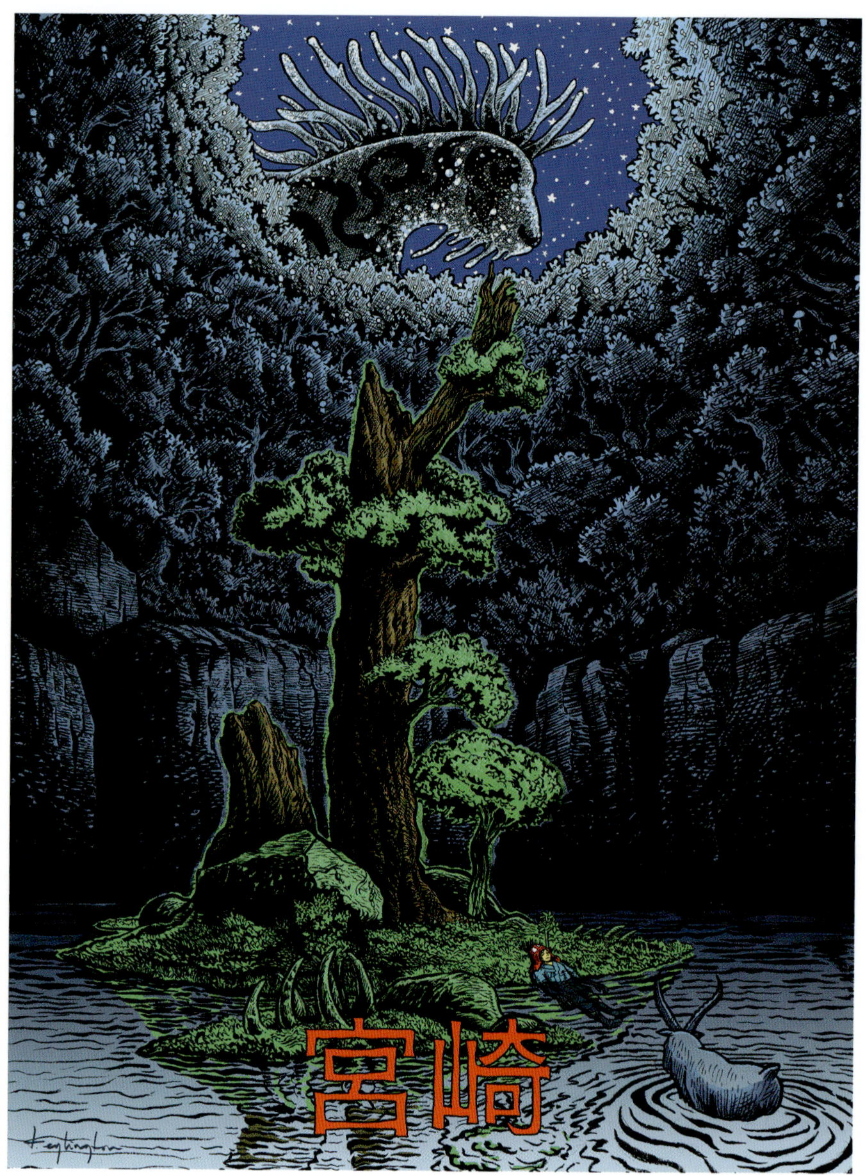

TOM EGLINGTON

ABOVE

At the Pool of the Forest
Archival pigment print. 11 x 17".

MAGGIE IVY

RIGHT PAGE

San and Siblings
Oil on treated paper. 11 x 17".

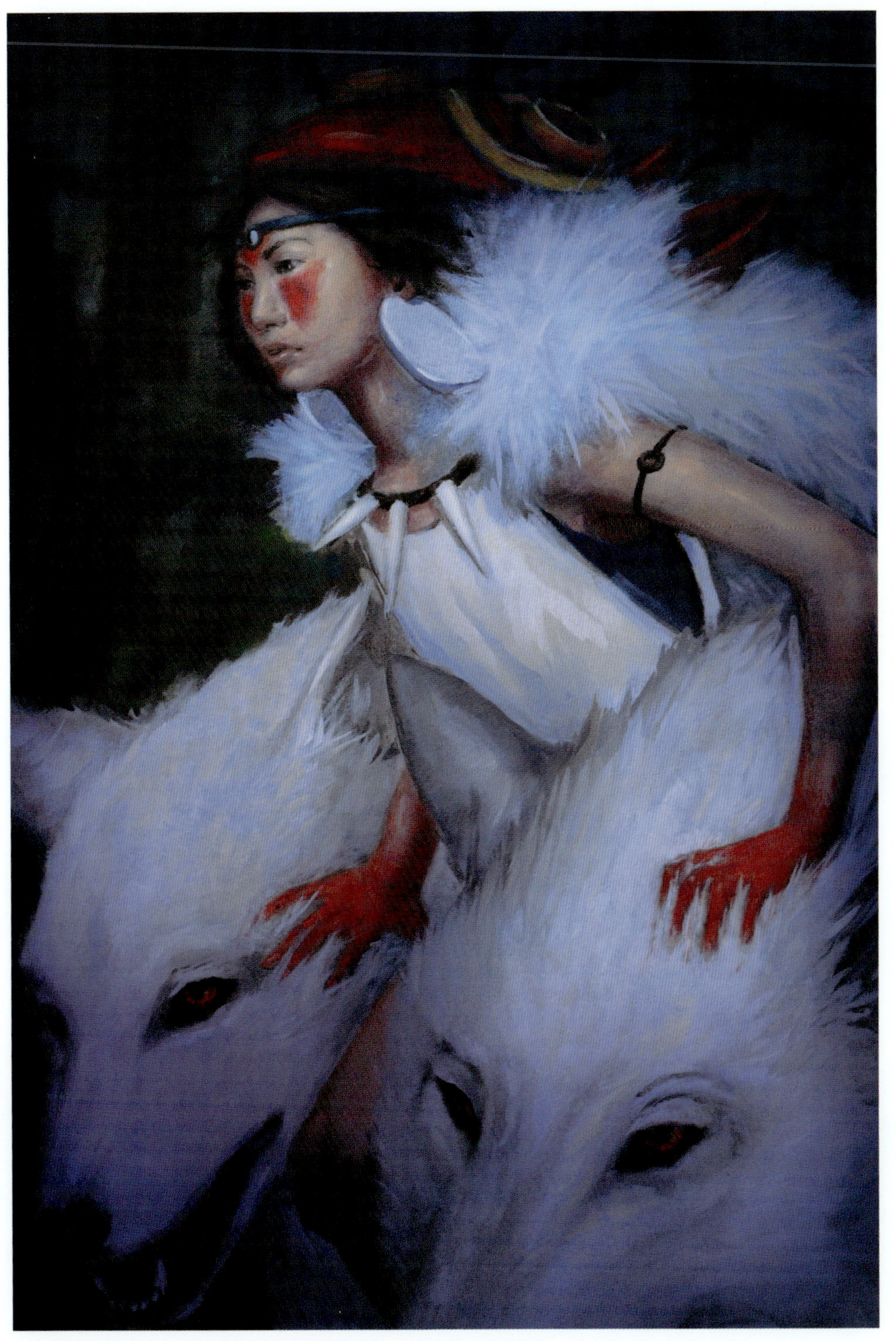

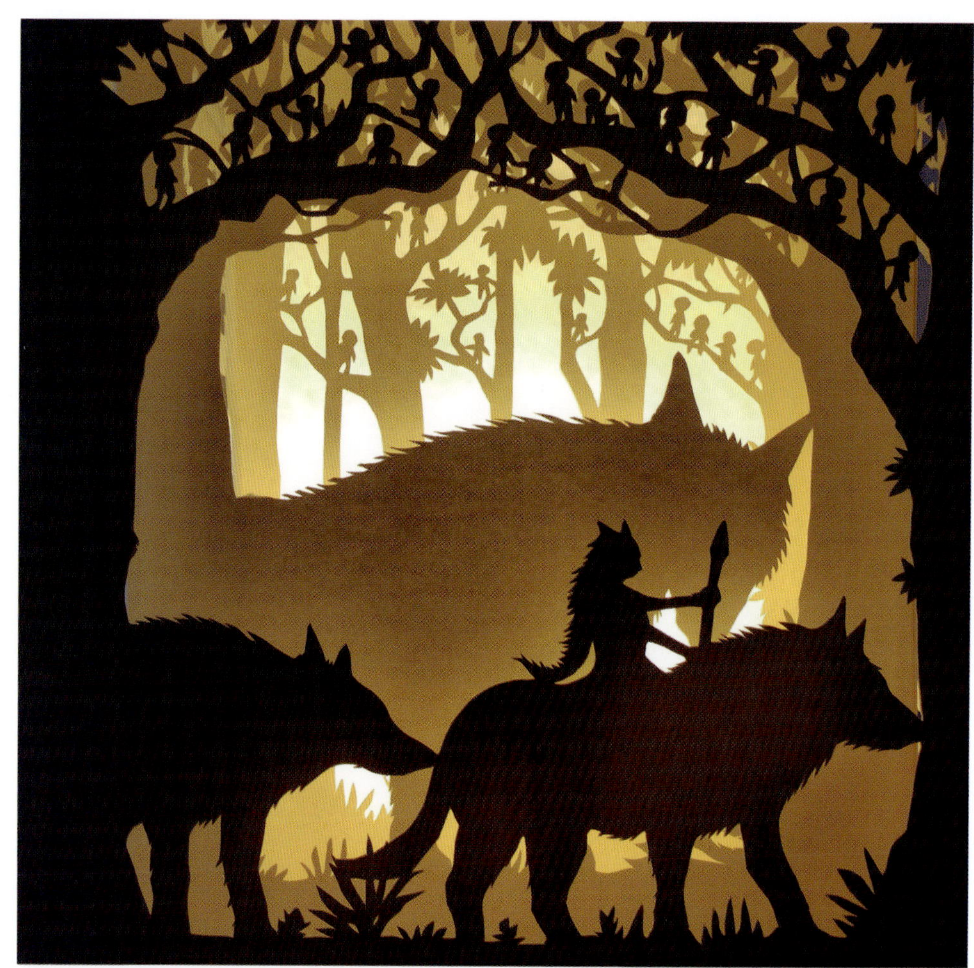

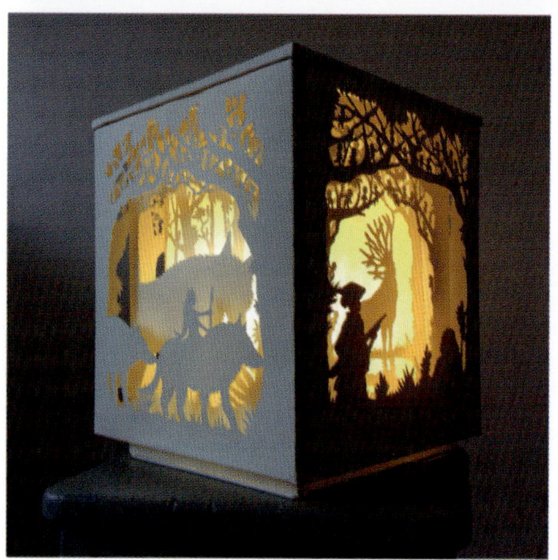

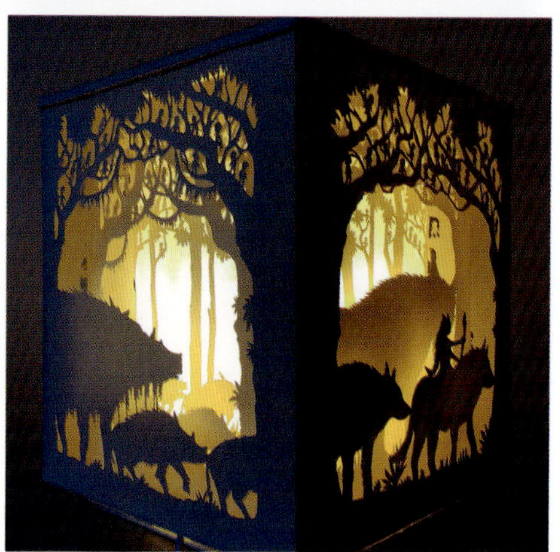

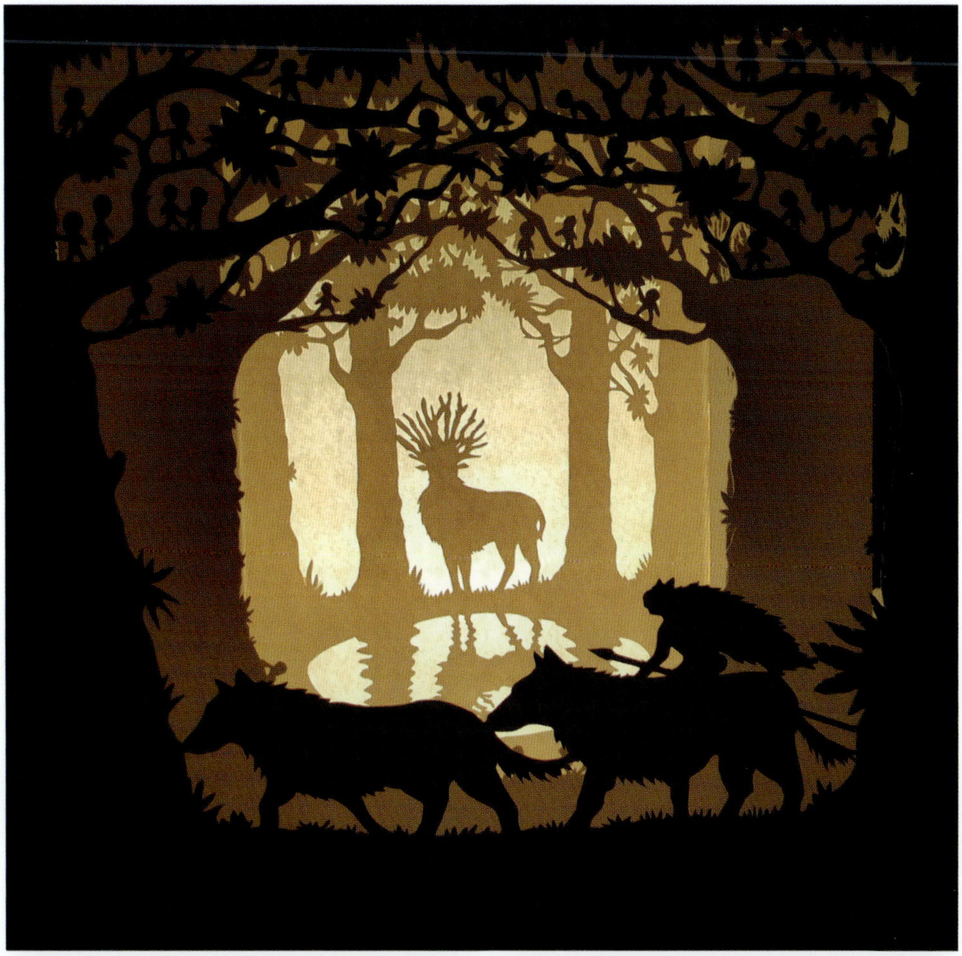

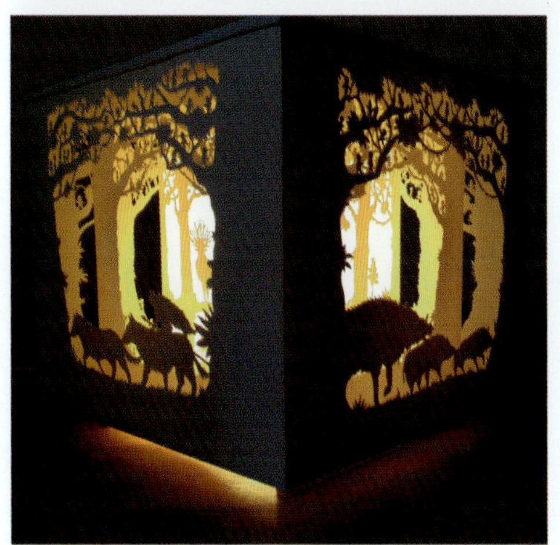

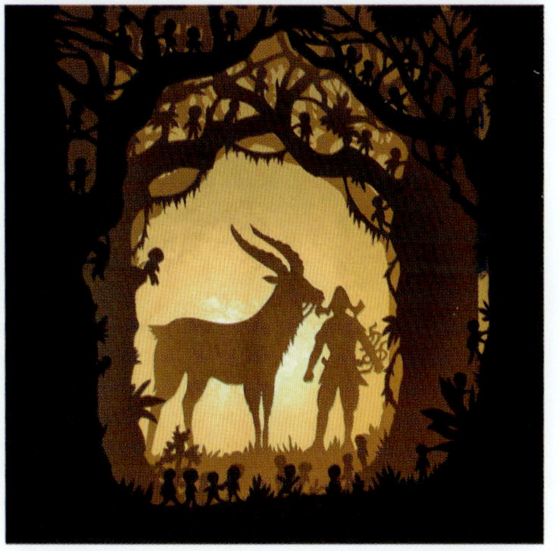

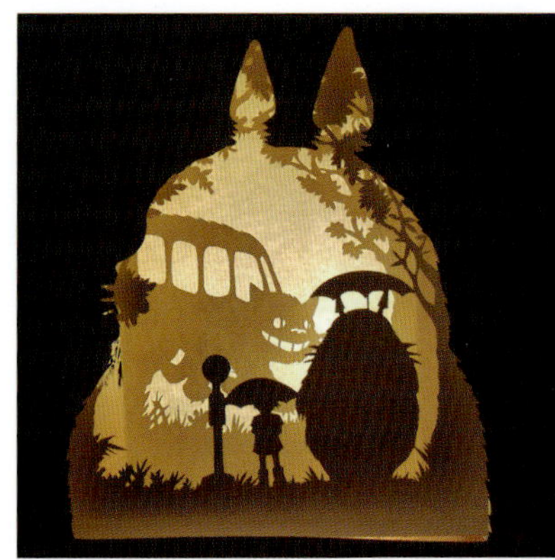

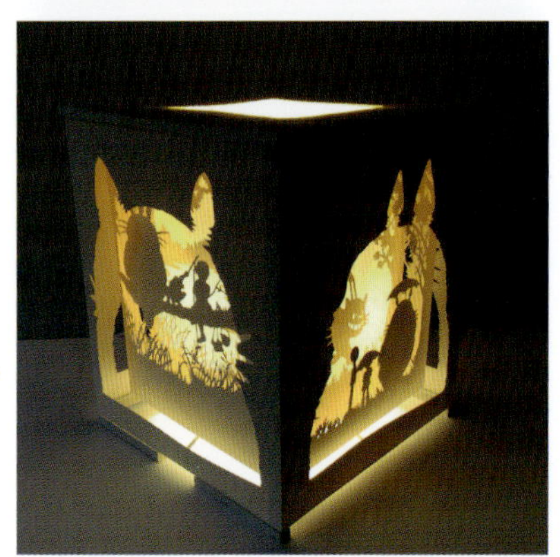

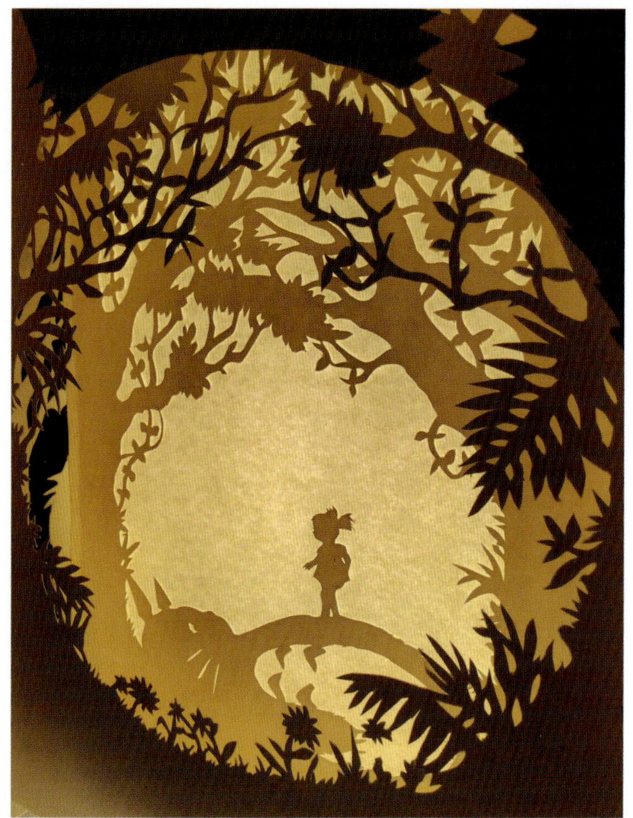

TOM EGLINGTON

PREVIOUS SPREAD, LEFT PAGE

Kodama Woods

Hand cut paper lantern: card, metal frame, light fitting, wood glue, fire retardant, LED bulb. 12.5 x 12.5 x 14.5".

PREVIOUS SPREAD, RIGHT PAGE

Princess Mononoke Illumination

Layered hand-cut 300 gsm card on metal frame, wood, standard light fitting, glue, flame retardant. 38 x 40 x 40".

ABOVE

Totoro Illumination

Layered hand-cut 300 gsm card on metal frame, wood, standard light fitting, glue, flame retardant. 36 x 30 x 30".

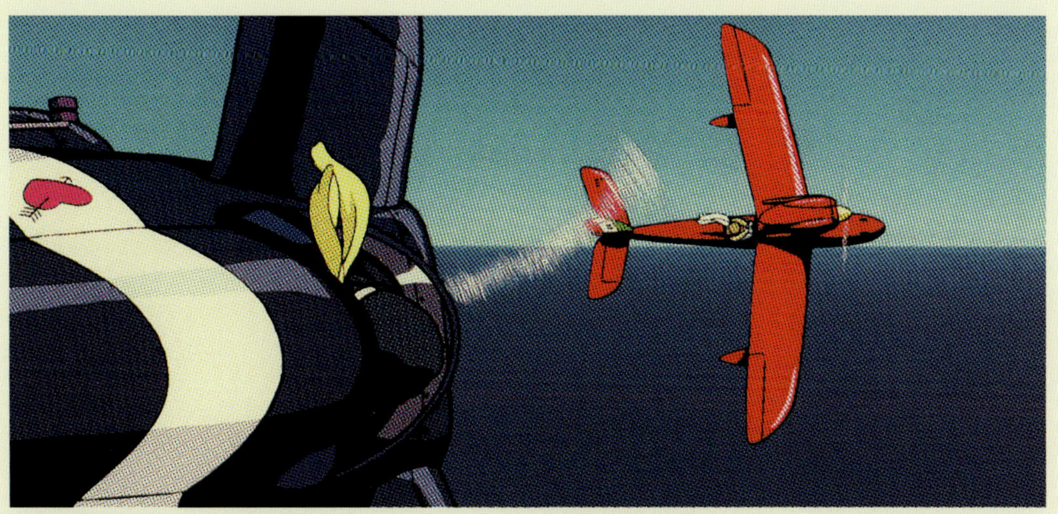

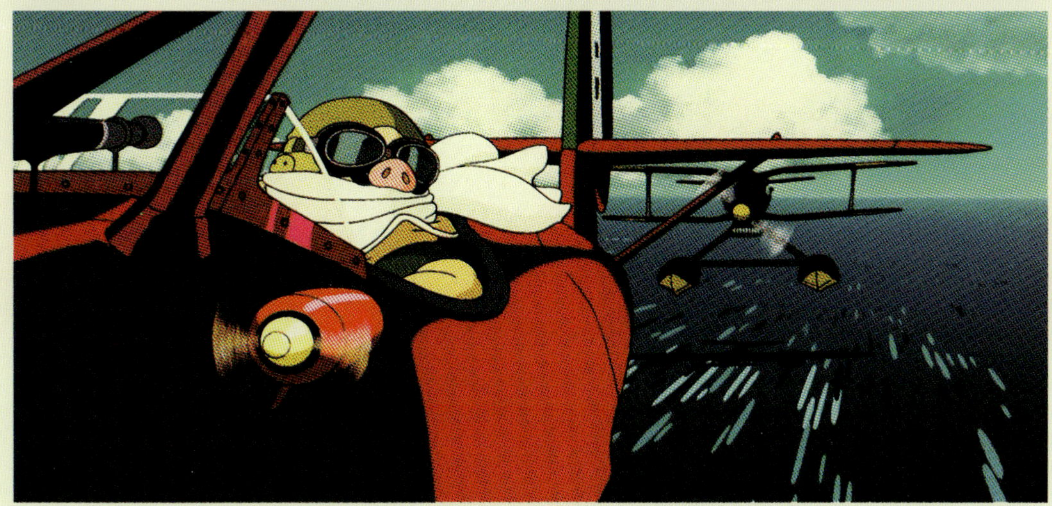

TIM JORDAN

TOP

Banking Pig

Four-color screen print. 36 x 18".

BOTTOM

When Pigs Fly

Four-color screen print. 36 x 18".

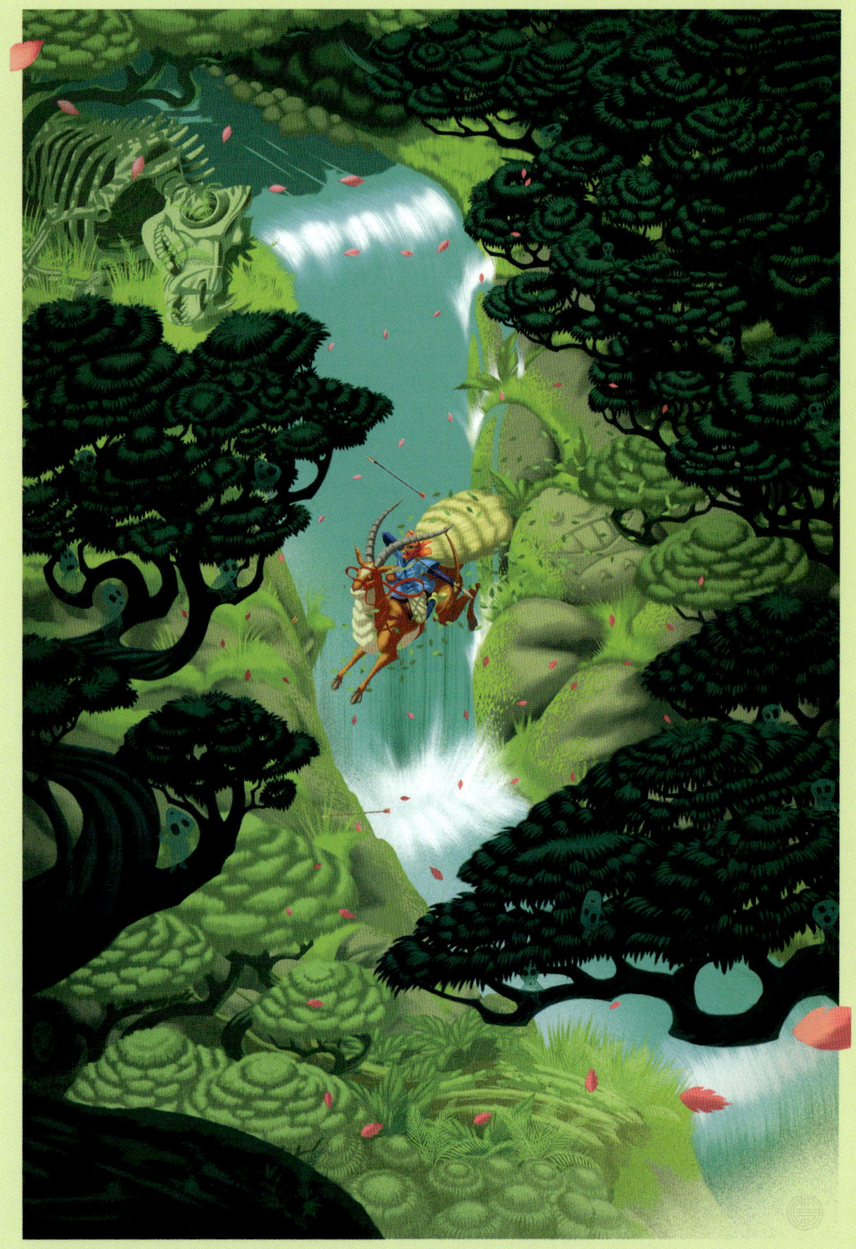

JAY GORDON

Ashitaka & Yaukul

Archival pigment print. 16 x 24".

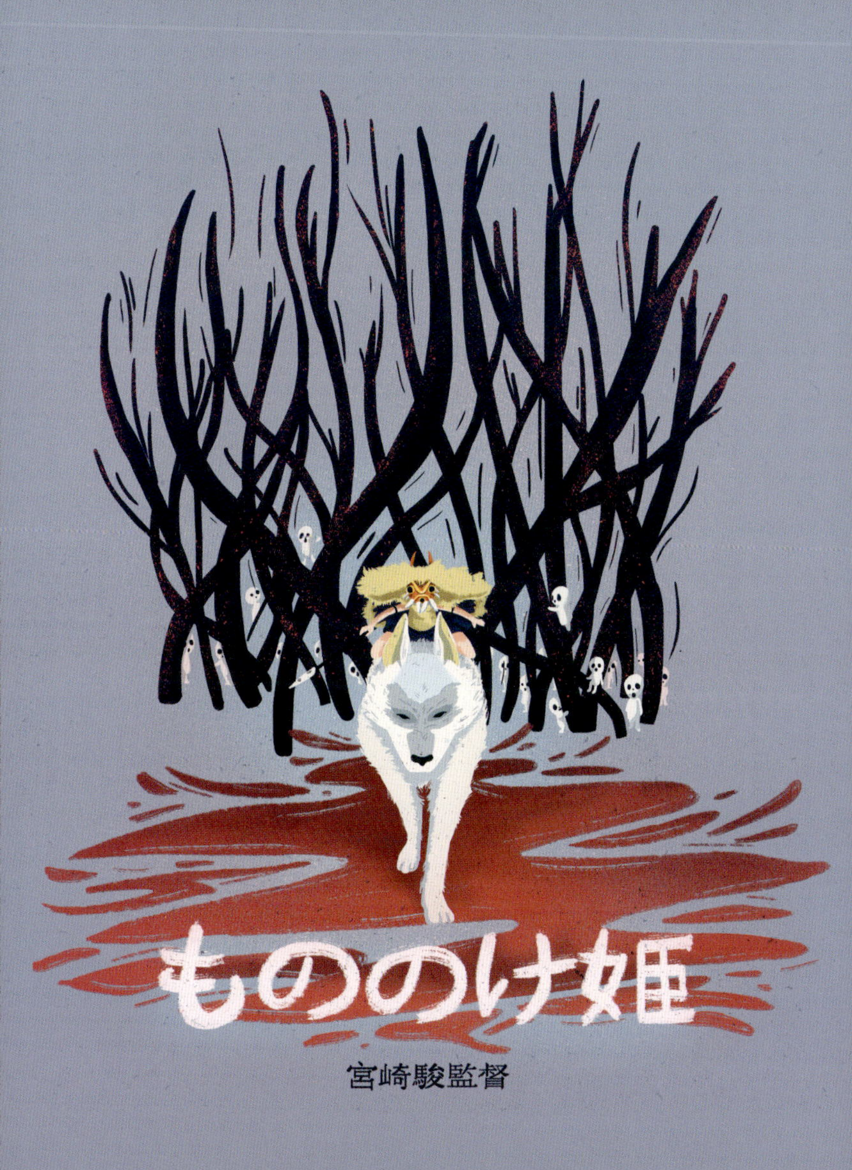

MARIA SUAREZ-INCLAN

Forest's Heart

Archival pigment print. 12 x 18".

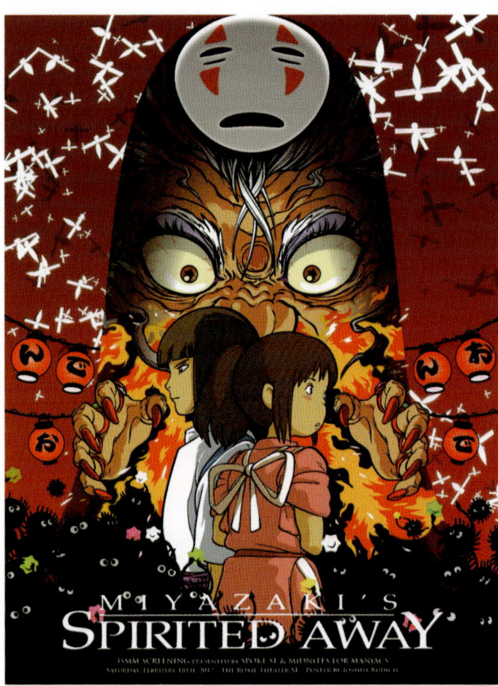

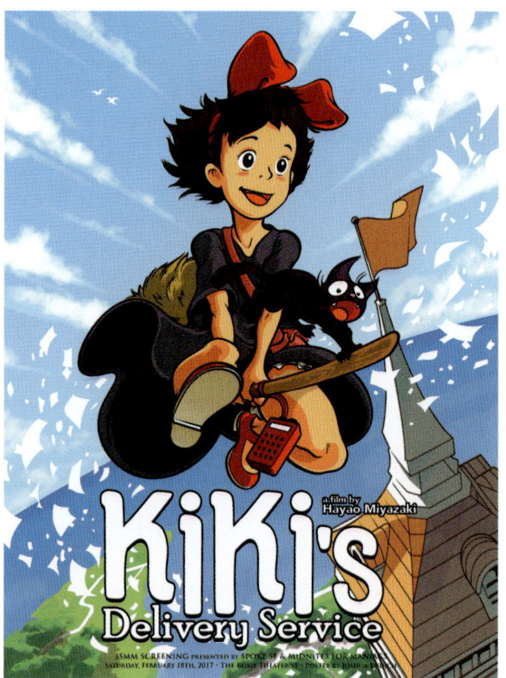

JOSHUA BUDICH

LEFT

Spirited Away

Screen print. 18 x 24".

RIGHT

Kiki's Delivery Service

Screen print. 18 x 24".

RIGHT PAGE

Ponyo (A World Where Everything Is Possible)

Seven-color screen print. 18 x 24".

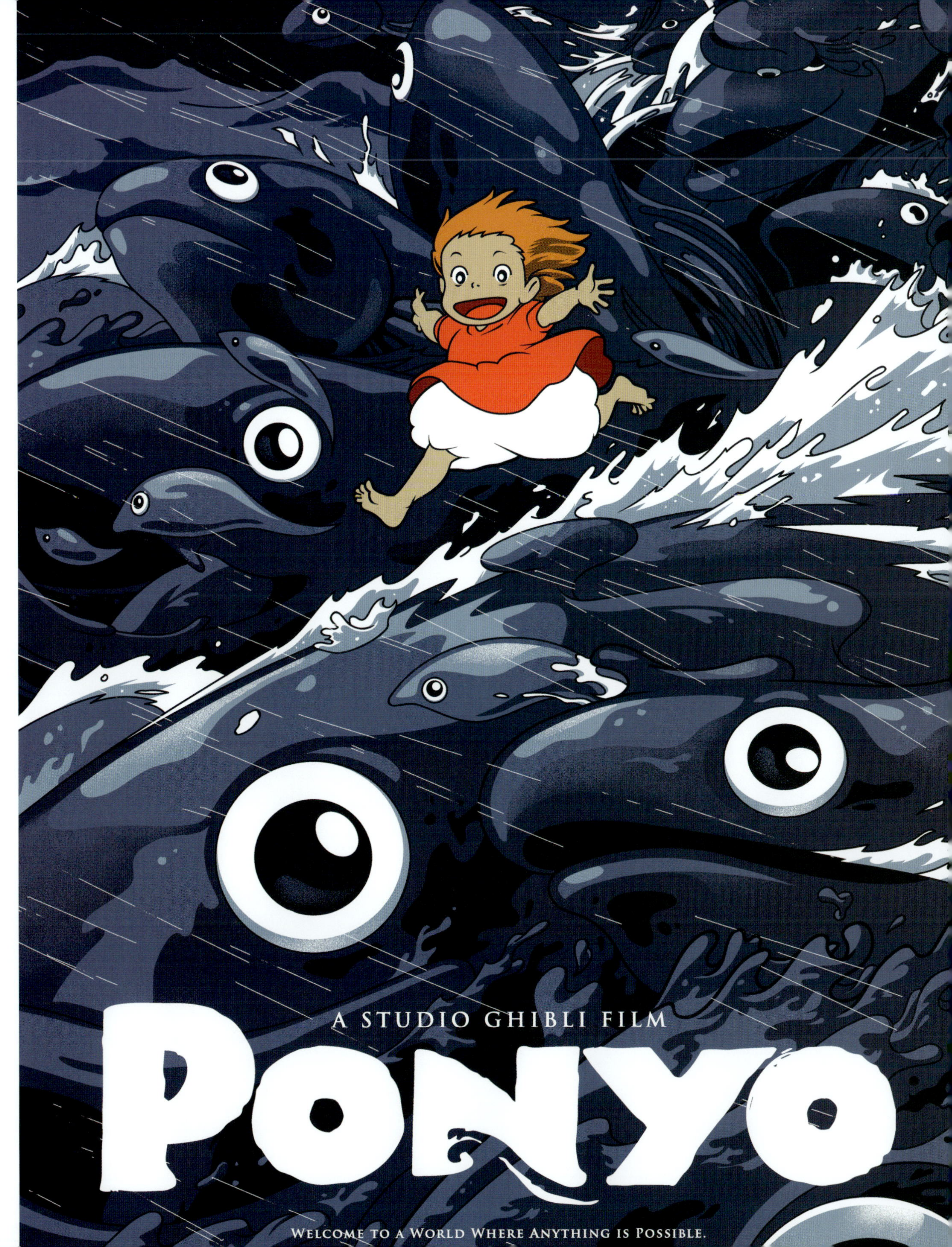
A STUDIO GHIBLI FILM
PONYO
WELCOME TO A WORLD WHERE ANYTHING IS POSSIBLE.

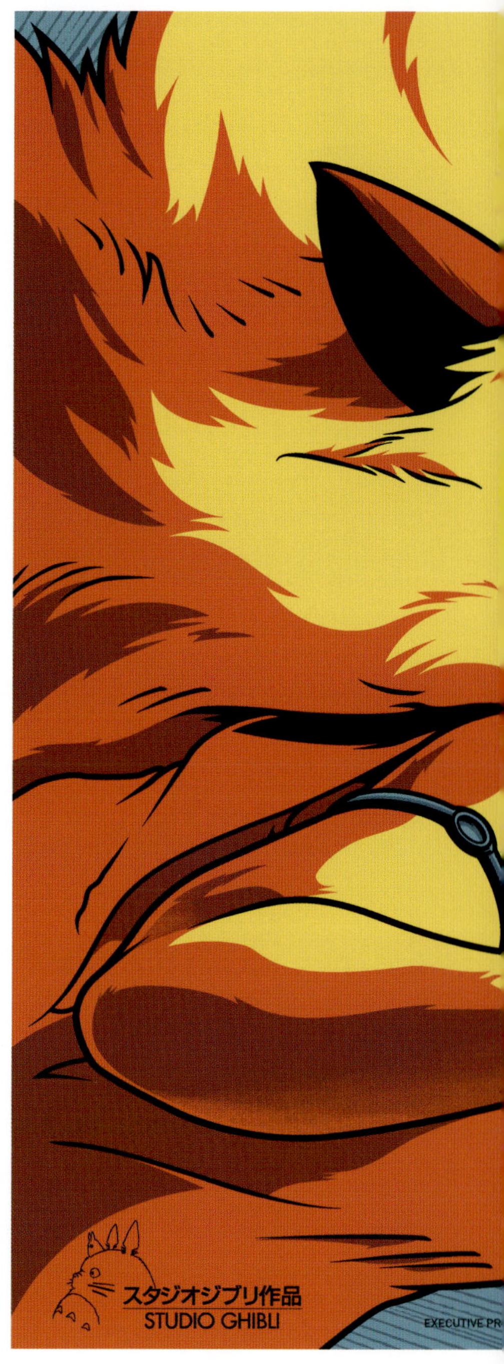

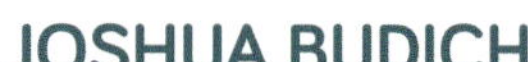

JOSHUA BUDICH

**There's A Demon Inside You.
It's Inside Both of You**
Screen print. 24 x 18".

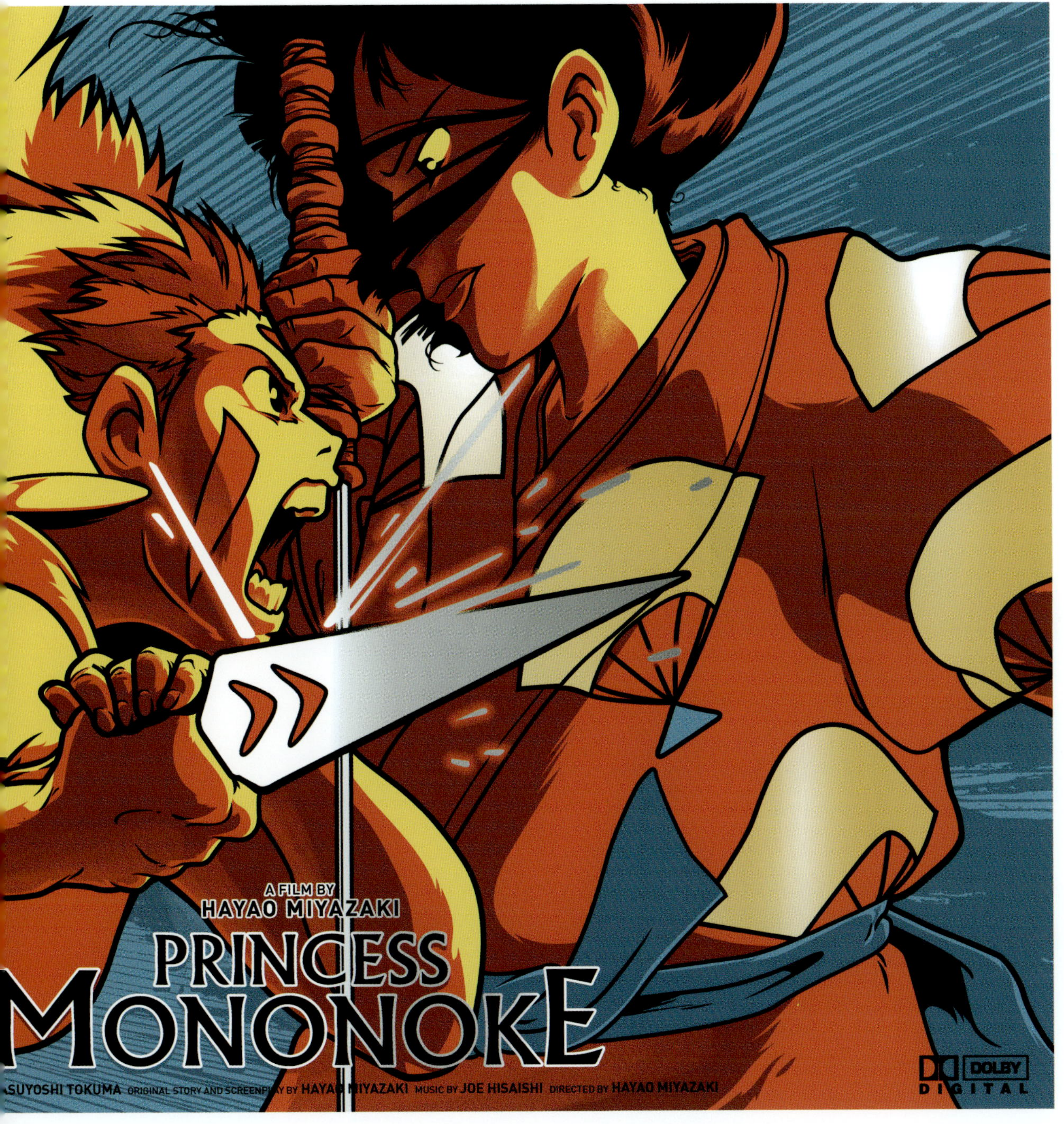
A FILM BY
HAYAO MIYAZAKI
PRINCESS
MONONOKE
SUYOSHI TOKUMA ORIGINAL STORY AND SCREENPLAY BY HAYAO MIYAZAKI MUSIC BY JOE HISAISHI DIRECTED BY HAYAO MIYAZAKI
DOLBY
DIGITAL

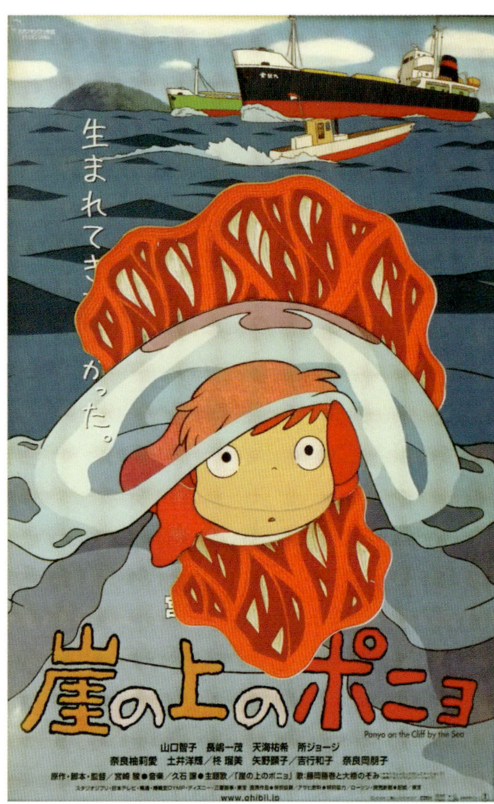

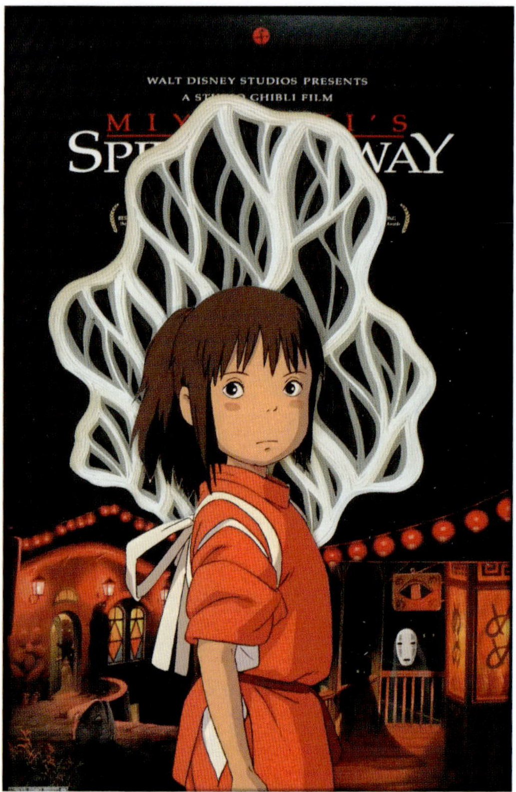

CHARLES CLARY

LEFT

Ponyo

Hand cut paper and found poster. 12 x 19".

RIGHT

Spirited Away

Hand cut paper and found poster. 12 x 19".

RIGHT PAGE

Princess Mononoke

Hand cut paper and found poster. 12 x 19".

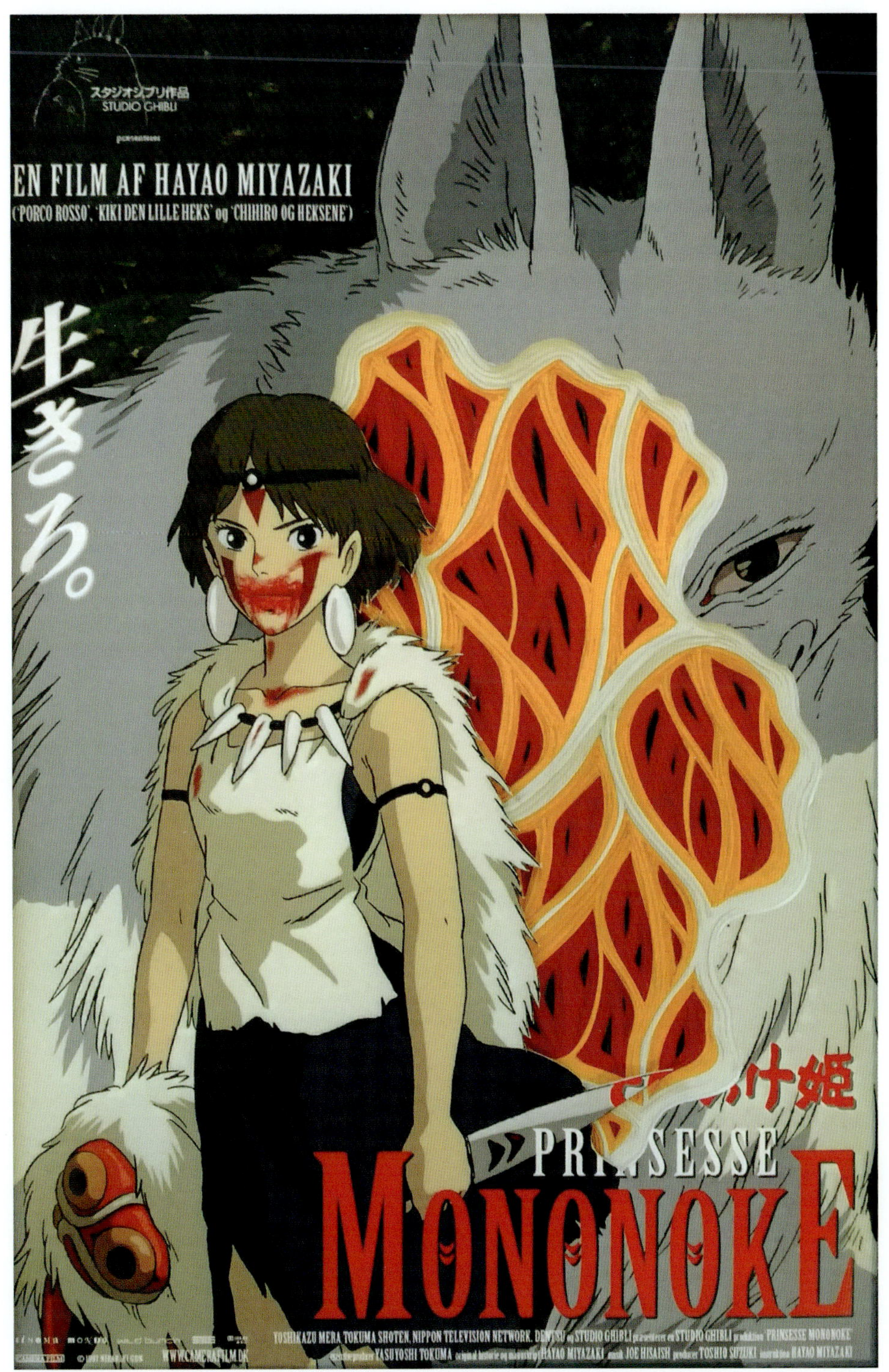
スタジオジブリ作品
STUDIO GHIBLI
EN FILM AF HAYAO MIYAZAKI
('PORCO ROSSO', 'KIKI DEN LILLE HEKS' og 'CHIHIRO OG HEKSENE')
生きろ。
PRINSESSE
MONONOKE
YOSHIKAZU MERA TOKUMA SHOTEN, NIPPON TELEVISION NETWORK, DENTSU og STUDIO GHIBLI
'PRINSESSE MONONOKE'
YASUYOSHI TOKUMA
HAYAO MIYAZAKI
JOE HISAISHI
TOSHIO SUZUKI
HAYAO MIYAZAKI
WWW.CAMERAFILM.DK

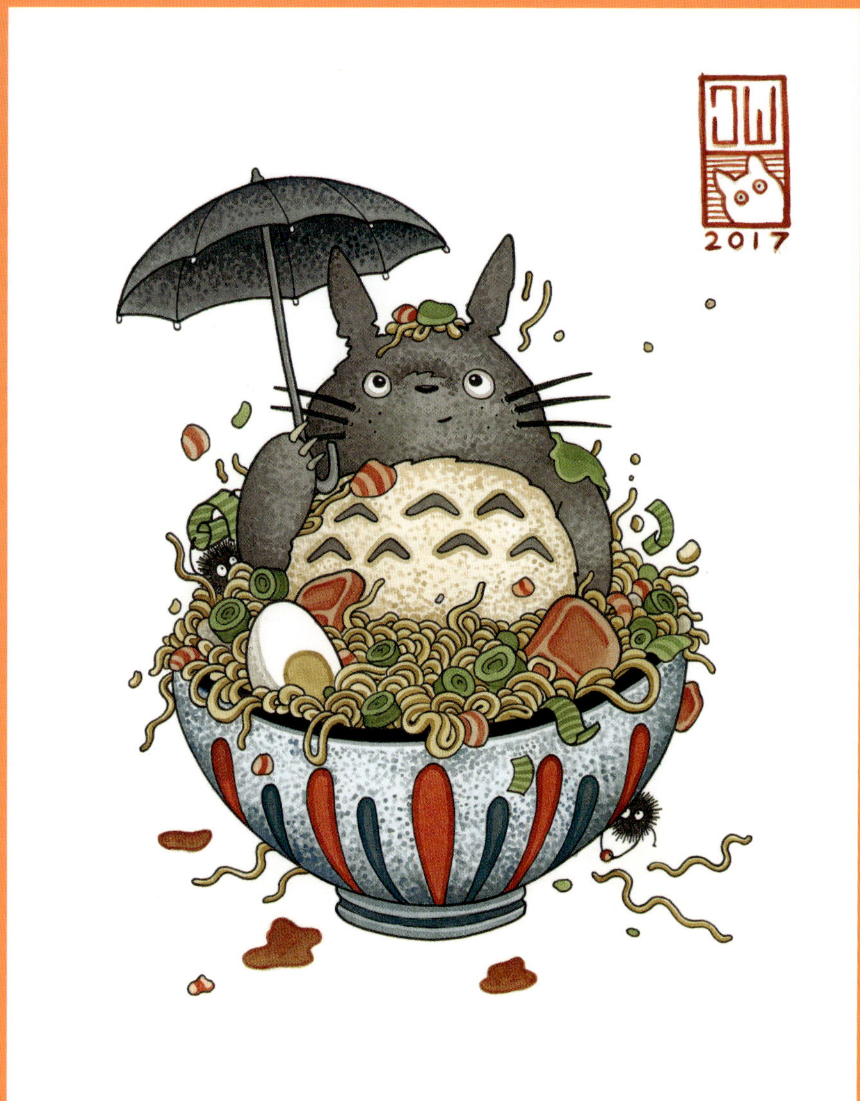

JAN WILLEM

ABOVE

Totoro Ramen
Acrylic watercolor and ink.
7.87 x 10.23".

KAYLA EDGAR

RIGHT PAGE

Nothing that Happens is ever Forgotten
Acryla gouache and chalk paint.
14.25 x 17.25".

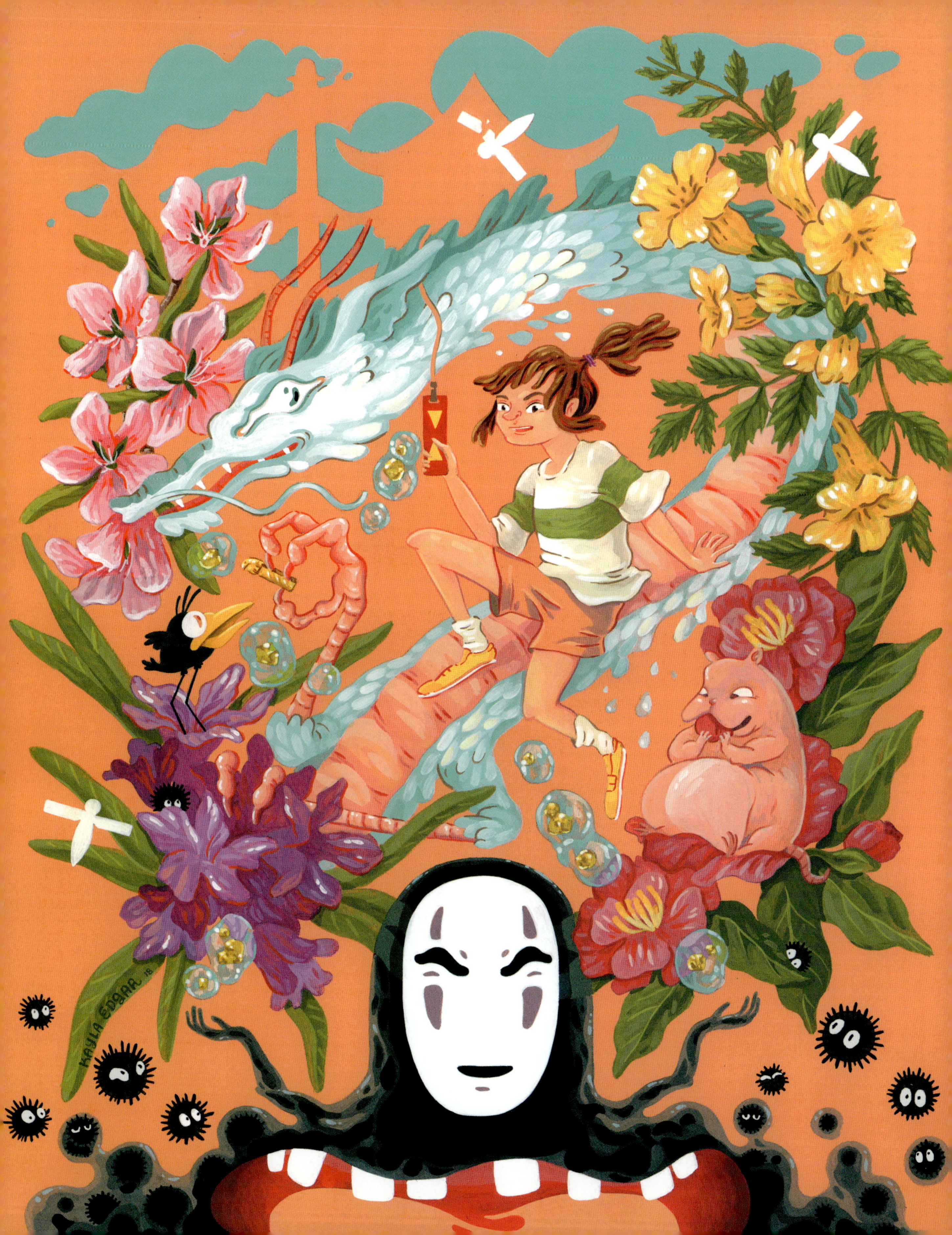
KAYLA EDGAR 18

CONCEPCIÓN STUDIOS

RIGHT PAGE

Hayao's Hero

Archival pigment print. 18 x 24".

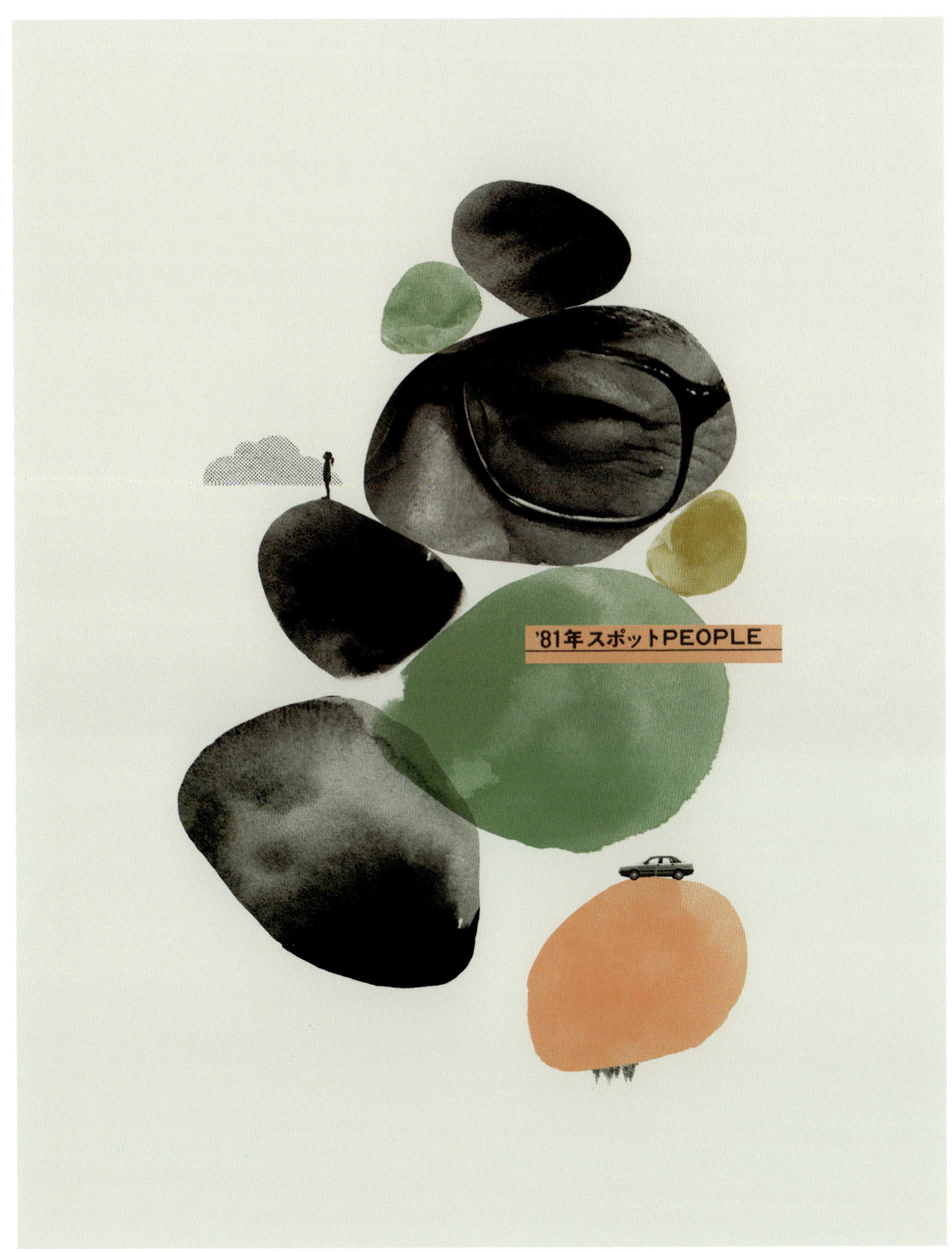
'81年スポットPEOPLE

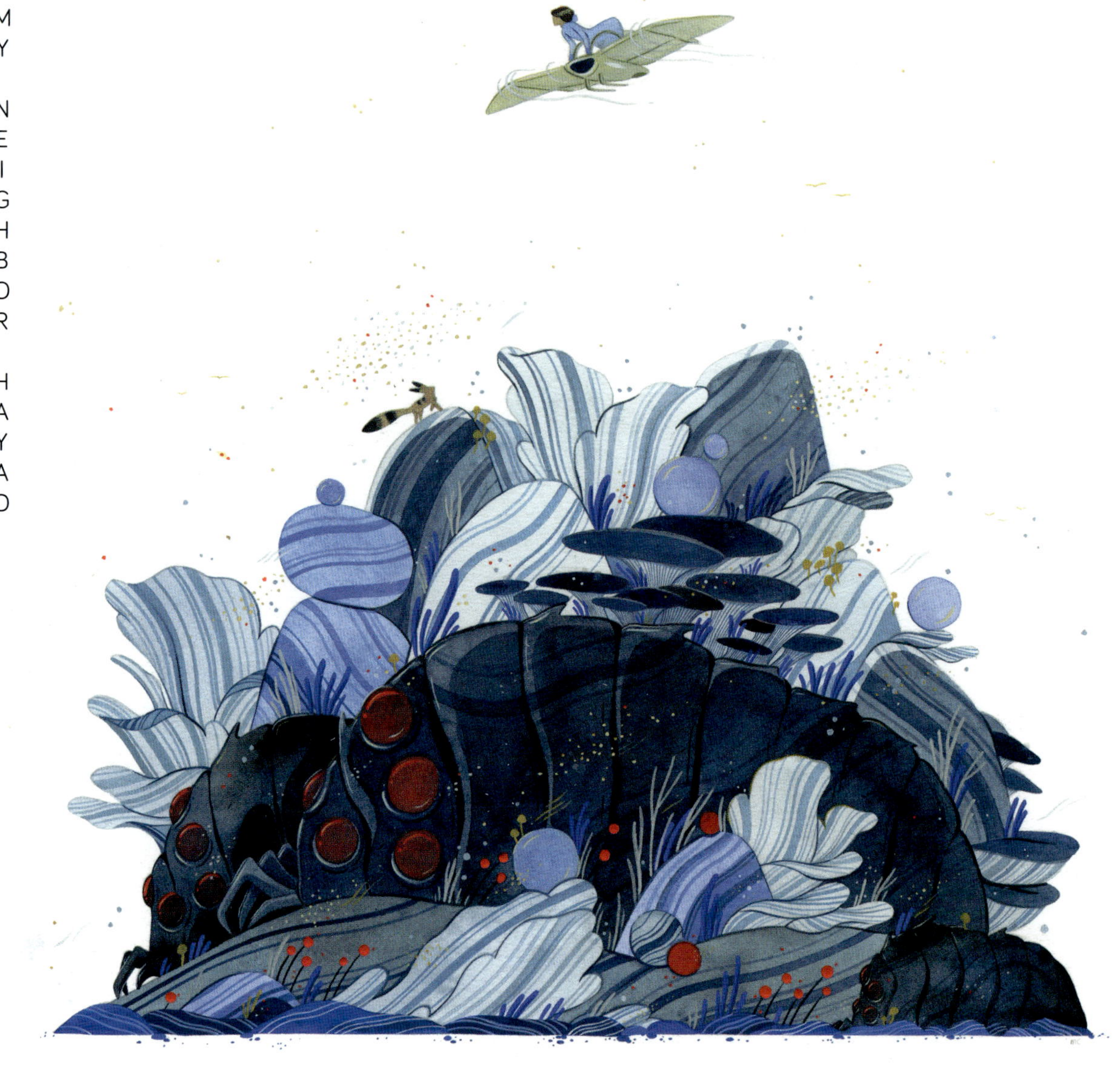

MAGGIE CHIANG

ABOVE

Nausicaä

Watercolor and acrylic gouache.
13.5 x 13.5".

RIGHT PAGE

Zeniba's Garden

Watercolor and acrylic gouache.
12 x 16".

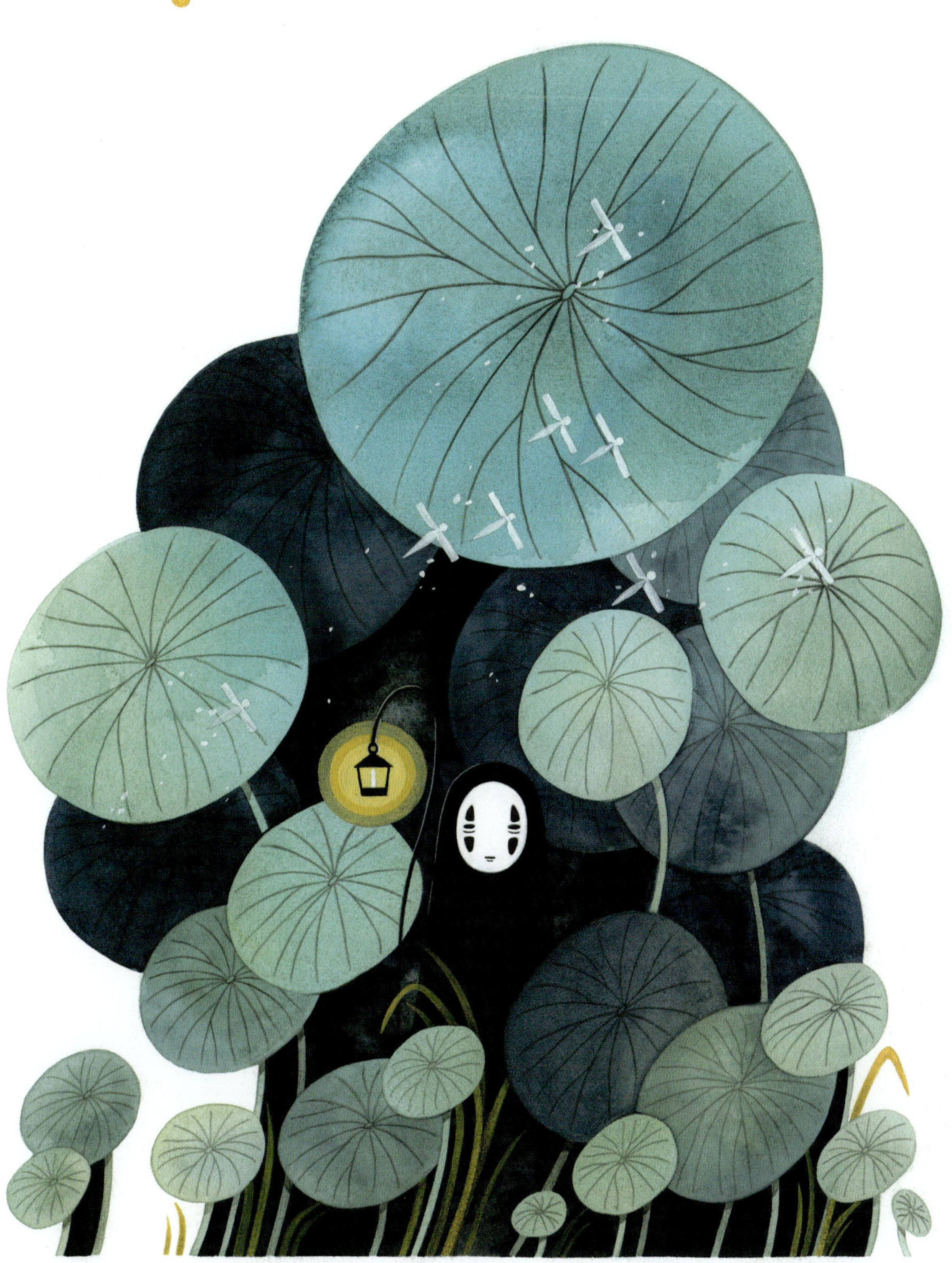

CRANKBUNNY

RIGHT PAGE

WWMD

Paper puppet. 12 x 16".

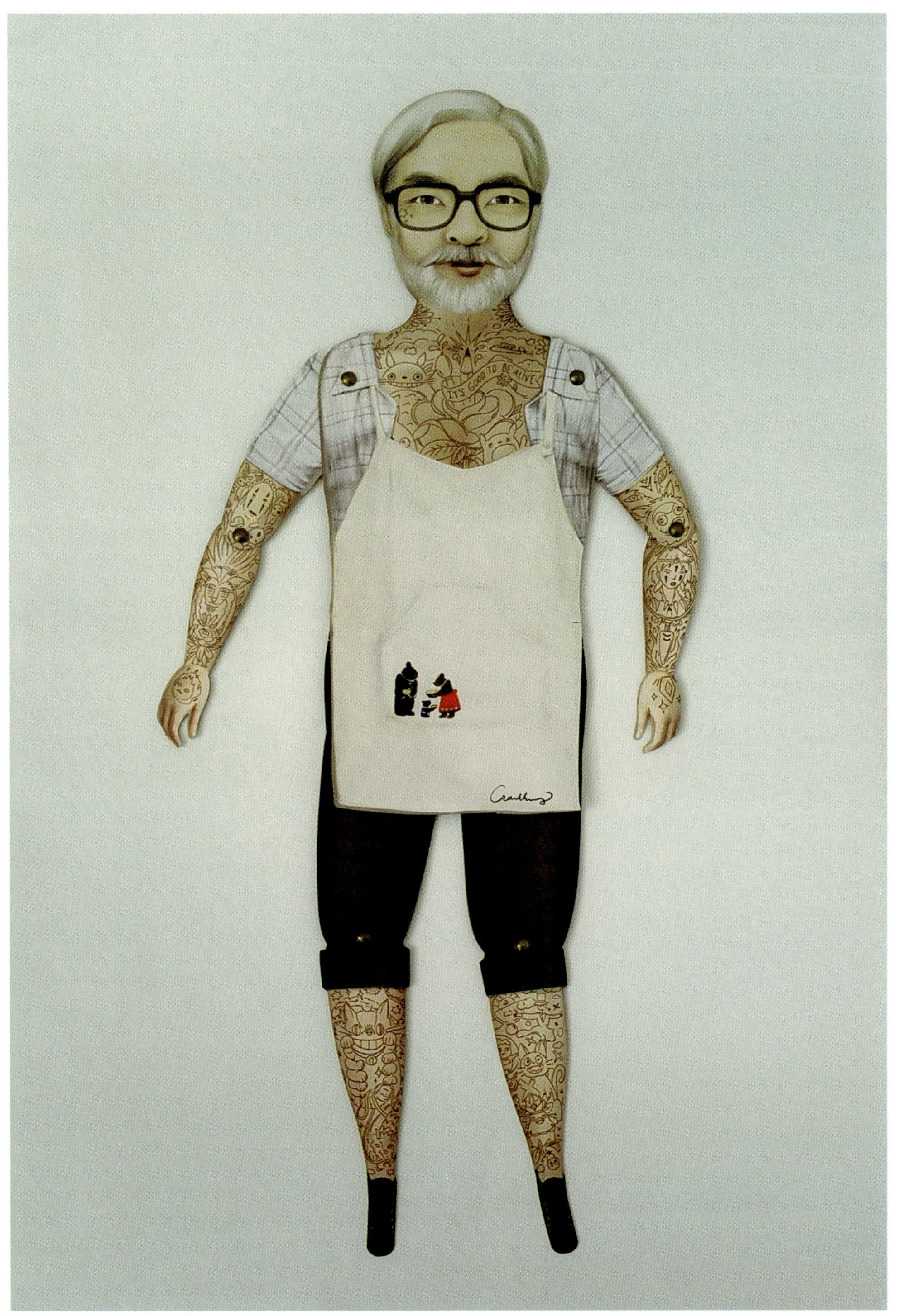
IT'S GOOD TO BE ALIVE

KATE SNOW

RIGHT PAGE

In Bloom

Watercolor and ink on paper.
11 x 14".

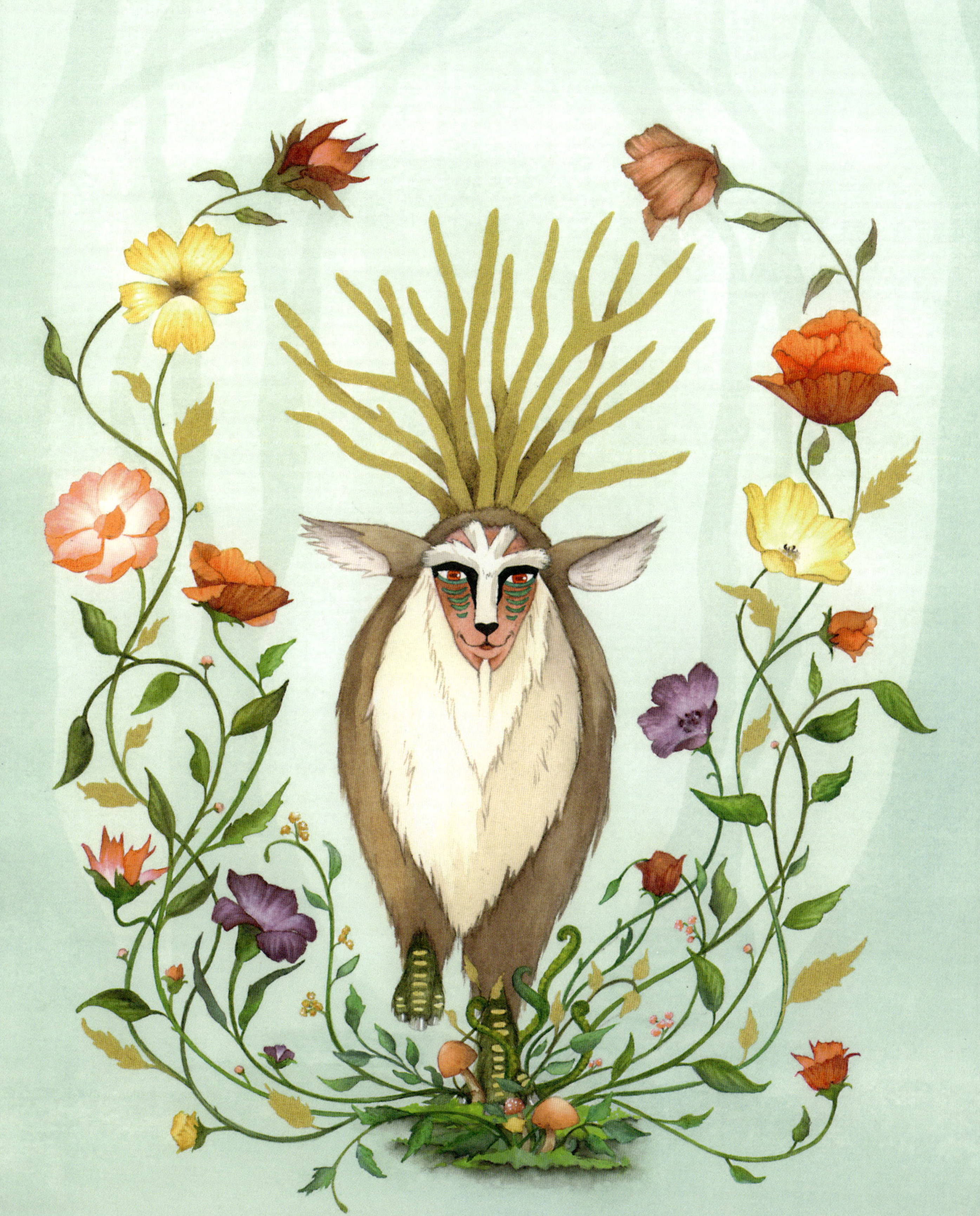

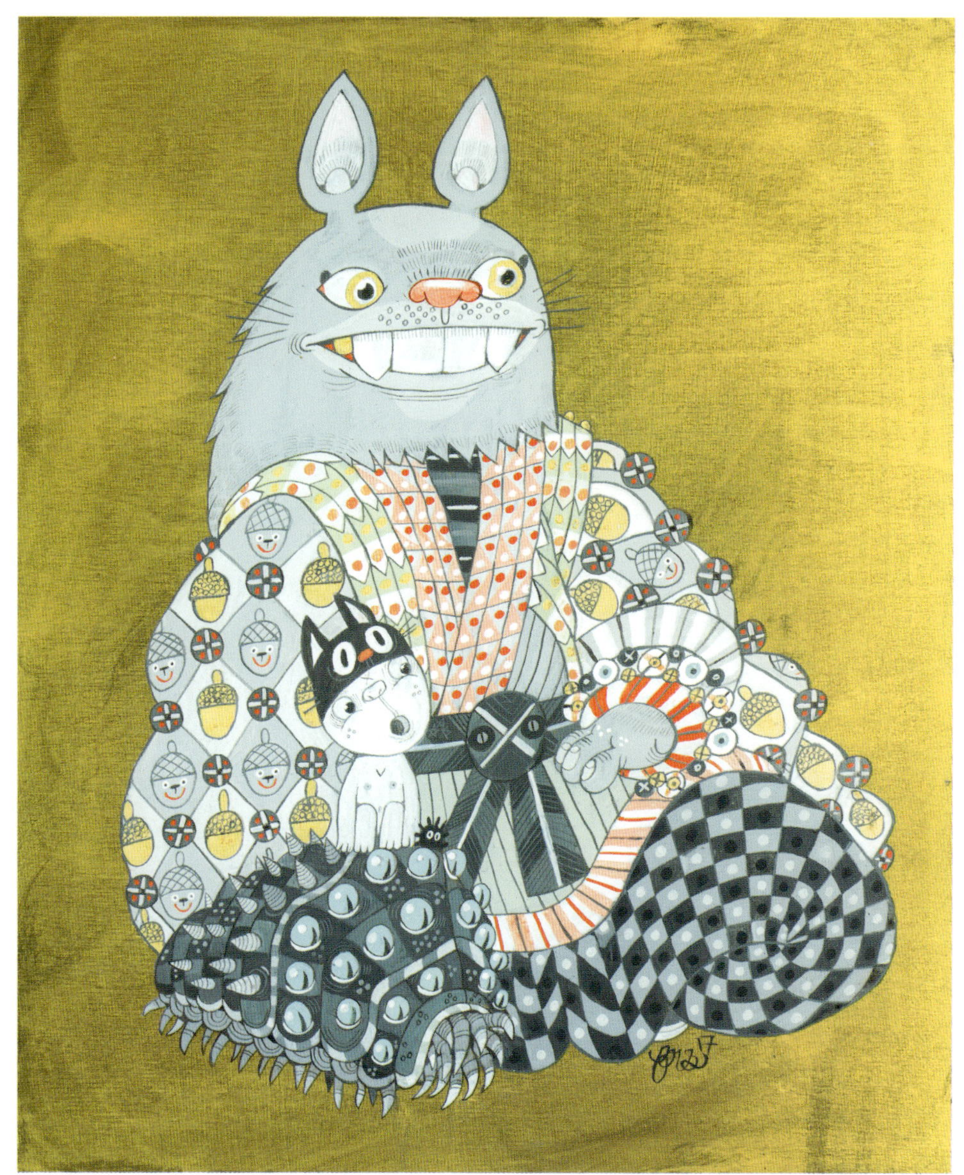

FERRIS PLOCK

ABOVE

My Own Private Totoro
Acrylic and gold leaf on panel.
16 x 20".

VALERIE SAVARIE

RIGHT PAGE

Cleansing of the Spirit
Altered book, acryla gouache and thread. 14.75 x 10.5 x 1.5".

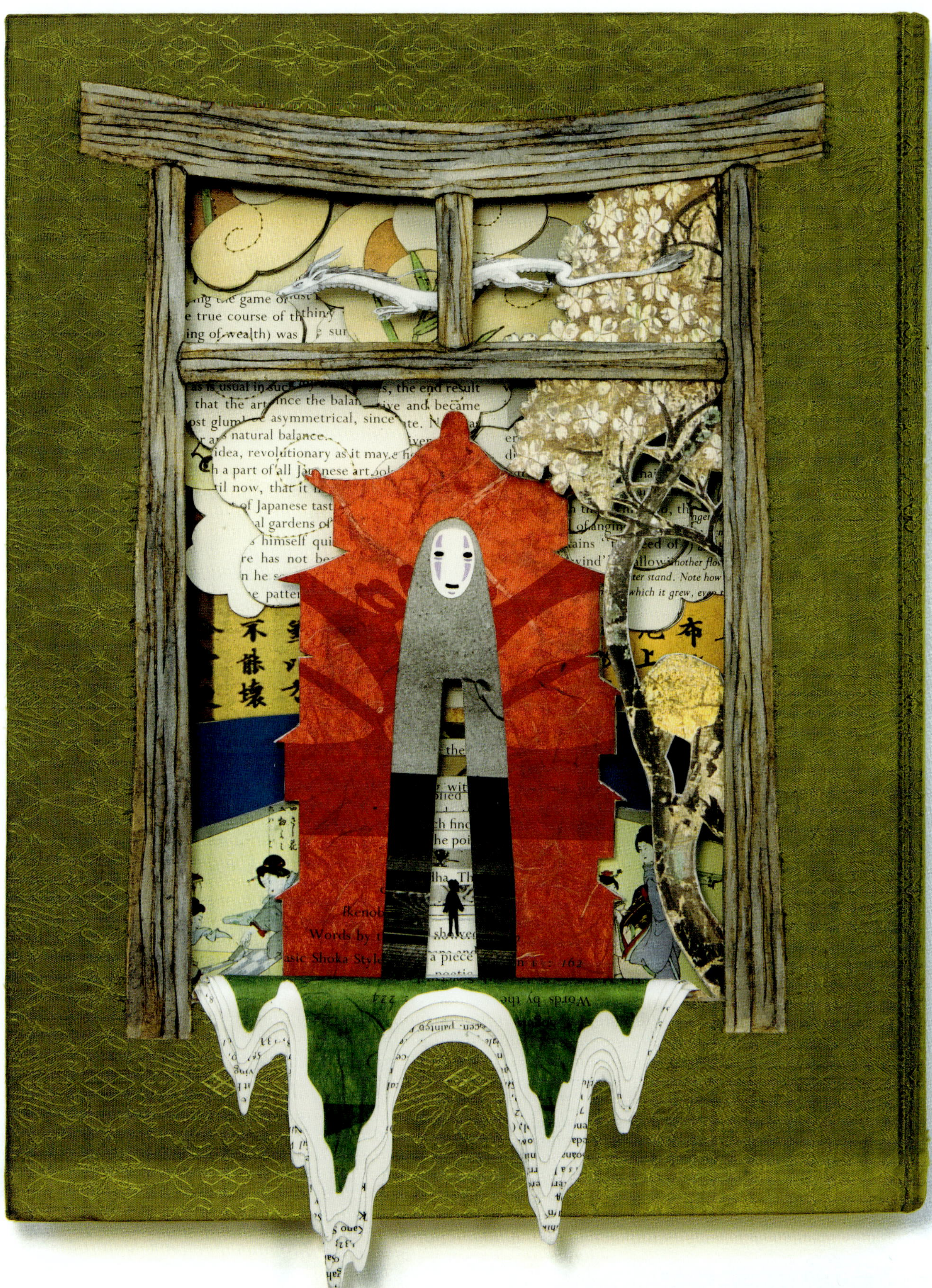

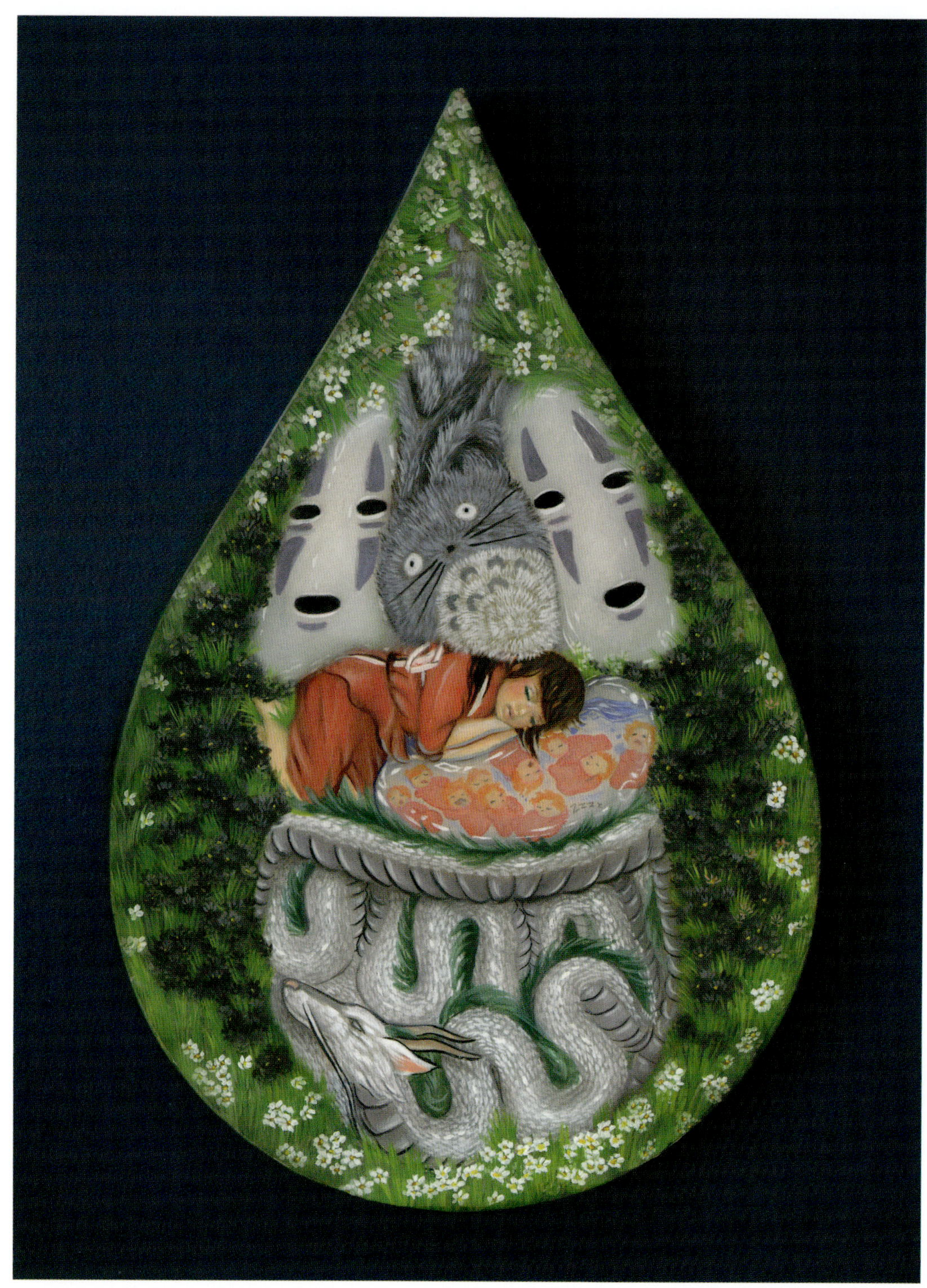

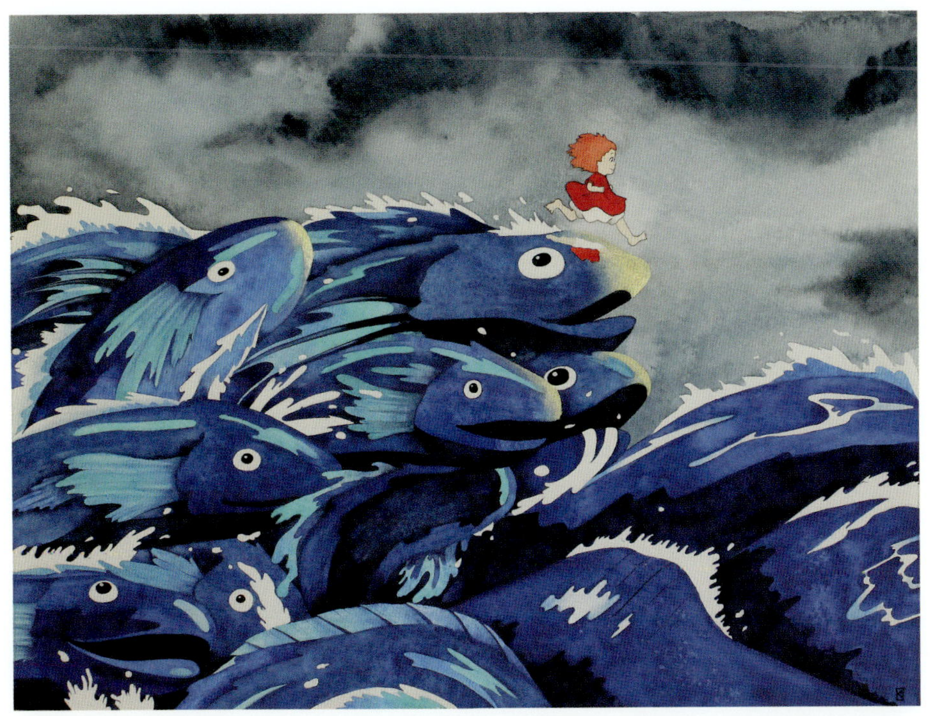

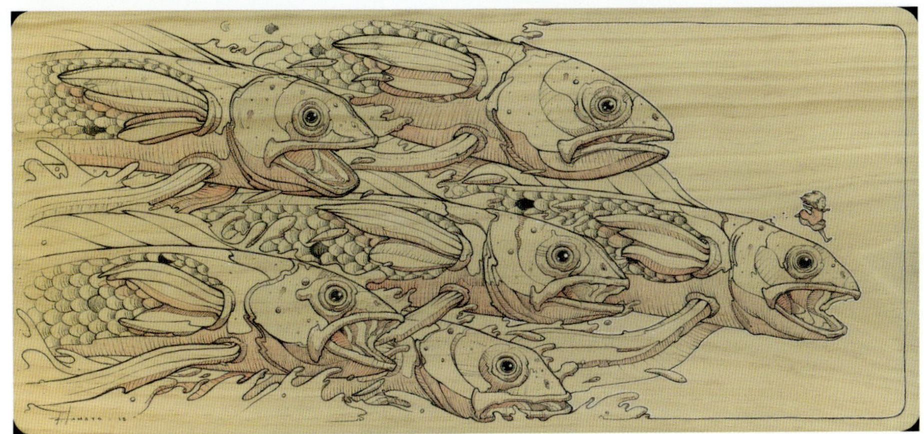

RELM

LEFT PAGE

Miyazaki Fan Anatomy

Oil on teardrop wood panel.
8.6 x 13.75".

KATE SNOW

TOP

Ponyo is Free

Watercolor and gold gouache.
14 x 11".

ROLAND TAMAYO

BOTTOM

Ponyo's Leap

Ink and pencil on wood.
24 x 11".

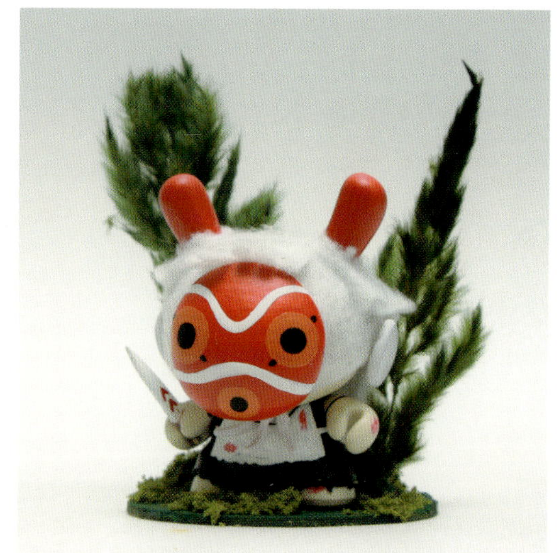

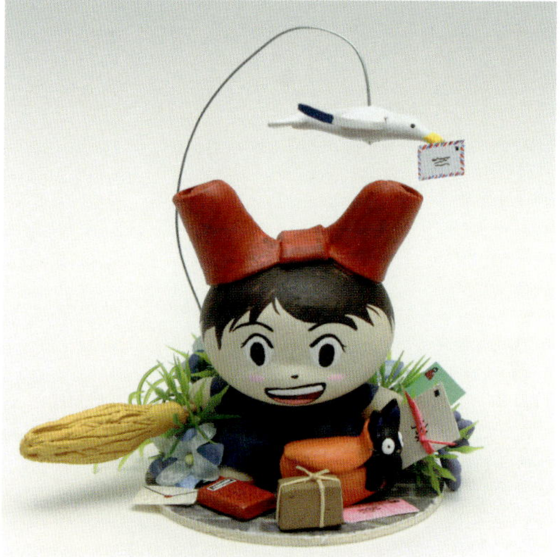

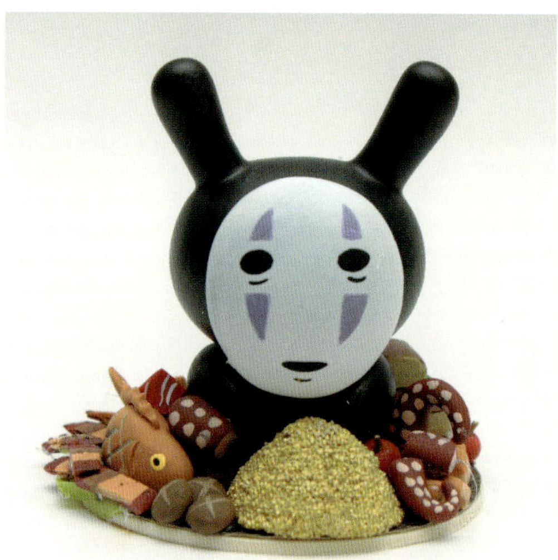

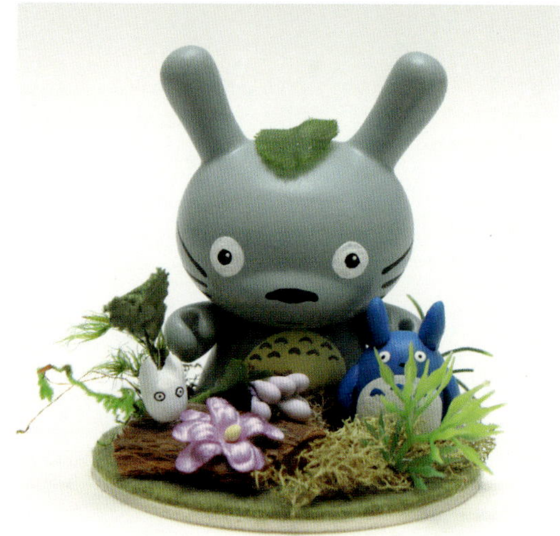

ZARD APUYA

TOP LEFT
Princess Mononoke
Vinyl toy, mixed media.
3.5 x 2.5 x 2.5".

BOTTOM LEFT
No Face
Vinyl toy, mixed media.
3 x 2.5 x 2.5".

TOP RIGHT
Kiki
Vinyl toy, mixed media.
4 x 2.5 x 2.5".

BOTTOM RIGHT
Totoro
Vinyl toy, mixed media.
3 x 2.5 x 2.5".

RIGHT PAGE, TOP
Cafe Miyazaki
Mixed media.
11 x 15 x 3.5".

RIGHT PAGE, BOTTOM
Miyazaki Wagashi
Mixed media.
6 x 10 x 2.5".

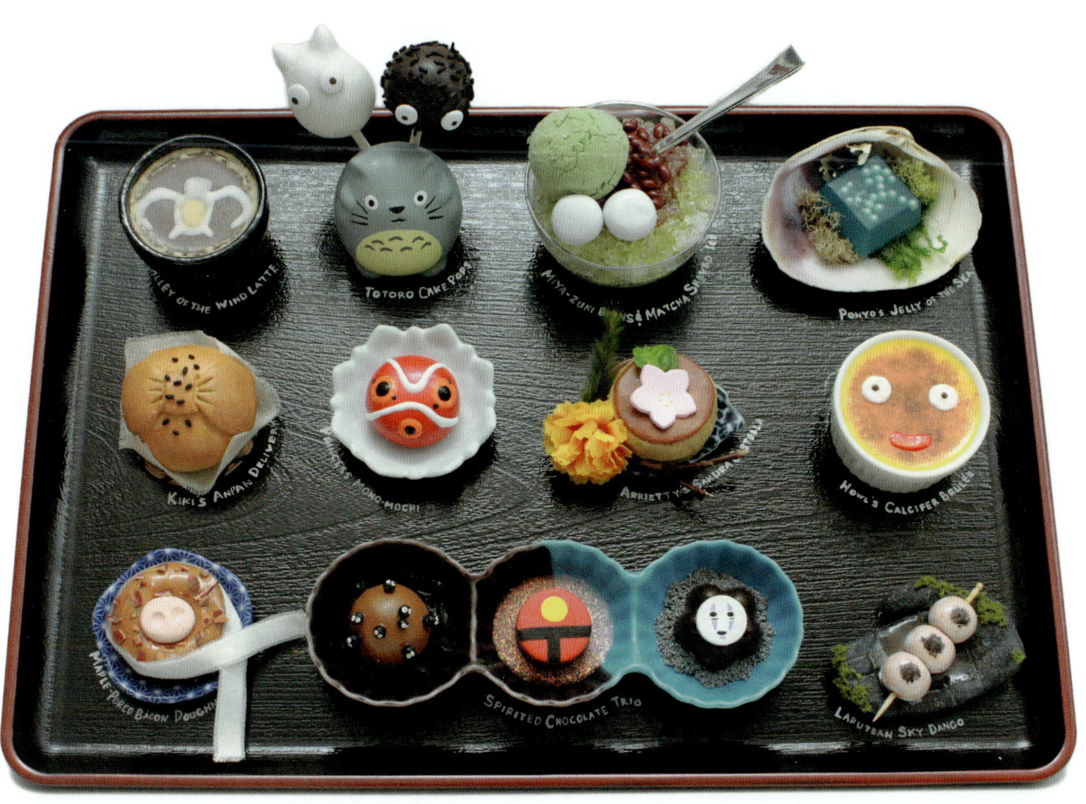
Totoro Cake Pops
Ponyo's Jelly of the Sea
Howl's Calcifer Brulée
Spirited Chocolate Trio
Laputean Sky Dango

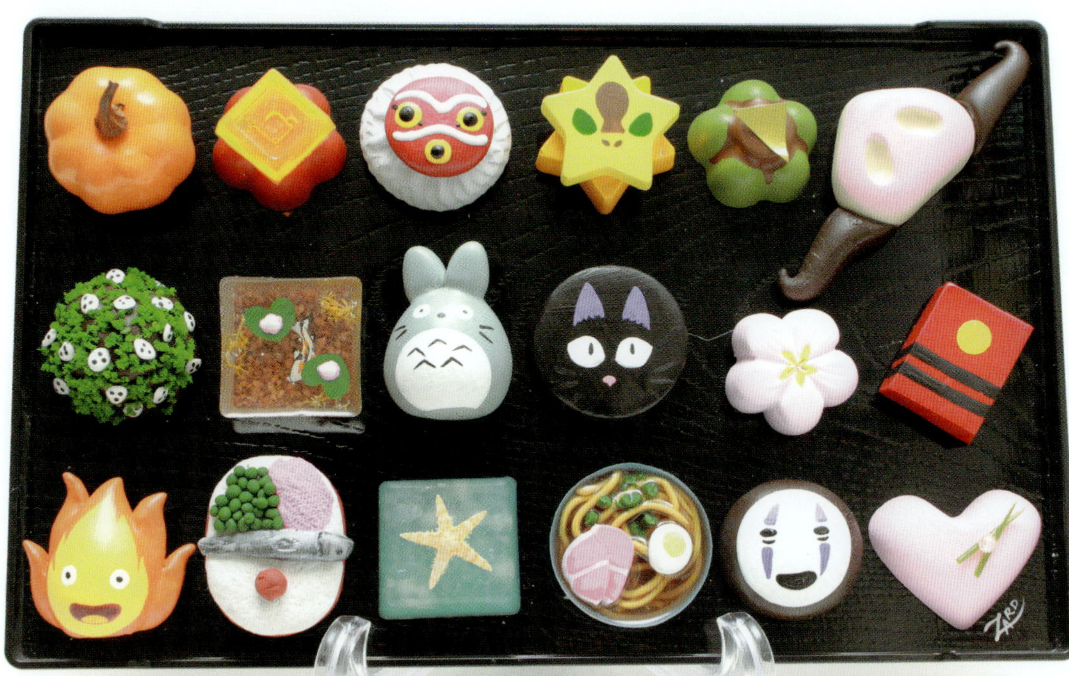

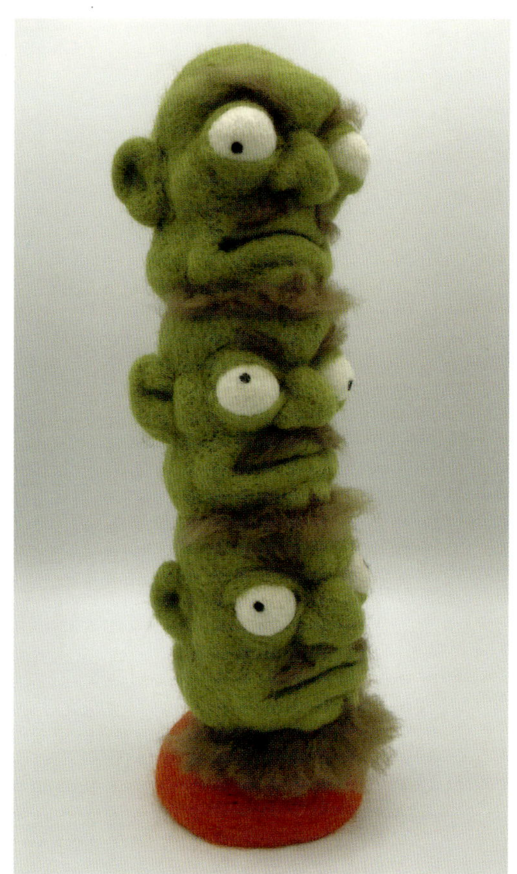

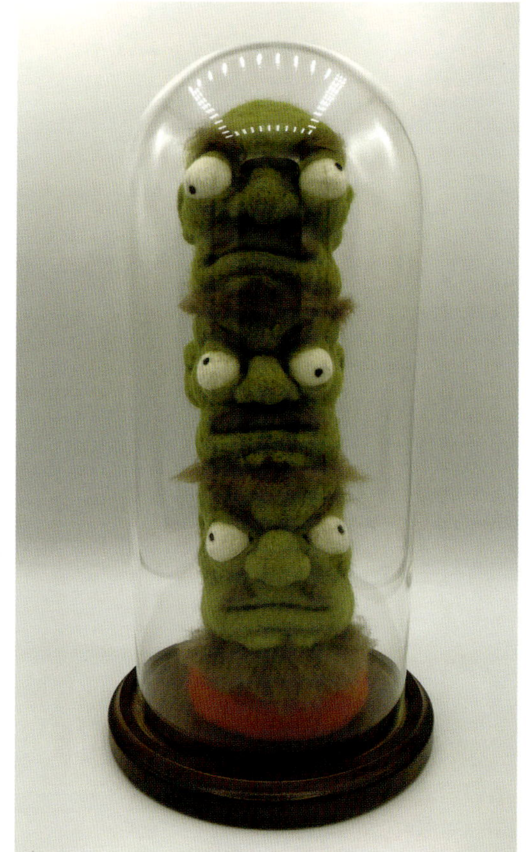

ED MIRONIUK

ABOVE

Kashira

Needlefelt sculpture.
4 x 12" (4 x 14" with glass dome).

DAVID MOSCATI

RIGHT PAGE

No Face

Mixed media on paper.
8 x 10".

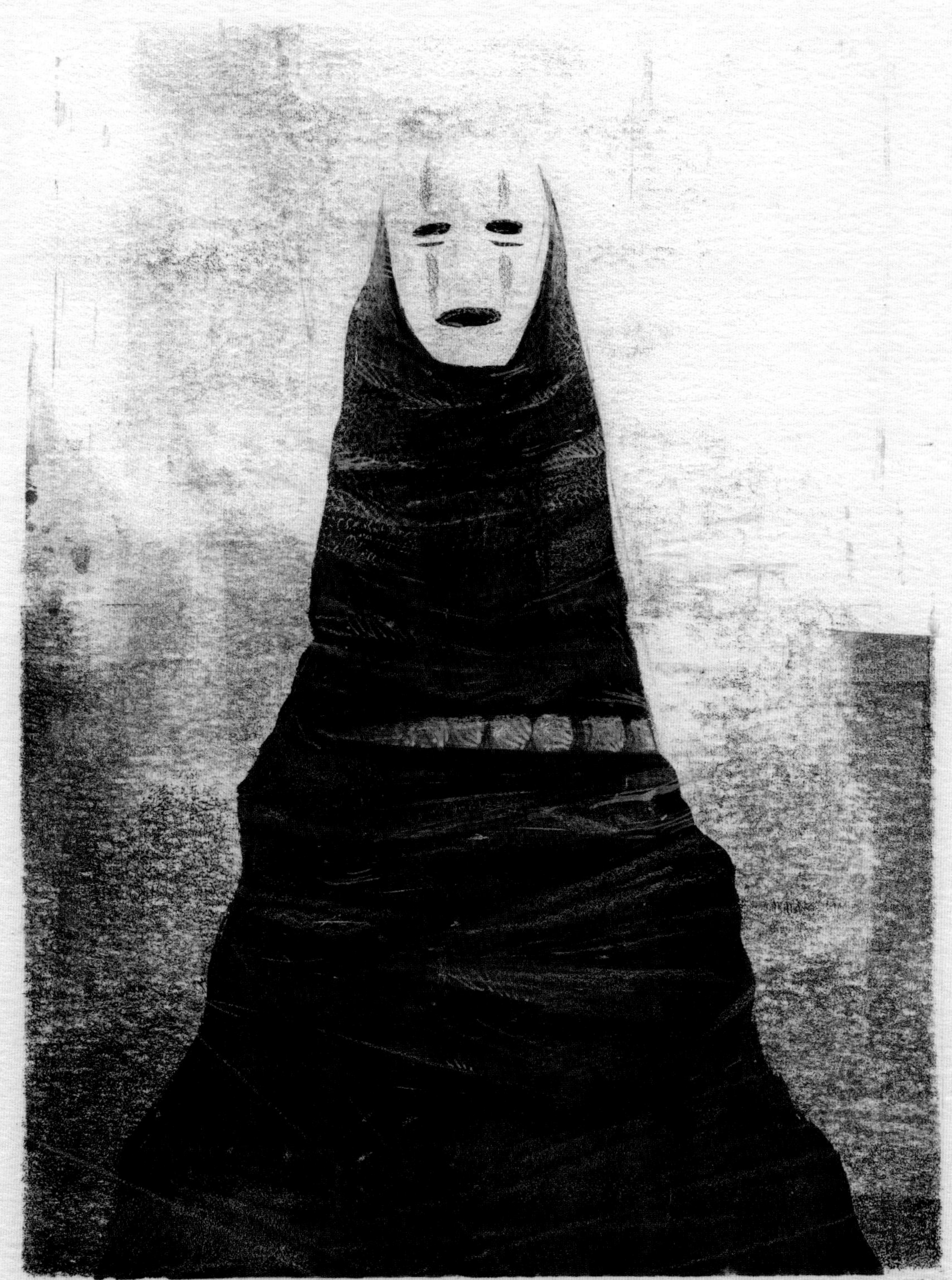
D.MOSCATI '17

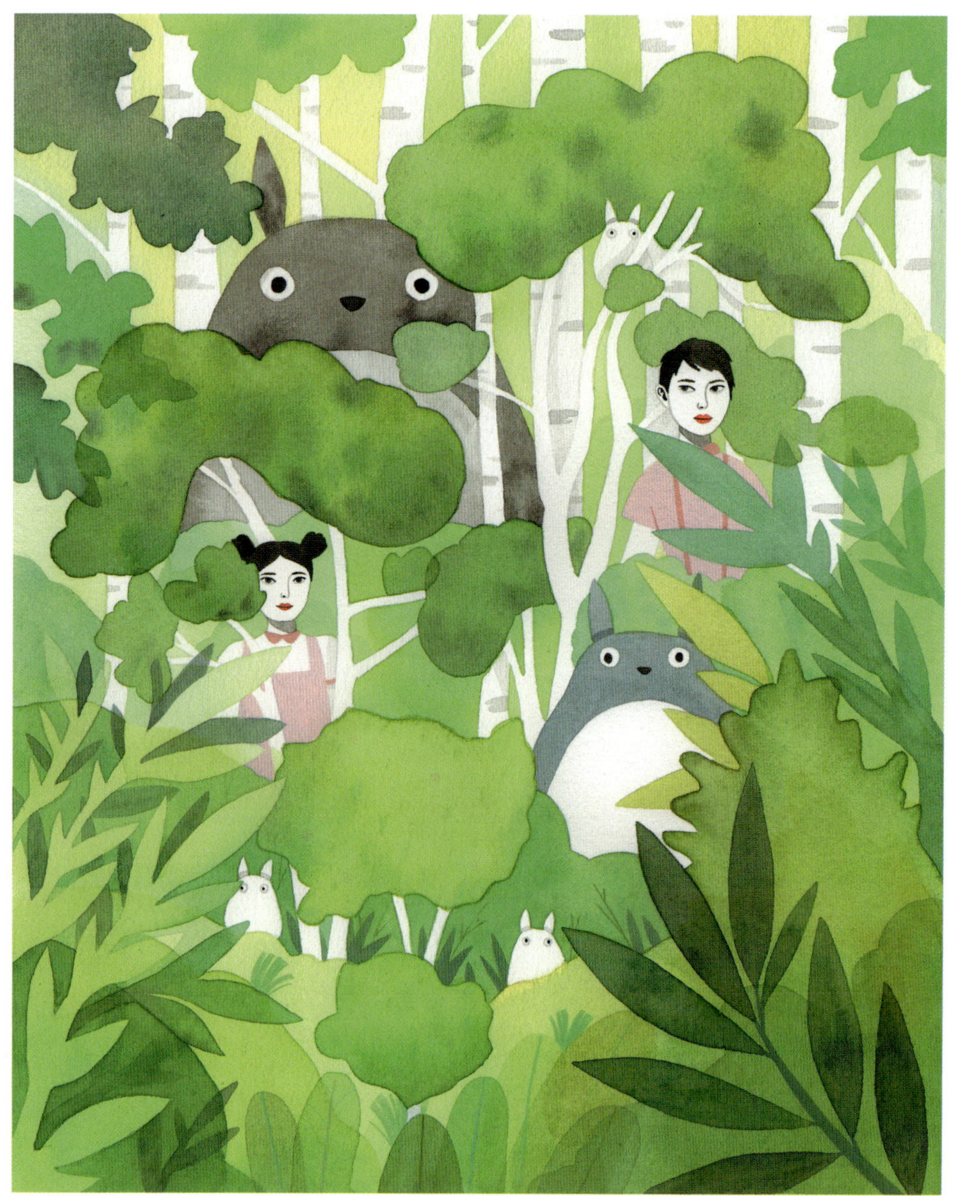

MONICA GARWOOD

ABOVE
Totoro's Forest
Watercolor. 11 x 14".

RIGHT PAGE
Meeting Totoro
Watercolor. 16 x 20".

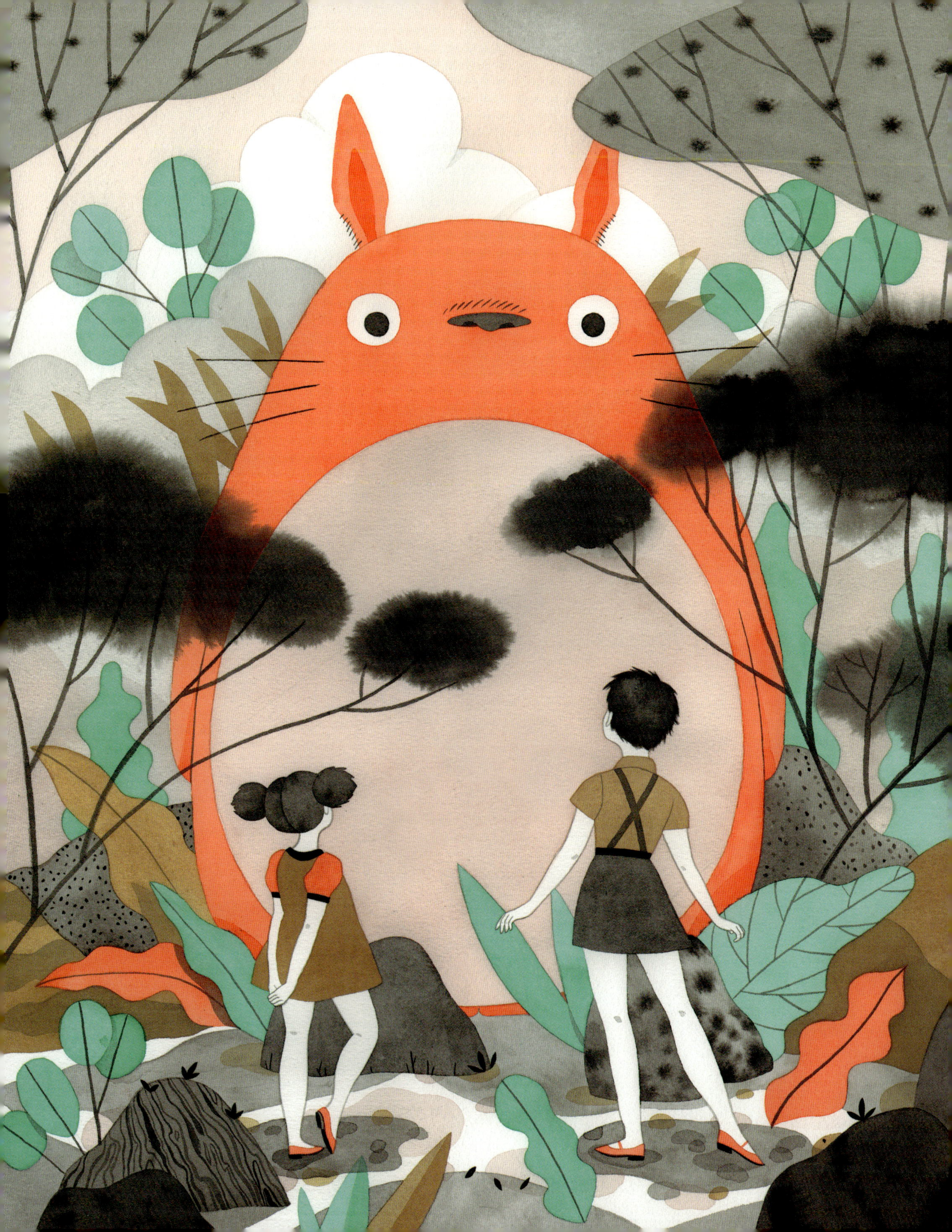

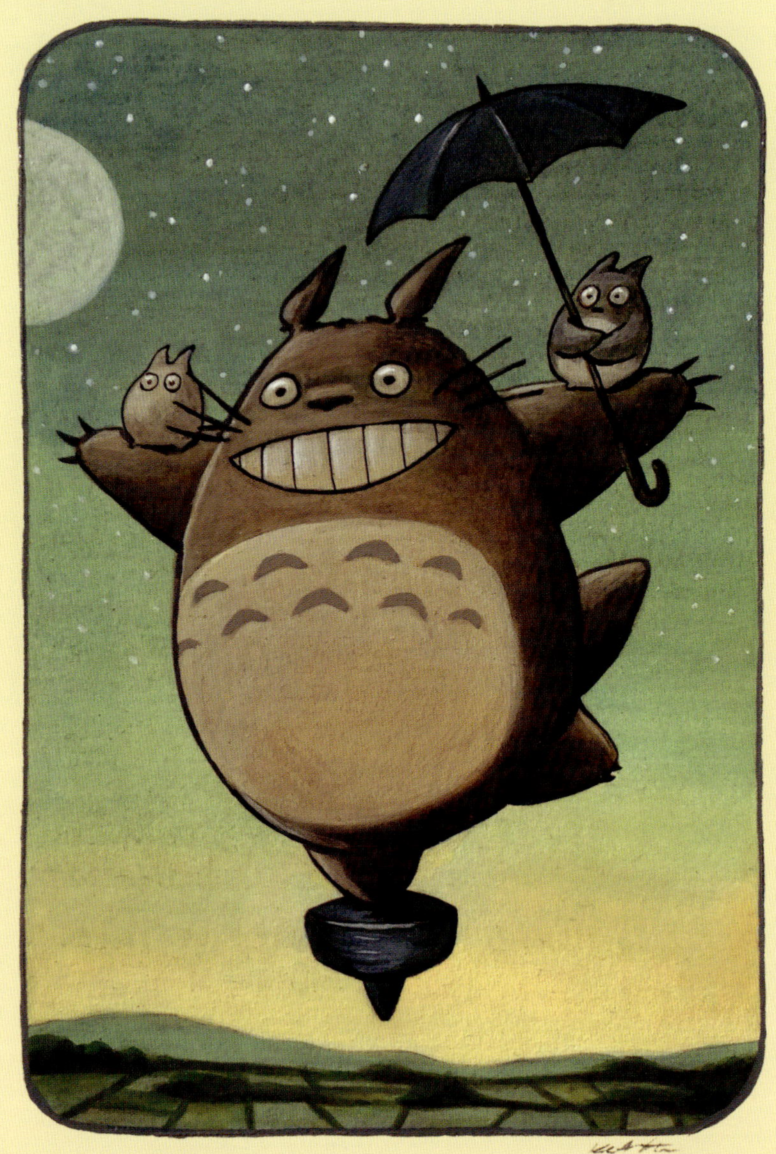

KEITH CARTER

ABOVE

To the Rescue
Acrylic on illustration board. 5 x 7".

DEREK BALLARD

RIGHT PAGE

Rather Be a Pig than a Fascist
Screen print. 9 x 24".

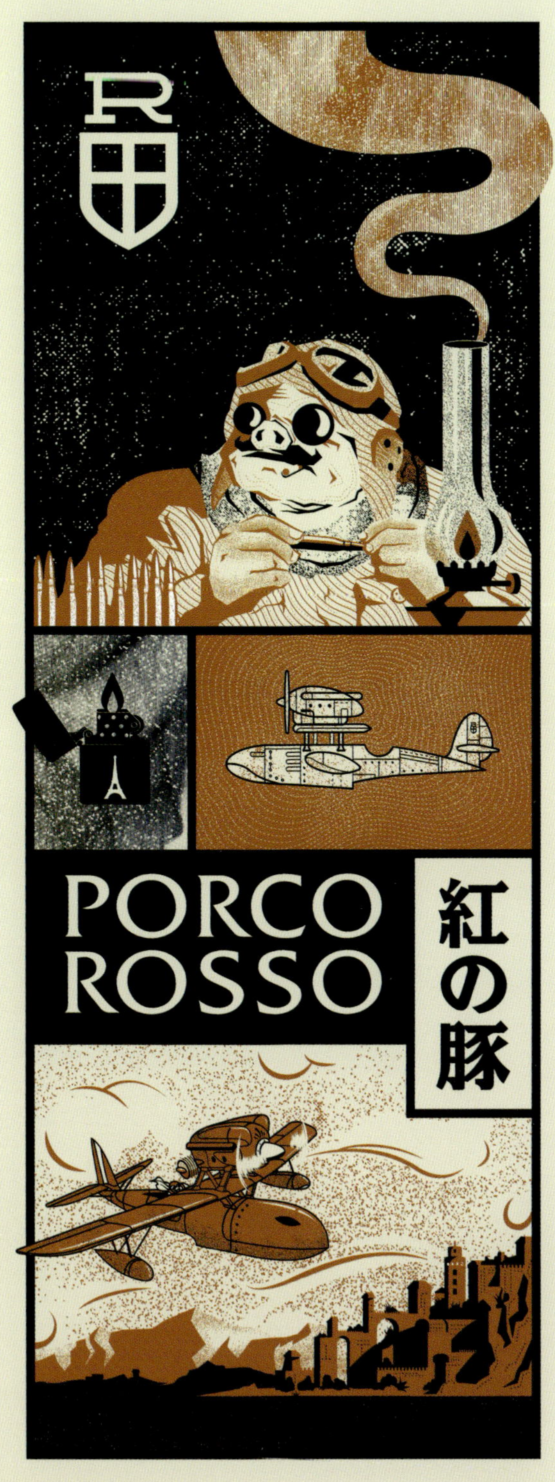
R
PORCO
ROSSO
紅の豚

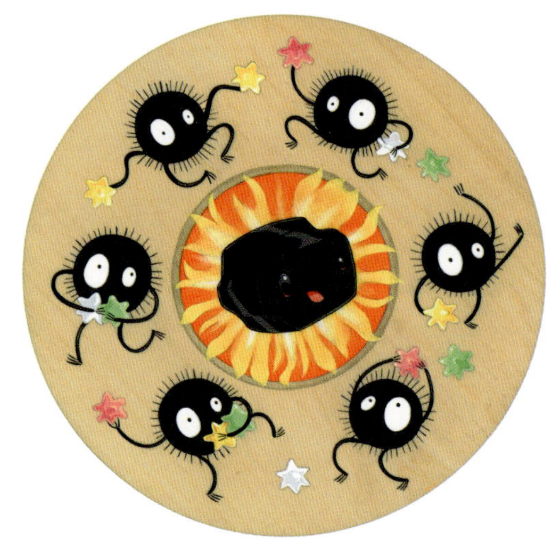

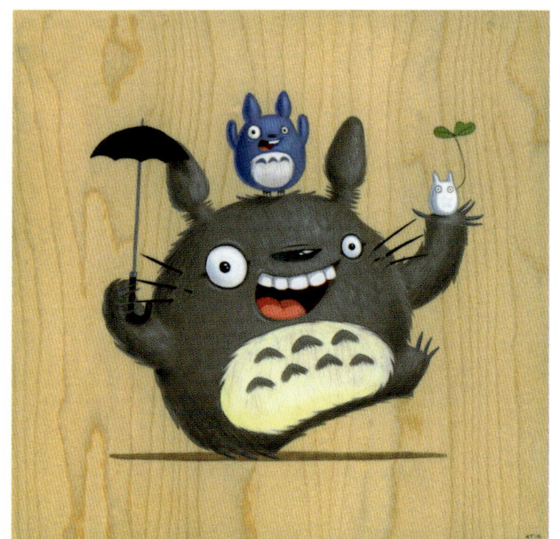

CUDDLY RIGOR MORTIS

LEFT
Susuwatari
Acrylic on wood. 10" diameter.

RIGHT
Totorooooo
Acrylic on maple. 8 x 8".

RIGHT PAGE
Teto
Acrylic on wood. 9 x 12".

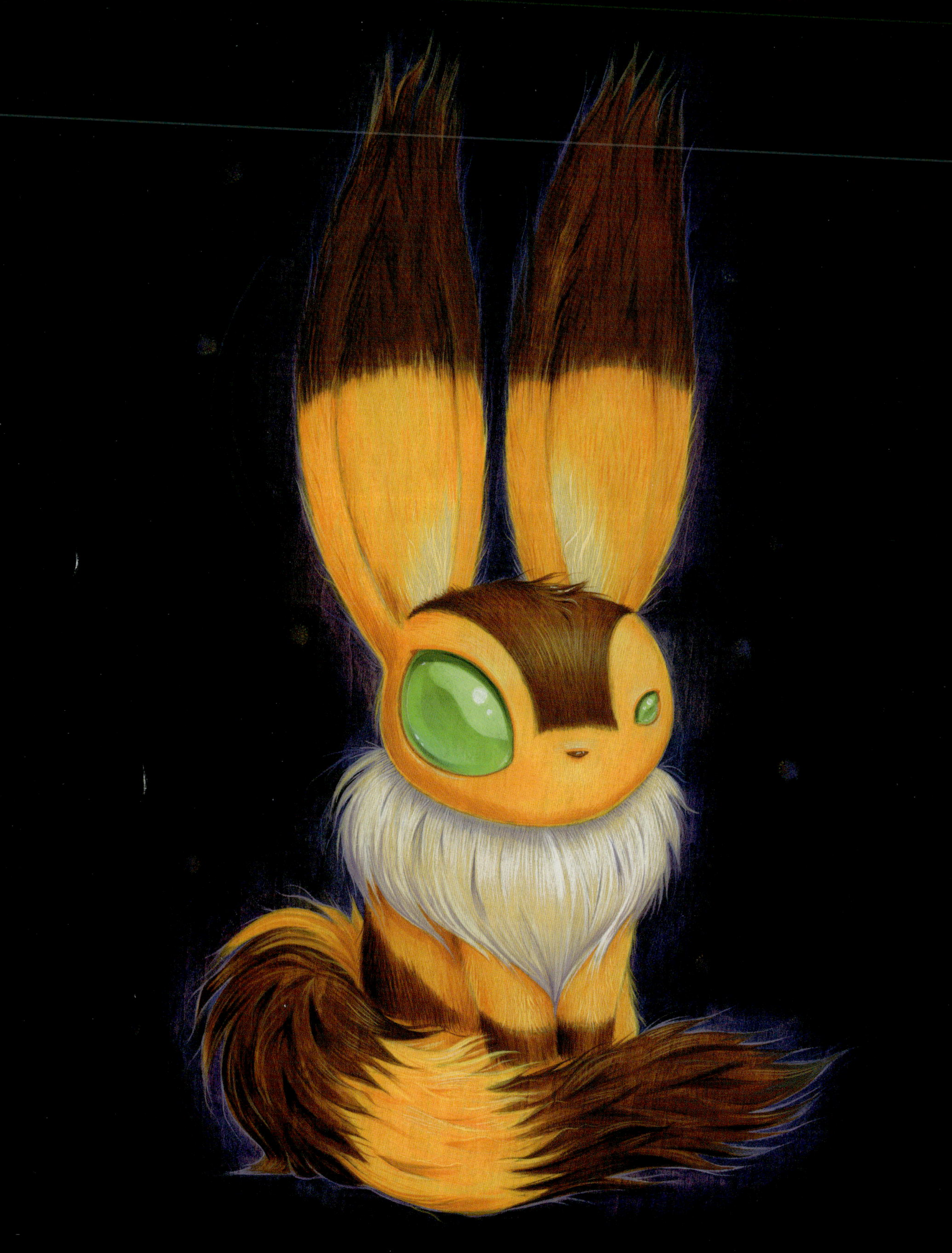

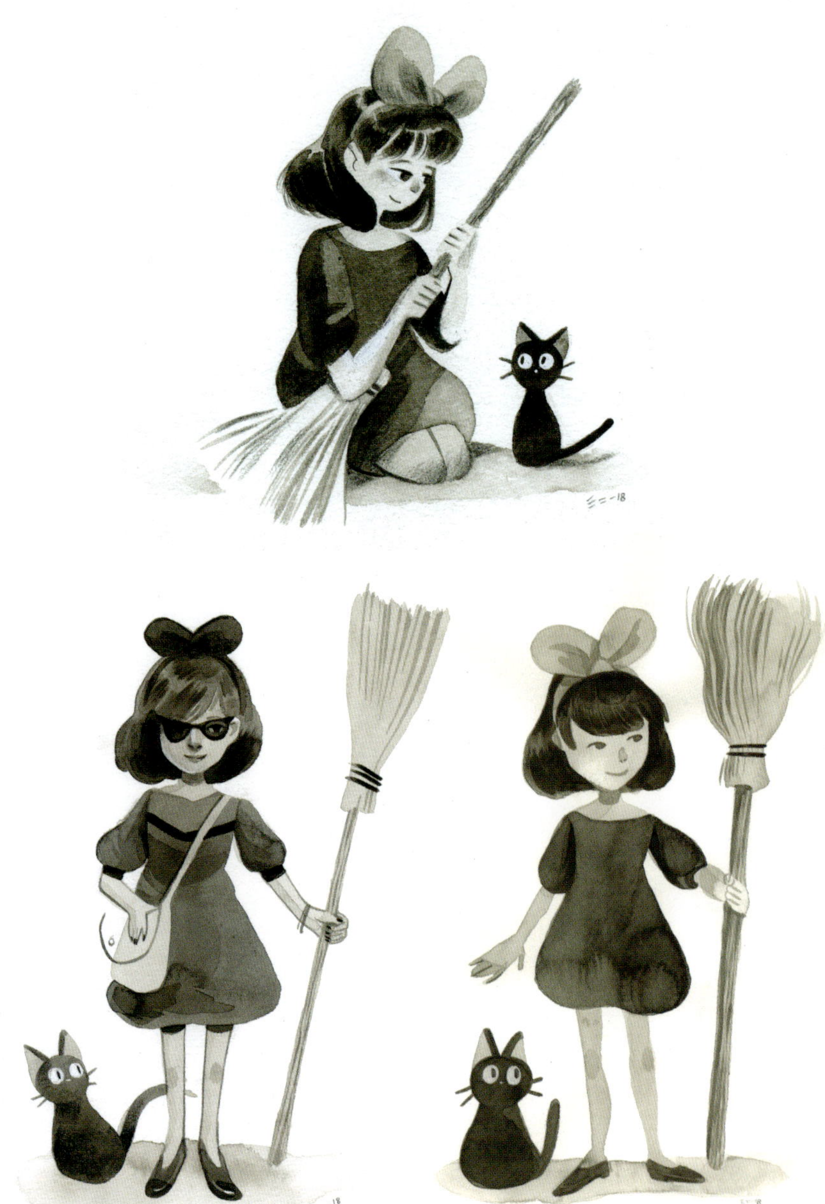

MINNIE PHAN

TOP

New Beginnings

Ink, color pencil and pen .
6 x 6".

BOTTOM LEFT

At Your Service

Ink, color pencil and pen .
7.5 x 10".

BOTTOM RIGHT

Witch In Training

Ink, color pencil and pen .
7.5 x 10".

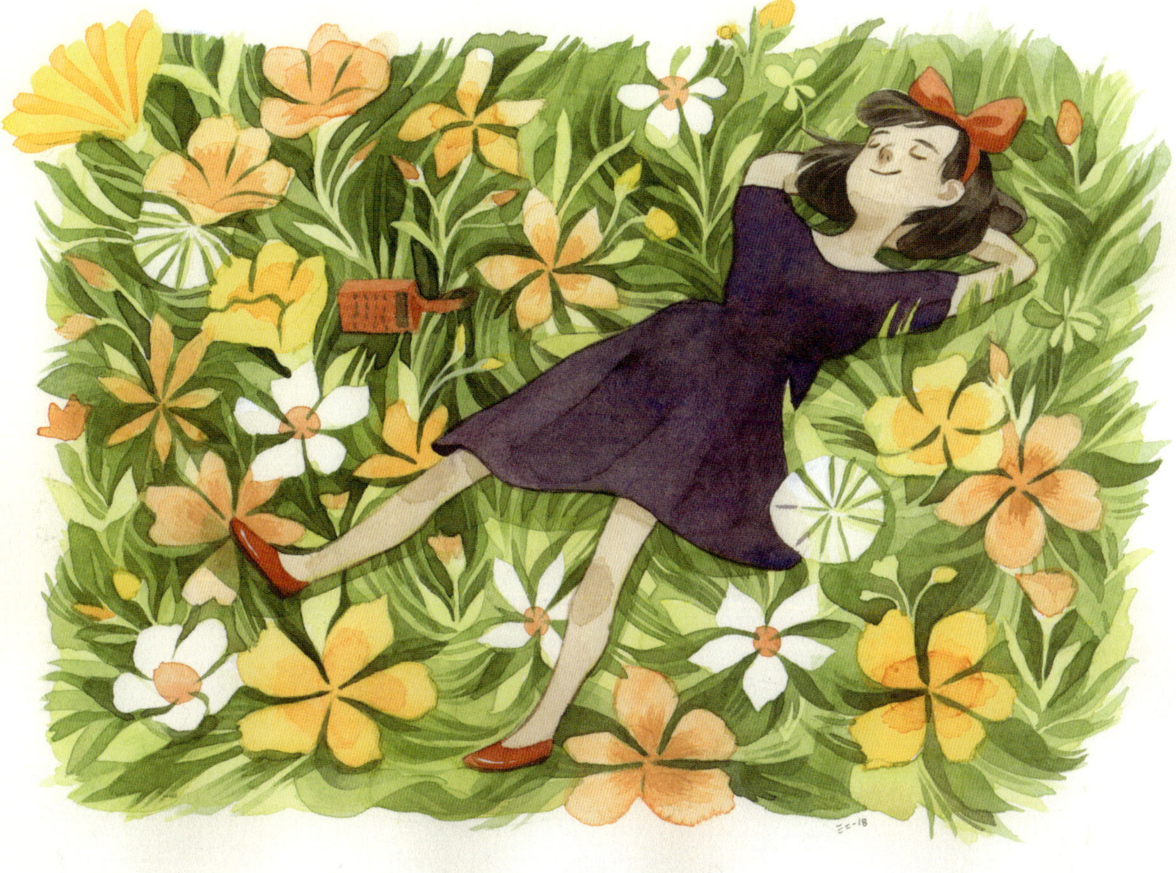

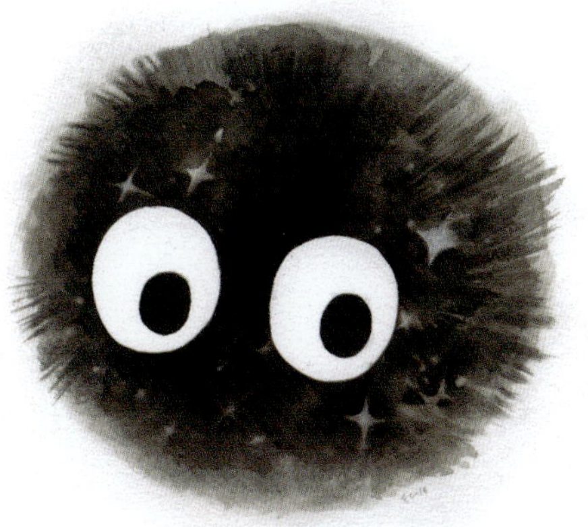

TOP

Today's the Day

Watercolor.
12 x 9".

BOTTOM

Little Friend

Graphite, ink, watercolor and color pencil. 9 x 9".

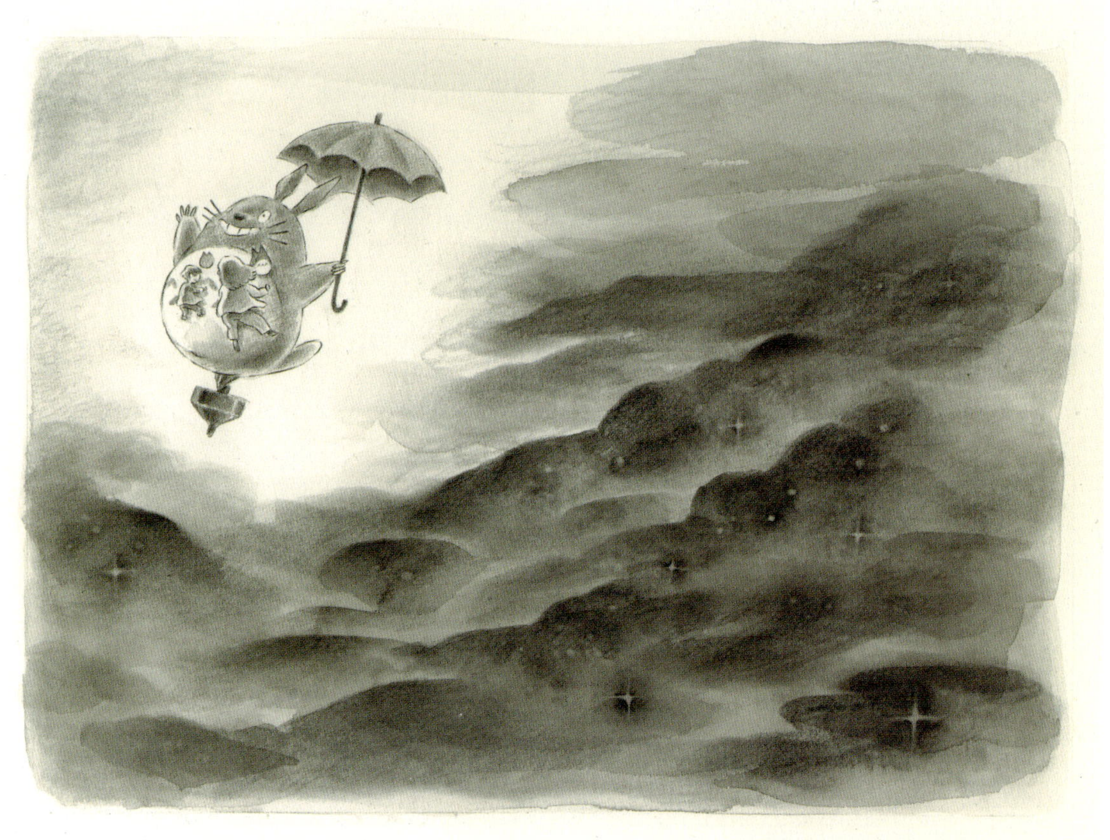

MINNIE PHAN

ABOVE

Into the Night

Risograph. 14.75 x 11".

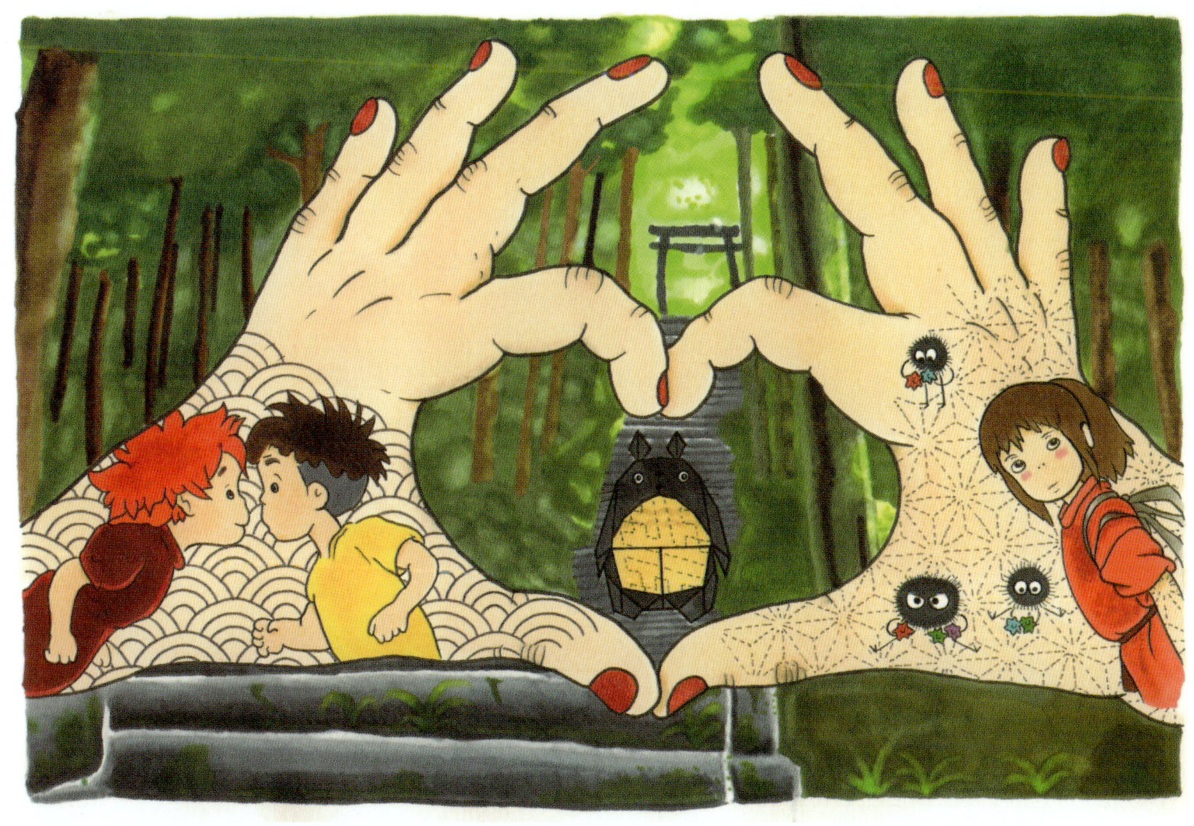

KEITH LIN

ABOVE

A Wild Totoro Appears!

Ink and watercolor on paper. 11 x 8".

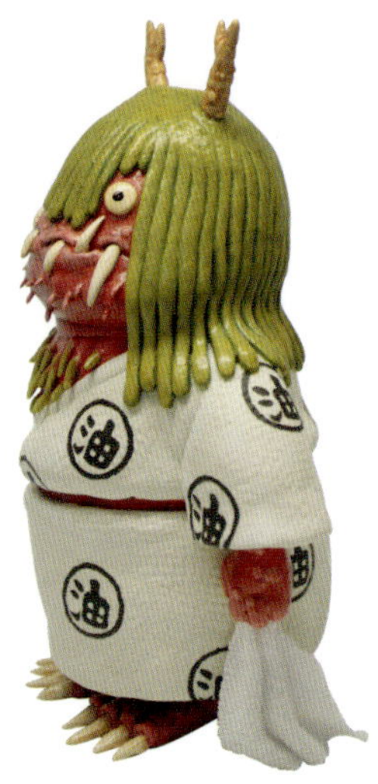

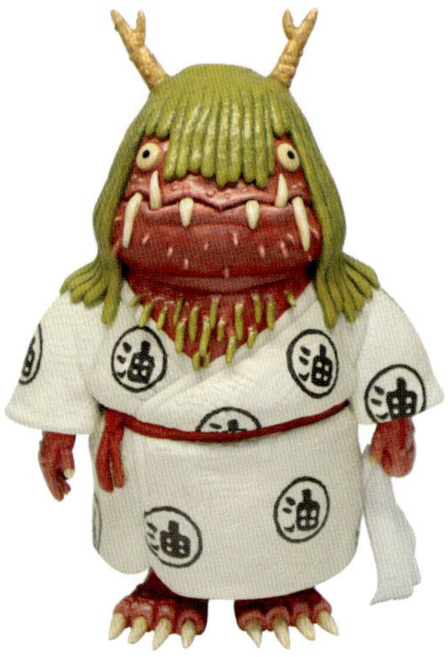

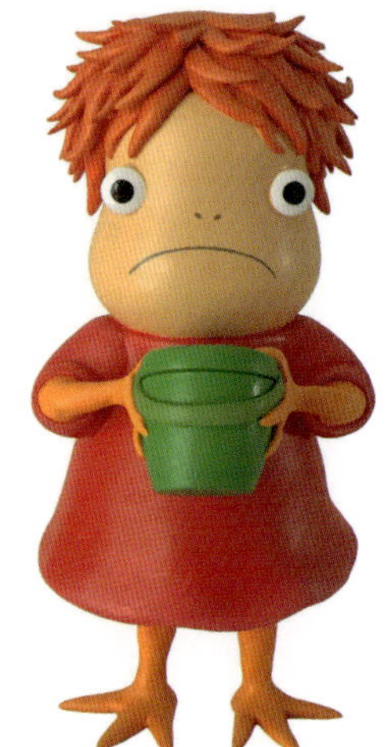

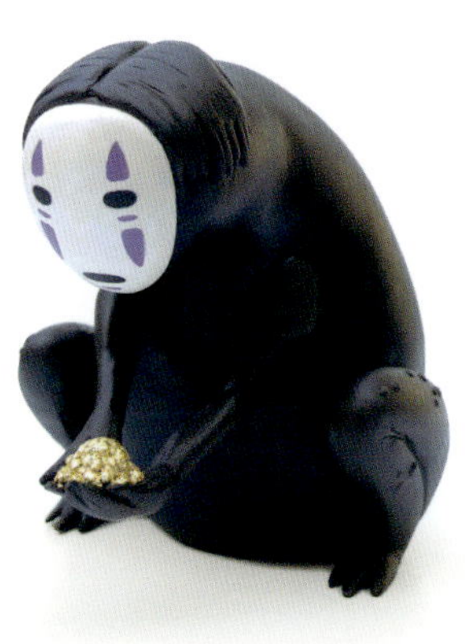

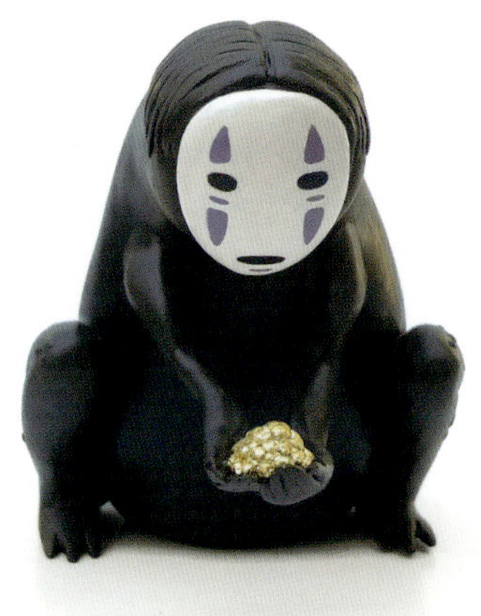

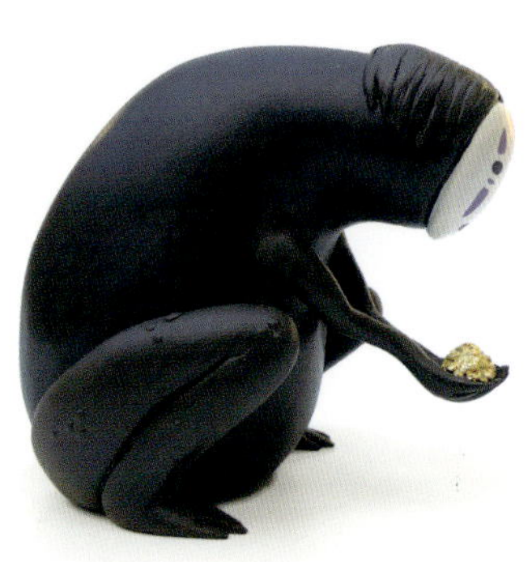

ERIC ALTHIN

TOP LEFT AND CENTER

Ushioni

Epoxy clay, acrylics, and imitation gold. 4 x 3.5 x 4".

TOP RIGHT

Mermaid

Epoxy clay. 7".

BOTTOM

Greed

Epoxy clay, acrylics, and imitation gold. 4 x 3.5 x 4".

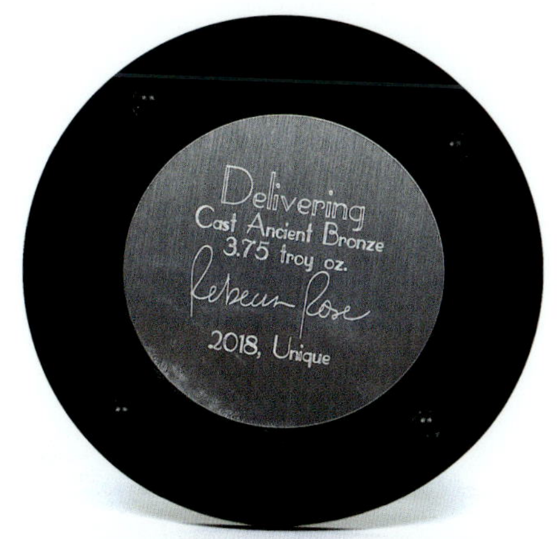

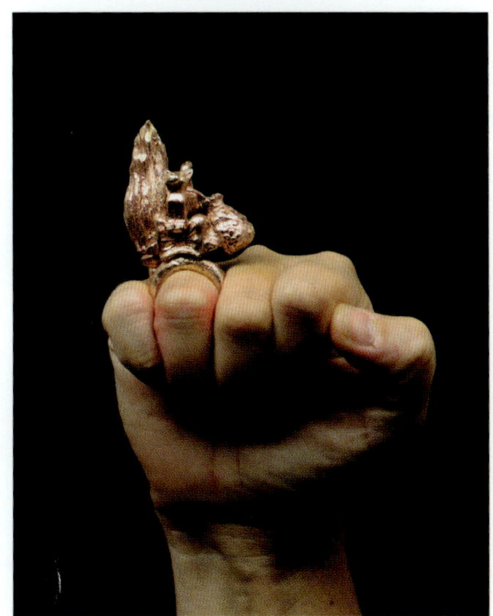

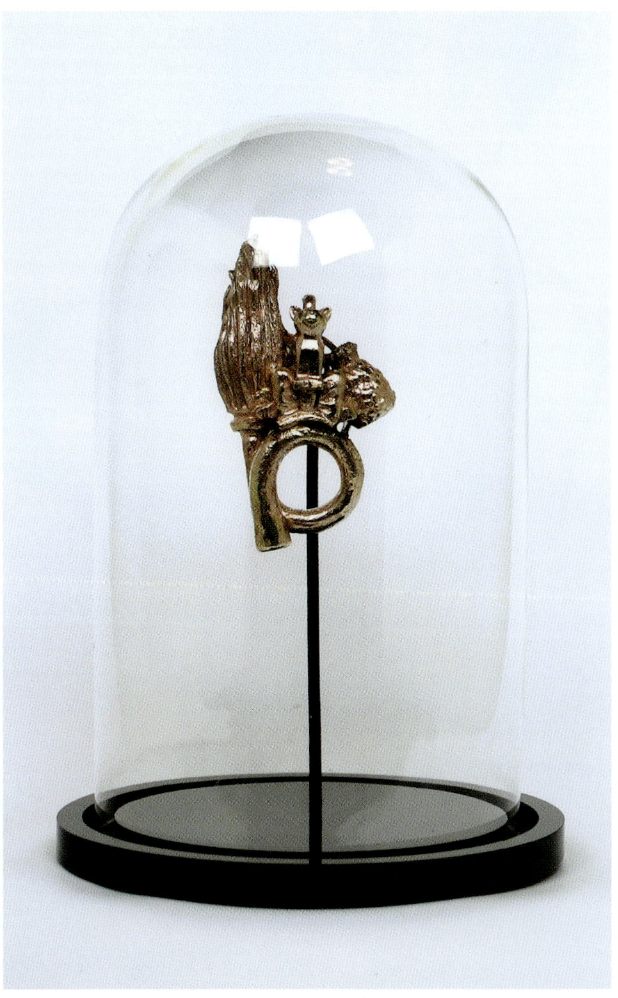

REBECCA ROSE

ABOVE

Delivering

3.75 troy oz. cast ancient bronze.
2.5 x 1 x 1.5" (8 x 4 x 4").

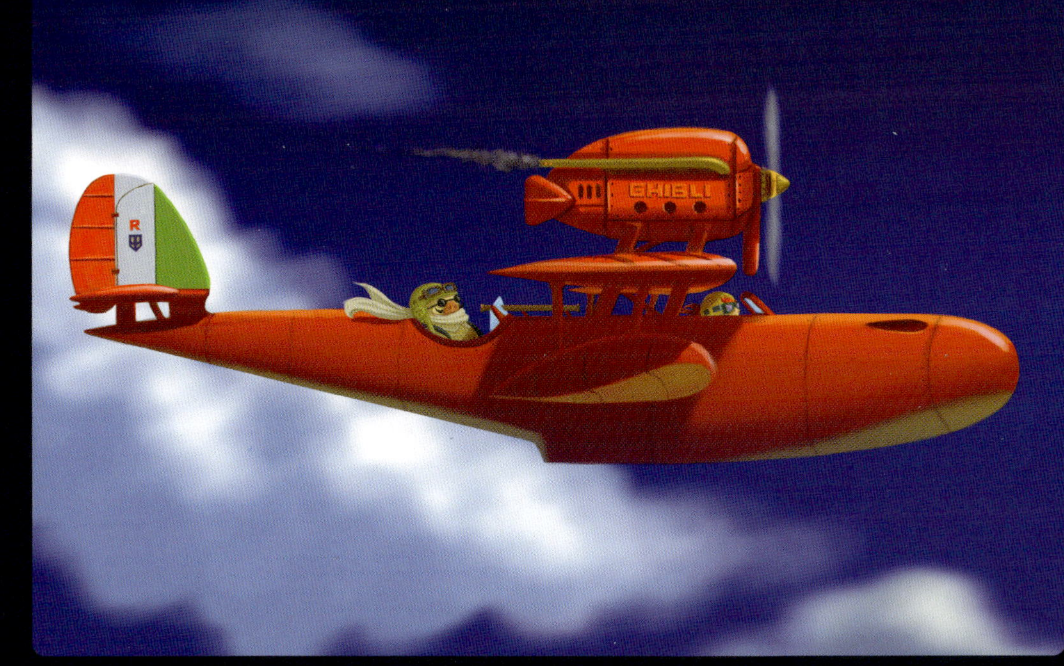

RUEL PASCUAL

ABOVE

Porco Rosso

Digital print. 19 x 13".

MAINGER (GERMAIN BARTHELEMY)

RIGHT PAGE

Spirited Away

Archival pigment print. 16 x 24".

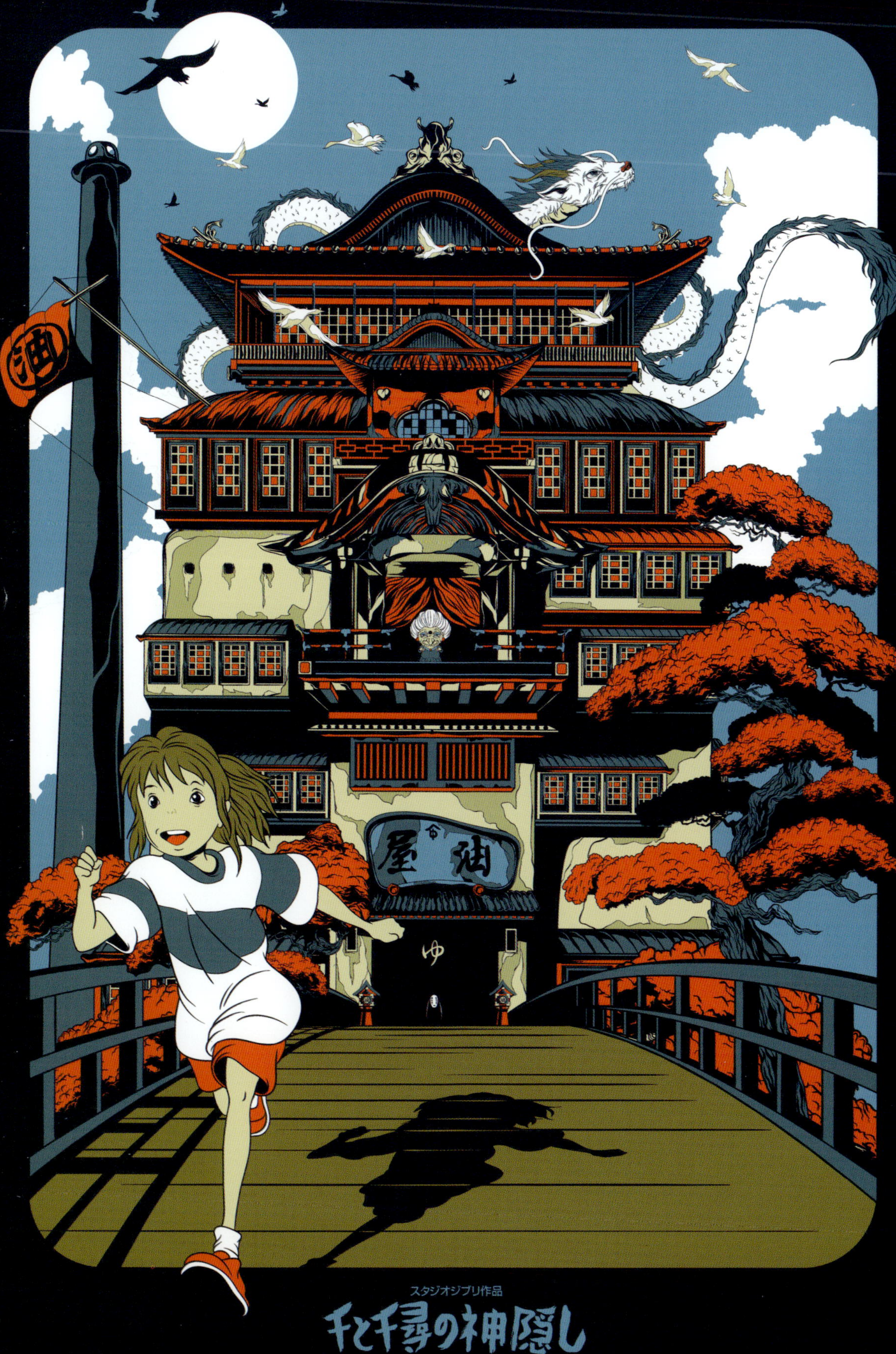
油
油屋
ゆ
スタジオジブリ作品
千と千尋の神隠し
MAINGER

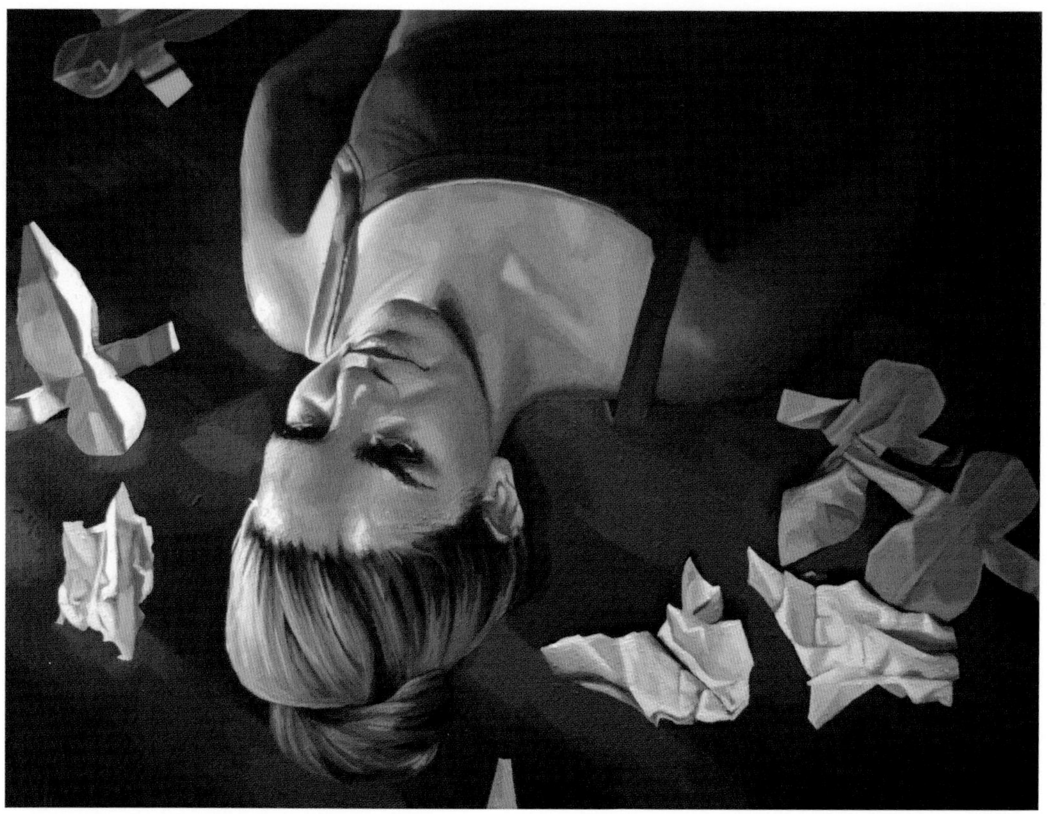

REBECCA MASON ADAMS

ABOVE

Julia vs. Shikigami

Acrylic on canvas. 18 x 14".

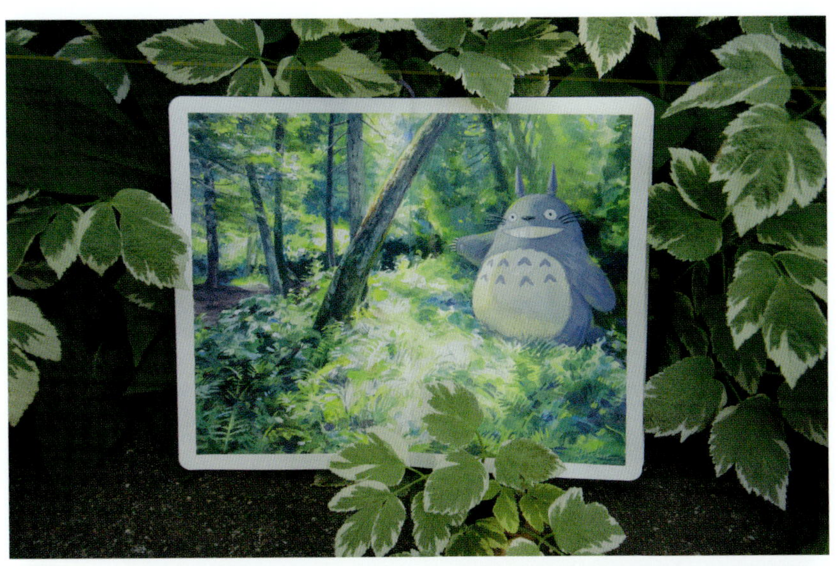

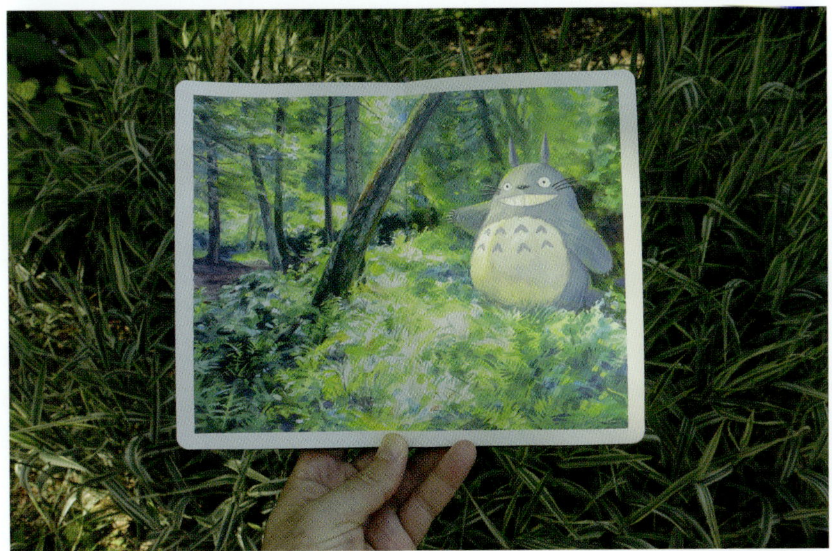

PRIMARY HUGHES

ABOVE

Keeper Of The Forest

Gouache on Moleskine sketchbook. 10 x 8".

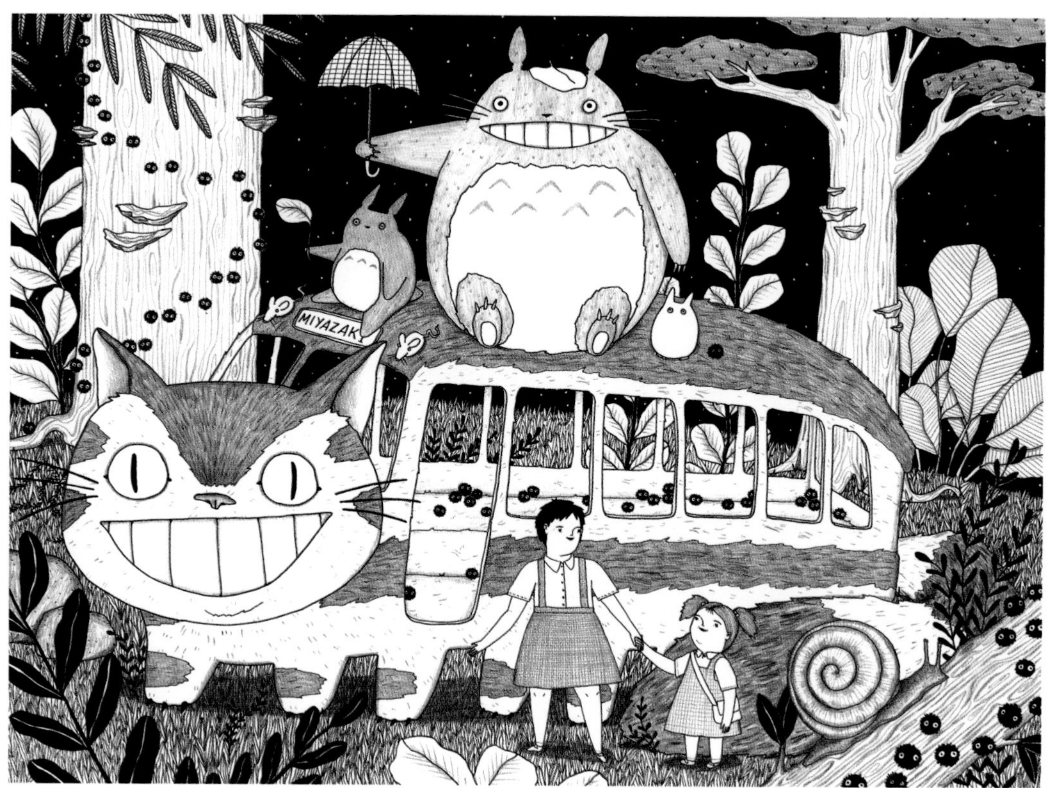

MAI LY DEGNAN

ABOVE

Catbus

Ink and graphite . 16 x 12".

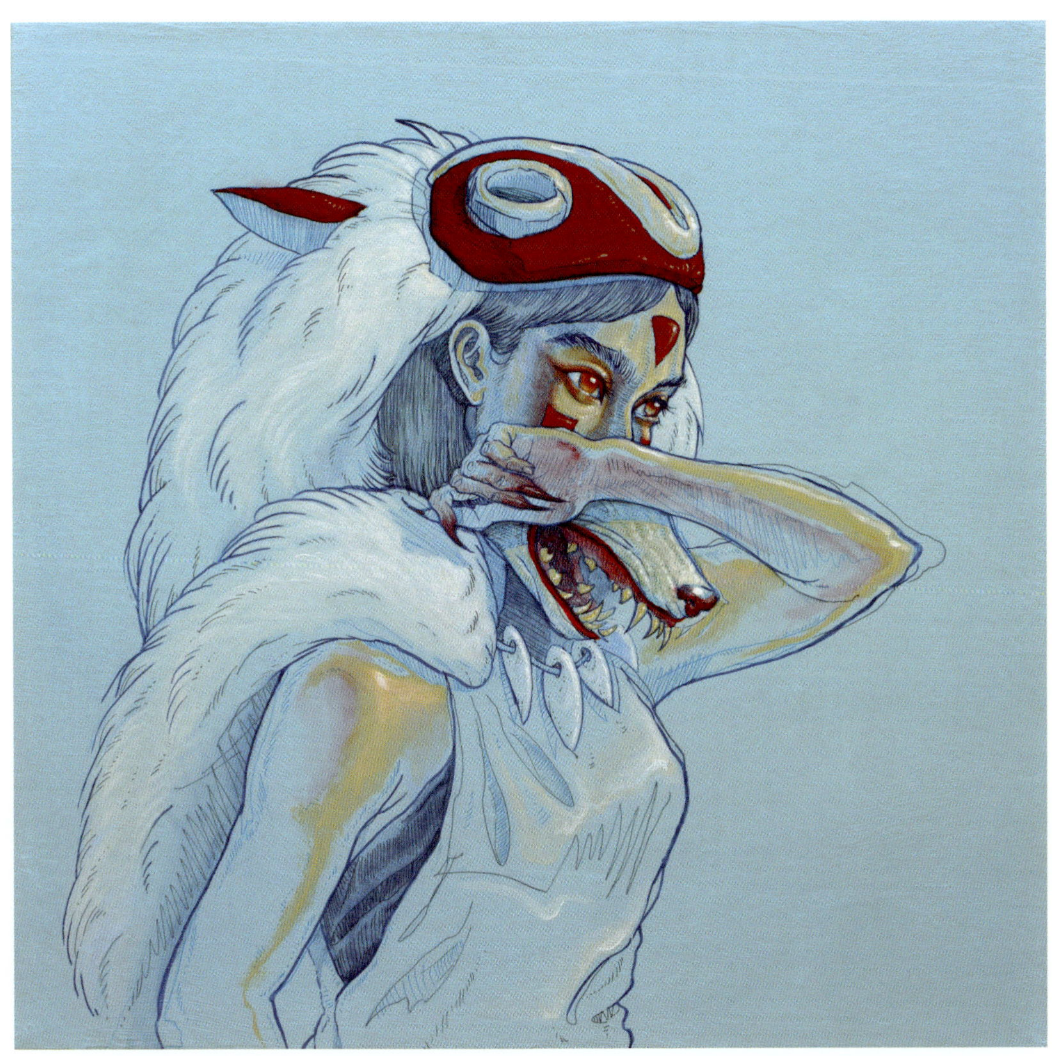

MANDY TSUNG

ABOVE

Mononoke

Ink and acrylic on canvas. 16 x 16".

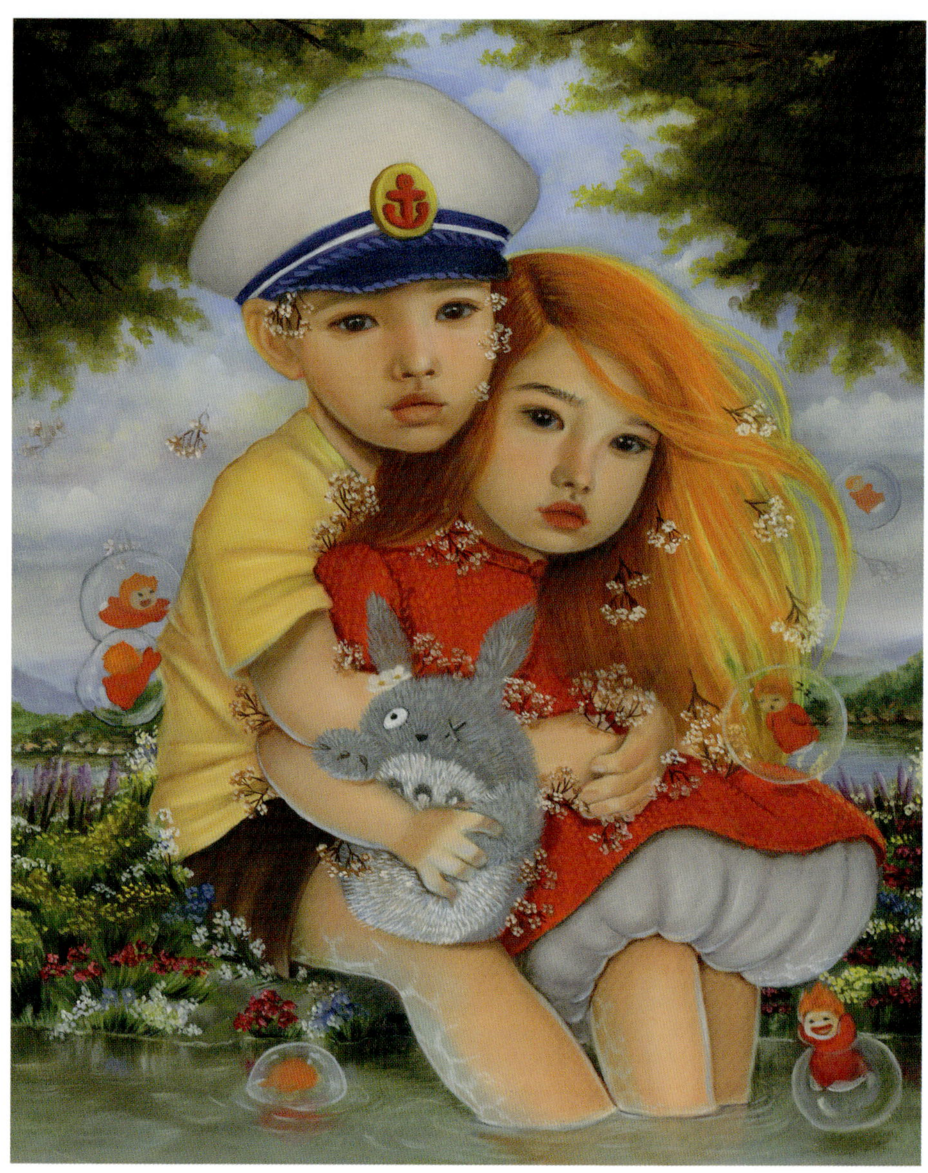

RELM

ABOVE

Sosuke & Ponyo
Oil on wood. 11 x 14".

VERONICA FISH

RIGHT PAGE

Arrietty in the Ivy
Gouache. 8 x 10".

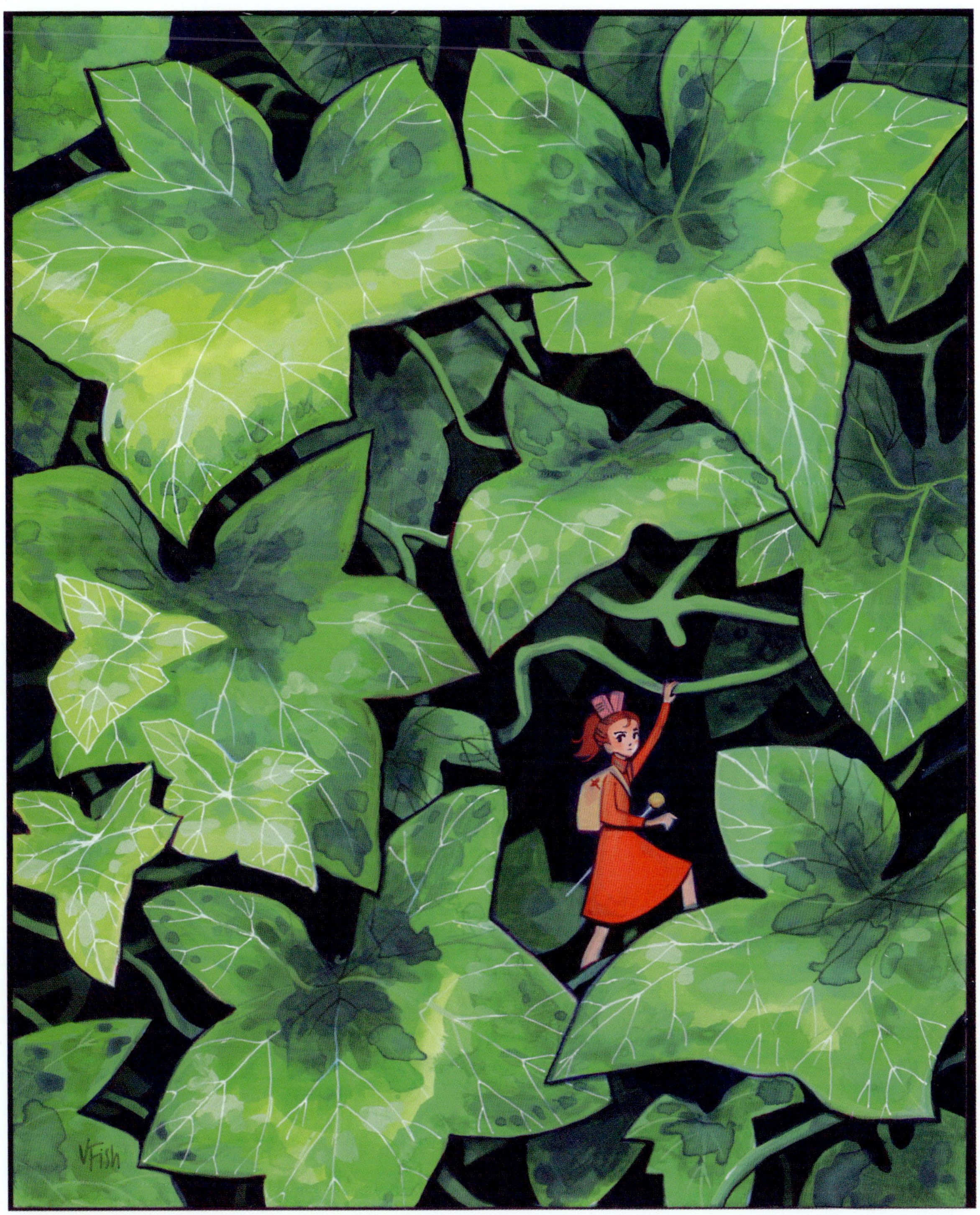
VFish

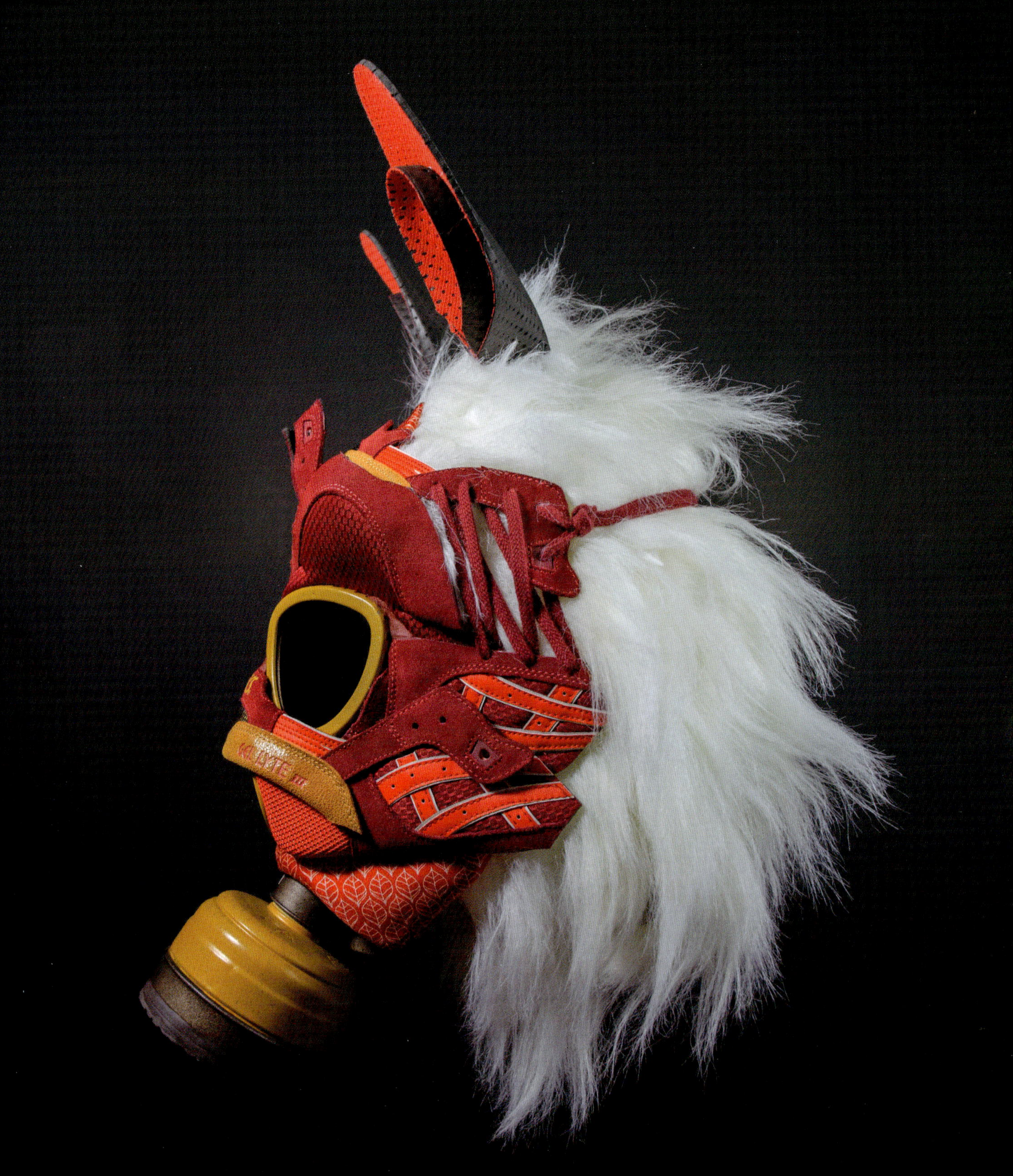

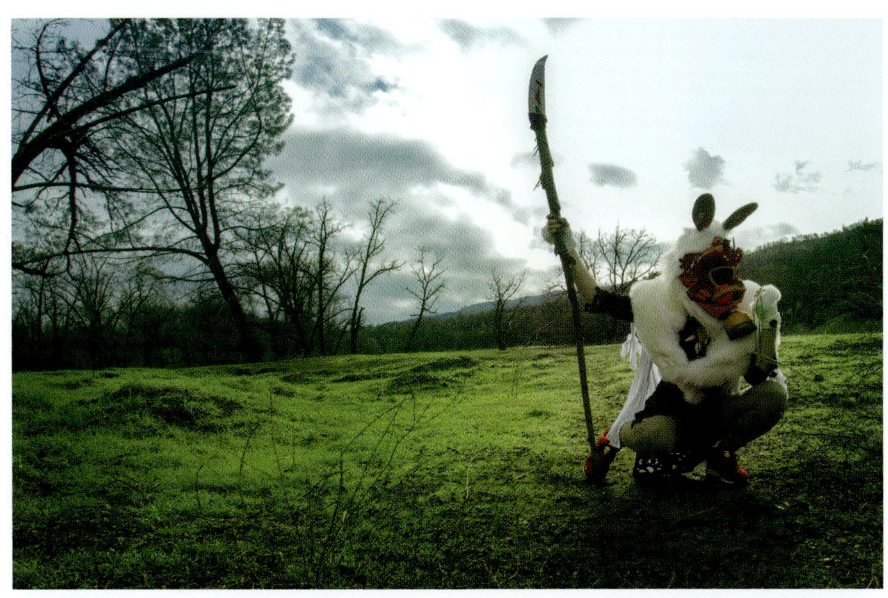

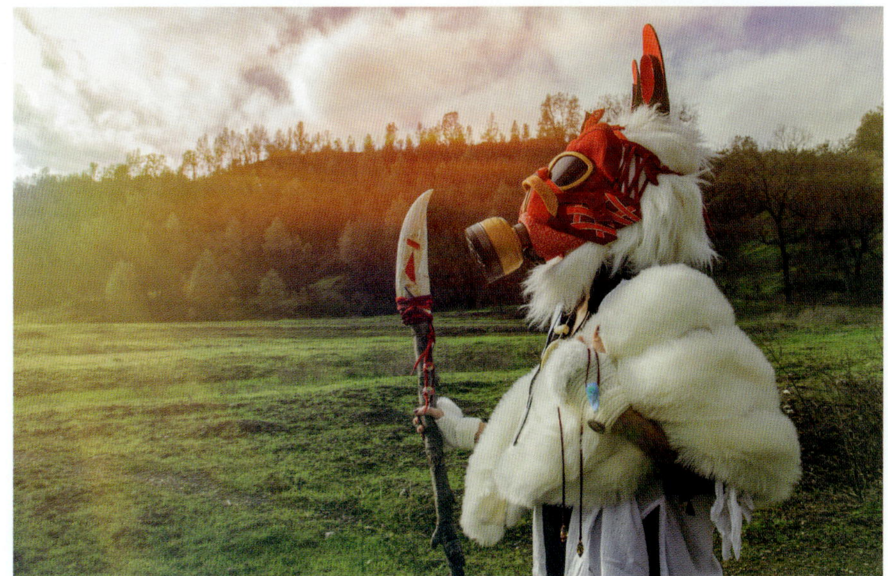

FREEHAND PROFIT (GARY LOCKWOOD)

THIS SPREAD

Princess Mononoke Gel Lyte III Gas Mask

Sneakers, faux fur & mixed media. 24 x 16 x 14".

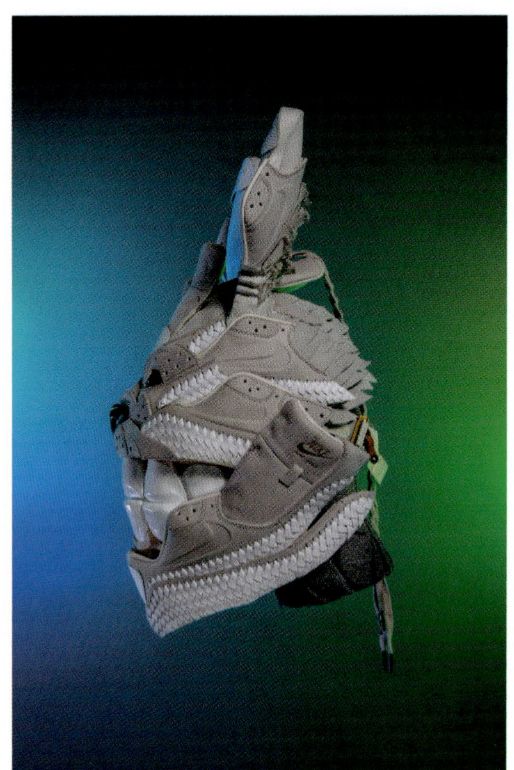

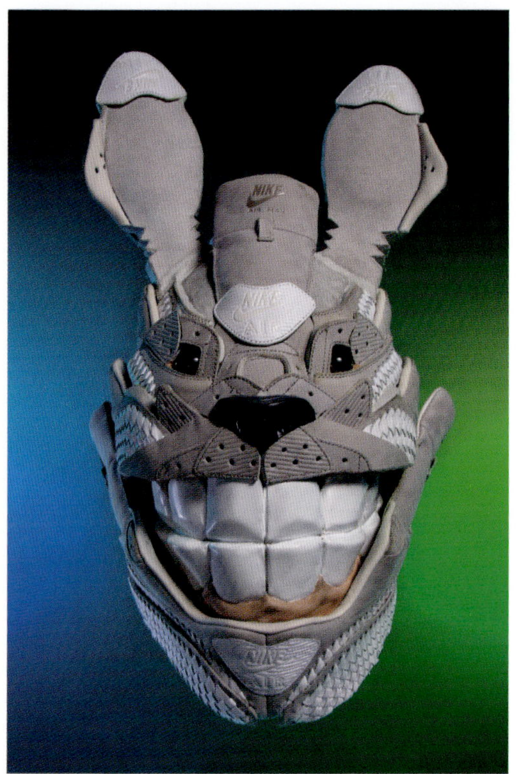

FREEHAND PROFIT (GARY LOCKWOOD)

THIS SPREAD

Totoro Air Max 90 Mask

Nike Air Max 90s, sculpting epoxy, thermoplastic, glass eyes, found objects. 24 x 16 x 12".

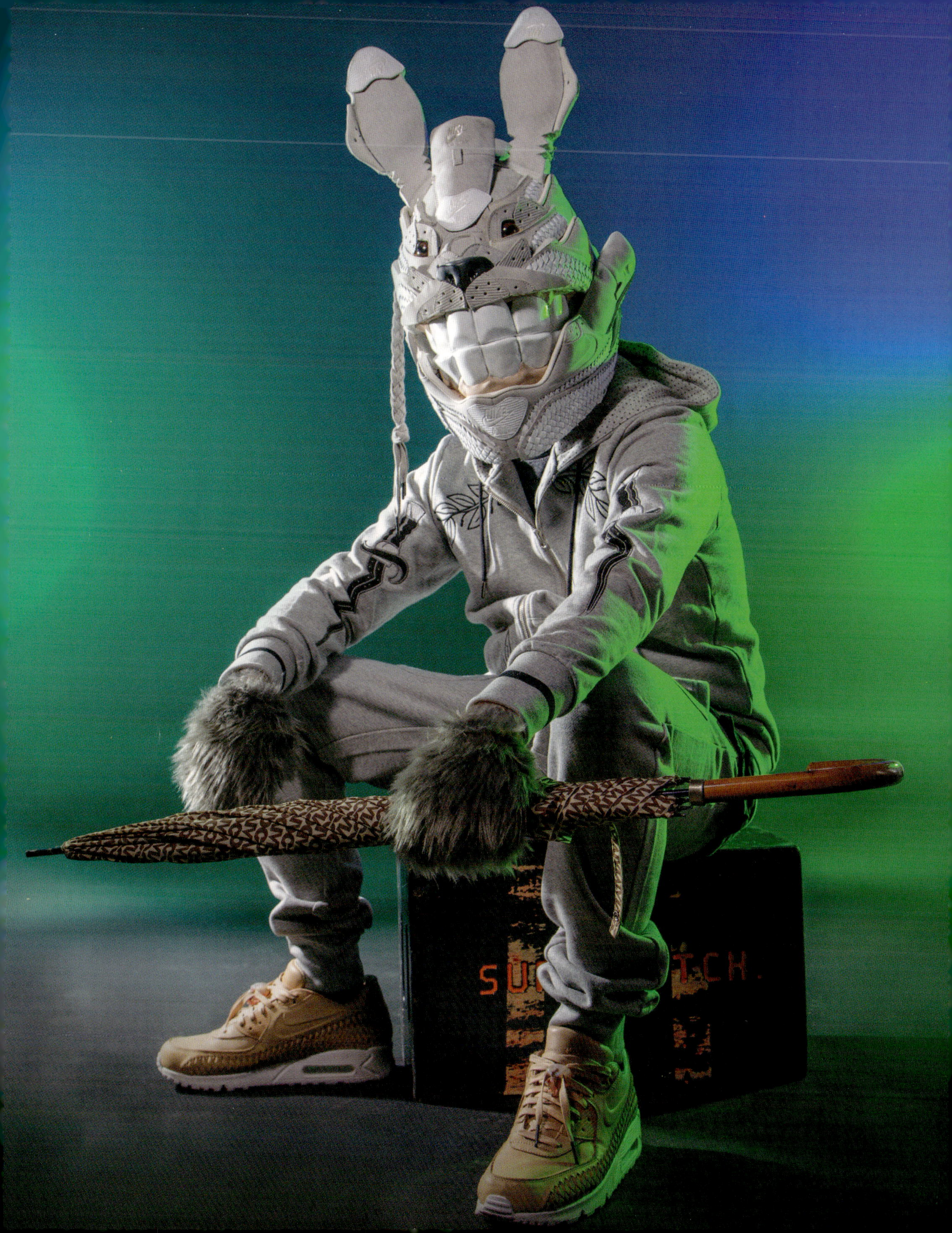

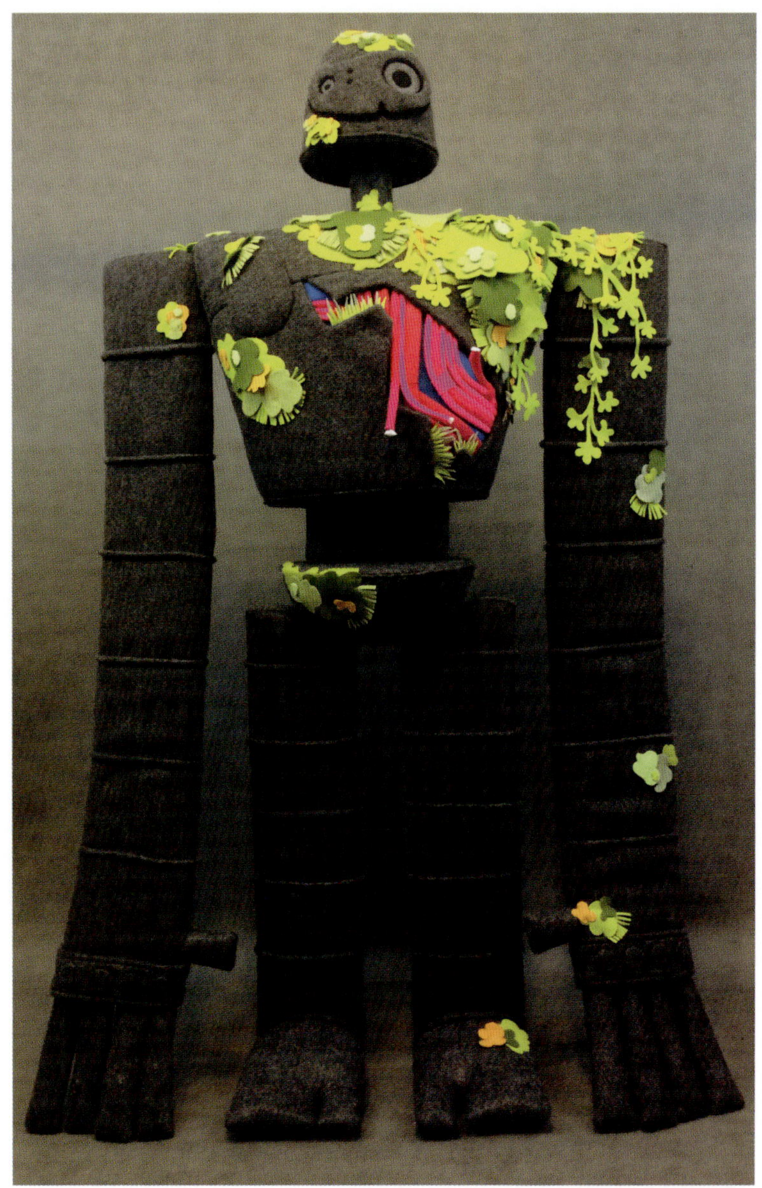

FELT MISTRESS

ABOVE

The Protector

Wool felt, mixed fibres. 25 x 50''.

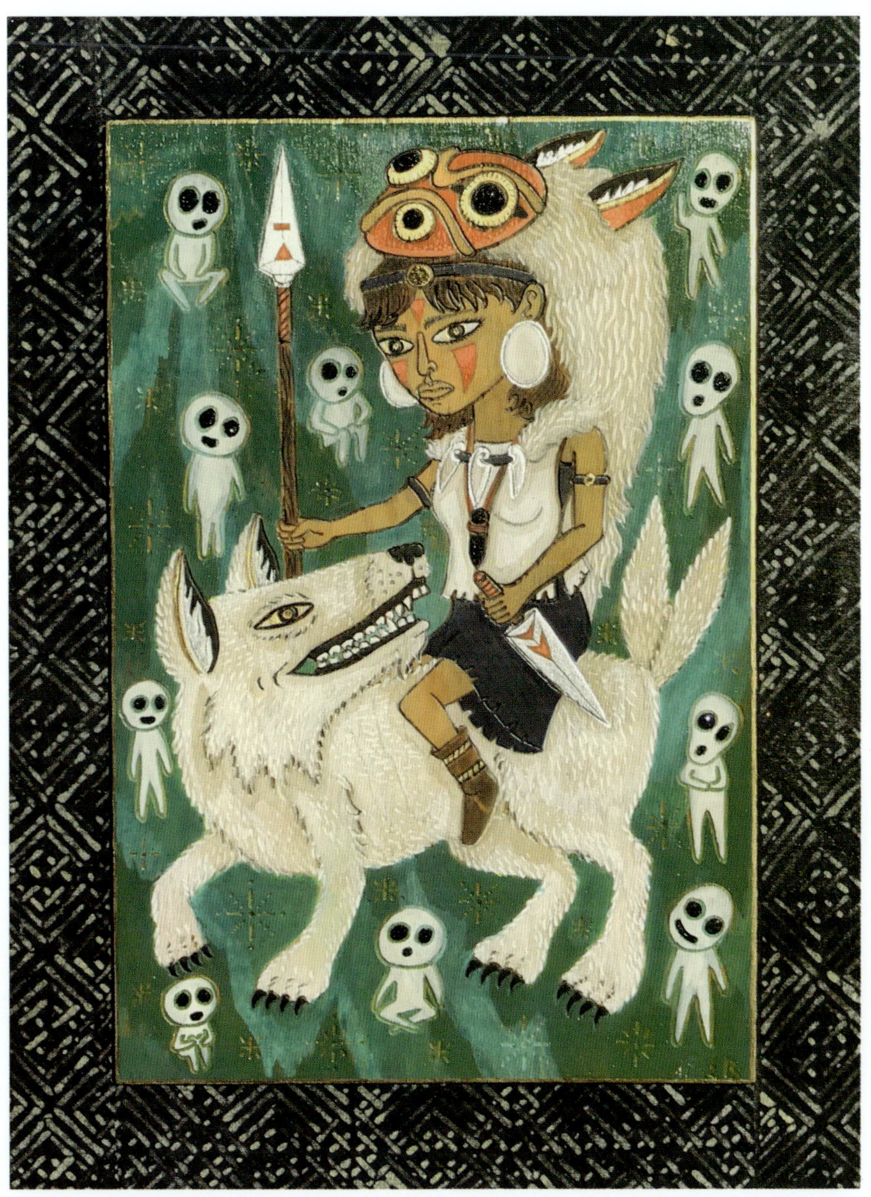

EVAN B. HARRIS

ABOVE

The Princess and the Wolf

Wood burned & acrylic paint trimmed with hand dyed fabric. 10 x 13.5".

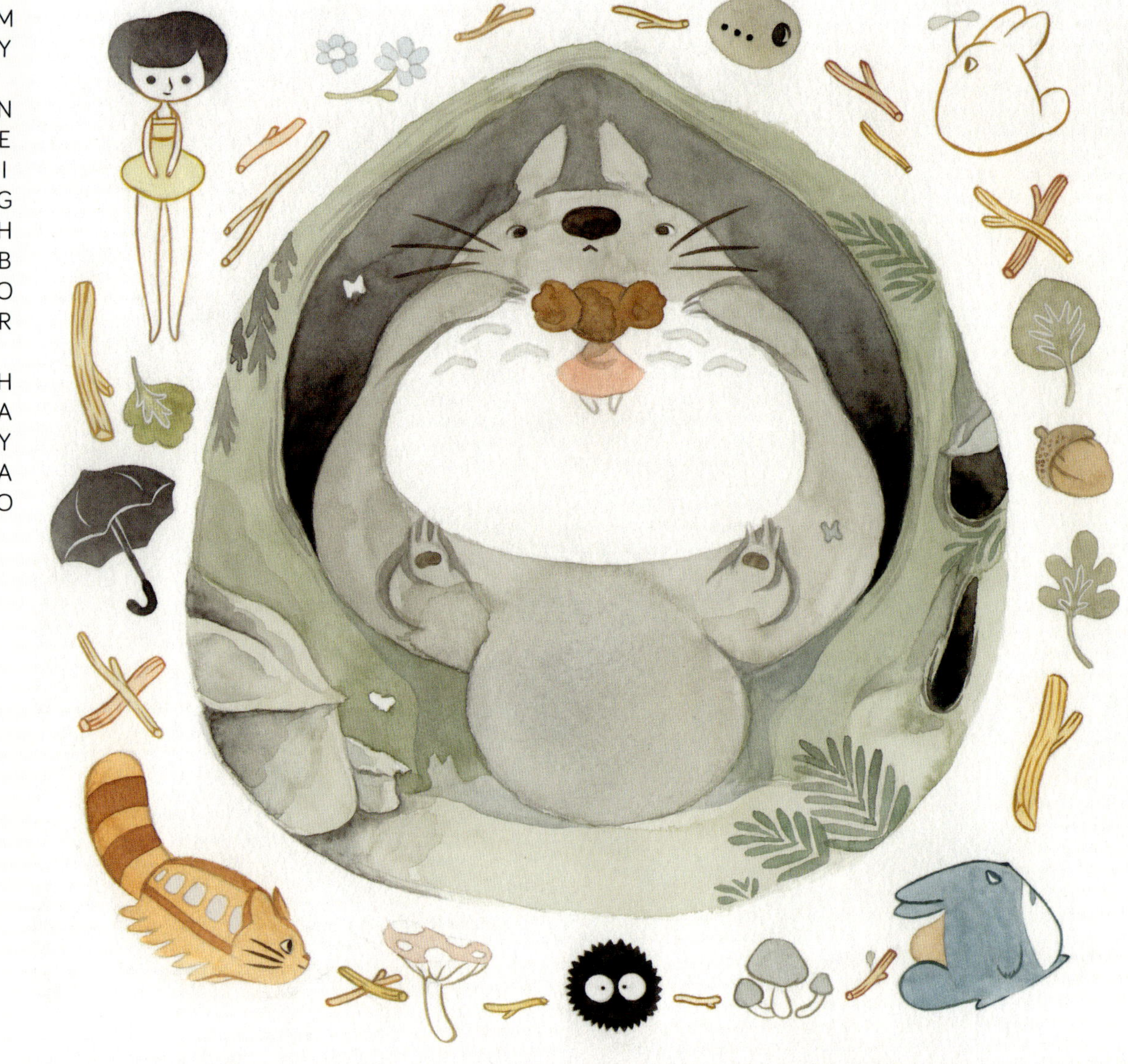

YOHAN SACRÉ

ABOVE

My Neighbor

Watercolor on paper. 9 x 9".

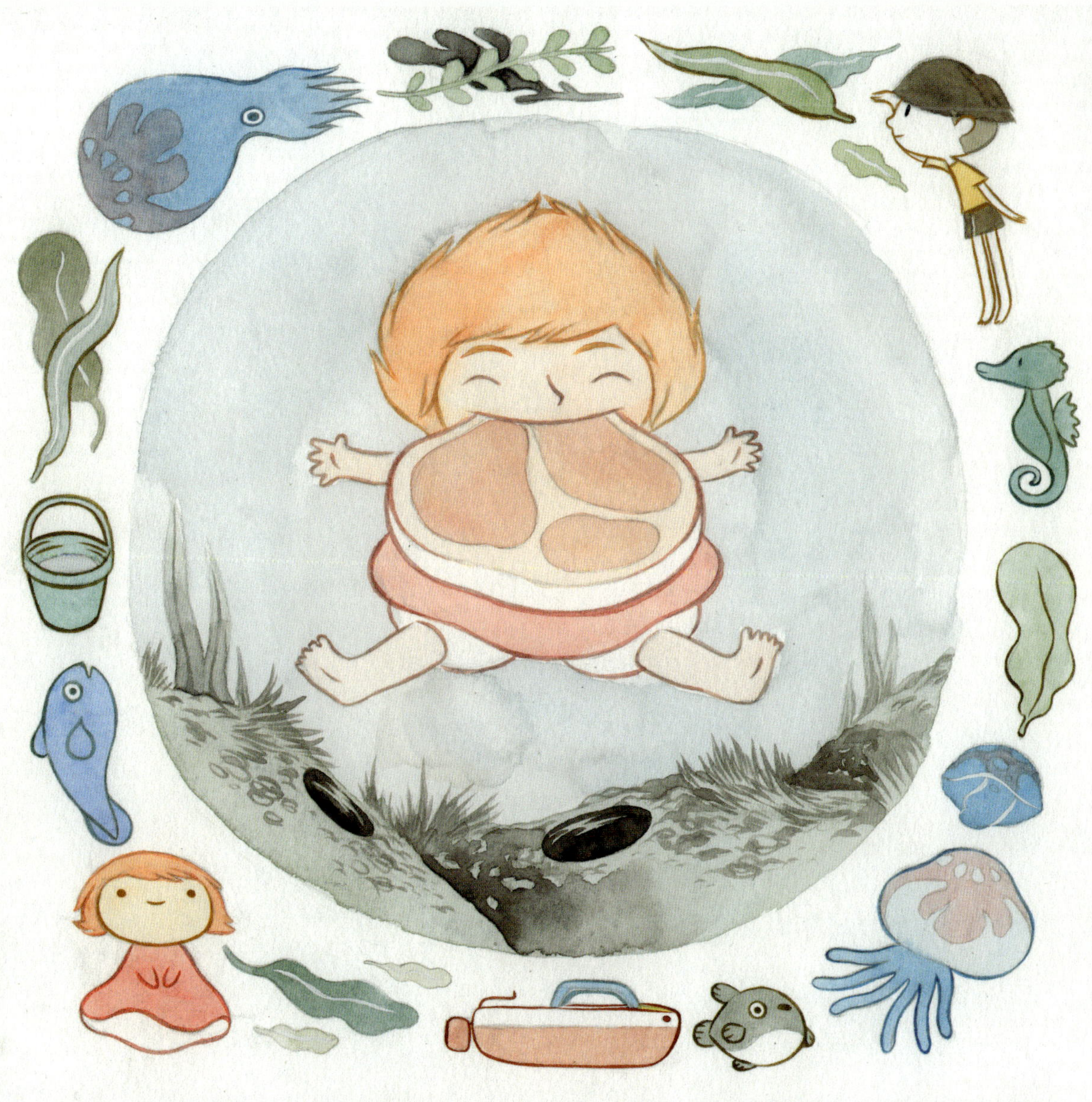

ABOVE

Ham

Watercolor on paper. 9 x 9".

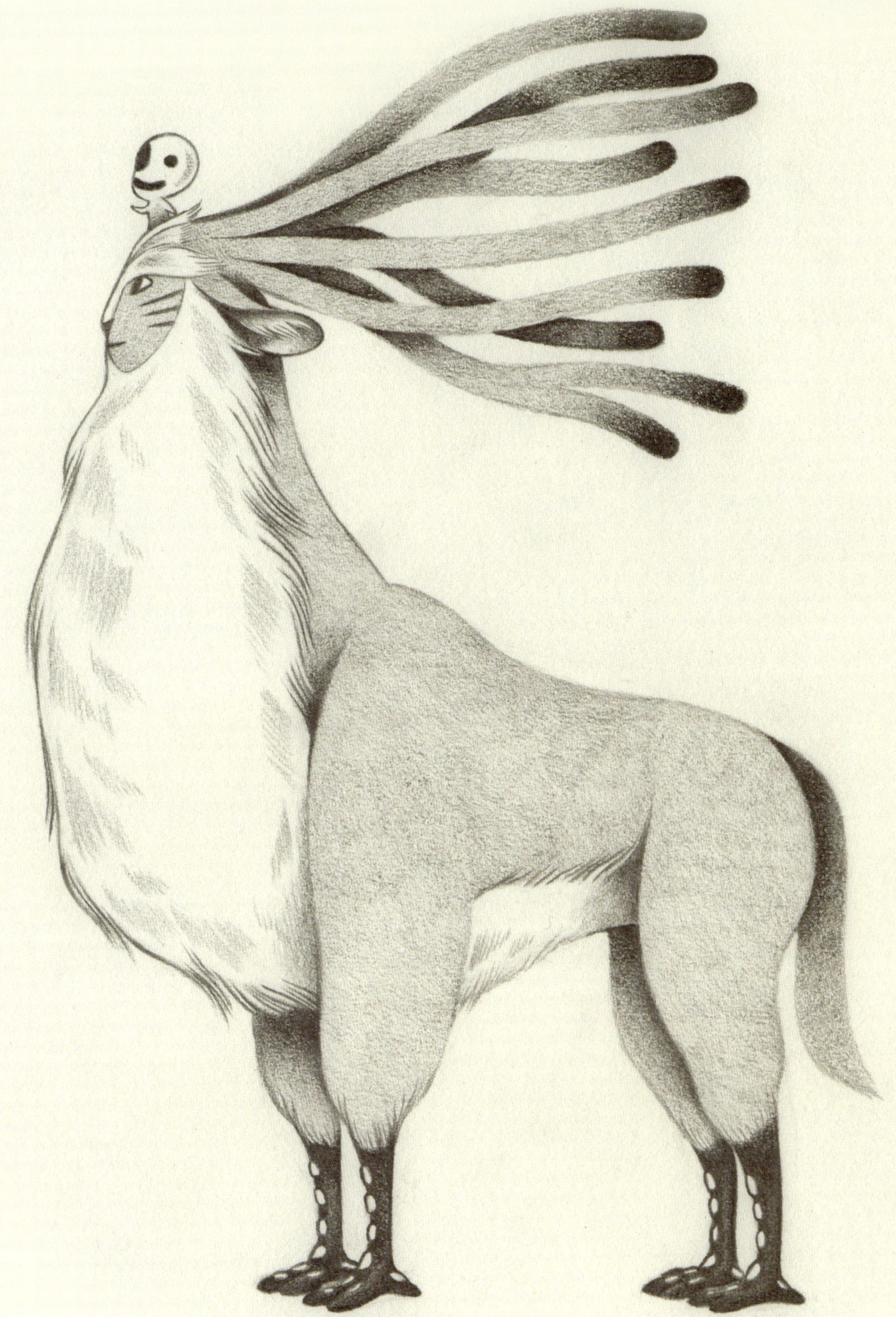

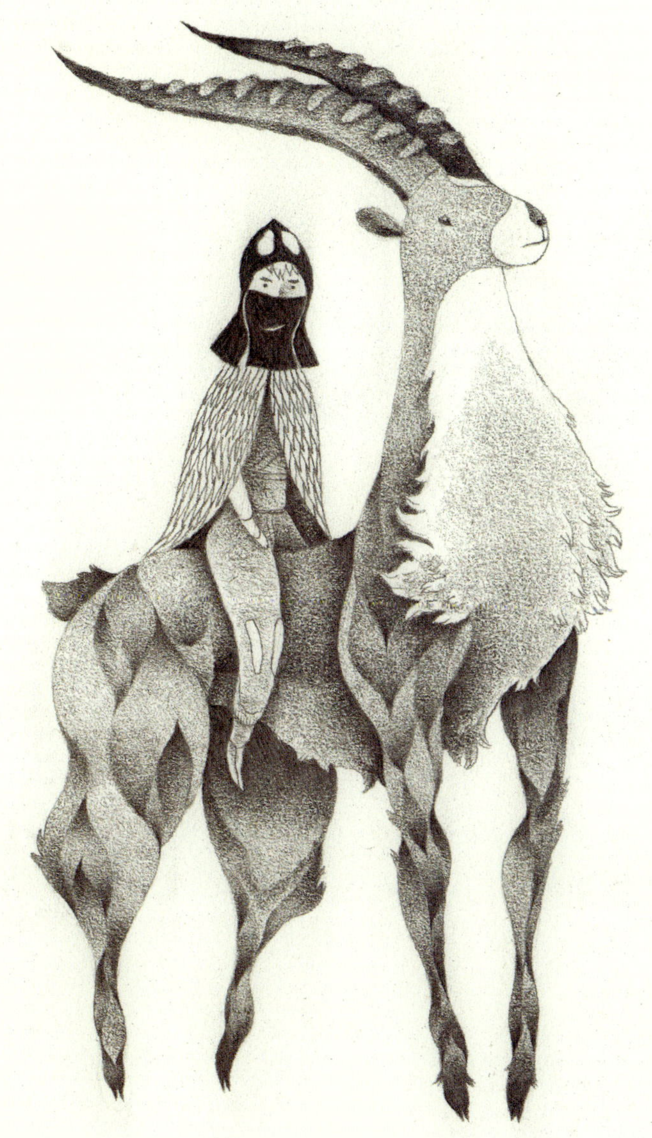

YOHAN SACRÉ

LEFT PAGE

Forest Spirit

Archival pigment print. 11 x 14".

ABOVE

もののけ姫

Archival pigment print. 11 x 14".

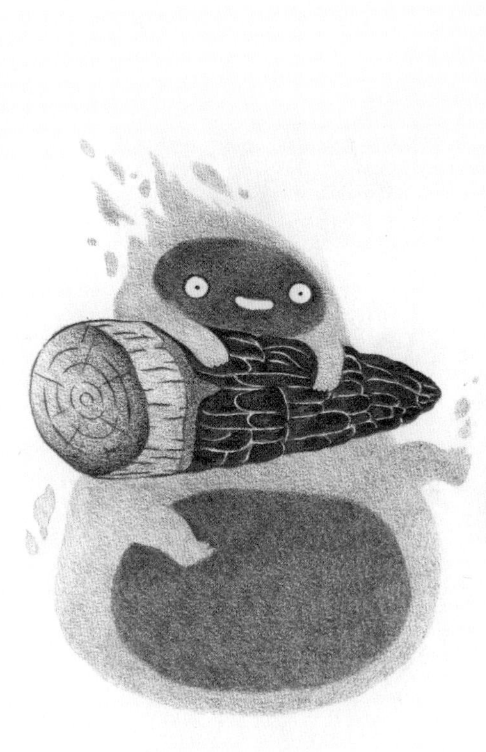

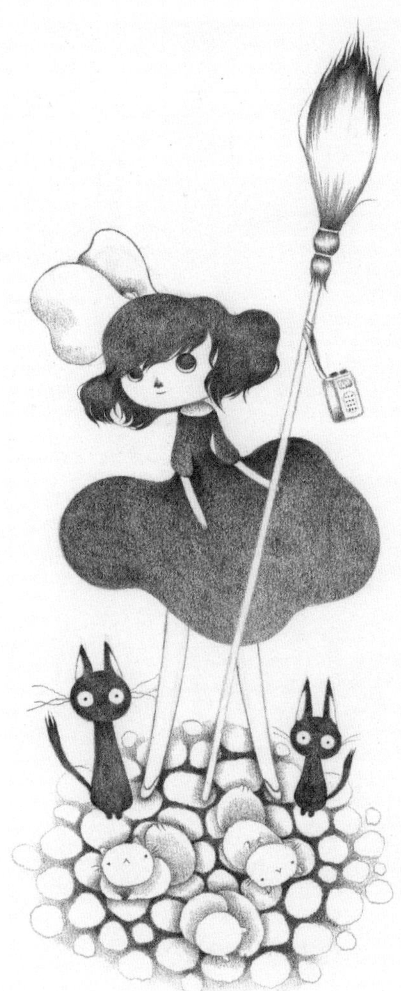

YOHAN SACRÉ

LEFT
Calcifer
Archival pigment print. 13 x 13".

RIGHT
Kiki
Archival pigment print. 8 x 10".

RIGHT PAGE
Hauru
Archival pigment print. 13 x 13".

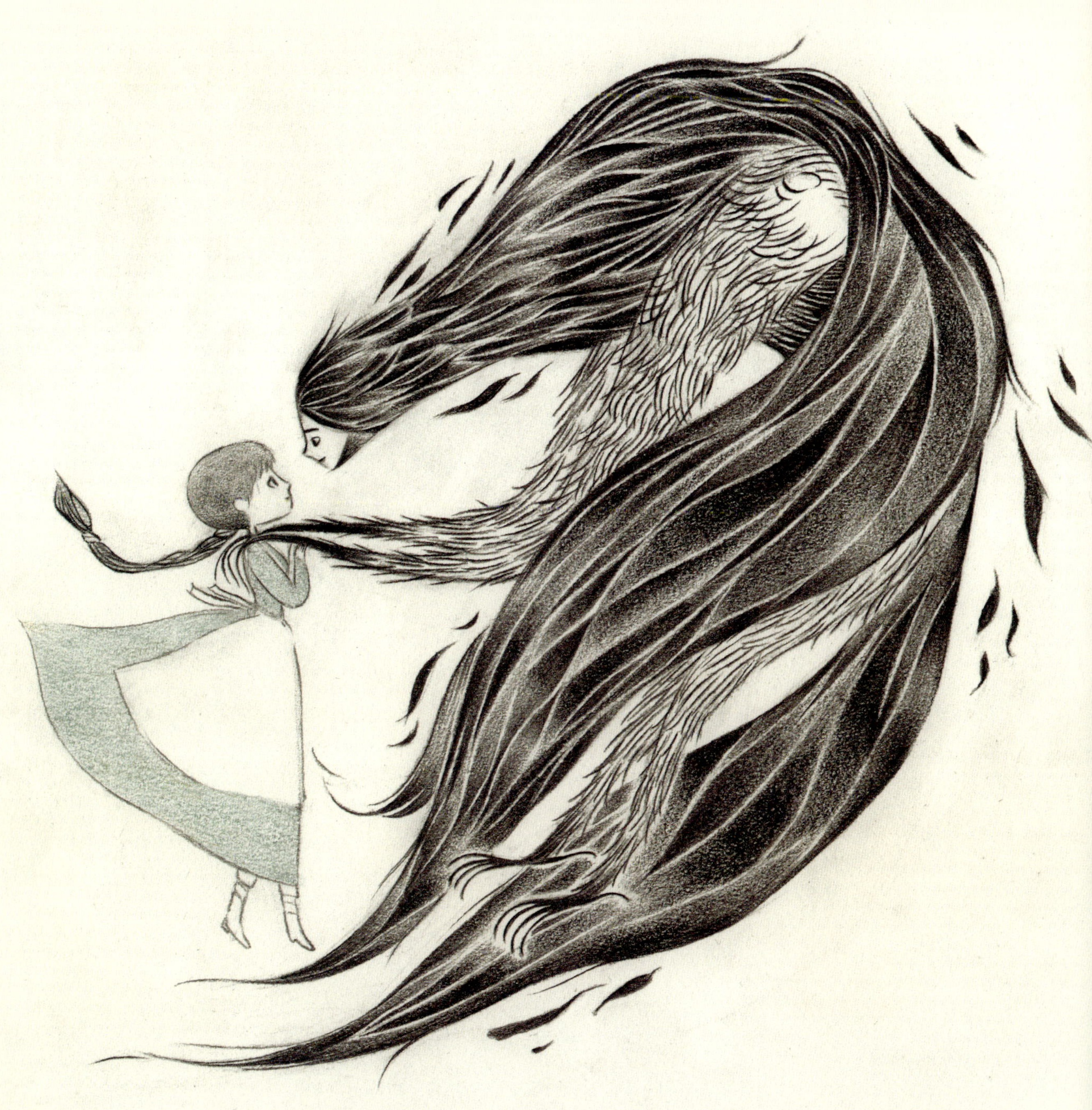

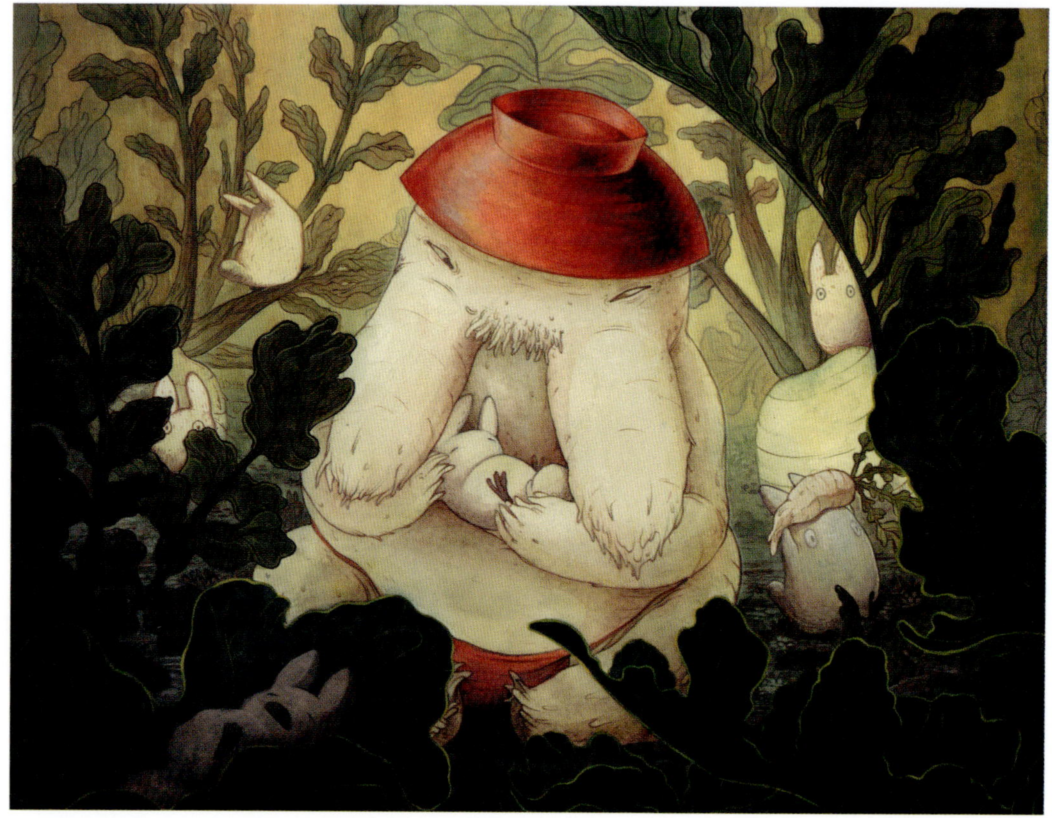

CORINNE REID

ABOVE

Afternoon Retreat

Watercolor, gouache, acrylic. 10 x 8".

RIGHT PAGE

Kawa no Kami

Archival pigment print with gold embellishments. 12 x 18".

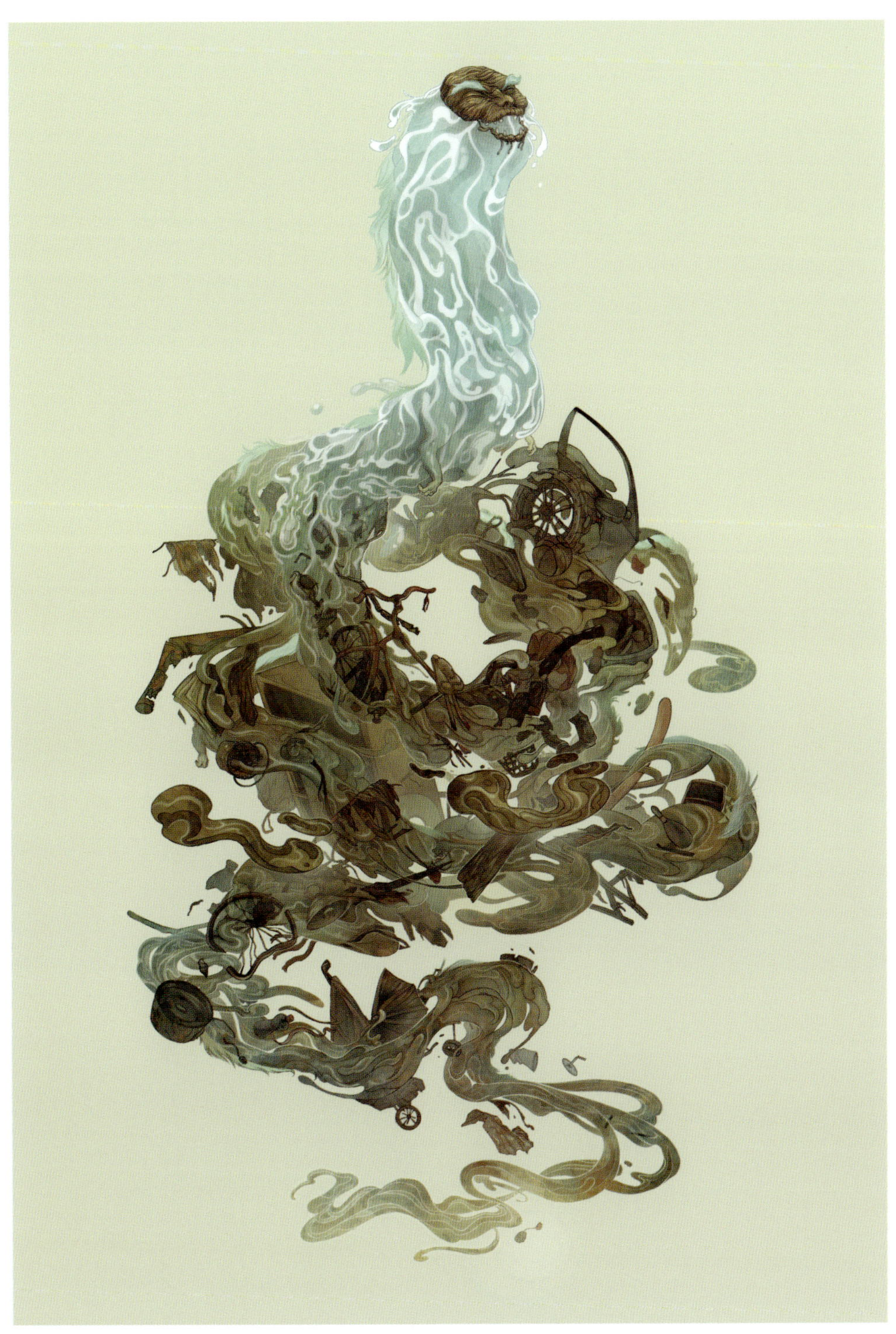

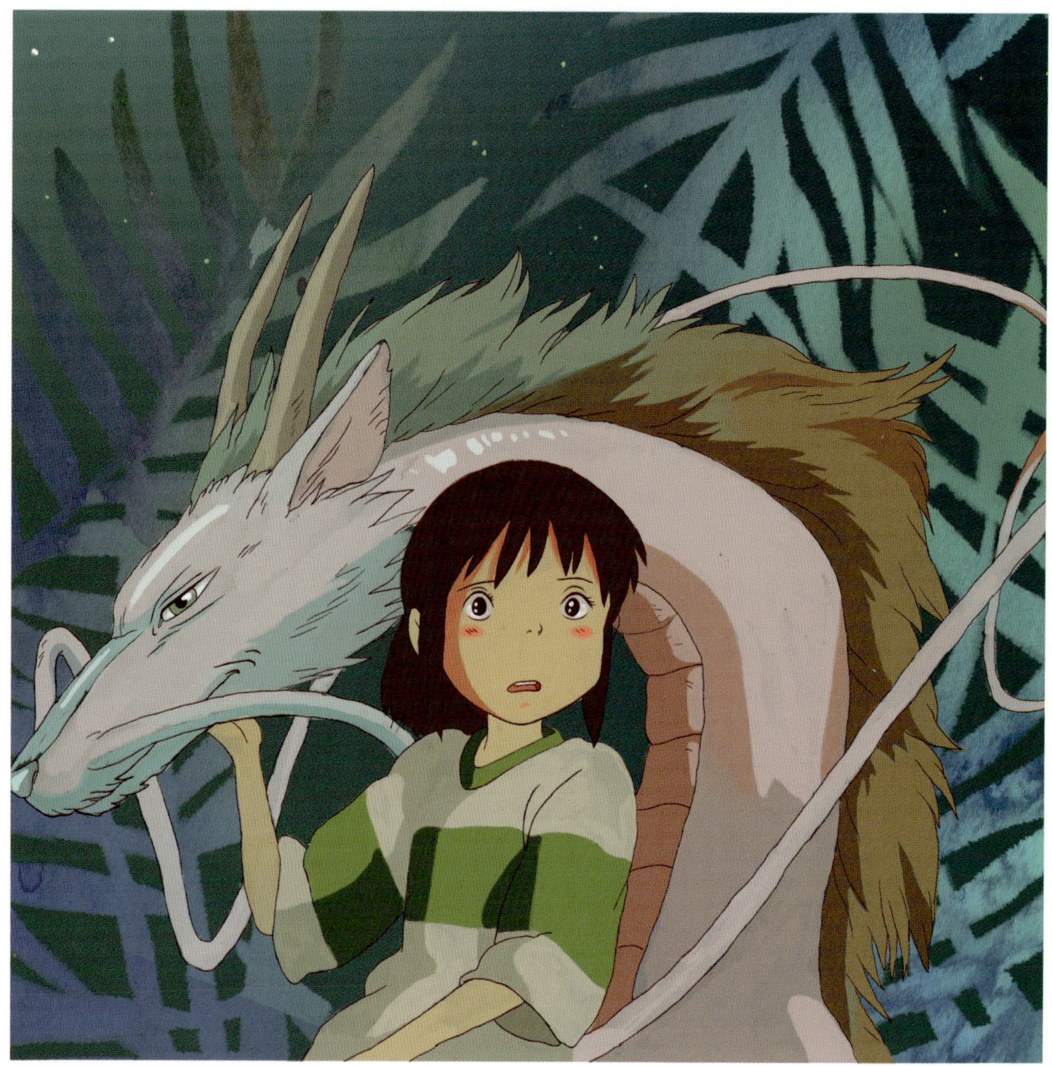

KEMI MAI

ABOVE

Haku and Chihiro

Archival pigment print. 12 x 12".

JAMES GILLEARD

RIGHT PAGE

Spirited Away

Archival pigment print. 18 x 24".

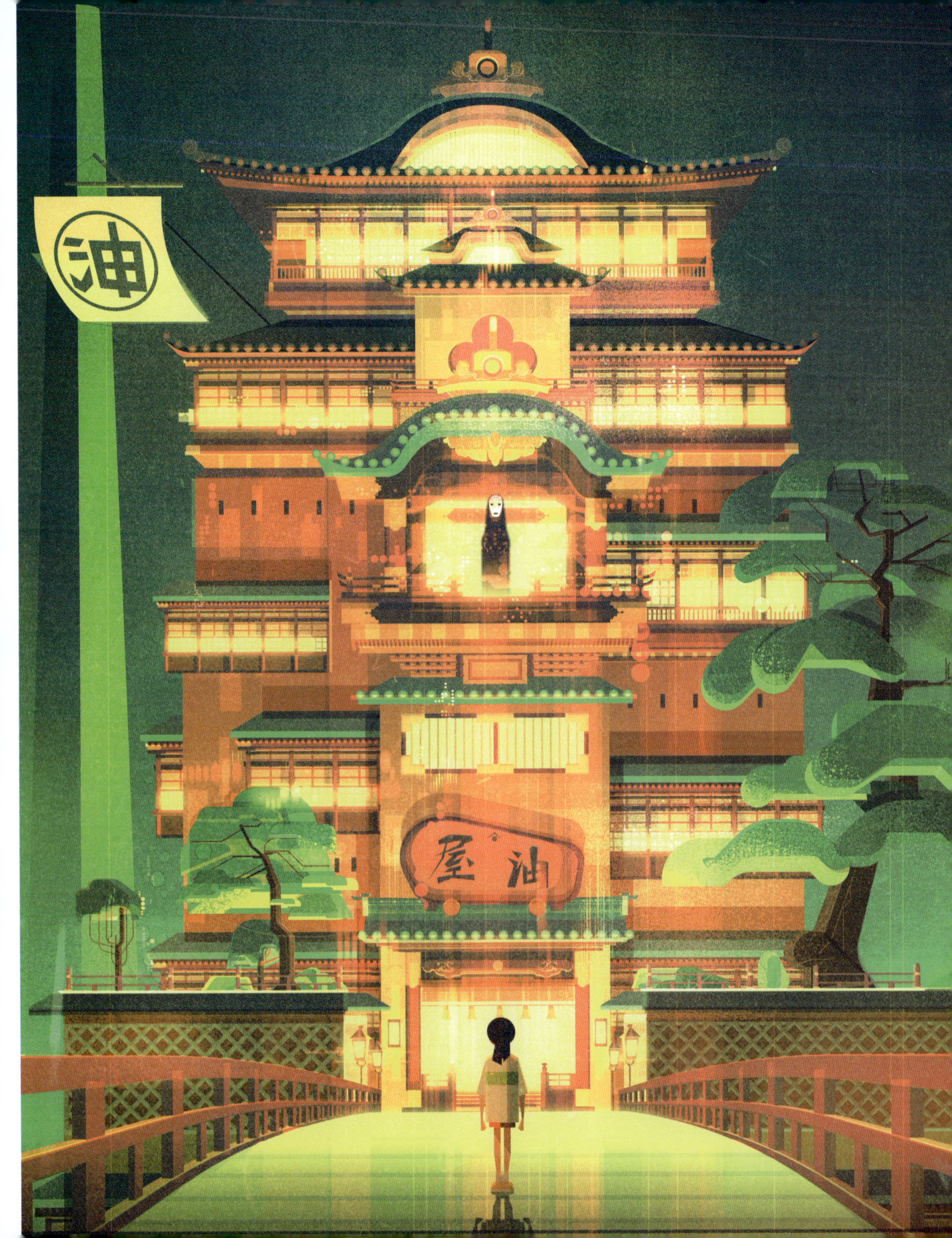
油
油屋

VAN ORTON

RIGHT PAGE

Spirited Away
Archival pigment print. 16 x 24".

NEXT SPREAD

Princess Mononoke
Archival pigment print. 24 x 18".

NEXT SPREAD

Porco Rosso
Archival pigment print. 24 x 18".

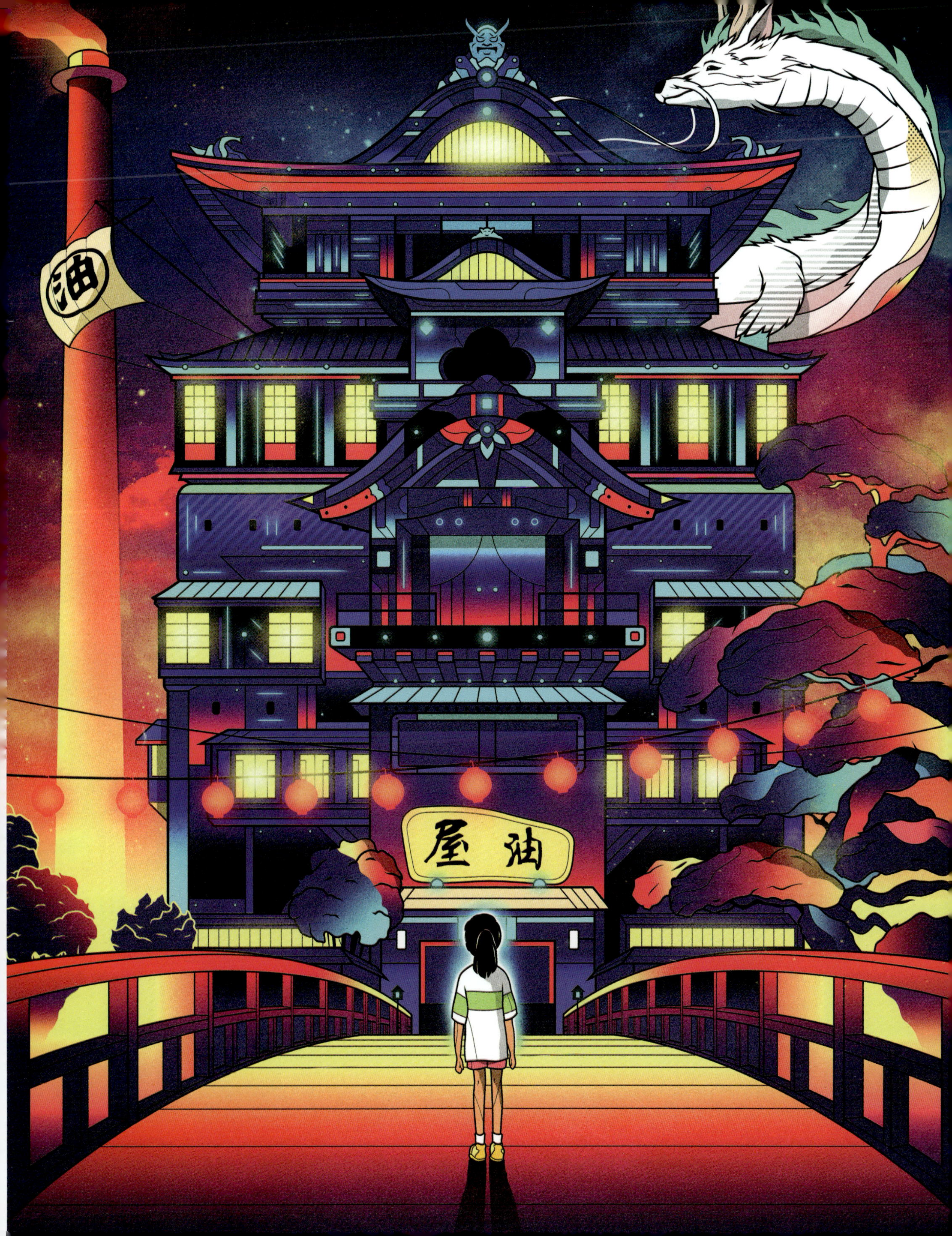
油
油屋

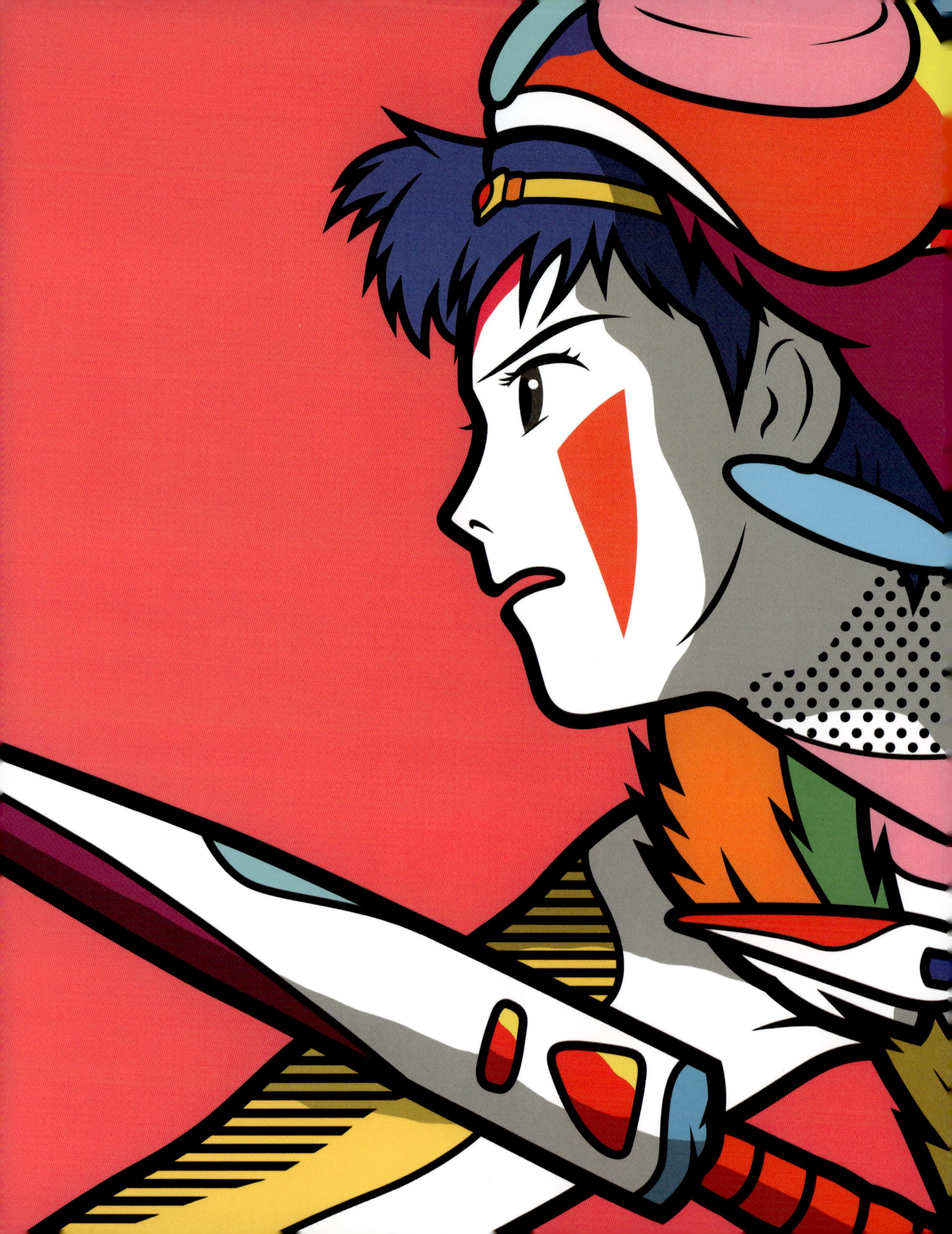

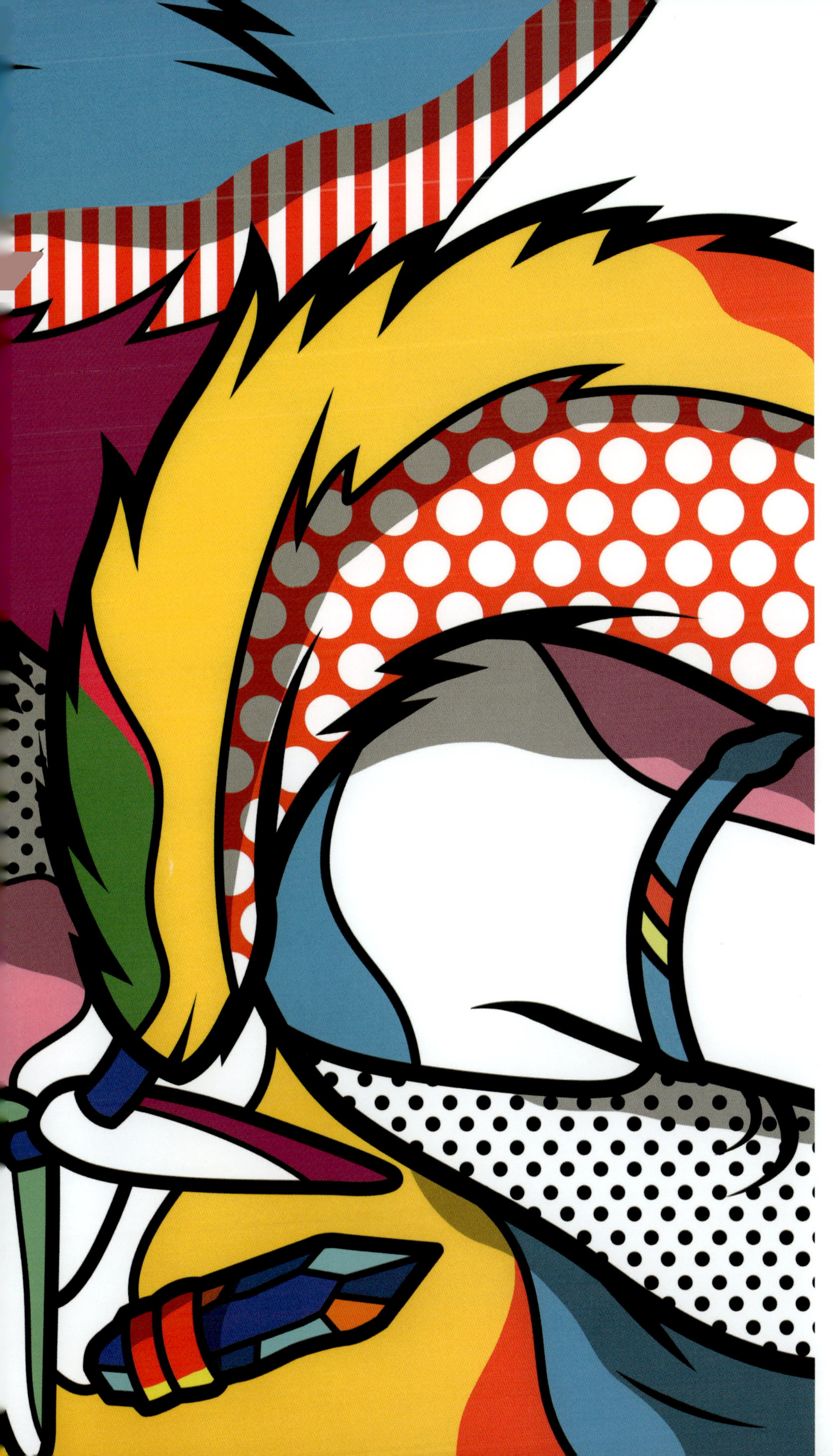

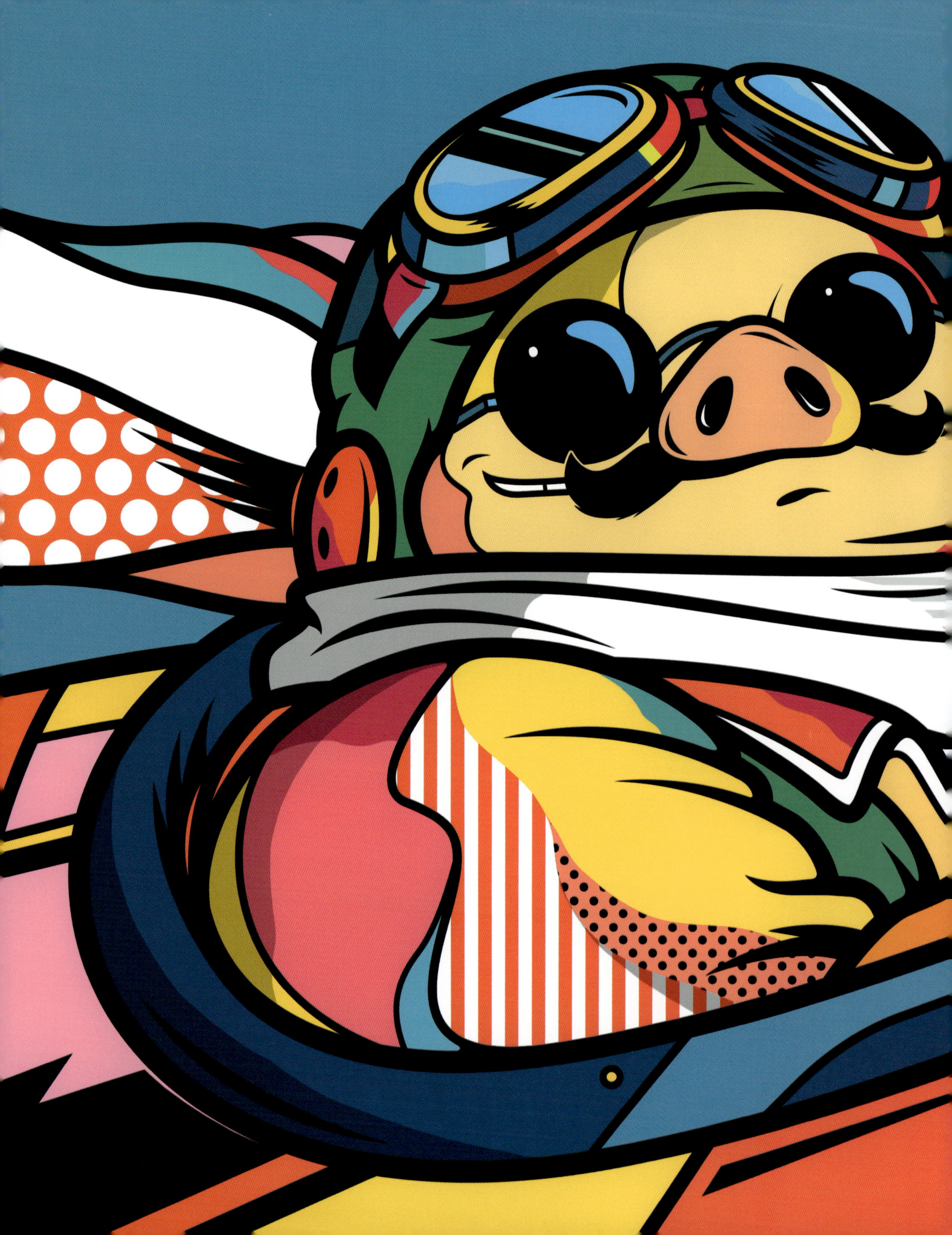

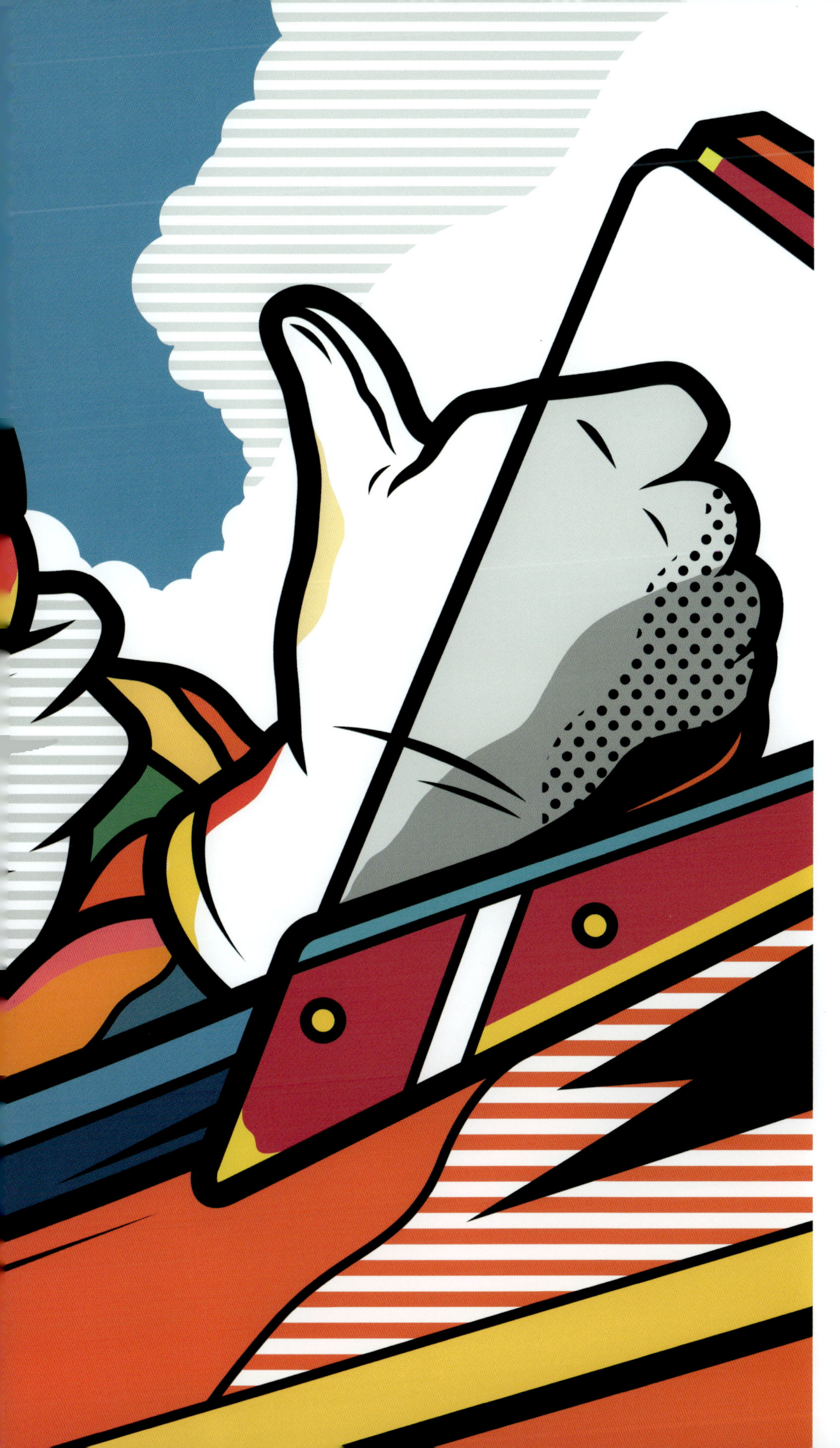

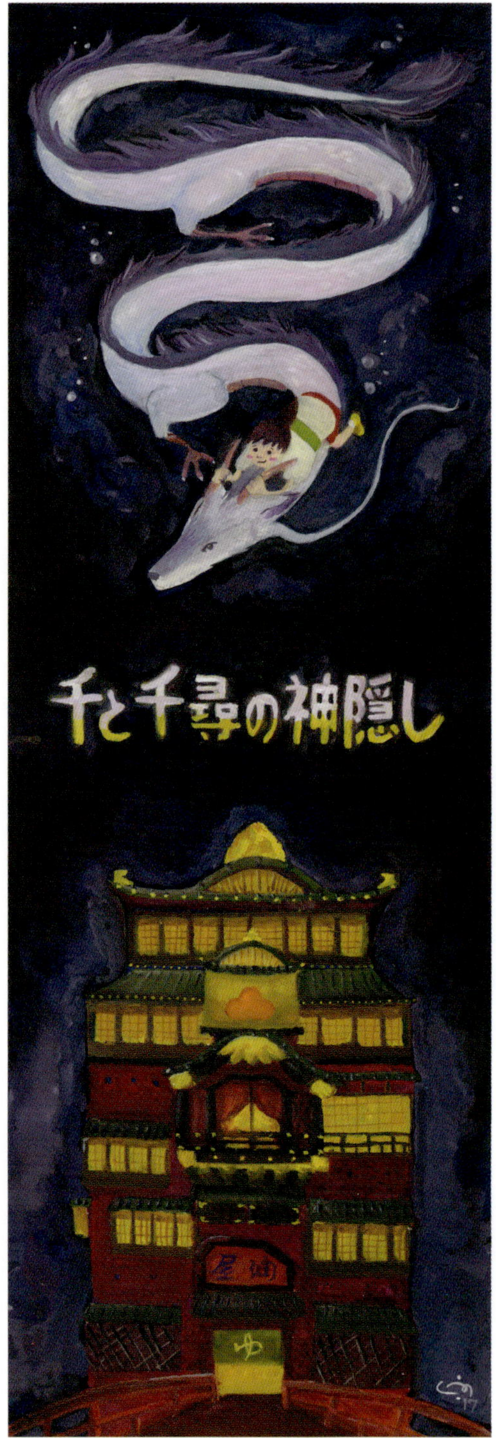
千と千尋の神隠し

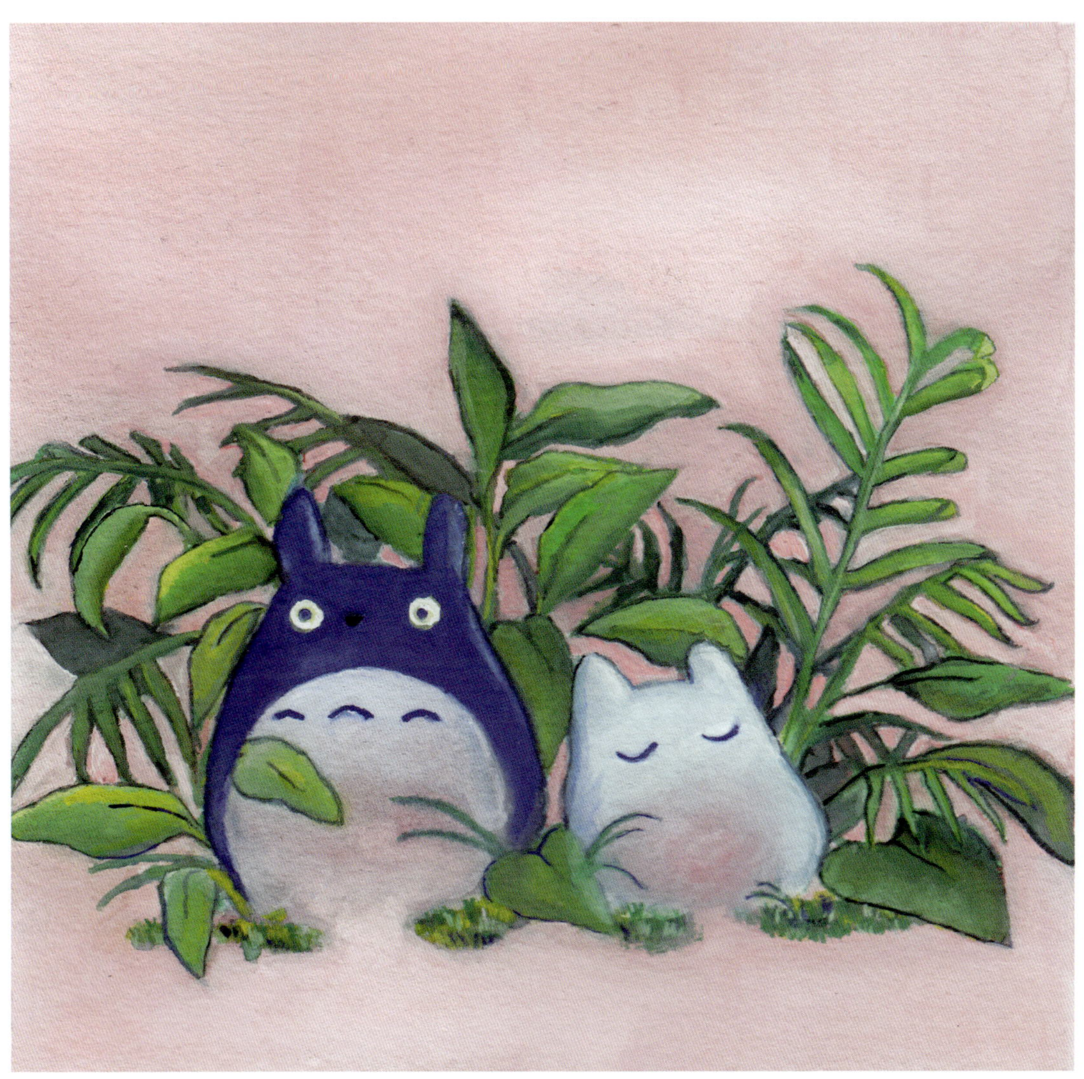

JEANY NGO

LEFT PAGE

Spirited Away

Gouache on paper. 6.75 x 18".

ABOVE

Totorrarium

Gouache on paper. 7 x 7".

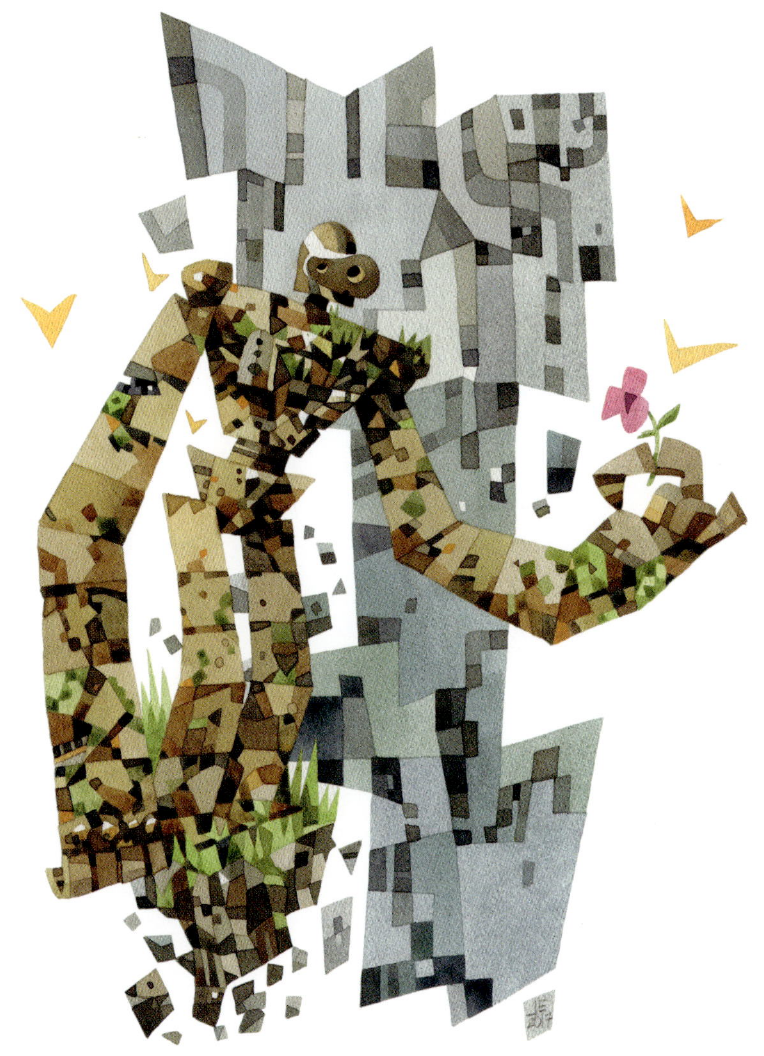

JONATHAN EDWARDS

ABOVE

Niwashi

Watercolor. 12 x 16".

RIGHT PAGE

Totoro No Mori

Watercolor. 12 x 17".

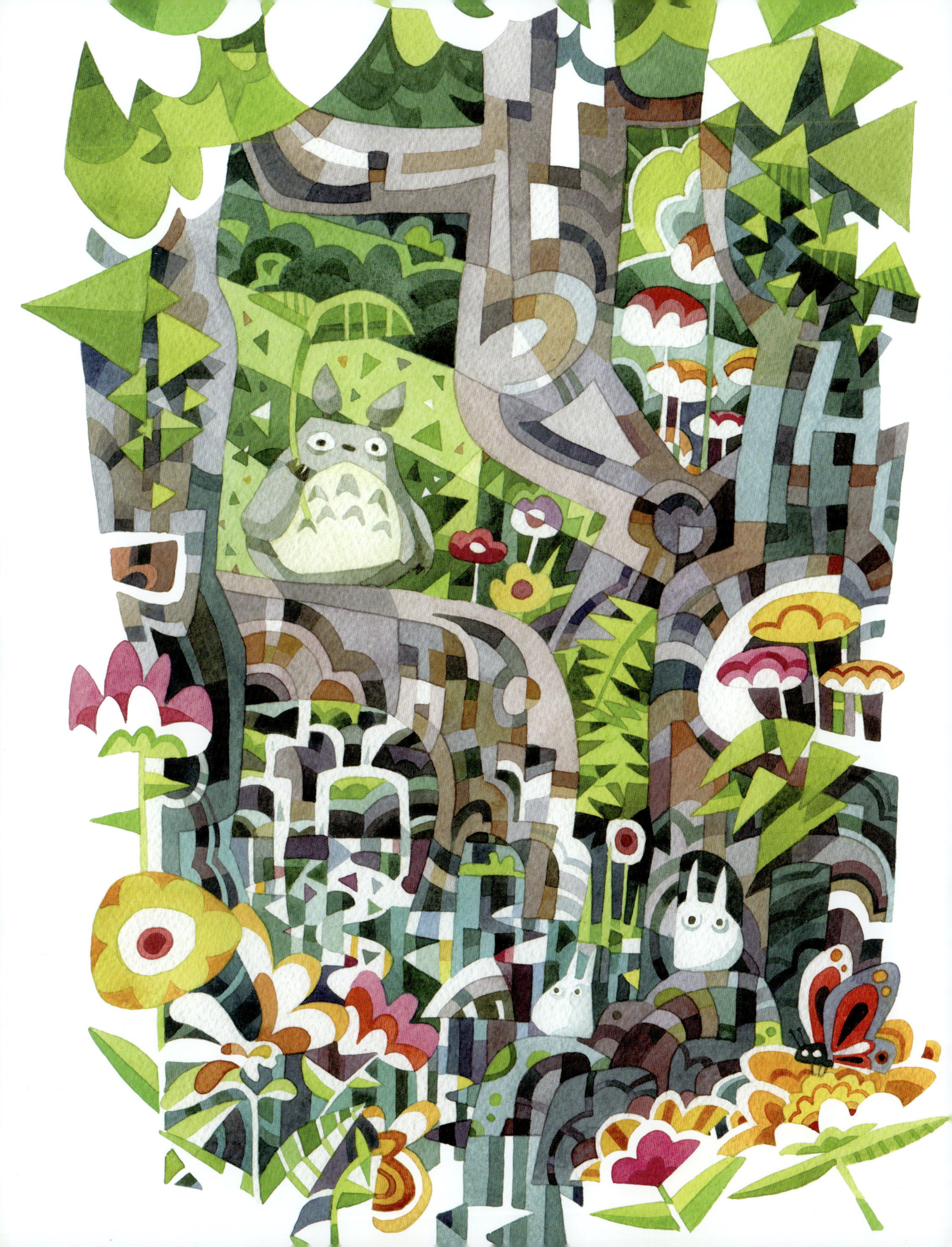

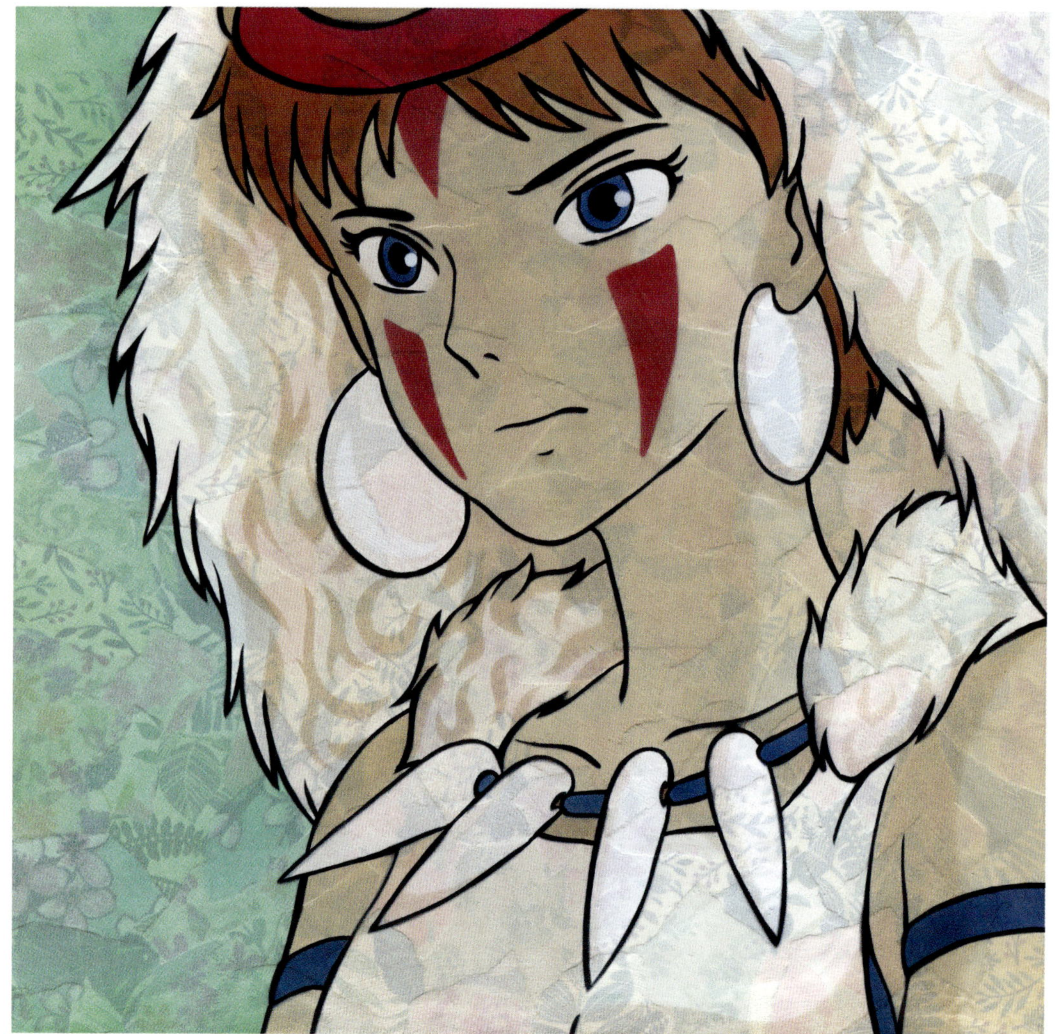

NICK COMPARONE

ABOVE

It's Time for Both of Us to Live

Eleven-layer stencil and spray paint on cradled panel. 16 x 16".

SARAH JONCAS

RIGHT PAGE

Princess Mononoke

Oil and acrylic on panel. 12 x 16".

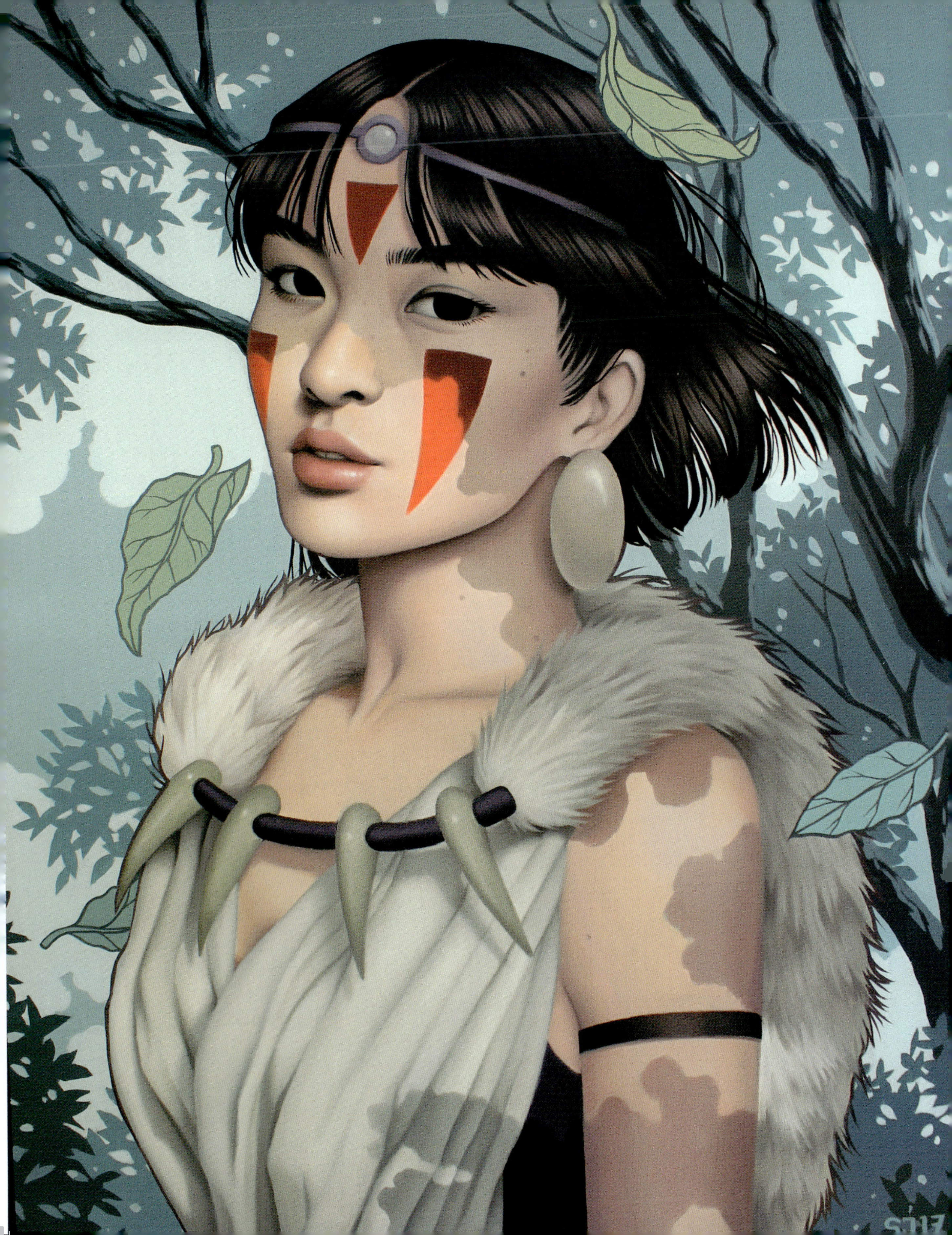

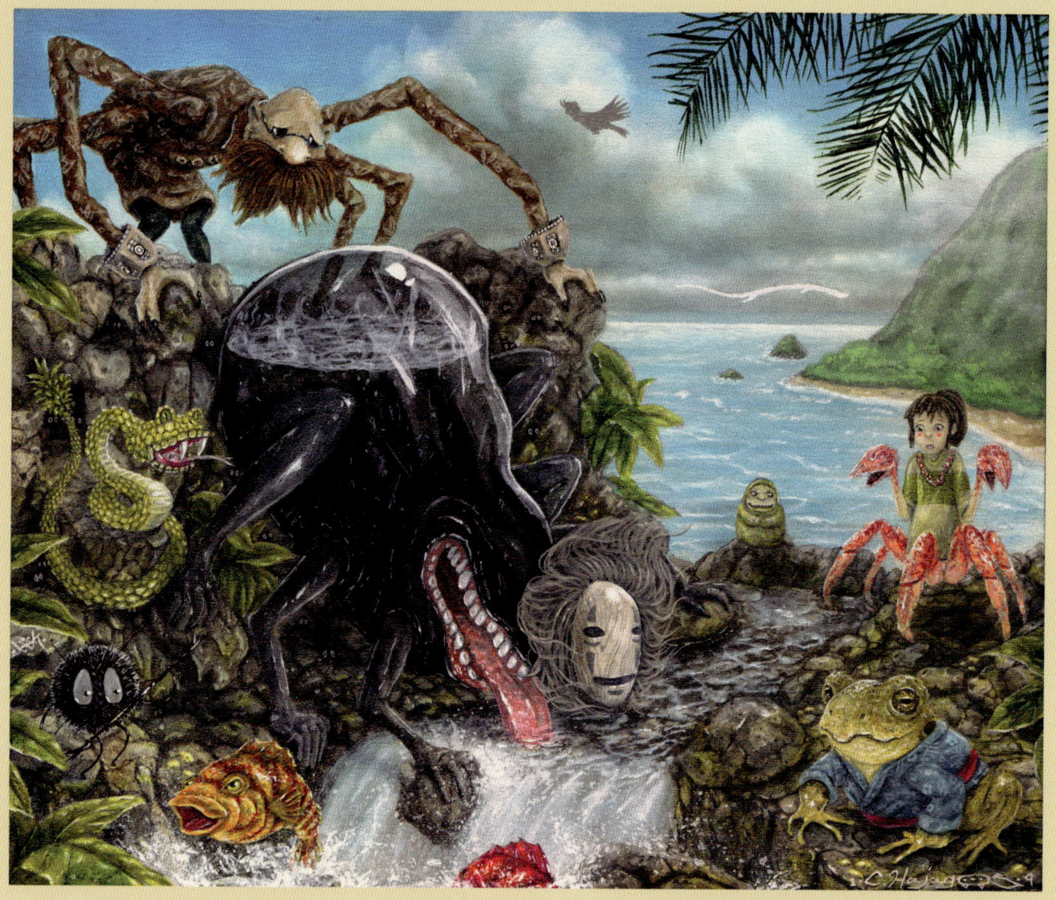

CAMERON HAJAGOS

ABOVE

Drink More Water No Face

Acrylic paint on wood panel.
12 x 10".

ARNA MILLER

RIGHT PAGE

They Cause Tsunamis

Five-color screen print on 100# paper.
18 x 24".

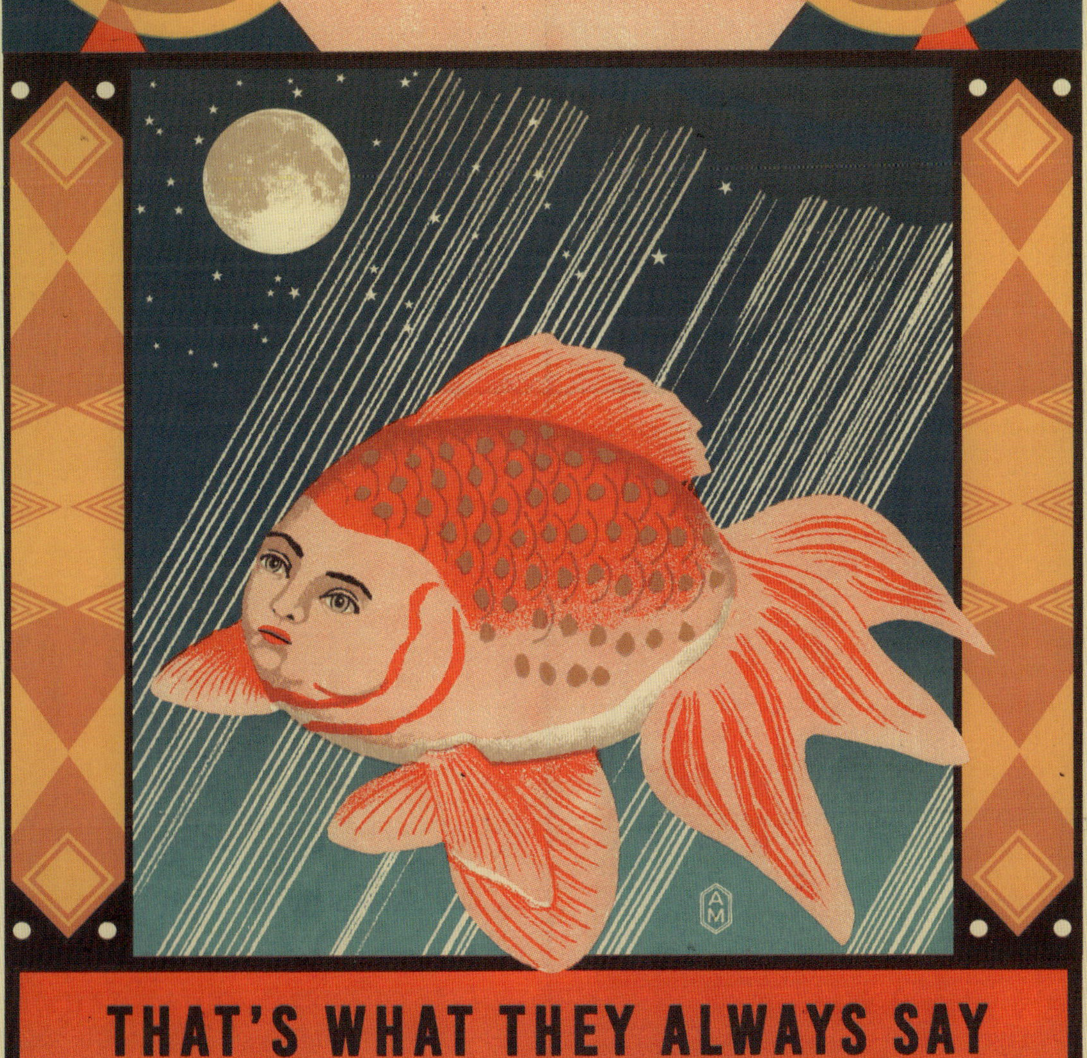
FISH WITH FACES
WHO COME OUT OF THE SEA
CAUSE
TSUNAMIS
THAT'S WHAT THEY ALWAYS SAY

CHARLES SANTOSO

RIGHT PAGE

Nap Time

Archival pigment print. 14 x 11".

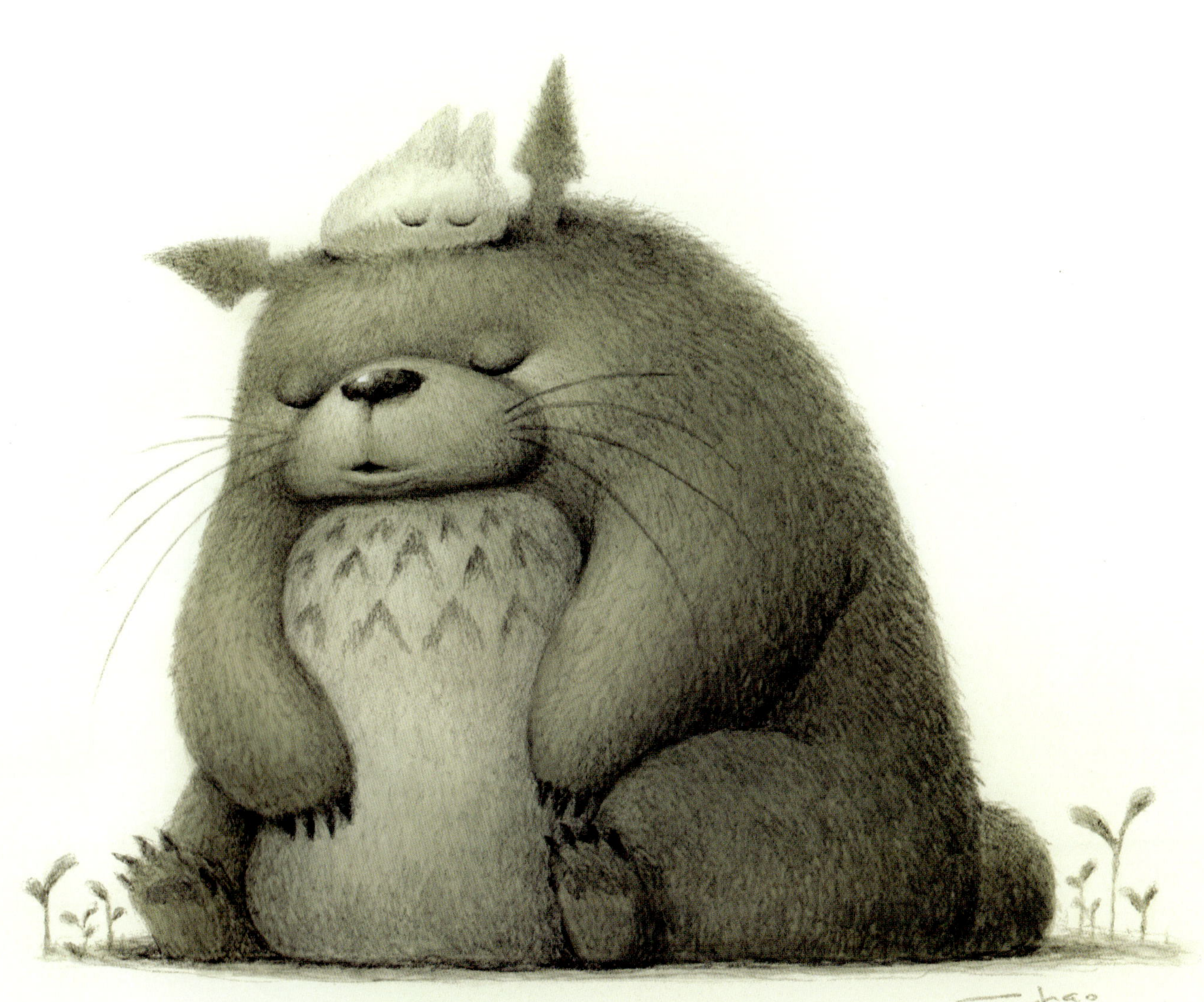
Chao

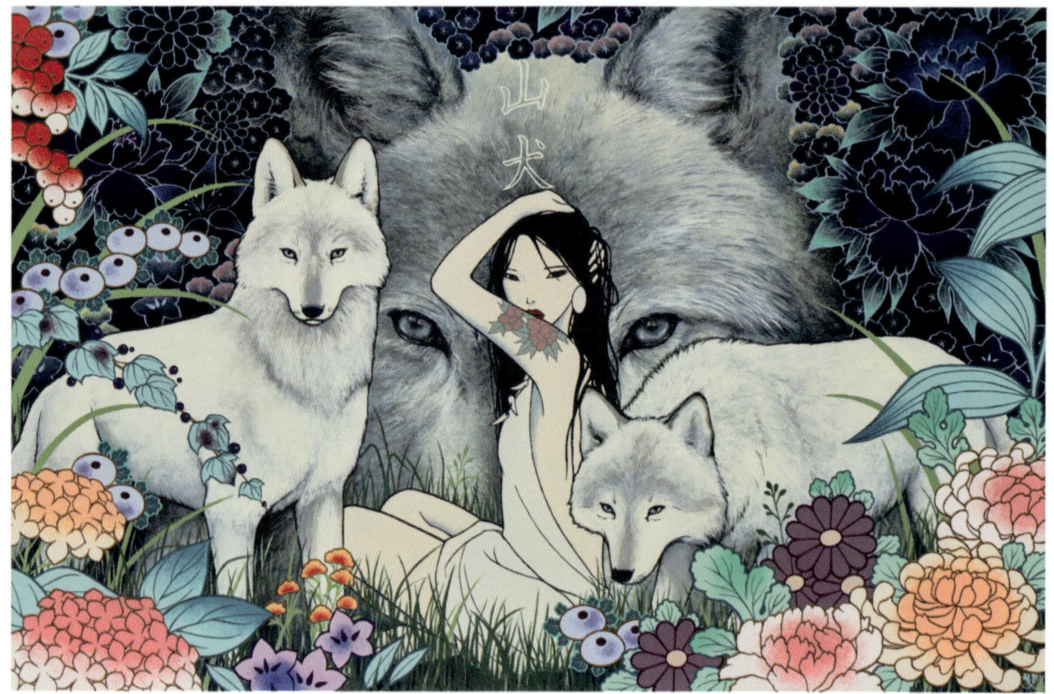

YUMIKO KAYUKAWA

ABOVE

Yamainu (Wild Dog)
Acrylic on linen. 18 x 12".

ANNIE STEGG GERARD

RIGHT PAGE

King of the Forest
Oil on canvas. 8 x 10".

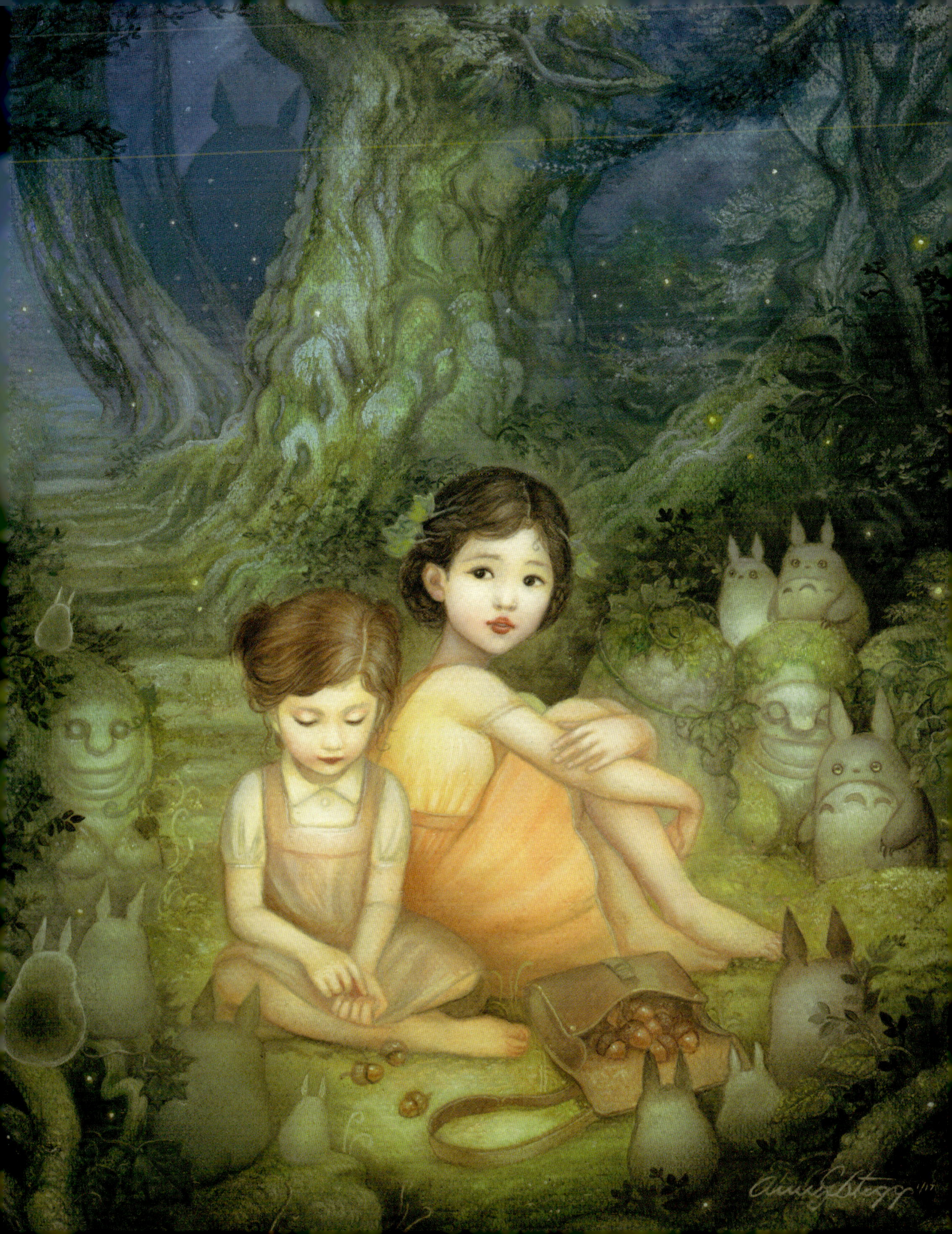

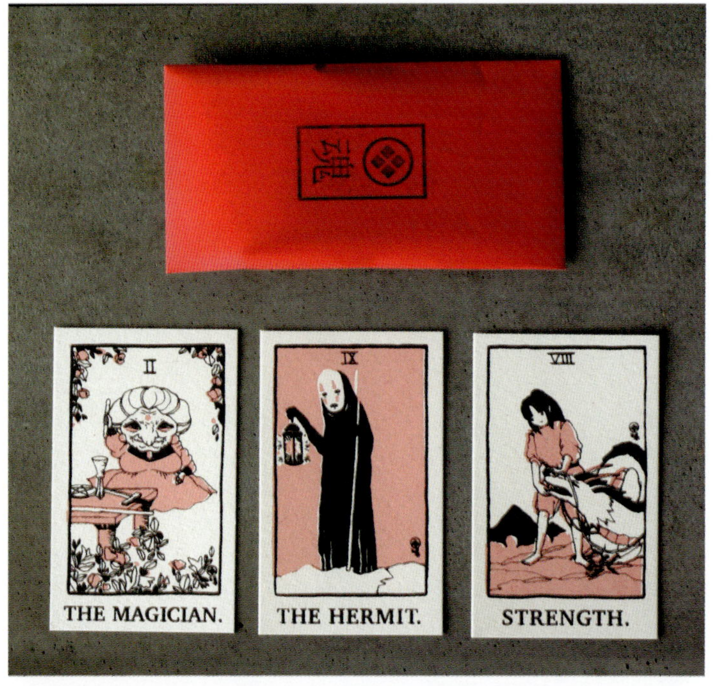

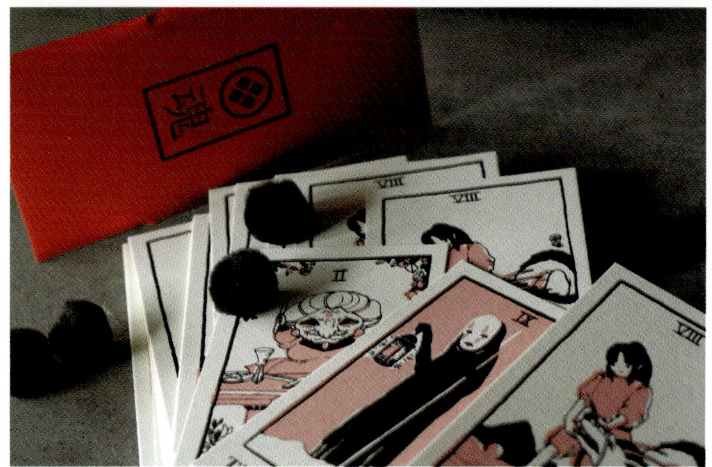

BRIGHTON BALLARD

ABOVE

Spirited Away Tarot Card Set
Risograph printed cards, stamped envelope. 3 x 6".

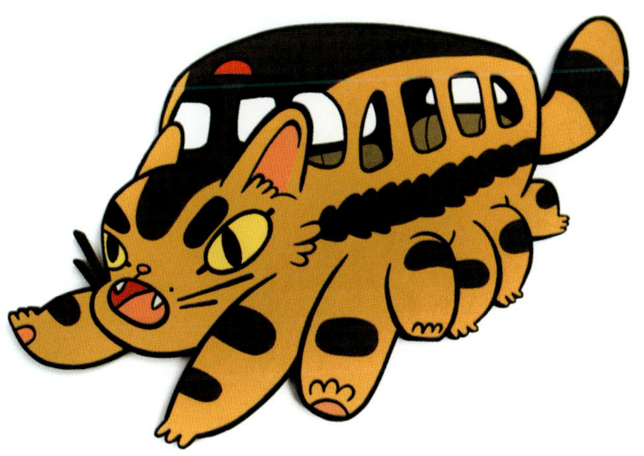

LAUREN GREGG

Catbus

Acrylic and cel vinyl on MDF. 16 x 10".

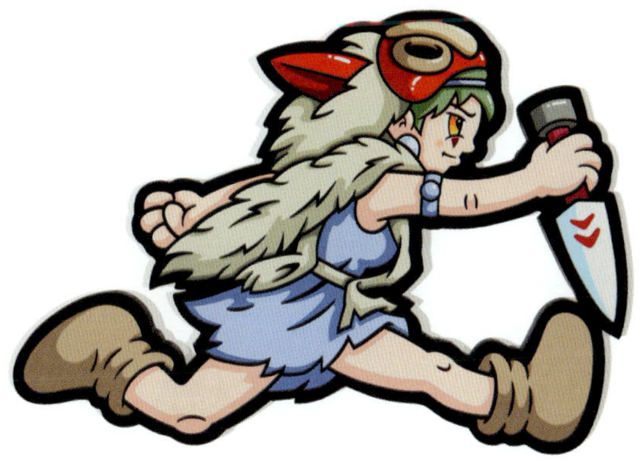

MATT RITCHIE

Princess MonoGOke

Wood and acrylic paint. 14 x 9".

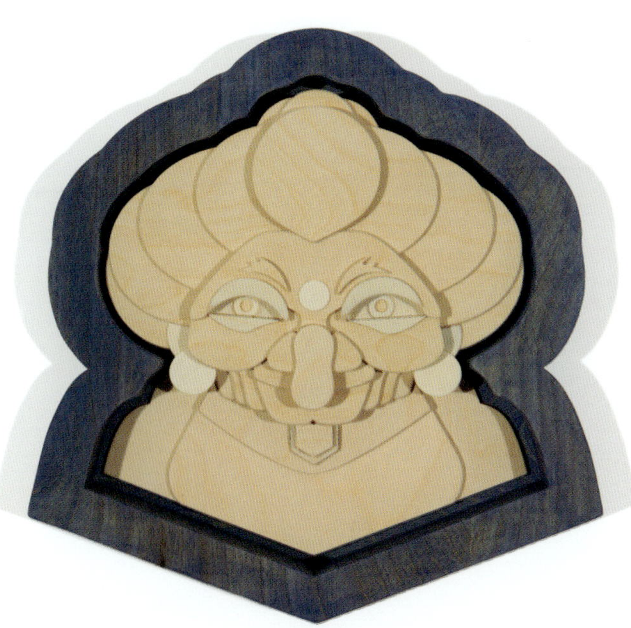

MILES RITCHIE

Zeniba

Wood. 12 x 12".

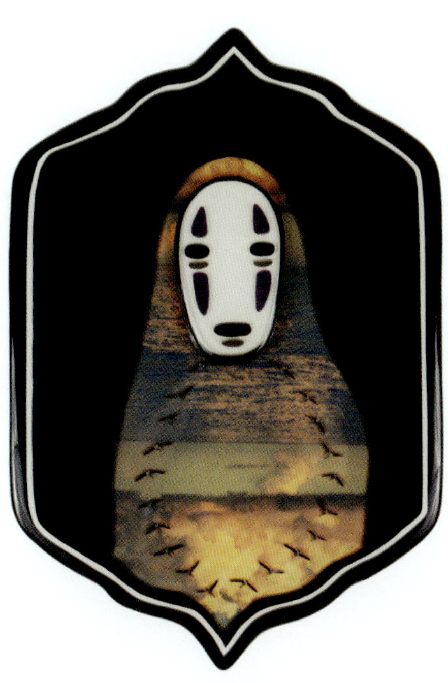

JAY RIGGIO

This Lonely Spirit

3D wood, paper, paint & layered resin assemblage. 16 x 23".

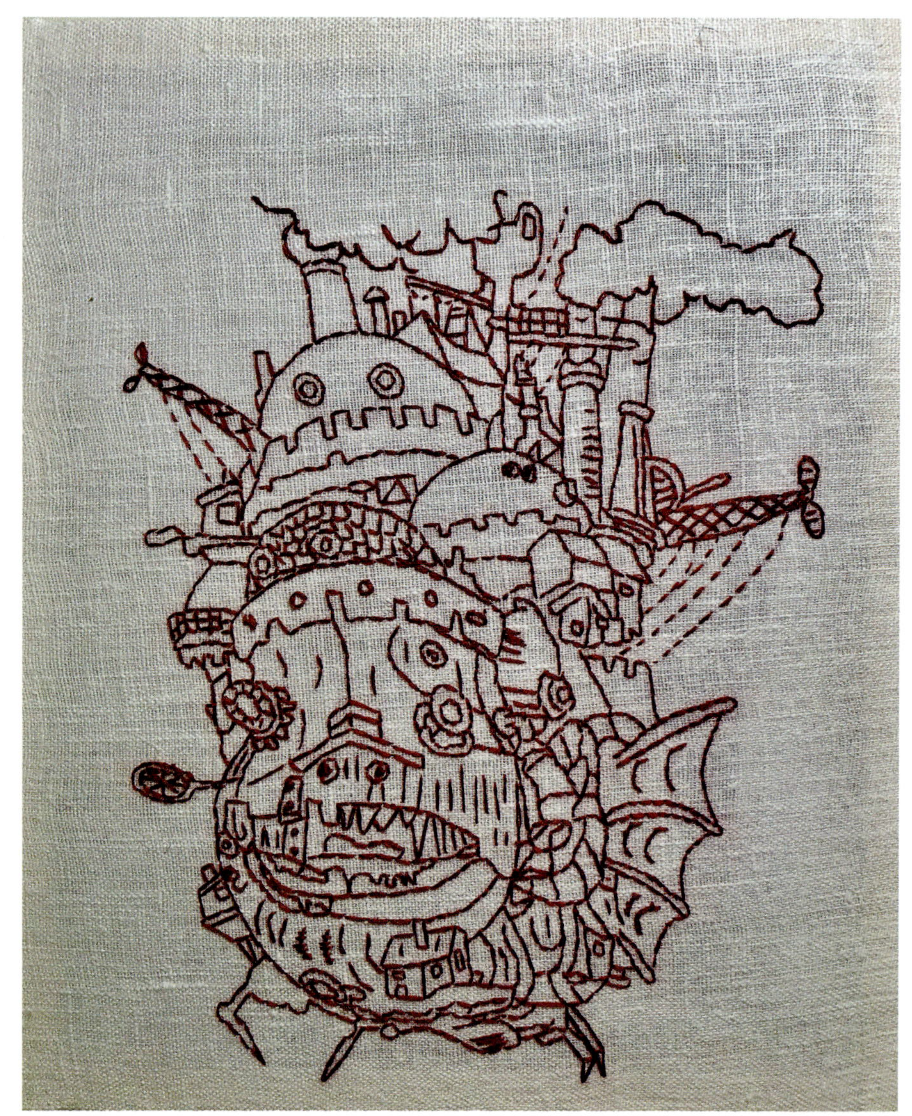

ELLEN SCHINDERMAN

ABOVE

The Castle

Hand embroidery. 9 x 11".

ALEX R. KIRZHNER

RIGHT PAGE

Mononoke the Curse

Acrylics and pencil on speciality paper. 16 x 20".

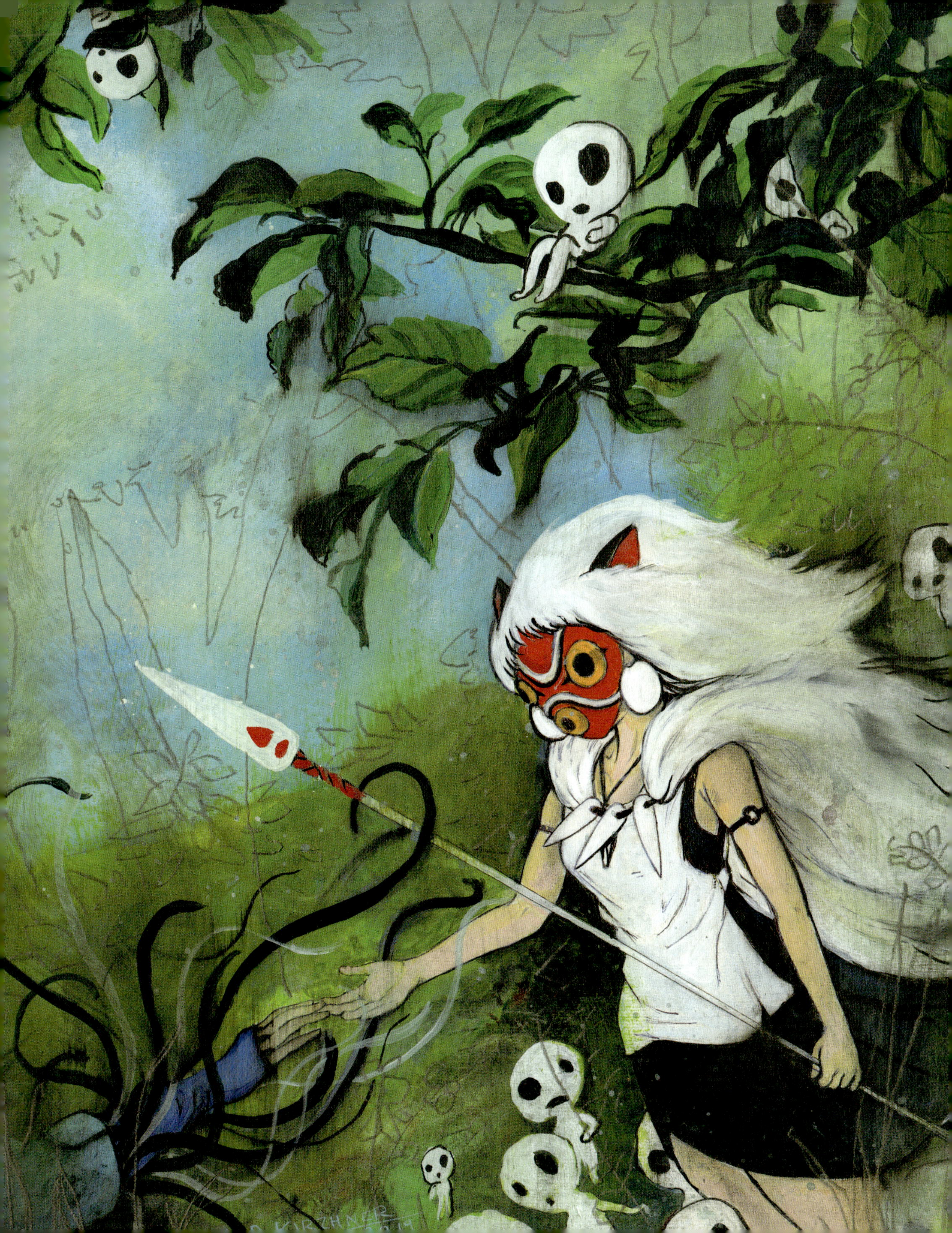

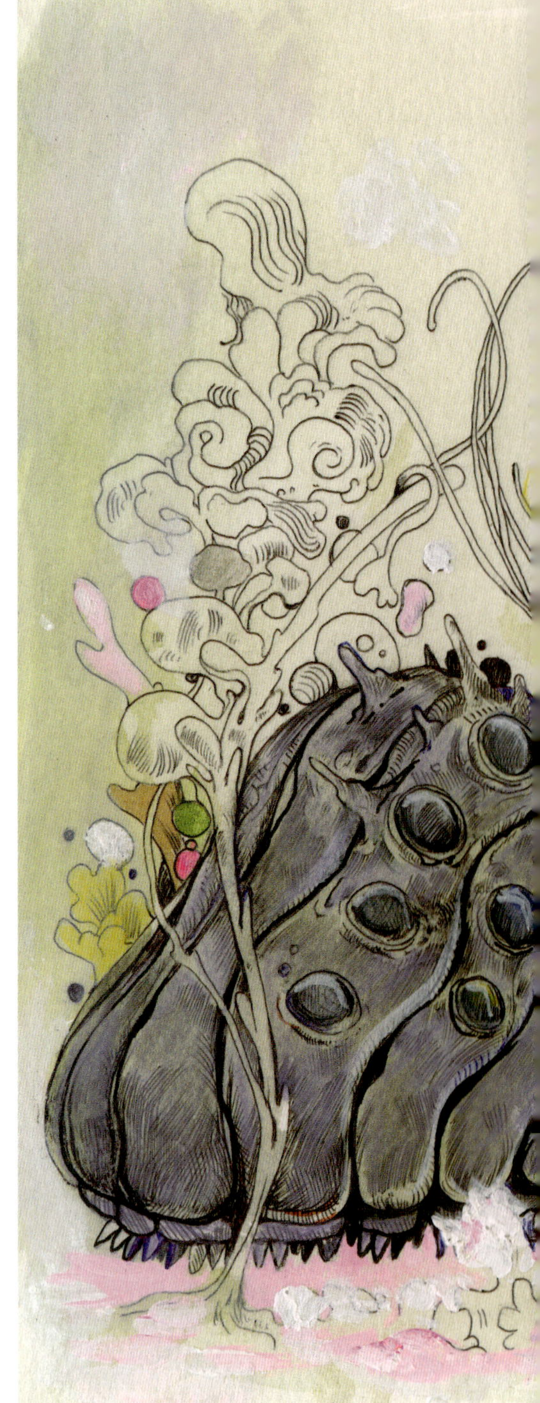

ALEX R. KIRZHNER

There is Nothing to Fear
Mixed media on printmaking paper.
14 x 11".

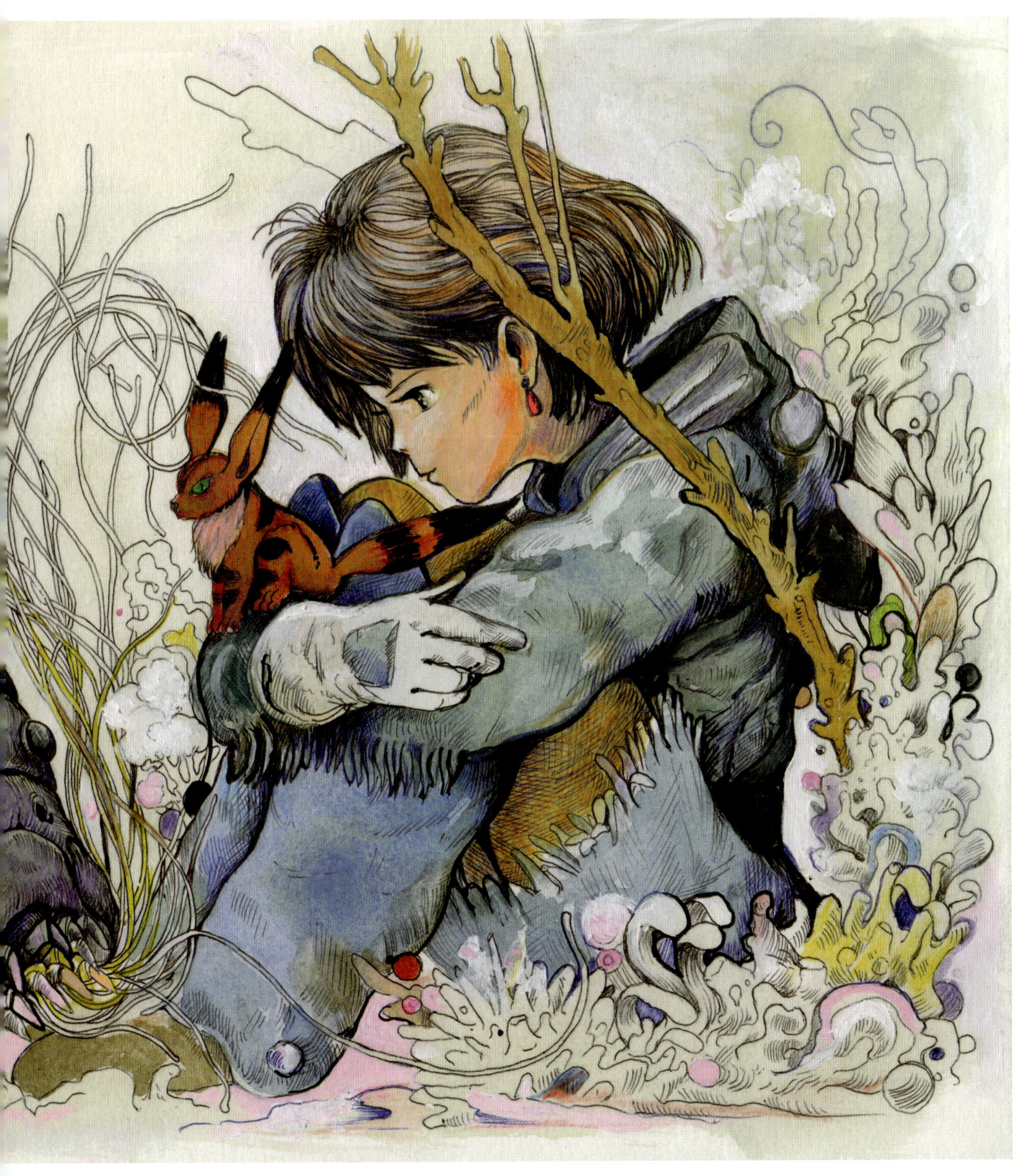

ALEX R. KIRZHNER

RIGHT PAGE, TOP LEFT

Kiki

Acrylic on printmaking paper. 5 x 7".

RIGHT PAGE, TOP RIGHT

Ashitaka

Acrylic on printmaking paper. 11 x 14".

RIGHT PAGE, BOTTOM LEFT

Howl Jenkins Pendragon

Acrylic on printmaking paper. 11 x 14".

RIGHT PAGE, BOTTOM RIGHT

San

Acrylic on printmaking paper. 11 x 14".

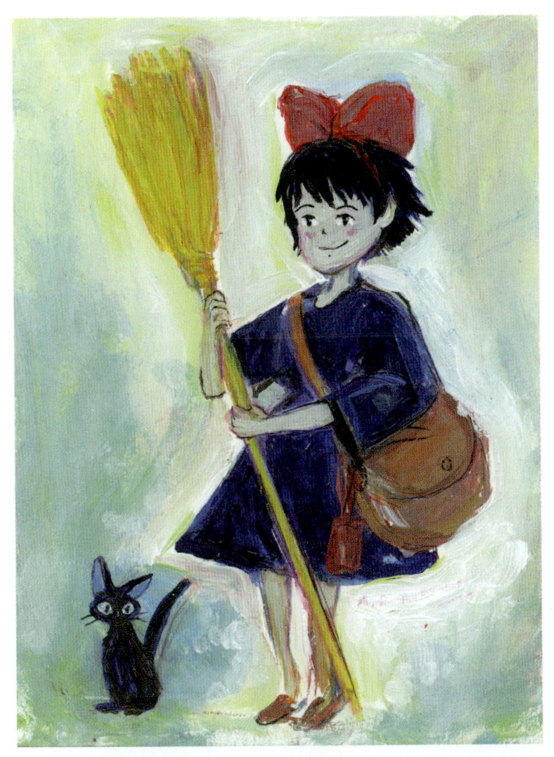

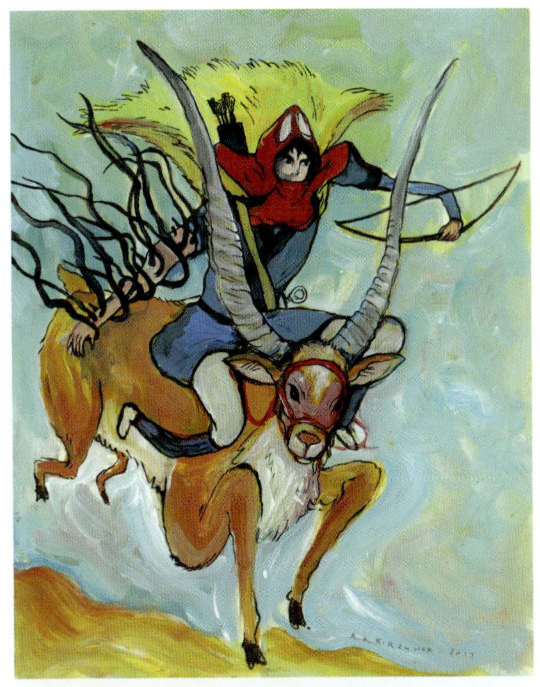

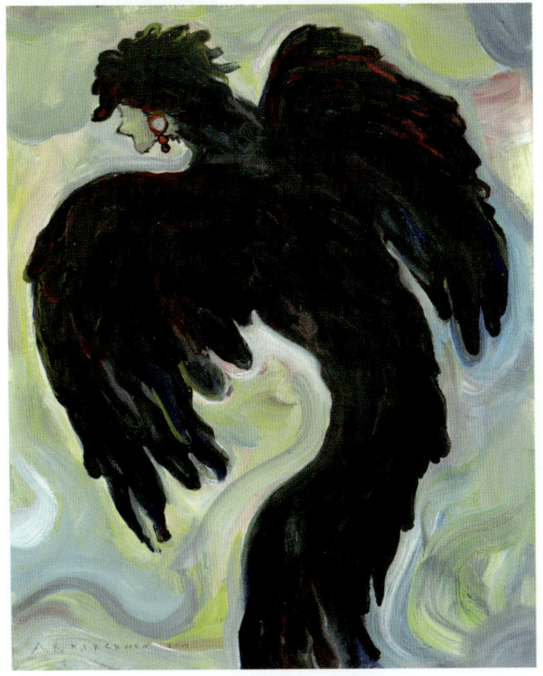

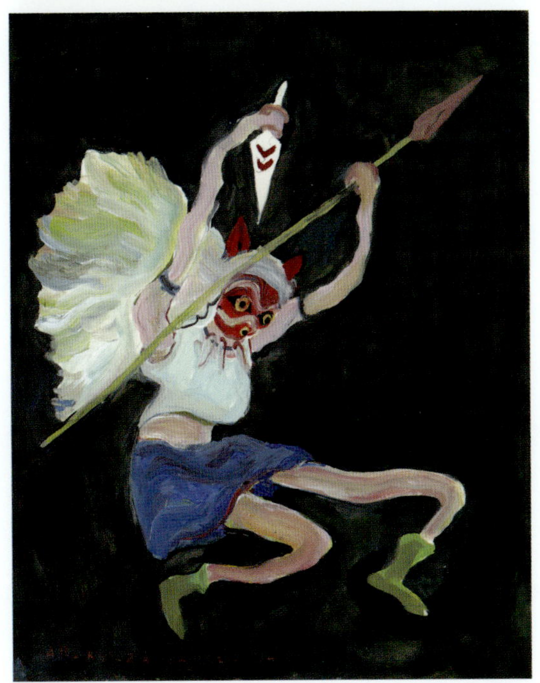

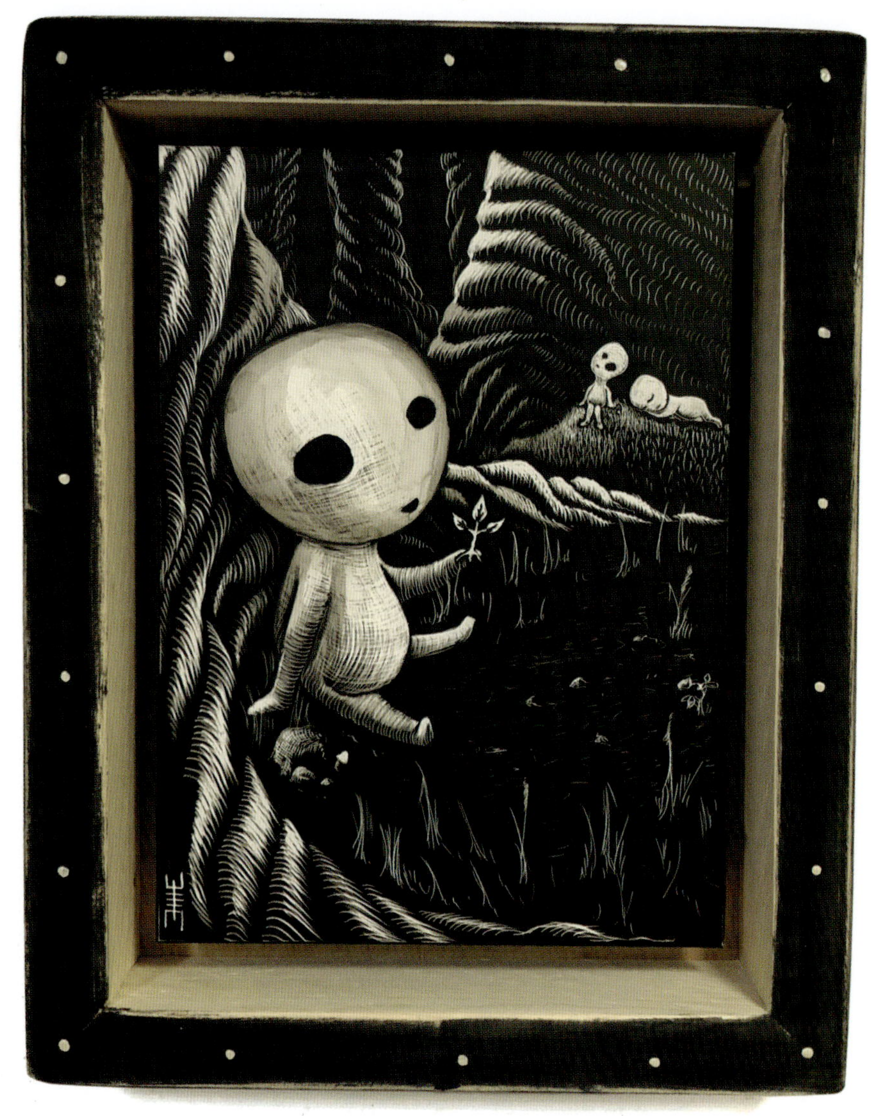

ELLIE RUSINOVA

ABOVE

Kodama 1

Scratch board. 7 x 9".

RIGHT PAGE

Kodama 2

Scratch board. 7 x 9".

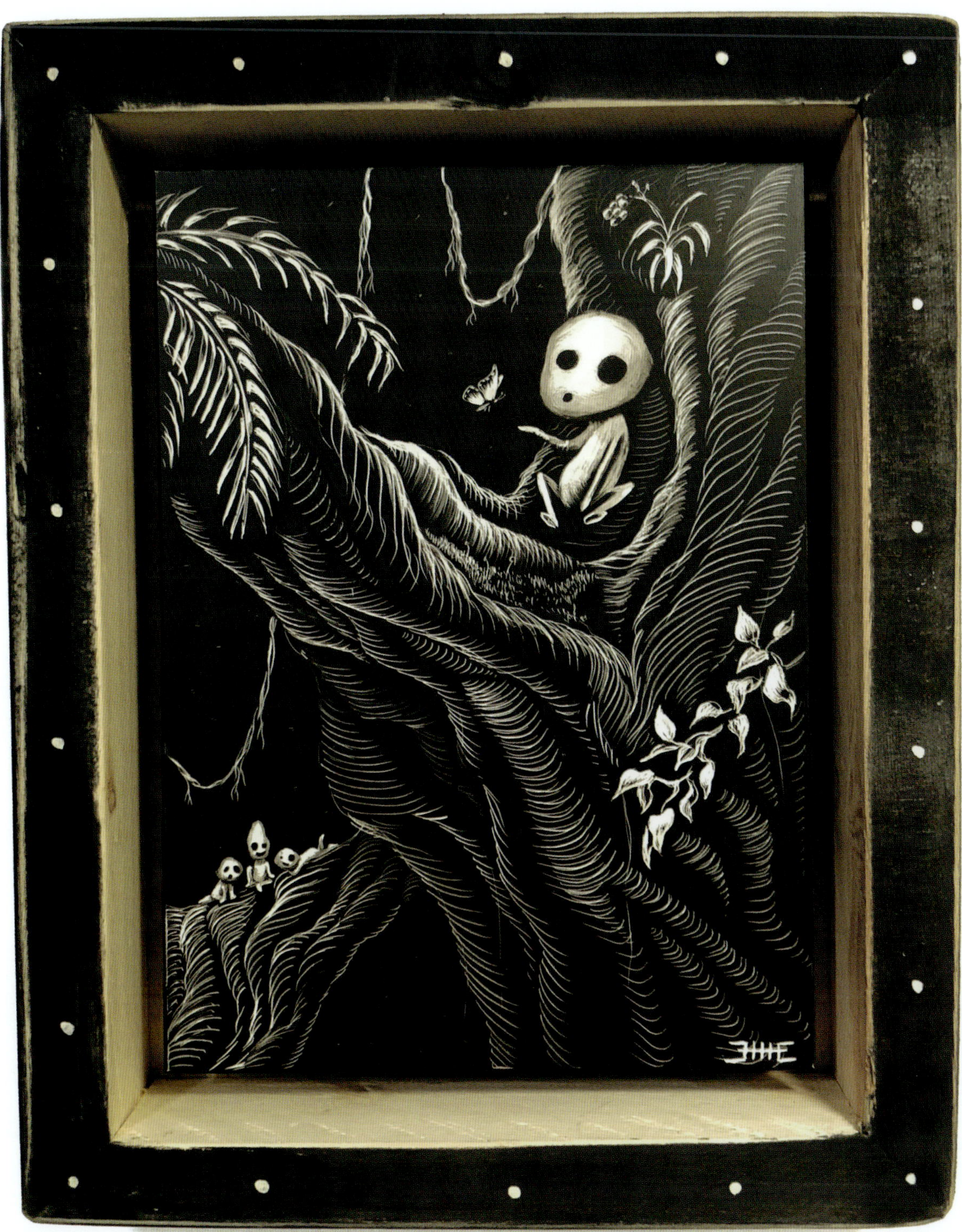

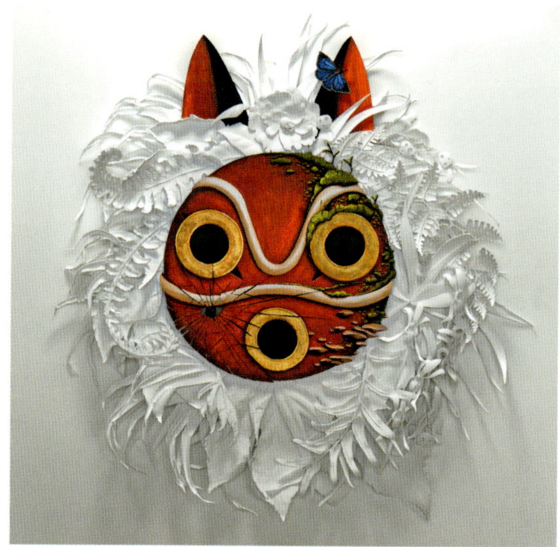

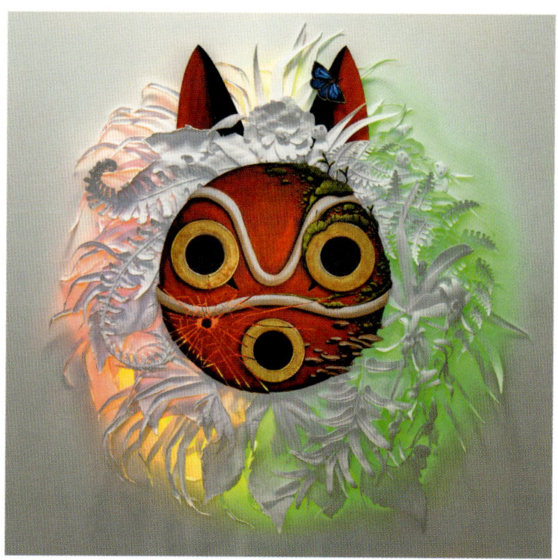

NICOLE LEE GROSJEAN

ABOVE

Shattered

Hand cut paper, watercolor, gouache, 22k gold leaf, & LED lights. 14 x 14".

JP NEANG

RIGHT PAGE

Youth of Ghibli

Graphite, watercolor and mixed media. 11 x 14".

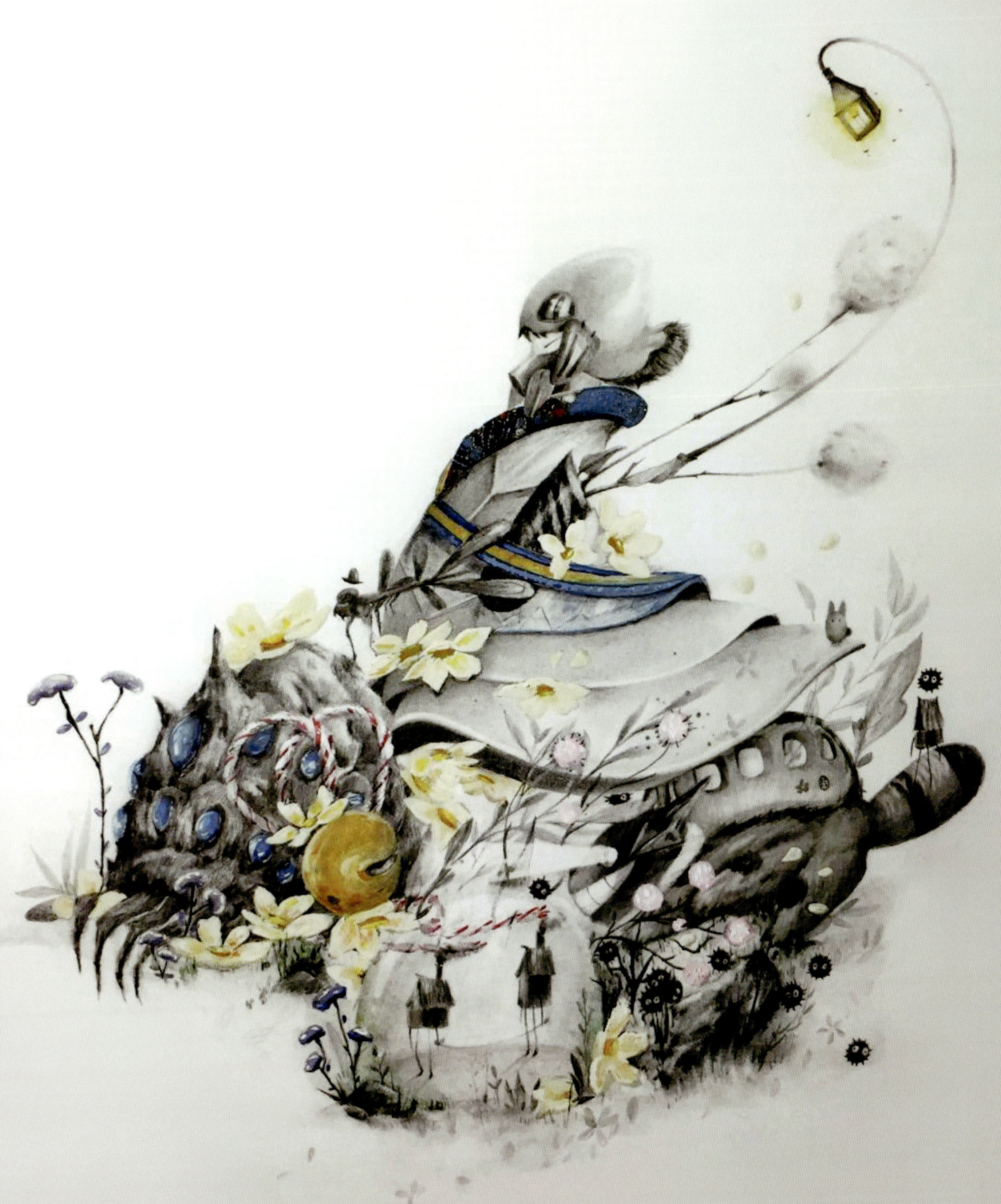

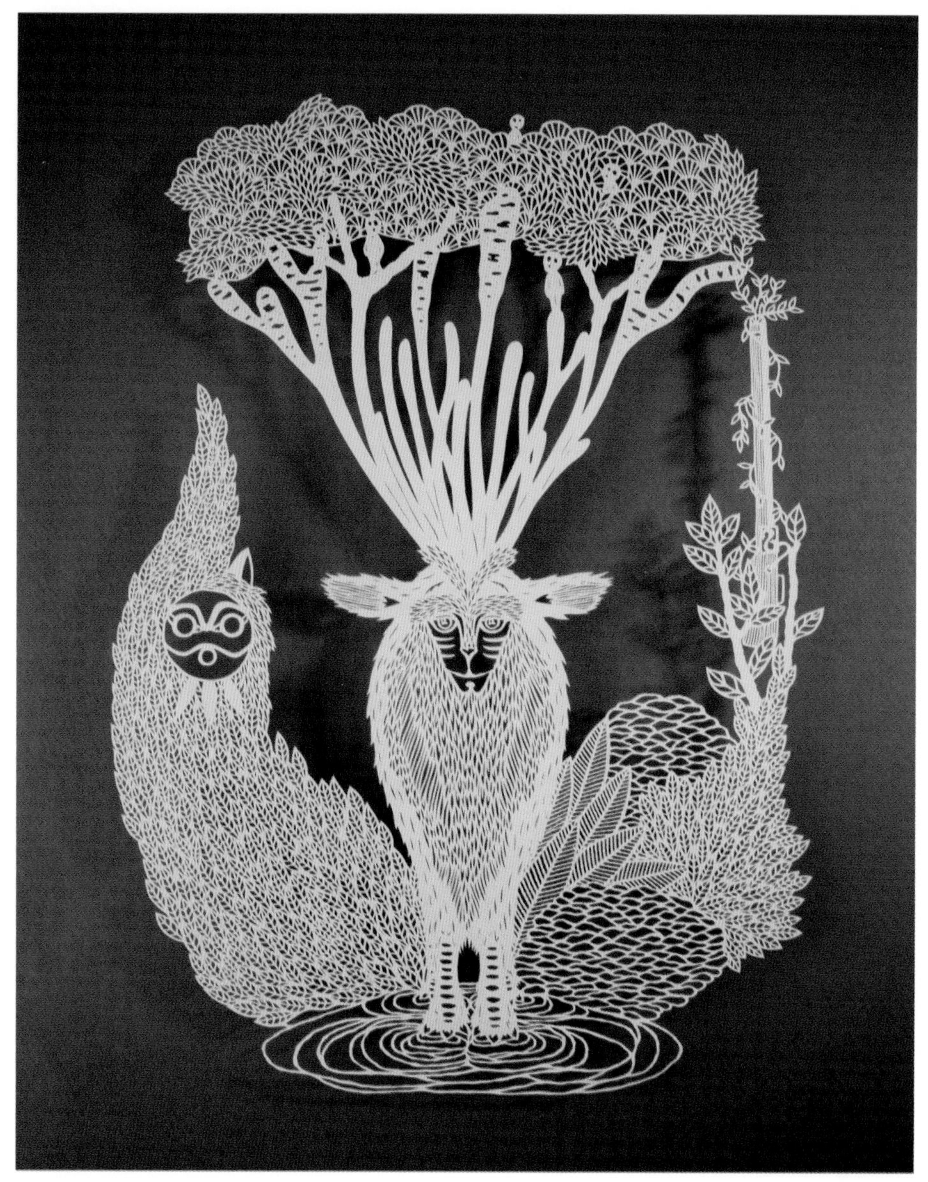

PIPPA DYRLAGA

ABOVE

The Forest Spirit

Hand cut paper. 8.5 x 12".

RIGHT PAGE

The Sky Gardener

Hand cut paper. 6 x 10.5".

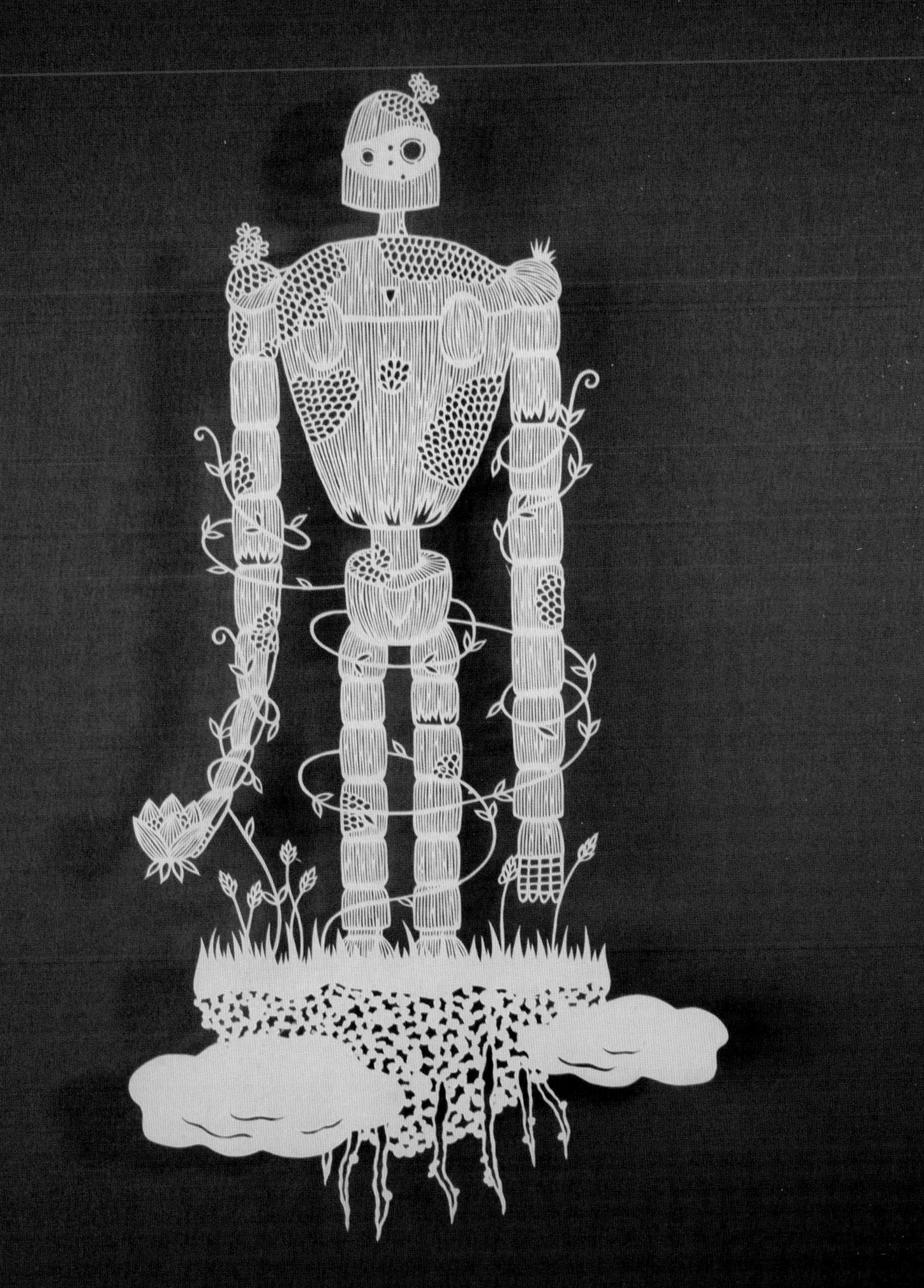

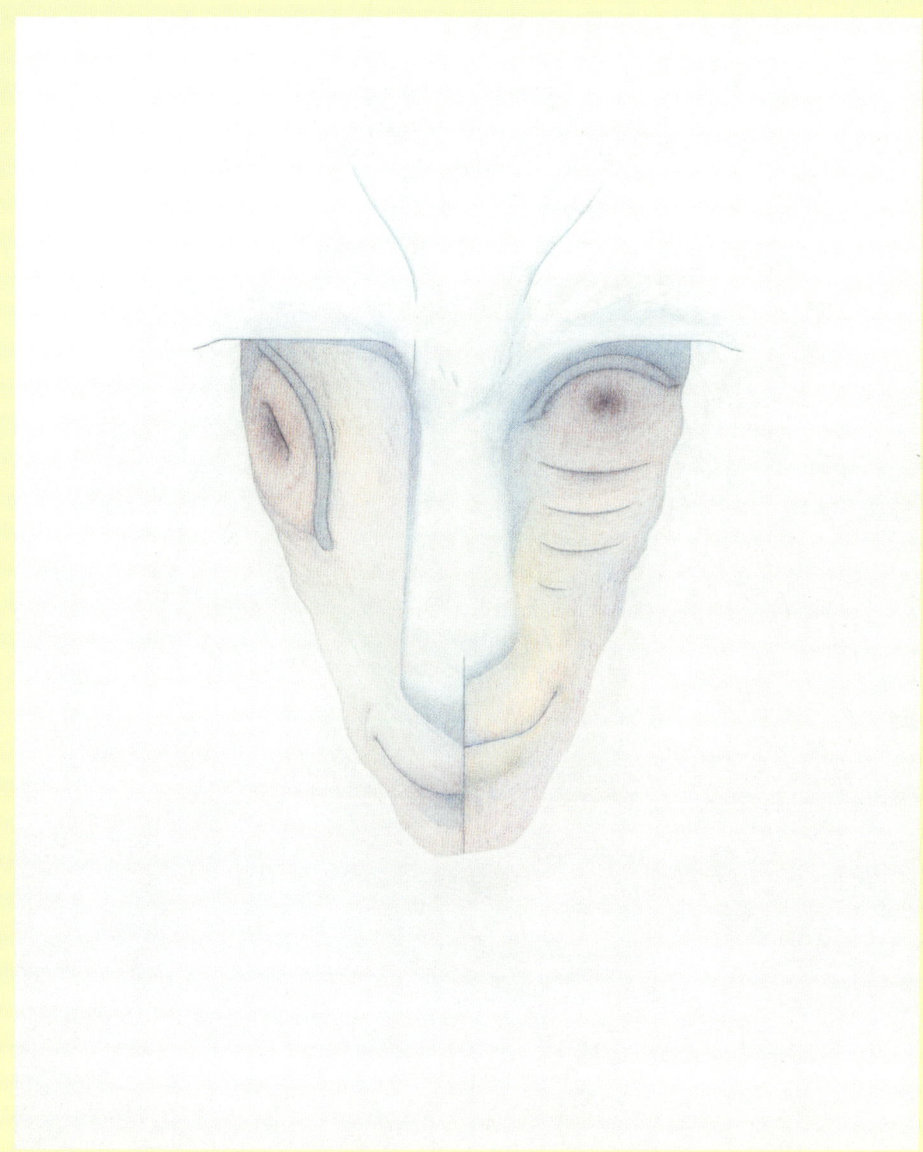

STEVE KIM

ABOVE

God of Life and Death

Colored pencil and graphite on paper. 11 x 8.5".

SUDI ROUHI

RIGHT PAGE

Mortido

Acryla gouache on cottonwood cold press paper. 8 x 10".

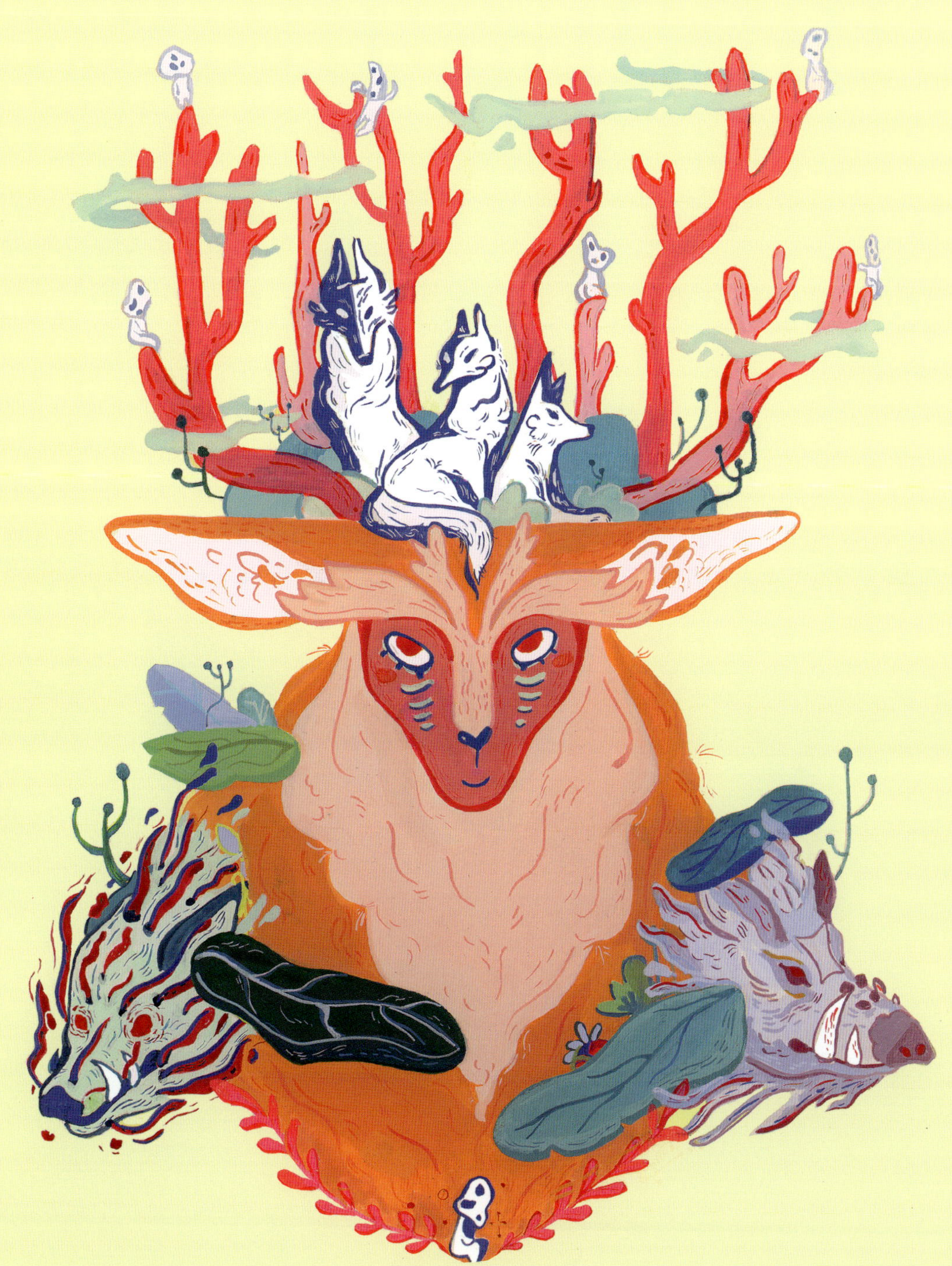

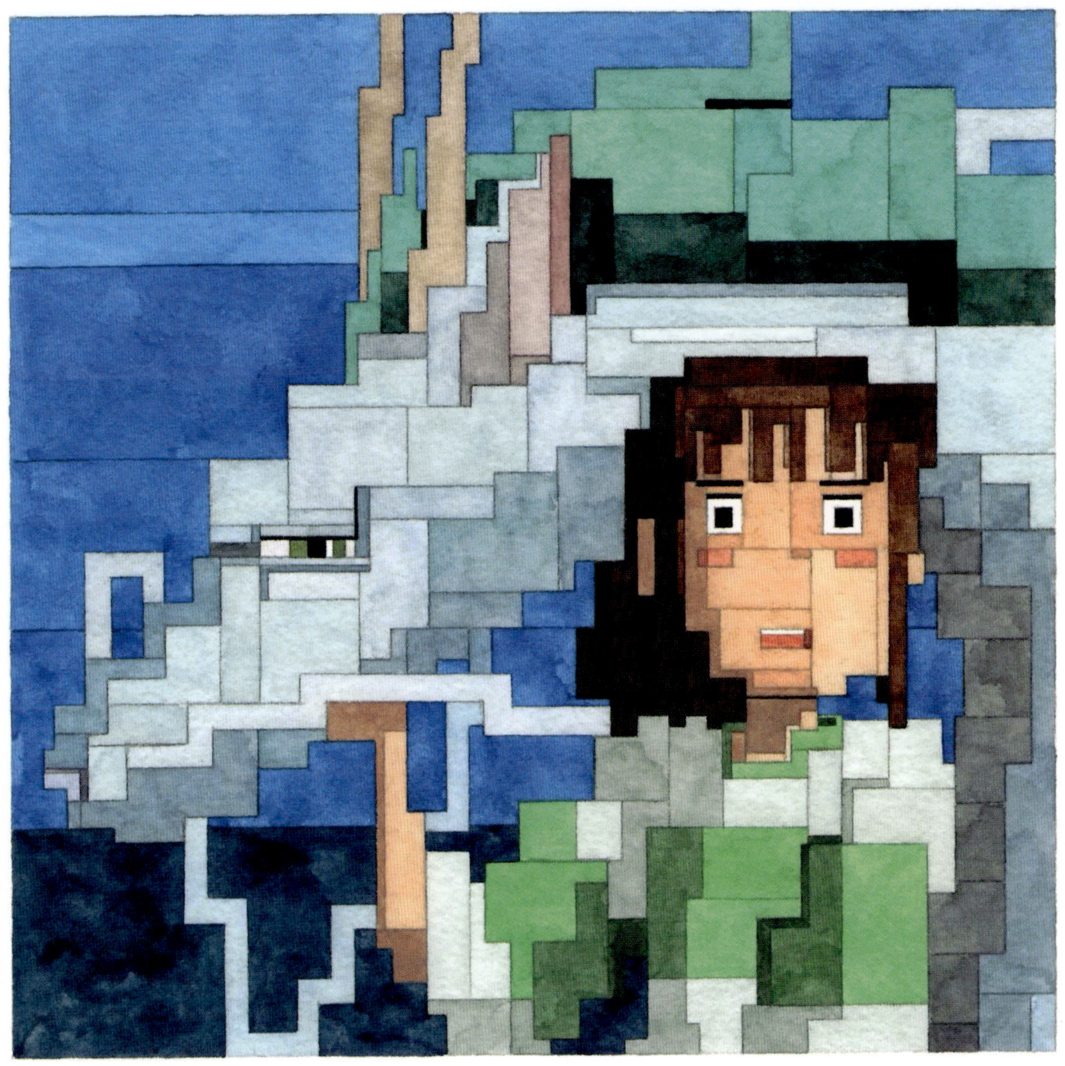

ADAM LISTER

ABOVE

Haku and Chihiro

Watercolor on paper. 8 x 8".

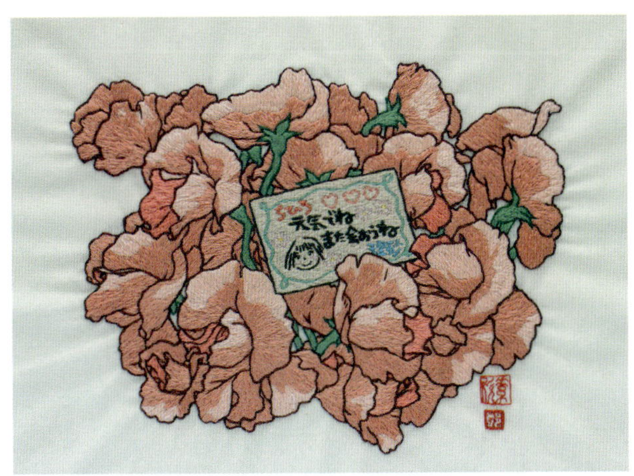

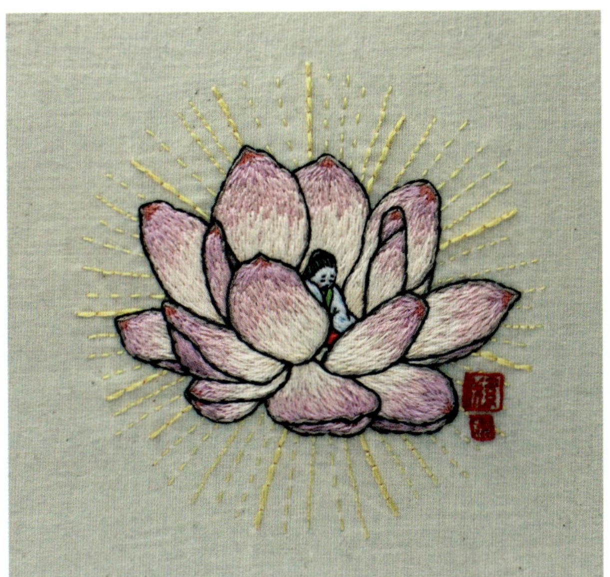

JESSICA SO REN TANG

TOP

Chihiro, Take care. See you soon. -Risa

Hand embroidery on fabric. 10 x 8".

BOTTOM

Divine Child

Hand embroidery on fabric. 6 x 6".

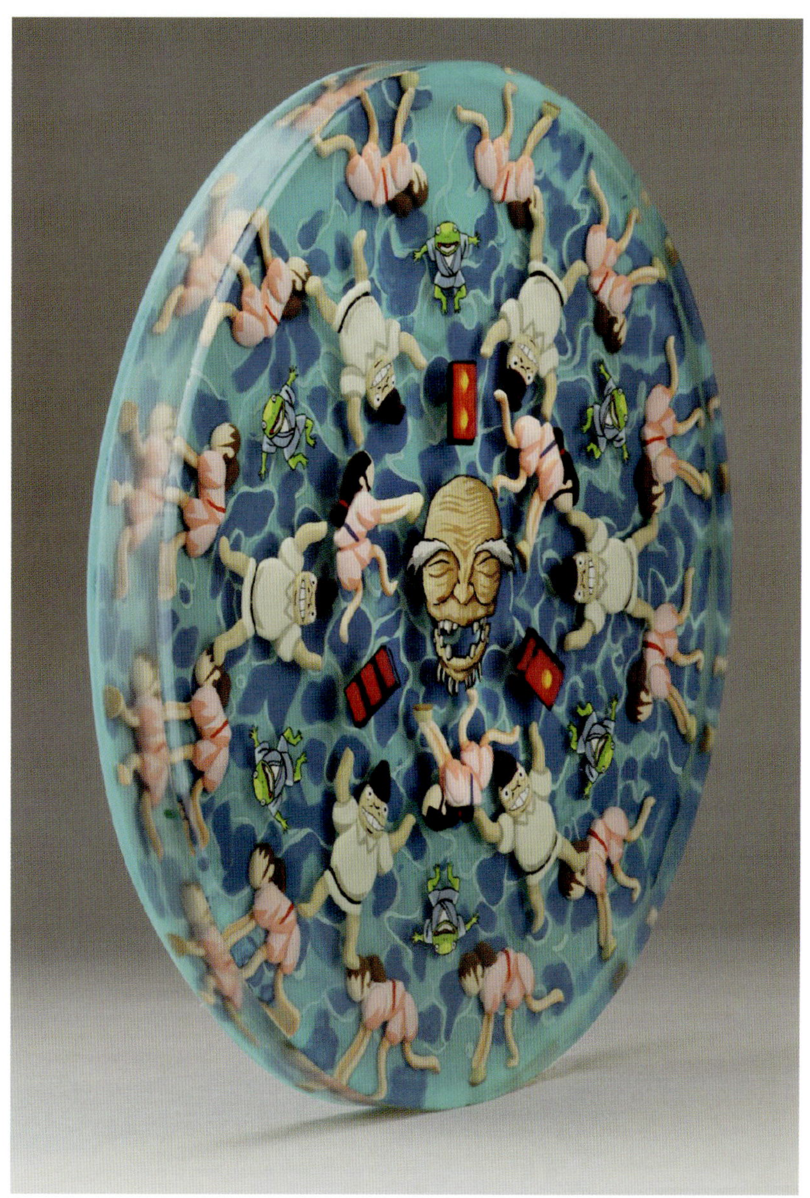

GEOFF TRAPP

ABOVE

Cleaning The River Spirit

Resin and acrylic paint. 11.5" diameter.

RIGHT PAGE

Spirited

Mixed media. 11" diameter.

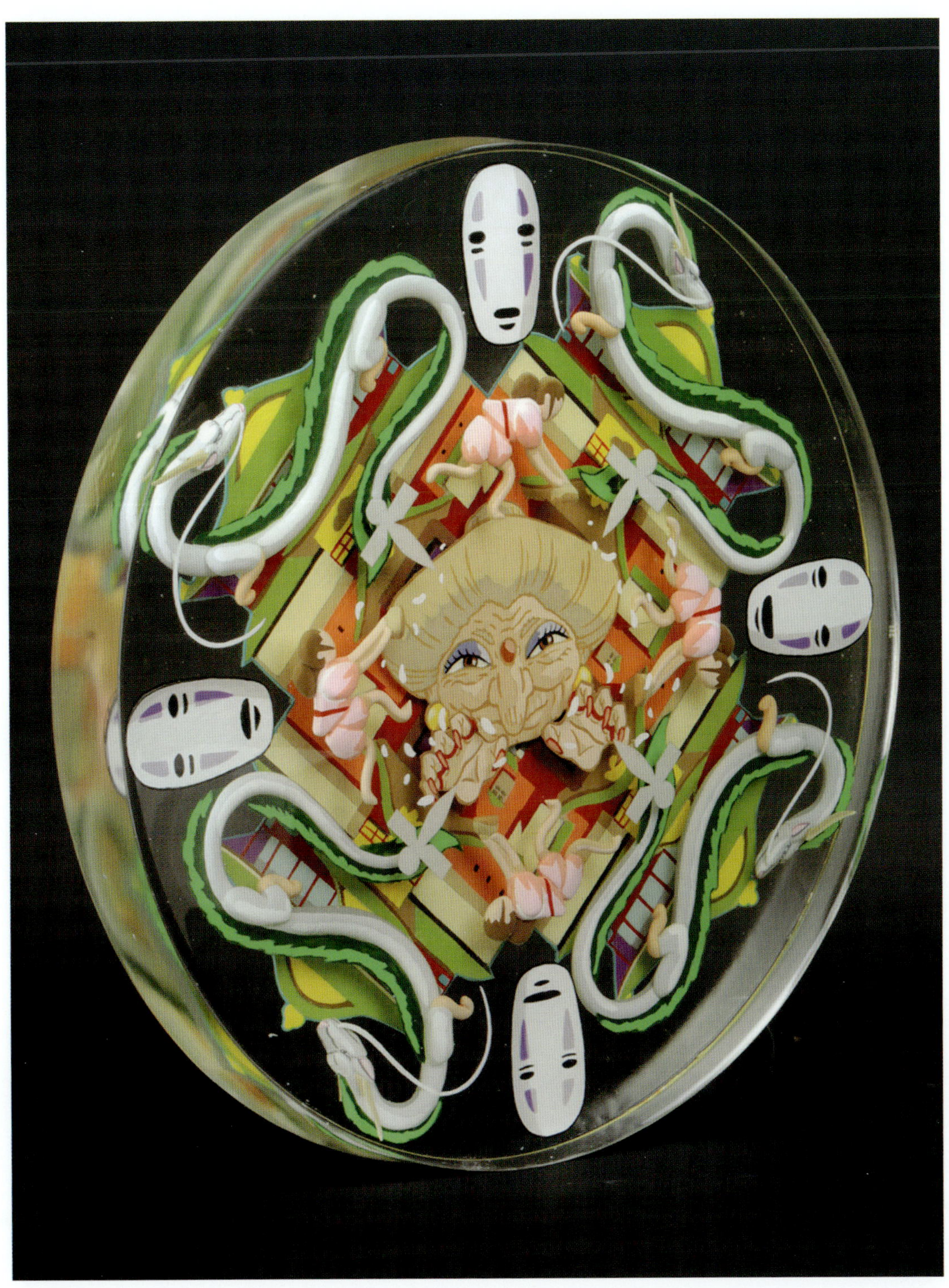

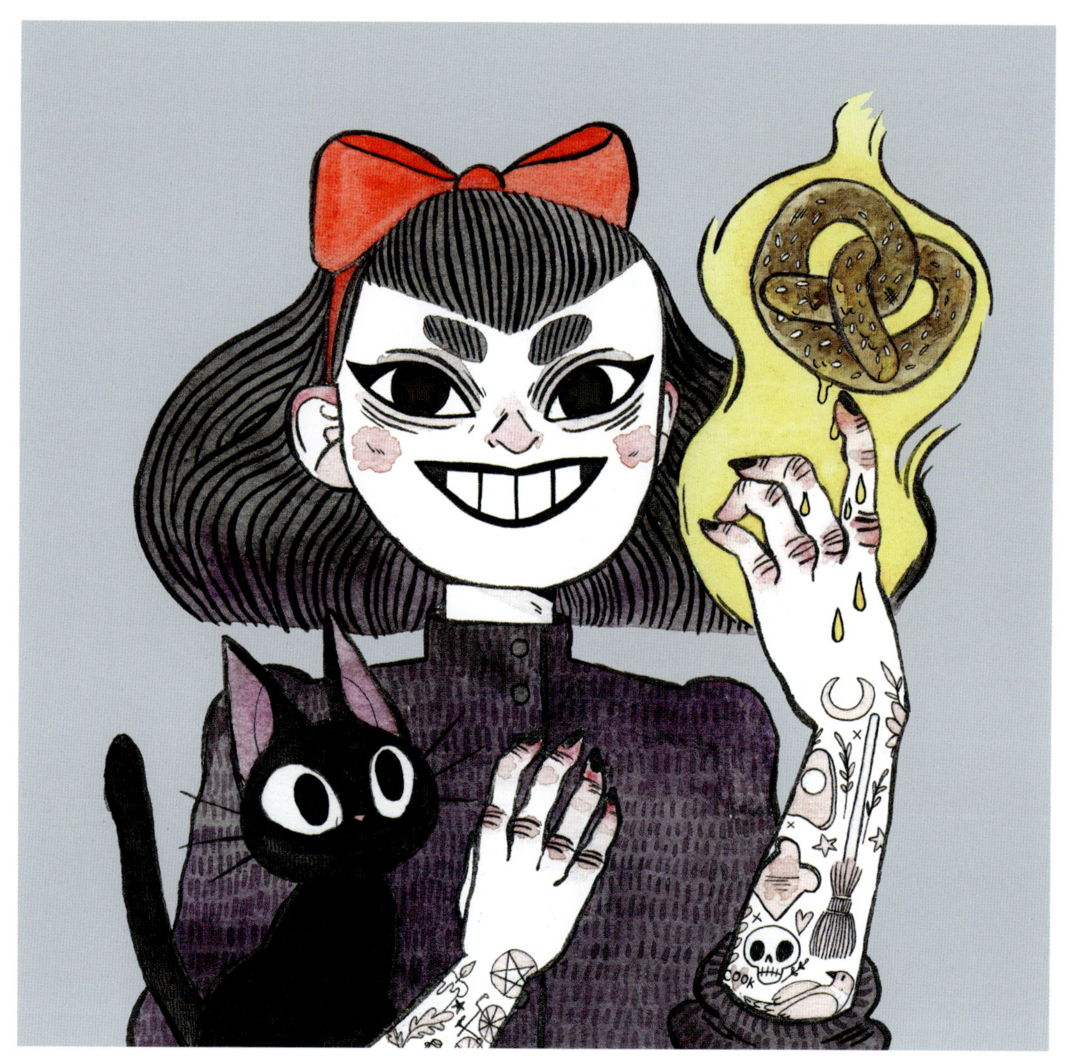

HEATHER MAHLER

ABOVE

Kiki Bakes

Watercolor, digital, mixed media. 10 x 10".

BRIAN MASHBURN

RIGHT PAGE

Moro

Oil on linen. 12 x 15".

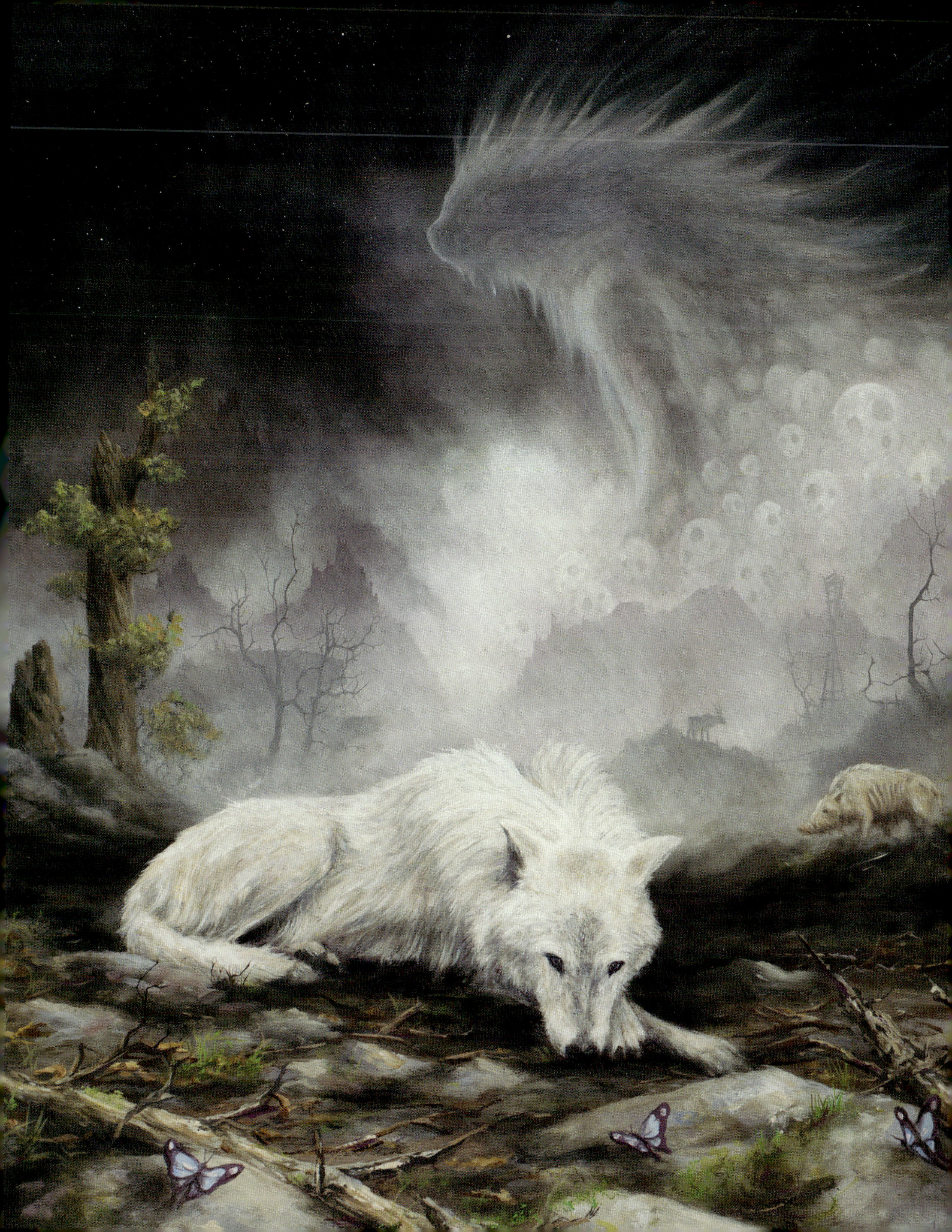

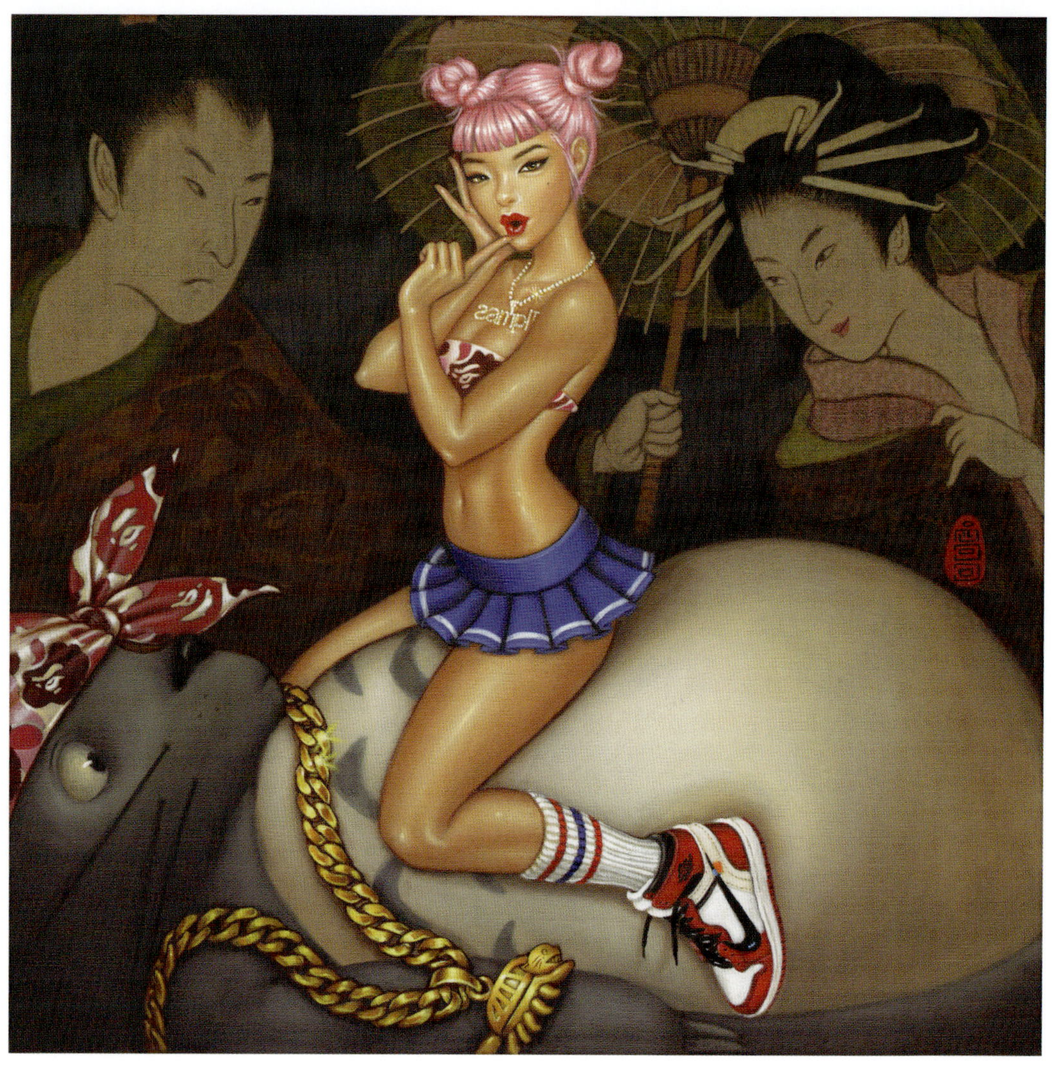

MIMI YOON

ABOVE

Luv My Neighbor

Acrylic on linen. 20 x 20".

J.A.W. COOPER

RIGHT PAGE

The Weave and the Weft-Alan Watts as Kamaji

Graphite, India ink and gouache. 8 x 11".

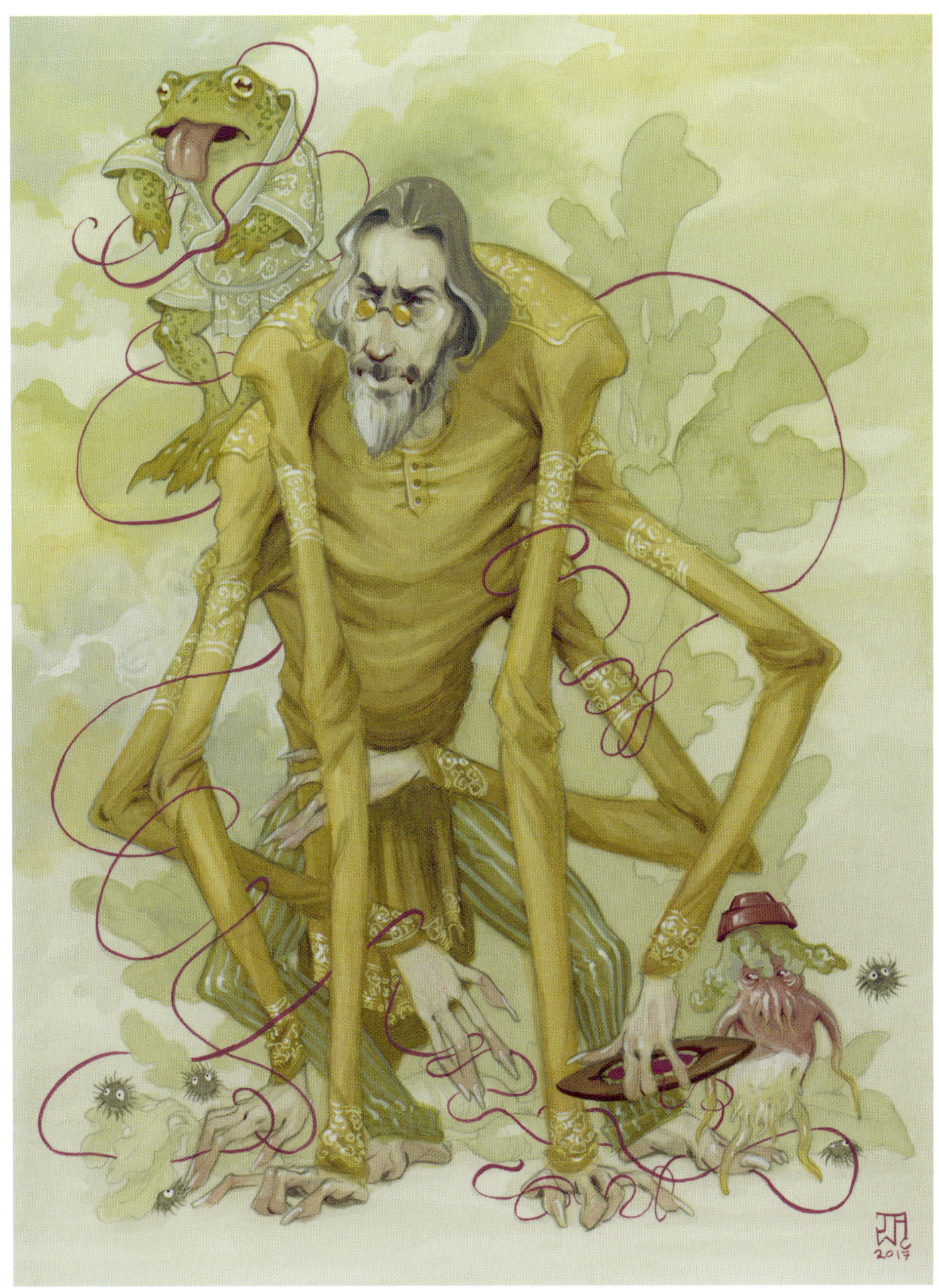

ADAM CALDWELL

Adam Caldwell is an artist, teacher and Oakland resident. He teaches drawing at the Academy of Art in San Francisco. His paintings juxtapose abstract and realistic styles to create collages that comment on social issues such as war and consumerism. They also question the nature of identity, gender and sexuality.

www.adamhuntercaldwell.com

ADAM LISTER

Adam Lister is a visual artist living and working in Beacon, New York. His work consists of geometric interpretations of iconic imagery and pop culture references. Lister has exhibited his artwork in galleries throughout the world, while also collaborating with numerous brands and other artists.

Instagram: @listergallery

ADAM ZISKIE

Adam is an illustrator and visual artist living in Berkeley, California. His artwork has been shown extensively in the Bay Area and has been featured in *Juxtapoz*, *Hi-Fructose*, and Supersonic Art. You can find him wandering around in the fog of the Bay.

www.adamziskie.com

ALEX R. KIRZHNER

Alex is an artist, Grammy-nominated art director and designer based in New York City.

www.newshadeofblack.com

ALINA CHAU

Alina Chau received her MFA from the University of California, Los Angeles. She spent over a decade working in the animation industry. Alina Chau's whimsical illustration style has been highly sought after for various art exhibitions world-wide. She is is currently developing her own children book publication and art projects.

www.alinachau.com

ALLISON REIMOLD

Allison Reimold is a Los Angeles native and nature enthusiast who currently works in the entertainment industry illustrating posters for film and TV.
She is a graduate of Otis College of Art and Design, and resides in Los Angeles with her muse, a French Bulldog named Penny.

Instagram: @allisonreimold

ANA ARANDA

Ana Aranda is an illustrator and visual artist based in San Francisco. You can find her work in children's books (Penguin, Lee & Low Books), murals and galleries in several countries. Her work is inspired by her native Mexico, the fantastical, childhood memories and music.

anaranda.com

ANNA TILLETT

Anna Tillett holds a B.F.A. in Illustration from Memphis College of Art, and has spent her days creating illustrations for popsicle shops, tees, films, and children's books. You can currently find her painting her next sour-faced sweet and eating all the pizza in the Beehive State of Utah.

www.annatillett.com

ANNIE STEGG GERARD

Annie Stegg Gerard has a special love for the eighteenth century Rococo painters who have had a large influence on her own method. She finds inspiration in their imagination, and the dreamlike palette and lively brushwork that combine to create a wonderful atmosphere of enchantment.

www.gallerygerard.com

ARNA MILLER

Denver artist Arna Miller creates screen printed illustrations of magical moments featuring an interesting character, often a cat or squirrel, and includes humorous text and sometimes fancy borders. With a background in architecture, and a respect for technical illustrations, inspiration is found in Asian firecracker and Victorian-era packaging.

www.arnamiller.com
Instagram: @arnamiller
Twitter: @arnamiller

AUDRA AUCLAIR

Audra Auclair is a Canadian artist whose work has spanned across many mediums. She specializes in exploring the surreal and beautiful female form with her transcendent fusion of fine art and illustration.

Instagram: @audraauclair

BEAU BERKLEY

Freelance artist living in Brooklyn, New York, with interests in pop culture art and design.

Instagram: @beauberkleyart

BENJAMIN CONSTANTINE

Painter, zine and comics maker living in Melbourne, Australia.

Instagram: @plumpe_ostere

BENNETT SLATER

A Canadian oil painter, Bennett utilizes traditional methods on wood panels. His work combines techniques from Flemish and Dutch still life disciplines, and the bold colors and forms from the pop art and surrealist schools. This dichotomy of contrasting disciplines and influences lends itself to thedualities explored in Bennett's work.

www.bennettslater.com

BETSY BAUER

Betsy Bauer is an illustrator working in publishing and animation based in Los Angeles. She loves being outdoors, cooking, and hunting for the perfect shrimp burrito.

www.betsybauerart.com

BRANDAN STYLES

Brandan Styles is a storyteller, tapping into the Universal Mythology that underlies and is within everything. His work is about creating visual poetry through the language of mythology, symbols and characters.

Instagram: @bzurk_demon

BRIAN MASHBURN

Brian Mashburn is an American artist based in Asheville, North Carolina.

www.brianmashburnart.com

BRIGHTON BALLARD

Brighton Ballard is an illustrator based in Salt Lake City, Utah. She's trained in watercolor painting and graphite drawing, and occupied most of her childhood with time spent over the page. She is the co-founder of NEUER GEIST, a design and risograph studio focused on keeping printed work alive.

Instagram: @neuergeist

BRUCE YAN

Bruce Yan is an artist and graphic designer based in Seattle, Washington. He's known for his clever interpretations of pop culture art from films, animations and comics.

www.bruceyan.com

CAMERON HAJAGOS

Cameron Hajagos is a surrealist painter based in Covina, California. He has been painting and drawing since early childhood. His artwork is inspired by nature and old cartoons he watched as a kid. He mainly works with acrylic paint and graphite. His artwork has been exhibited in Gallery1988 and Spoke Art.

Instagram: @Highsyrup

CAMILLA D'ERRICO

Camilla d'Errico is making waves in comics and low brow art with her manga-influenced style, expanding into designer toys, fashion, merchandise and video games. Camilla has distinguished herself through her ability to seamlessly weave comic art and manga with surrealist elements, wrapping it all together with an extensive emotional palette.

www.camilladerrico.com

CANDACE JEAN

Candace J. Andersen is an illustrator working in the suburbs just outside of Salt Lake City. She uses traditional media to complete her pieces, finding inspiration in old books, good animation, folklore and the natural world.

shop.candacejean.com

CAROLINE CALDWELL

Caroline Caldwell is an artist, writer and bad girl based in Brooklyn. She co-curates Art in Ad Places, a guerrilla community service project that replaces advertisements with artwork.

Instagram: @Dirtworship

CASEY WELDON

Casey Weldon is a Seattle-based fine artist and commercial illustrator. By using to the iconography of today and yesterday's popular culture, his work aims to awaken a feelings of nostalgia within the viewer, though often along with a sense humor, melancholy and longing for times lost.

www.caseyweldon.com

CHARLES CLARY

Charles Clary has shown regionally, nationally and internationally and has been included in numerous print and online interviews including *WIRED Magazine*, *Paper Art Now*, *PUSH Paper*, and *500 Paper Objects*. He is represented by Paradigm Gallery in Pennsylvania and RO2 gallery in Texas.

Instagram: @charlesclary

CHARLES SANTOSO

Charles Santoso loves drawing little things in his little journal and dreaming about funny, wondrous stories. He gathers inspiration from his childhood memories and curiosities he discovers in his everyday travels.

www.charlessantoso.com

CHRIS SKINNER

UK-based illustrator. Clients include Marvel, DC, Mondo, Bottleneck Gallery, Arrow Films, Studio Canal, The Folio Society.

www.chrisskinnerart.co.uk

CHRISTOPHER UMIMGA

Christopher Uminga is a painter and illustrator who has spent the last ten years developing a unique style that blends together creepy and cute. He has created art for DC Collectibles, Disney, Marvel Comics and Puma.

Instagram: @uminga720

CHRIS WALKER

Wild's & Co - An Old Fashioned Commercial Art Department Circa 1932! Hand Painted Advertising, Posters, Novelties & Movie Work.

Instagram: @wildsandco

CONCEPCIÓN STUDIOS

Concepción Studios is an award-winning design studio based in California with clients like Paul McCartney, Lady Gaga, David Bowie and Beyoncé. It has earned international recognition with works published in *The New Yorker*, *Rolling Stone*, *Time*, and *Print Magazine*, along with album art aired on the *Tonight Show*, *Conan*, and *Jimmy Kimmel Live*.

Instagram: @concepcion_studios

CORINNE REID

Corinne Reid is an illustrator and designer specializing in publishing, editorial and fine art. She uses unconventional imagery to cultivate emotional connections with her audience and adopts a narrative melody with accentuating tones of the natural world. Her work is award winning and globally recognized, making its way to Australia, Europe and North America.

www.corinnereid.com
Instagram: @rinfishe

CRANKBUNNY

Some things in life are slick, hip and blatantly obvious. But for Norma V. Toraya, who's known as Crankbunny, these are exactly the things she shies away from. Instead, Crankbunny is more inclined to explore storytelling through curiosity and timeless concepts while working as an animator, director and illustrator.

www.crankbunny.com

CROWDED TEETH

Michelle Romo is an illustrator and maker of things from Los Angeles, California. She is on an endless pursuit of drawing blobs with faces, cats in sweaters, and monsters who would really like to hug you.

www.crowdedteeth.com
Instagram: @monstromo

CUDDLY RIGOR MORTIS

Kristin Tercek has been painting under the name Cuddly Rigor Mortis since 2009. Her work has been shown in galleries and museums all over the world from New York City to Los Angeles to Paris to the Disneyland Resort in California. She still can't believe it.

www.cuddlyrigormortis.co

DAN GRISSOM

Dan Grissom is an illustrator, print-maker, painter and musician based in Austin, Texas. He runs a screen printing and letterpress studio called Biscuit Press out of his garage.

www.biscuitpressatx.com

DAVID MOSCATI

David is an award-winning artist residing in Atlanta with his equally creative better half and a cat whose namesake loves a damn fine cup of coffee. Inspired by scotch, and a good science-fiction novel, David often finds himself attempting to save the world one piece of art at a time.

Instagram: @moscativision

DEAN STUART

Since 2007, he's been cultivating his career both as an illustrator and a fine art painter out of his studio in Oakland. His interests are in creating surreal dreamlike worlds and narratives. He finished his first published illustrated and painted fairy-tale called *Finders Keepers* which can be seen on his website.

www.deandraws.com
Instagram: @deangus

DEREK BALLARD

Derek Ballard is a graphic designer whose career has taken him around the world, with work appearing in New York, San Francisco, Los Angeles, London and Salzburg. He is inspired by time spent outdoors, whether alone on a bike or with his wife, Brighton. Derek is the co-founder of NEUER GEIST.

www.neuergeist.com

ED MIRONIUK

Ed Mironiuk lives and works in New Jersey. He received his BFA from Parson School of Design. Inspired by his wife Kristin Tercek's toys and paintings he transitioned from illustration to wool sculpture. The resulting cuteness and happiness has become the driving factor in his work.

www.edmironiuk.com

EDWIN USHIRO

Edwin Ushiro is an artist from Maui who now resides in Los Angeles. After graduating from Art Center College of Design, his artwork has been exhibited in venues worldwide, including Villa Bottini in Italy, the Museum of Kyoto, the Honolulu Museum of Art and the Japanese American National Museum.

Instagram: @edwinushiro

ELLEN SCHINDERMAN

Ellen Schinderman is an autodidactic artist who uses stitch to see things anew. Her work comes from a need to celebrate women, femininity and sexuality in all its shades and aspects.

www.schindermania.com

ELLIE RUSINOVA

Ellie Rusinova is an artist known for her theatrically spiritual art from a variety of influences ranging from mythology to folklore, surrealism and occultism, blended together into thoughtful, humorous and slightly dark imagery that radiates with energy.

Instagram: @Ellie_Rusinova

EMILY DUMAS

Emily is a licensed illustrator and surface designer in Massachusetts. Her work has adorned a variety of retail products and has been exhibited and sold at tradeshows and galleries across the US. Her work includes handlettering, inspiration from her love of food and bright, bold colors.

Instagram: @emilydumas_illustration

ERIC ALTHIN

Eric Althin, AKA Sad Salesman, is a Brooklyn-based artist and character designer. Eric launched his own art-toy brand Sad Salesman in 2017 and won the Designer Toy Award for Breakthrough Artist in 2018. He also creates characters for mobile games and showcases his sculptures in exhibitions across the country.

Instagram: @sad_salesman

ERIC BONHOMME

Miami-based artist Eric Bonhomme has been perfecting his craft for several years. Originally a fine arts painter, he has moved on to more contemporary subject matters and incorporates his comic book influences. He has been experimenting with mixed medias and mythology concepts exploring unique narratives and rich details in his worlds.

Instagram: @skullbashhero

EVAN B. HARRIS

Everything in life is ART... the little things matter.

www.bloodmoongallery.com
Instagram: @evanbharris

FELT MISTRESS

Felt Mistress AKA Louise Evans is a UK-based stitcher who creates a range of one-off bespoke creatures in collaboration with her partner illustrator Jonathan Edwards. Their work has been exhibited all over the world and used in fashion shoots, ad campaigns, music videos and films.

Instagram: @feltmistress

FERNANDO REZA

Fernando Reza, professionally known as Fro, is a graphic artist/illustrator living in Los Angeles, where his company, Fro Design Co., is based. Much of his art contains hidden clues that, for 2,000 years, the Knights Templar have hidden and protected the secret bloodline of Jesus Christ.

www.frodesignco.com

FERRIS PLOCK

Ferris Plock is a San Francisco-based artist who lives within the city with his wife, Kelly Tunstall (Plock's partner in the artistic duo KeFe), and son. Plock brings a dedicated focus to his work that is paired with a wild sense of originality. Through a variety of mediums, he creates highly detailed works, often character-based paintings on wood panel, that combine contemporary pop culture with the aesthetic of Japanese ukiyo-e woodblocks. Plock has created illustrations for many high-profile clients, has been involved in solo and group exhibitions both nationally and abroad.

www.ferrisplock.com
Instagram: @ferrisplock

FREEHAND PROFIT (GARY LOCKWOOD)

Freehand Profit is a Los Angeles-based artist best known for creating one of a kind masks from deconstructed sneakers. They explore identity and consumerism in a world plagued by war, environmental destruction and civil unrest, with inspirations from the roles of masks in ancient civilizations, comics, anime and hip-hop.

www.freehandprofit.com

GEOFF TRAPP

For over a decade Geoff Trapp has worked in toy development at NECA where he is a model painter, with experience in toy design and packaging illustration. Since graduating from the Mason Gross School, he has shown his artwork at Gallery1988, Hero Complex Gallery and Spoke Art amongst others.

www.geofftrappdidit.com

GEORGE TOWNLEY

Designer and illustrator living in London with a passion for americana, film and architecture.

Instagram: @george.townley

GERMAIN BARTHELEMY (MAINGER)

Graphic designer and illustrator for ten years, he mainly works on alternative movie posters.

www.mainger.com

GINA HENDRY

Gina Hendry was born in 1994, is from Upstate New York, and lives and works in California.

www.ginapierikhendry.com

GREG GOSSEL

Greg Gossel was born in 1982 in western Wisconsin. With a background in design, his work is an expressive interplay of many diverse words, images, and gestures. Gossel's multi-layered work illustrates a visual history of change and process that simultaneously features and condemns popular culture.

Instagram: @greggossel

GUILLAUME MORELLEC

French graphic designer and illustrator living in Paris. His passion for video games and cinema cultivates his fondness for design more and more everyday. He is working in children's publishing, fashion and is regularly exhibited in international galleries.

www.guillaumemorellec.com

HARRY MICHALAKEAS

Harry Michalakeas is a Dallas-based British contemporary artist whose current work primarily focuses on the psychological dualities one experiences in today's world.

Instagram: @harry_michalakeas

HEATHER MAHLER

Heather Mahler is an artist based in Salt Lake City. Her work depicts bold women and animals, sharing body positivity and strength. Her drawings reflect how we all choose our identity and celebrate feminity. Pop culture and geekdom is a big part of her work too, for it is an escape from stress.

www.heathermahler.com

IVONNA BUENROSTRO

Ivonna Buenrostro is an artist based in Mexico. Her work is inspired by her love of comics and movies.

Instagram: @ivonnabuenrostro

JAMES GILLEARD

James Gilleard is an illustrator and animator from the UK, residing in New York and working for Blue Sky studios. He is influenced by many things including glitch art, vaporwave, impressionism, mid-century architecture and early 3D video games, to name a few. Slightly obsessed with Japan, he regularly visits to see his wife's family.

Twitter: @jgilleard

JAMES R. EADS

James R. Eads is a Los Angeles-based artist with a background in traditional printmaking and painting. He uses motion and color to create impressionistic dreamlike paintings. James takes a feeling of discovery and scatters it throughout his work, offering a glimpse of the underlying magic of everything.

Instagram: @james.r.eads.art

JAN WILLEM

Illustrator and tattoo artist based in Rotterdam, The Netherlands.

Instagram: @janwillemtattoo

JASON STOUT

He's had a lot of good fortune and fun as an artist in Austin, Texas. He has knocked around all kinds of work: design, illustration, animation on Richard Linklater's *A Scanner Darkly*. He is currently in service to this town he loves as art director of the legendary alt-weekly *The Austin Chronicle*.

www.jasonstout.com

J.A.W. COOPER

J.A.W. Cooper was born in England, grew up in Kenya, Sweden, Ireland, and Southern California, and currently lives in smelly downtown Los Angeles. Cooper works commercially as an illustrator and as an art director for TV/movie advertising campaigns and spends copious amounts of time camping and hiking.

www.jawcooper.com

JAY GORDON

Jay Gordon is a Cape Town-based illustrator with a love for drawing, film, graphic novels, Golden-Age illustration and weird fiction. Jay's influences range from the classic pulp art to the cinematography of Deakins, Alcott and Kubrick. His tools of choice are Photoshop, a Wacom Cintiq and a Bialetti Espresso Maker.

www.jaygordondraws.com

JAY RIGGIO

Jay Riggio is a self-taught visual artist from New York. Riggio's mixed media works depict dream-inspired stories through unique, surrealistic visual pairings: a reflection of the artists interpretations on life, love, humor and the human condition. Jay currently lives and works in Los Angeles.

Instagram: @jayriggioart

JAYDE CARDINALLI

Jayde Cardinalli is a California-based designer and illustrator with a BFA in Graphic Design. She is skilled in hand-drawn and digital techniques, animation, product design, and art direction. Jayde's illustrations were recently featured on clothing for GUCCI. Her work can also be found in editorials including *Elle*, *Vogue* and *Vanity Fair*.

Instagram: @jayde.cardinalli

JEANY NGO

Jeany is a designer's illustrator and artist. She loves playing with lights, shadows and moods in her artwork. Hayao Miyazaki's fantastic storytelling and strong leading characters is an influence in her life and work.

Instagram: @gojeanyn

JESSE RIGGLE

Jesse Riggle is a painter and illustrator who has been working professionally for more than a decade. He has shown work in galleries across the US and has done illustration for books, games, and magazines. When not making art Jesse is probably travelling or petting some cats.

www.jesseriggle.com

JESSICA SO REN TANG

Jessica Tang is a first-generation Chinese-American artist. Born and raised in San Francisco, she received her BA in Studio Art at Mills College in Oakland in 2013. Her work has been exhibited in San Francisco, Portland and New York. She currently maintains a studio in South San Francisco.

Instagram: @jessicasorentang

J.M. DRAGUNAS

Illustrator living in northern Ohio with his lovely wife, Jenn. Currently working on his creator owned book, L.C. Noir.

Instagram: @jmdragunas

JONATHAN EDWARDS

Jonathan Edwards is an illustrator and comic artist with a long and diverse career. He has produced illustrations and comics for publishers worldwide as well as concept artwork for films and television. His character design work includes the vinyl toy Inspector Cumulus and many collaborations with his partner Felt Mistress.

Instagram: @jontofski

JORDAN BOLTON

Jordan Bolton is a photographic poster artist from Manchester, England, where he creates posters that focus on how films use set design to communicate their story to an audience. All objects are made by hand then photographed.

Instagram: @jordanboltondesign

JOSE MERTZ

Based in Miami, Florida, Jose Mertz has a dreamy style that is inspired from science fiction, anime, ancient cultures and the supernatural.

www.josemertz.com
Instagram: @josemertz

JOSEY TSAO

Josey Tsao is an illustrator and designer based in Los Angeles working in illustration, design and conceptual artwork for animation, publishing,and themed entertainment design.

Instagram: @joseytsao

JOSHUA BUDICH

Joshua Budich is an independent illustrator working for galleries, movie studio and media outlets worldwide. Inspired by a love for the pop culture of his youth, his focus is on art that celebrates film, TV, toys, etc. He lives in the Baltimore/DC area with his wife and their two children.

www.joshuabudich.com

JP NEANG

An artist and creative director, from California , JP's work has been showcased in various galleries internationally. She pushes boundaries with colorless images that evoke stillness and playfulness, from small scale thumbnail landscapes to Japanese-inspired monsters. She has also been an advocate of creative education for all youth for eight years.

Instagram: @jpneang

JUSTIN HILLGROVE

Mostly self-taught, Justin Hillgrove ("Imps and Monsters") paints monsters, robots and other such nonsense, as well as working on tabletop games, comics, books and toys at his studio in Washington State.

www.impsandmonsters.com

JUSTIN VAN GENDEREN

Justin Van Genderen is a graphic designer with a bachelor of fine arts and a minimalist retro style. He creates movie posters, comic and pop culture icons as well as science graphics. He is charting his own pop culture trek to success in Chicago, where he opened his own company, 2046 Design.

2046Design.com

KATE SNOW

Kate Snow is an artist who mainly works in photorealistic watercolor. Her pieces are featured in multiple galleries in California and New York and have appeared in various art magazines and publications. Kate's work ranges from fun illustration to hyper realism, often focusing on pop culture. She resides in Southern California.

Instagram: @katesnowart

KAYLA EDGAR

Kayla Edgar is a freelance illustrator and gallery artist who enjoys getting lost in the details while creating elaborate designs full of playful characters and whimsical narratives. She calls Colorado, where she graduated from RMCAD with a BFA in illustration, home and can be found hanging with her cat/human family.

www.kaylaedgar.com

KEITH CARTER

Keith was born in 1978 in Tacoma, Washinton. He went to Western Washington University where he received his BA in Fine Art. He later went to Pacific Northwest College of Art in Portland. He currently lives in Portland, and spends most of his time painting pictures of animals and people.

www.kcarterart.com

KEITH LIN

Tattooist/artist/pop culture nerd.

Instagram: @keithatlin

KELLY MCKERNAN

Kelly McKernan is an independent artist based in Nashville, Tennessee. Her work is created with watercolor and acryla gouache.

www.kellymckernan.com

KELLY TUNSTALL

Kelly Tunstall is a San Francisco-based artist known for her paintings of elongated, large-eyed female figures, experimental yet classically grounded, layered works that merge graphic expression, stylized representation, surrealism and sketch. Tunstall works with collage, pencil, acrylic, spray paint, pen and ink, and gold leaf, sometimes in collaboration with husband Ferris Plock.

Instagram: @kellytunstall

KEMI MAI

Kemi Mai is a painter who lives and works in Manchester, UK.

Instagram: @kemimai

KEVAN HOM

Kevan is an artist based in San Francisco, California. Through his background in illustration, he focuses on conveying simple story moments by combining his interests in nature and fantasy. Miyazaki's films such as *Princess Mononoke*, *Spirited Away* and *My Neighbor Totoro* have been big childhood favorites for him.

Instagram: @kevanhom_art

LAUREN GREGG

Lauren Gregg is an illustrator who lives in Athens, Georgia. She has made things for Nickelodeon, Disney Television, *Yo Gabba Gabba* and even commercials about tampons and homeless pets. She is tall with a friendly disposition.

www.laurengregg.com

LAUREN YS

Lauren YS is a Los Angeles-based artist. With bouts in academics, literature and writing, teaching, illustration, and animation, the impact of these phases of her career add up to a robust style of murals and fine art, influenced by dreams, mythology, death, comics, love, sex, psychedelia, animation and her Asian-American heritage.

Instagram: @squid.licker

LEILANI BUSTAMANTE

Leilani Bustamante was born in California and is a graduate of the Academy of Art University.
She grew up between the suburbs and rurality, her inspirations for their simultaneous decay and growth. Her work explores death, rebirth, beauty and spoil, the loveliness of the macabre and the mournful influence of osteological motifs.

www.leilanibustamante.co

LEONARDO SANTAMARIA

Leonardo Santamaria is a first-generation Filipino-American freelance illustrator working across a variety of industries. In addition to producing commercial work, he also regularly exhibits his paintings at galleries across the United States. He currently lives and works in Los Angeles.

www.leonardosantamaria.com

LIZ VOWLES

Liz Vowles explores the line between art and craft through the intricate stitchwork of free-form embroidery. Her work addresses themes related to her passions for media and sustainability. Threadpainting allows her to tap into an intuitive, creative mode free from the insecurities and overly analytical tendencies in her day-to-day life.

Instagram: @peanutbutterjellycat

MAGGIE CHIANG

Maggie Chiang is a full-time artist and part-time dreamer. Her work evokes a longing for adventure and the pursuit of the unknown. A central theme is the relationship between humanity and nature, oftentimes the underlying thread that ties together her work and establishes her individual artistic voice.

Instagram: @mcmintea

MAGGIE IVY

She is a freelance illustrator and artist currently living and working in the Ozark area.

www.maggieivy.com

MAI LY DEGNAN

Mai Ly Degnan is an illustrator and professor based in Baltimore, Maryland. Much of her work is inspired by relationships, childhood mischief and humor. She has a passion for telling stories and creating characters. Mai Ly enjoys depicting people in familiar everyday situations, always with a twist of irony and humor.

www.mailydegnan.com

MANDY TSUNG

Mandy was born in Banff, but spent most of her formative years in Calgary and Hong Kong. After completing a BFA in Sculpture at The AUArts in 2007, she moved to Vancouver where she now paints and tattoos full-time. She has exhibited in numerous galleries around the world.

Instagram: @mandytsung

MAR CERDÀ

Mar Cerdà is an illustrator who creates watercolor prints and in little dioramas made of cut papers. She lives in Barcelona, has displayed her dioramas pieces in galleries around the world, has worked for clients like *The New York Times*, *Entertainment Weekly*, *Architectural Digest*, Christian Louboutin, Deloitte and as a children illustrator.

www.marillustrations.com

MARIA SUAREZ-INCLAN

Maria Suarez-Inclan is a Spanish illustrator living in London. She tries to balance advertising life with illustration. She enjoys watching animation films, reading comic books and listening to 1950s music.

www.msinclan.com

MATT DYE / BLUNT GRAFFIX

Trouble maker.

www.bluntgraffix.com

MATT RITCHIE

Matt Ritchie is a Bay Area artist that works in many mediums. Matt enjoys rollerskating, coffee, chips and salsa and his cat Marcie. Matt spends his days as a park ranger and his nights making art.

Instagram: @rat136

MAX DALTON

Max Dalton is a graphic artist living in Buenos Aires, Argentina. He has been drawing since he was two or three years old and began to take it seriously around the age of thirteen. Today he works as a freelance illustrator for advertising, editorial and personal artistic projects.

www.max-dalton.com

MAX KAUFFMAN

Max Kauffman's paintings shift between abstraction and figuration by blurring the distinction between real and imagined, conscious and unconscious. He investigates how we draw comfort from inanimate objects and habitats that we occupy, letting them shape us. Kauffman currently lives and works in Denver with his cat Lady Drew.

www.kauffmanartistry.com

MEGHAN STRATMAN

Meghan Stratman is a paper-collage artist based in Lincoln, Nebraska. Common subjects in her work include plants and animals, pop culture, ghosts, adventures, brave girls and the occasional monster.

www.bunnypirates.com
Instagram: @bunnypirates
Twitter: @bunnypirates

MICHAEL TUNK

Michael Tunk uses photographs and magazines from the 1800s-1980s to re-contextualize them. From refused detritus he spins yarns of gold. He takes the weight from a hoarder's home and fixes it into aesthetic candy, never photoshopped. He uses Xacto blades and what's left of the bones in his wrists.

Instagram: @michael_tunk

MILES RITCHIE

Miles Ritchie is an artist out of the San Francisco Bay Area. Heavily inspired by the movies he watches, Ritchie's latest series titled *Pop Ply Portraits* features stylized hand cut and painted layered wooden portraits of the characters from those films.

Instagram: @milesritchie

MIMI YOON

For artist Mimi Yoon, there is no concrete definition for art. To her it is simply that "art is." Mimi's artwork vibrates with tangible and sensual beauty and honesty. It subtly allure then climaxes to demand attention and is immediately unforgettable.

Instagram: @mimiyoon

MINNIE PHAN

Minnie Phan is an illustrator and cartoonist located in Oakland, California. She graduated from California College of the Arts in Illustration and enjoys making colorful pictures with whimsy. She focuses on themes of cultural heritage, diversity, personal stories, and the invisible things that shape who we are.

www.minniephan.com

MONICA GARWOOD

Monica Garwood is an illustrator and painter from San Francisco. She graduated from California College of the Arts with a BFA in Illustration and Visual Studies. She specializes in watercolor and gouache conceptual and narrative illustration. Clients include Google, *The New York Times*, Pinterest, Facebook, and Penguin Books.

www.monicagarwood.com

NAN LAWSON

Nan Lawson is an Angelenos artist. She's a contributor to art galleries across the country with a pop culture focus. She worked with companies such as the Academy Awards, LucasFilm, Disney, HBO, Nickelodeon and HULU. She also works with clients for animation visual development, book and editorial illustration.

Instagram: @nanlawson

NATE UTESCH

Nathaniel is a music industry art director moonlighting as an electronic musician from his home studio in Fort Wayne, Indiana.

www.nthnl.com

NICK COMPARONE

Nick's work is composed of hand drawn and cut stencils, spray paints and collage. Giving new lifc to an overabundance of printed materials, these books, prints and patterns form the basis of each painting. From layers of paint the final work emerges in a display of depth and overlaying tones.

www.designanddestroy.com

NICK STOKES

Nick Stokes is an art director and illustrator who talks too much.

www.itscolortime.com
Instagram: @nick___stokes

NICOLE LEE GROSJEAN

Nicole Grosjean is an illustrator with a passion for handmade art and attention to detail. Her layered paper artwork combines fantasy and craftsmanship to build complex worlds of her own designs as well as those from pop culture films.

www.paperfauna.com
Instagram: @nicolegrosjean
Twitter: @NLGrosjean

PEACH MOMOKO

Japanese illustrator working with Marvel and *Heavy Metal Magazine*.

Instagram: @peachmomoko60

PIPPA DYRLAGA

Pippa is a paper artist, printmaker and illustrator based in Yorkshire, England. All work is hand cut from a single sheet of paper. She uses a traditional art form to create contemporary works inspired by nature, pop culture and the things around her.

www.pippadyrlaga.com

PRIMARY HUGHES

Primary Hughes can often be found exploring the landscape along the coast of Lake Superior with his plein-air watercolor kit. His paintings revel in the interplay of light and color, and the emotional impact in quieter moments of determination, thoughtful reflection and preparation for a thing that must be done.

www.primaryhughes.com

REBECCA MASON ADAMS

Rebecca Mason Adams is an artist based in Rhode Island. She graduated in 2006 with a BFA in photography. Her paintings focus on black and white portraiture referencing stylized and graphic photography and film. She transitioned into painting after school, utilizing her skills in photography and lighting to aid her.

www.rebeccamadams.com

REBECCA ROSE

Rebecca Rose is an award-winning sculptor and art jeweler. Her body of work, Sculpturings, is a hybrid of small sculpture and wearable art cast in precious metals using the lost wax casting process. Rose consistently shows globally. She is in various magazines and has been filmed for PBS documentaries.

www.sculpturings.com

RELM

Inspired by colors, patterns and attention to detail, most of his pieces range in influence taken from his background in fashion design, the intricacies of nature coupled with his own life experiences. He finds ways to apply this to the subject instead of having it simply fade away into the background.

Instagram: @relmartist

REUBEN NEGRON

Reuben Negron is a contemporary realist best known for his highly detailed, figurative watercolor paintings. He currently lives and works in the Blue Ridge Mountains and is represented by H Gallery in Paris, and by Blue Spiral 1, located in Asheville, North Carolina.

www.reubennegron.com

RHYS COOPER

Australian illustrator Rhys Cooper has proudly created work for bands QOTSA, The Bronx, Misfits, Metallica, Nine Inch Nails, Pearl Jam, Foo Fighters and many others along with film studios, Mondo, Star Wars and Marvel. Rhys' art prints can also be found in pop culture galleries around the world.

Instagram: @studioseppuku

ROLAND TAMAYO

Roland is a devoted husband, and father to fast growing twin boys. His love of Miyazaki's films has happily carried over to them, so they are thrilled that their dad has a part in this book. His family and loves are often reflected in his paintings and drawings.

Instagram: @tamayosoup

RUEL PASCUAL

Ruel Pascual has been an artist for over twenty years, fifteen of which spent working in the vfx and video game industry. He's an art director at Night School Studio. His personal work consists of paintings, sculptures and drawings, a living breathing extension of him in his eyes.

Instagram: @roozilla

RYAN BERKLEY

Ryan Berkley is a self-taught illustrator best known for his detailed drawings of animals in addition to his pop culture and comic-book influenced art. He splits his time between client work, gallery shows and creating new art.

Instagram: @theberkleys

SAM GILBEY

He's been drawing for as long as he can remember, and illustrating professionally since 2004. His distinctive painterly illustrations have been featured in books, magazines, comics and exhibitions worldwide. He has also contributed to more than fifty pop culture group exhibitions in the UK and US over the last five years.

Instagram: @samgilbey

SARAH JONCAS

Sarah Joncas was born in 1986 and grew up in both Hamilton and Niagara Falls, Ontario. She graduated from the Ontario College of Art and Design's BFA program in 2010 and currently works and resides out of Mississauga, Ontario.

www.sarahjoncas.ca

SCOTT HOPKO

Scott Hopko has owned Hopko Designs, an advertising/design agency for the past twenty-one years, providing communications needs to clients around the world. Taking projects from initial concept to finished product, Scott is highly skilled in fulfilling all aspects of design and production.

www.hopkodesigns.com

SERGIO LOPEZ

What he hopes to bring to the world is an understanding of the importance of beauty for the human soul by creating the most beautiful awe-inspiring works he's capable of, and helping others create their art at the greatest capacity, then communicating why these works matter.

www.themainloop.com

STACEY AOYAMA

Stacey Aoyama is an illustrator and designer working for Disney Consumer Products. She graduated from University of California with a degree in Visual Arts. Her career ambitions included astronaut, ballerina, orthodontist; however, her consistent passion for being creative prevailed. She currently lives in California with her husband, son and a cat named Ramona.

Instagram: @bluemt23

STACEY ROZICH

Stacey Rozich is a Los Angeles-based artist and illustrator. She crafts folk-art inspired scenarios in watercolor that play with boundary between the mortal world and the realm of dreamtime. Her storybook work is brought to life through lush patterning, symbolism and nostalgia.

Instagram: @Staceyrozich

STEVE KIM

Artist and illustrator based in Oxford, Mississippi.

Instagram: @stvkmco

SUDI ROUHI

Sudi Rouhi is an Iranian-born American illustrator and designer whose work is influenced by strong women, body positivity and mythology.

www.sudirouhi.com

TIMOTHY DOYLE

Tim Doyle — founded Nakatomi Inc., a silkscreen pop-art studio in Austin, Texas, — in 2009. He's been working in the silkscreen print industry for fifteen years now, producing work for galleries and clients around the world. He is currently art directing and producing tour poster series for bands like Metallica and Weird Al.

Instagram: @timothypdoyle

TIM JORDAN

Tim Jordan is a graphic designer and printmaker who lives, works and plays in Eugene, Oregon. His work revolves around pop art topics and portrayal of various celebrities. He is a frequent collaborator with Blunt Graffix.

Instagram: @timjordandesign
Twitter: @TimJordanDesign

TOM EGLINGTON

Tom Eglington is a multi-disciplinary artist working in the UK. He is self-taught and has been creating paper art since 2012, developing a style that mixes folk tale imagery with pagan, surreal and pop culture influences.

Instagram: @tomtheeggeglington

TRACIE CHING

Living in Washington, DC, Tracie Ching is a self-taught illustrator, specializing in portraiture featuring digital cross-hatching and a limited palette – a tendency-turned-style after years of working on silkscreen prints. While commissioned for projects including commercial design, editorial illustration and gallery work, Tracie Ching is known for her alternative movie posters.

www.tracieching.com

VALERIE SAVARIE

Valerie Savarie is a mixed-media artist based in Denver, Colorado. Know for her altered book sculptures which she considers a "reanimation of old books." Using vintage books as the centerpiece of her artistic creations, she retells the stories within through cutting, carving, stitching and character illustrations.

www.valeriesavarie.com

VAN ORTON DESIGN

Van Orton are twin brothers from Italy. Their art is influenced by pop culture, inspired by stained-glass windows of churches and evolved with geometric inserts and lines of light. The term Vanortonized describes their mark.

www.vanortondesign.com

VERONICA FISH

Veronica Fish is a comic artist, painter and illustrator. Her clients include Marvel, Disney, Archie Comics, Dark Horse Comics, Valiant, IDW, Boom! Studios and Conde Nast Publishing. She lives with her husband and fellow artist, Andy, in Massachusetts.

Instagram: @itsveronicafish

YOHAN SACRÉ

Yohan Sacré was born in Belgium on June 7, 1989. Mainly a children's illustrator and author of self-taught comic, he is inspired by monsters, nature and childhood.

Instagram: @yohan.sacre

YUMIKO KAYUKAWA

Yumiko grew up in the small town in Hokkaido, Japan. In this pristine, natural surroundings, she found her love of wildlife which later became an important theme of her work. Yumiko draws inspiration from American pop culture such as rock n' roll, film and fashion and has lived in Seattle since 2005.

www.sweetyumiko.com

ZARD APUYA

Zard is an artist born-and-raised on the island of Guam and is now based in San Diego, California. He's always loved art as a child and has evolved over the years. He now dabbles in vinyl toy customization and his creations are inspired by something we all love—FOOD.

www.zardapuya.com

THANKS

Spoke Art Gallery and Ken Harman Hashimoto would like to thank, first and foremost, the many talented artists who have contributed to this project over the years, neither this exhibition or corresponding book would have been possible without you.

To the thousands of art and film lovers who have visited our exhibitions in San Francisco, New York City, Los Angeles, and Honolulu—thank you for attending our shows and supporting our artists, your support means the world.

To Isabel Fondevila and Jesse Hawthorne Ficks, thank you for hosting our Miyazaki film festival in 35mm at the Roxie Theater in San Francisco every year. Being able to screen these movies in the original 35mm format with subtitles at an independent theater is truly a blessing in this age of digital projectors and corporate multiplexes.

To Peter Adamyan, Shaun Roberts, Jessica Ross, Dasha Matsuura, Jennifer Rizzo, Raul Barquet, Lyndsie Fox and Hector Esqueda, thank you for all your hard work and unwavering confidence in our gallery and what we do. A very special shout out to Iggy, Tubey, Meera, Pupusa and Otis, you're the real superstars here.

Finally, to Miyazaki-sama and everyone at Studio Ghibli—thank you for the decades of entertainment and inspiration.

MICHAEL TUNK

Mononoke Hime (detail)

Analog collage with Micron pen and vellum paper. 19 x 16".

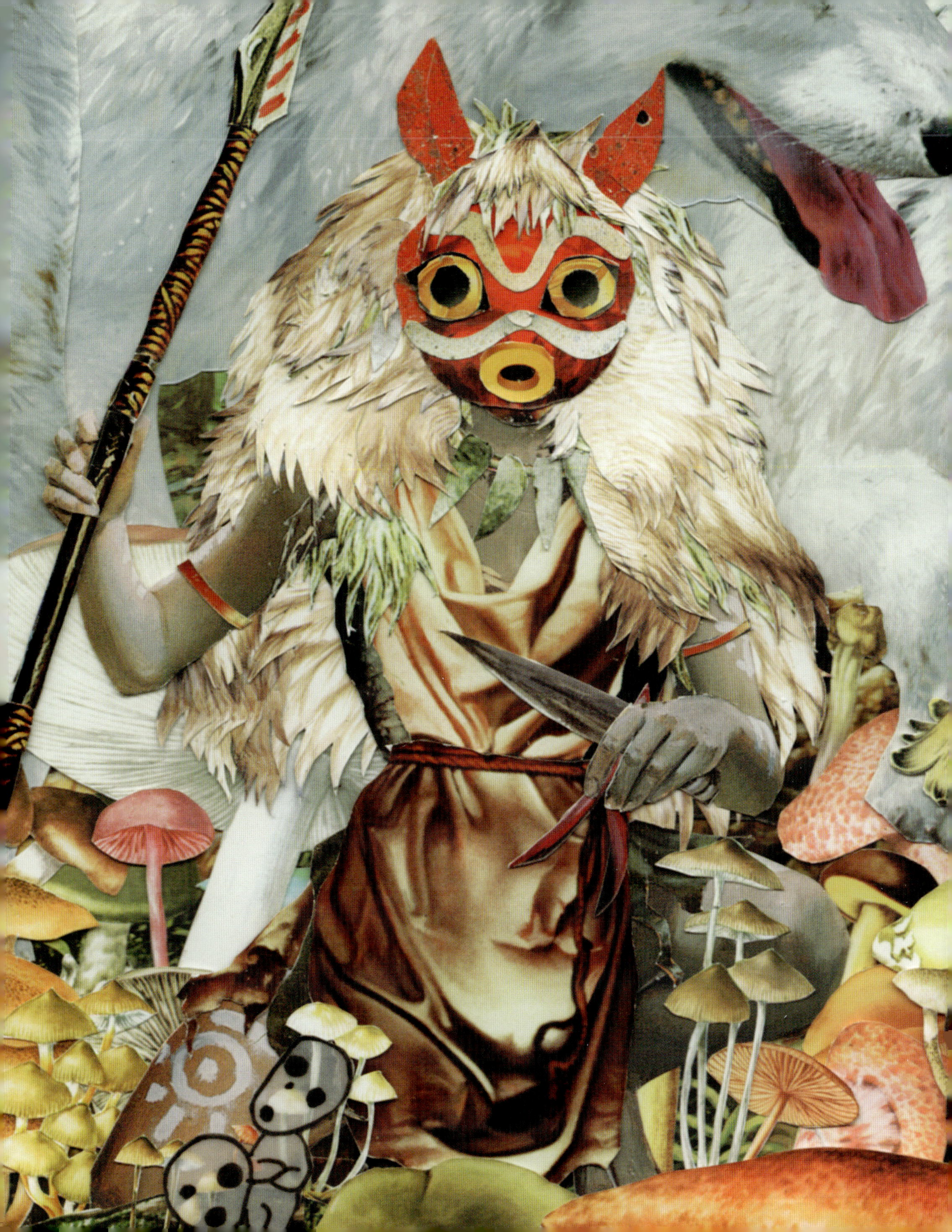

MINNIE PHAN

Spark

Acrylic, watercolor, gouache and colored pencil. 10.75 x 10.75''.

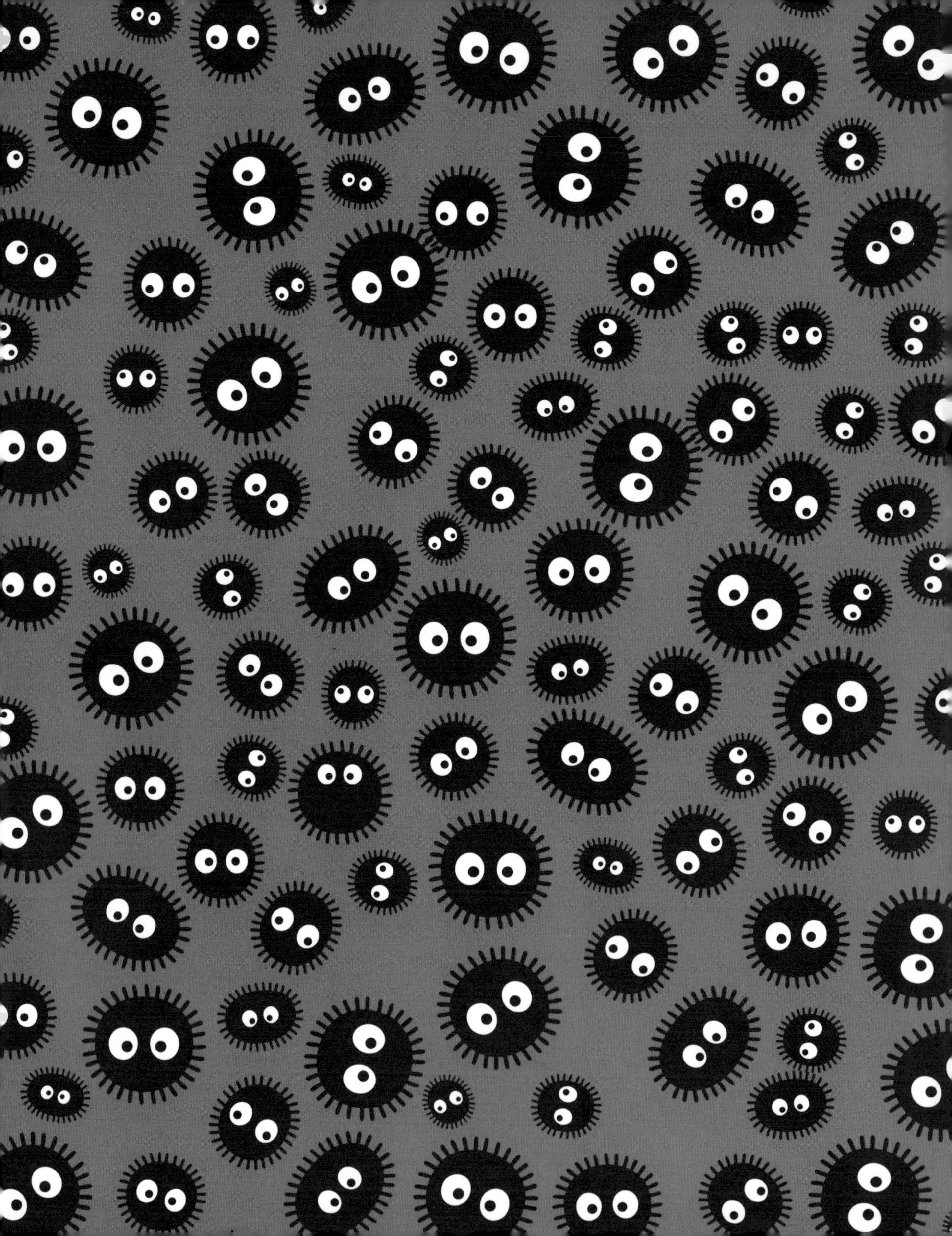